Spirit Possession and Spirit Mediumship in Africa and Afro-America

Garland Reference Library
of Social Science
(Vol. 56)

Spirit Possession and Spirit Mediumship in Africa and Afro-America

An Annotated Bibliography

Irving I. Zaretsky
Divinity School and Law School
The University of Chicago

Cynthia Shambaugh
Anthropology Department
The University of Chicago

Garland Publishing, Inc. • New York & London
1978

Library of Congress Cataloging in Publication Data

Zaretsky, Irving I
Spirit possession and spirit mediumship in Africa and
Afro-America.

(Garland reference library of social science; v. 56)
Previous ed. published in 1966 under title:
Bibliography on spirit possession and spirit mediumship.
1. Spiritualism—Africa—Bibliography. 2. Spiritu-
alism—America—Bibliography. I. Shambaugh, Cynthia,
joint author. II. Title.
Z6878.S8Z36 1978 [BF1242.A35] 016.1339'096
ISBN 0-8240-9823-4   78-4181

Printed on acid-free, 250-year-life paper
Manufactured in the United States of America

Contents

v

LISTS OF JOURNALS, NEWSLETTERS,
PERIODICALS SURVEYED

Preface

The present bibliography is a greatly enlarged, revised and updated edition of the *Bibliography on Spirit Possession and Spirit Mediumship*, compiled by Irving Zaretsky and published in 1966 by Northwestern University Press. Shortly after publication in 1966, the bibliography was sold out and remained out of print for the past decade. The present edition has been compiled in response to numerous requests of the present editors to bring the bibliography once again into print.

We want to express our appreciation and thanks to those individuals who were of invaluable assistance to this project. We are indebted to Professor Elizabeth Colson of the Anthropology Department at the University of California, Berkeley, for her knowledgeable help in the collection of sources and for her continuous encouragement. Professor Ralph Austen of the History Department at the University of Chicago gave generously of his time and helped us clarify various research issues as they arose. Professor Stephen Glazier of the Anthropology Department at the University of Connecticut, Storrs, shared with us his excellent bibliographic collection of African materials, and we express our gratitude to him. Dean Joseph Kitagawa and Professor Martin Marty of the Divinity School at the University of Chicago extended to us warm hospitality and support throughout the duration of this project.

Although it is impossible to cite them individually, the staff of the Regenstein Library at the University of Chicago provided us with excellent services. The curator, Hans E. Panofsky, and bibliographers, Daniel Britz, Maidel Cason, Mette Shayne and Judith Rosenthal, of the Africana collection at the Northwestern University Library were extremely helpful in suggesting new areas of source materials.

Great appreciation is extended to Rehova Arthur, Evelyn

vii

Gueno, Cheryl Harrell and Frances Paul of the Divinity School at the University of Chicago for their inestimable patience in typing the first draft of the bibliography, and to Beatrice Gibson who expertly produced the final copy.

We are grateful to Marilyn Locker for her expert editorial assistance.

Mr. Walter Pflaumer briefly served as research assistant on this project at Princeton University during 1971.

This bibliography has been compiled during the past several years with generous support from several foundations. We are deeply grateful to these foundations and to their representatives who have made this work possible and encouraged us along the way: The Lilly Endowment, Inc., and their representatives, Robert Lynn, George Lawrence and Robert Lecky; the Wenner-Gren Foundation for Anthropological Research and its Director, Mrs. Lita Osmundson; the Lucius N. Littauer Foundation and its President, Mr. Harry Starr; The Edward W. Hazen Foundation and its President, William Bradley; and the Anthropology Research Institute, Inc., and its Secretary, Gary Kardos, M.D.

Chicago, Illinois   Irving I. Zaretsky
January, 1978   Cynthia Shambaugh

Introduction

In compiling this bibliography, our aim has been to provide the researcher with an introduction to published works containing ethnographic data on, and analysis of, spirit possession and spirit mediumship in North and sub-Saharan Africa and in some Afro-American communities in the Western Hemisphere. The latter are included to the extent that they shed light on the African phenomena, their diffusion and the historical ties between the African continent and the Americas. The listings may not exhaust the subject matter, and extensive research on a particular spirit cult, ritual or ethnic group may lead the scholar beyond the sources cited in this compilation.

A. Method of Compilation: Research orientation, scope of material surveyed, special topical problems

The usefulness of a bibliography to a researcher lies, in part, in understanding exactly what has been compiled and annotated. In the area of spirit possession and spirit mediumship, this is particularly important because of confusion over the definitions of these phenomena and the multiplicity of verbal and nonverbal behavior covered by these terms.

In determining which areas to investigate and, later, what to include in the bibliography, we were guided by several decisions. First, we wanted to explore the published material from approximately 1850 to 1977. This time span was manageable and encompassed most of the significant published material.

Second, these phenomena have attracted the attention of researchers around the world; consequently, we scanned the English, French, German, Portuguese and Spanish literatures. Because of the preponderance of research in English and French, we made greater use of texts in these languages.

Third, in order to achieve as comprehensive a survey as possible, from 1966 to 1977 we researched the Africana collections of the following libraries: the University of California Libraries at Berkeley, the Regenstein and Harper Libraries of the University of Chicago, the Widener Library of Harvard University, the Howard University Library, the Firestone Library at Princeton University, the Northwestern University Library, the Museum of Natural History Library at the Smithsonian Institution and the Sterling Library at Yale University.

In each of these libraries we surveyed potential sources such as accounts by missionaries and travelers, anthropological ethnographies, historical monographs and professional journals from major African, American and European institutions dealing with anthropology, art, music, philosophy, psychology, psychiatry, religion and sociology. (Lists of the journals, newsletters and periodicals surveyed appear at the end of this volume.) We also examined collections of conference papers and various publications of abstracts (although whenever possible the original article was searched and cited instead).

Fourth, in annotating the material we attempted to remain true to the choice of language, orthography and flavor of the original text and minimized standardization of highly divergent material. It has been our individual, yet shared, experience in this research area that it is useful from the outset for a scholar to have a sense from the annotation of what the original source is likely to yield, before he or she embarks on what may be an extensive library search.

Finally, we approached the subject matter holistically. While as anthropologists we may have an *a priori* preference for the wide-angle lens of the holistic approach, it is, objectively, a particularly useful one for a bibliography on this topic. This compilation should be useful to scholars from a variety of fields having their own disciplinary interests in the topic. The holistic approach, as we have used it, means casting a wide net for potential sources covering the various aspects denoted and connoted by our topic. Spirit possession and spirit mediumship are conceptual labels whose referents are sometimes elusive. They may refer to such things as idiosyncratic or shared cultural beliefs in spirit forces; private or public rituals and ceremonies in which such beliefs may be embedded; explicitly or implicitly articulated institutions; folk categories and analytic categories; a multiplicity of verbal and nonverbal behavior which may be symptomatic of the phenomena, and yet not be so labelled by an author. We have included, therefore, not only ethnographic descriptions in which the specific terms "spirit possession" and "spirit mediumship" (or their counterpart terms in an indigenous language) are used, but also ethnographic accounts that mention phenomena so akin to those described under spirit possession and spirit mediumship that the scholar ought to be aware of them when analyzing this topic for a particular region, historical period or ethnic group.

The problem of citing relevant data on spirit possession and spirit mediumship was not easy to resolve. The descriptions and symptomatology of the phenomena are numerous and depend largely upon the particular aspects of these phenomena that are emphasized by the culture and are familiar to the observer, and upon the particular questions the observer brings with him to the field. Among the symptoms frequently encountered in the literature are convulsions, hysteria, frenzied dancing, trembling, glossolalia (speaking in tongues), wild behavior, vacant stares, depressed activity and illness.

Once we discovered in a published work any mention of spirit possession and spirit mediumship, or a description of allied phenomena which could be conservatively construed as symptomatic of it, we included the citation, no matter how brief that description was.

To locate relevant material in a publication, we first went to the subject index of a monograph. We found that such material has been indexed under a plethora of terms, all of which had to be scanned. These terms include ancestors, ancestor spirits, cults, demons, demonology, devils, devil worship, deities, evil spirits, evil eye, epilepsy, fetishes, gods, healers, hysteria, illnesses, impersonation, masquerading, mediums, mediumship, nature spirits, obsession, possession, religion, shamanism, spirits, spiritism, spiritualism, sorcery, trances, ventriloquism, voodoo, witchcraft and wizardry. There are many more.

Where indices were not available, we scanned the texts for information. In all cases we checked footnotes and bibliographic citations for further material on a given cult, ethnic group or region.

B. Working Definition of Spirit Possession and Spirit Mediumship

We have taken into consideration all of these difficulties and have evolved a working definition of spirit possession and spirit mediumship. We exercised very little censorship in order to allow the scholar to sift through the various labels, symptoms and world views evident in the sources he chooses to investigate.

The five elements of our definition are:

(1) An individual becomes ill or enters into a state of dissociation by means of various inductive techniques such as drumming, hyperventilation, sleep deprivation and dietary restrictions.

(2) His behavior is recognized as not that of his usual self, according to a folk interpretation.

(3) This apparently aberrant behavior is attributed by the society to the control exercised by some external or transpersonal agent.

(4) This external agent has inspired the individual to act in a certain manner by means of having "entered into" or "mounted" him, thus taking over and/or displacing the individual's own personality and acting in its stead.

(5) The agent acting through the individual communicates, with varying degrees of coherence, a specific message pertaining to the life of the possessed individual, his illness or condition, the lives of others in the community or the state of the society in general.

B (1). Element 1—Possession illness and possession trance. The first element of the definition highlights a common distinction in the use of the term "possession." First, possession is used as an etiological explanation of disease, both in cases where the individual feels himself to be possessed by a spirit, deity, ghost, ancestor, power and so on, and in more general cases where the individual's subjective experience is simply one of being ill. Second, possession refers to a specific trance state in which the individual is said to be possessed by one of the various agents.

In the first usage we encounter a major issue of theoretical import: whether or not the "possessed" individual is manifesting behavior that can be described in medical or psychiatric terms as epileptic, neurotic, psychotic or schizophrenic. Although there *are* cases where such interpretations are valid, caution must be exercised in their application, since in many instances the possession state is neither irreversible nor long-term, and the individual who has the ability to become possessed displays a great degree of control over his behavior and shoulders even more social responsibility than the average member of his society. Moreover, the onset of a spirit-sent "illness" is only one of three ways in which an individual is chosen to participate in the possession state. He can also consciously embark on a personal quest to become a vehicle for the spirits, or he can be chosen by heredity or by the rest of the society to fulfill such a role.

The second distinct use of the term "possession" centers on the trance state. Although there is debate over the necessity of trance to the manifestation of such possession-related phenomena as glossolalia, a recent article by Vincent Crapanzano (1977b, Bib. 392, p. 7) defines spirit possession as "any altered state of consciousness indigenously interpreted in terms of the influence of an alien spirit." His use of the term "altered state of consciousness" emphasizes the importance both of trance behavior and, more generally, of the recent psychological research into various states of consciousness. A definition of states of consciousness, reworked from Arnold Ludwig's 1969 article (Bib. 1070) reads as follows:

> States of consciousness are mental states, induced by various physiological, psychological, or pharmacological maneuvers or agents, which can be recognized subjectively by the individual himself (or by an objective observer of the

individual) as representing a sufficient alteration in subjective experience of psychological functioning from an identifiable state of consciousness previously experienced by that individual.

When the phenomenon of possession is approached along this avenue of research, several interesting issues develop. For example, confusion in definition is evident in the use of the word "trance," for it has been employed as an all-inclusive term to cover many analytically distinct types of behavior. Thus, further research is necessary to determine the similarities and differences between possession trance and various other states of consciousness such as hypnosis and meditation.

Nonetheless, the occurrence of a possession state may be analyzed as consisting of five distinct steps: (1) the preliminary preparation, such as ceremonial libations or ritual baths, that serves to promote greater receptivity to the trance state; (2) the techniques of induction into a trance state, the most important of these being the use of percussion instruments to achieve the "sonic driving" effect on the cortical brain-wave patterns; (3) the possession state itself, involving two major phases (discussed below); (4) the exodus or recovery from the state, usually described as an abrupt cessation with accompanying emotional reactions ranging from euphoria to pain and exhaustion; and (5) the aftereffects of the state that depend largely upon the attitude the specific individual has towards the state of being possessed as prescribed by cultural patterns for postpossession behavior.

There appear to be two major phases to the possession state. First is a period of dazed, mute inaccessibility during which the individual displays such behavior as fidgeting, crying, looking oppressed, swaying or huddling. This may last only a few seconds and gives way to a second, longer phase of greater physical excitement, marking the possession of the trancer's body by a spirit or deity. In many cultures this process is thought of as the spirit "mounting" its "horse," and the subjective experience is of something coming down from above one's head.

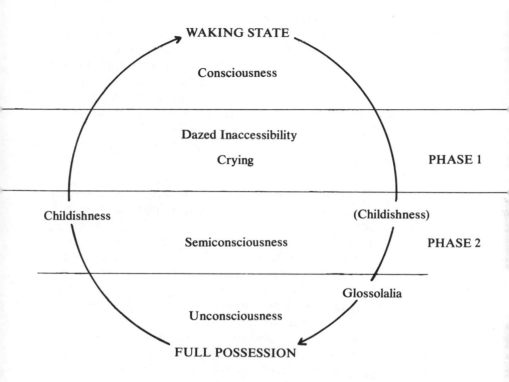

In this figure, two arching arrows are used to indicate the descent from the waking state into the full unconscious—that is, posttrance amnesic—possession state, and the ascent into wakefulness. The trance may stop at any point along the descending or ascending arcs and remain there without being elaborated further. Thus, the trance may never go beyond the initial confused inhibitory phase. If it does, the first aspect of Phase 2 encountered is behavior not socially appropriate to the individual relative to his social status. One instance of such behavior is childishness: naughty, childlike behavior displayed with a high degree of consciousness. This aspect is parenthetical for the descending arc because it is recorded more frequently during the ascent back into consciousness. The second aspect of Phase 2 is marked by the complete unconsciousness of the trance. It is in the initial moments of this aspect that glossolalia, speaking in tongues, may occur. At the lowest point on the descending arc is the full possession trance. The body of the possessed quivers continually in a fine tremor, and the spirit manifests its own personality by both vocal and behavioral actions. As the trance terminates, the childlike aspect, or nonappropriate behavior, occurs frequently, and the dazed, inhibitory phase usually lasts for only a short while, unless specific learning to prolong recovery from trance has been acquired.

B (2). Elements 2 and 3—Social interpretations of possession. The investigation into the psychological development of the possession state constitutes only one avenue of research. Returning to our working definition, the second and third elements elucidate another approach. Here the emphasis is on the social interpretation of the individual's behavior, thus highlighting the cultural framework in which the state occurs. Crapanzano (1977b, Bib. 392, p. 10) speaks of spirit possession as being an idiom that "gives the event structure, thus precipitating its context, relates it to other similarly constructed events, and evaluates the event along the ideosyncratic and (culturally) standardized lines. Once the experience is articulated, once it is rendered an event, it is cast within the world of meaning and may then provide a basis for action." He goes on to say (p. 11) that whatever the ontological status of the possessing spirits may be, it is necessary to study them as they are articulated in a culture without reducing them to fit Western psychiatric terminology (which usually centers around the issue of psychological projections). Therefore, research into the folk definitions and descriptions of illnesses, of the spirits and of the abilities and types of knowledge that accompany the possession state is of utmost importance. Unfortunately, only in recent years has research in the form of detailed case studies begun. (V. Crapanzano and V. Garrison's *Case Studies in Spirit Possession* [1977a, Bib. 391] is a fine example.)

B (3). Elements 4 and 5—Relationship between possession and mediumship. Elements 4 and 5 in our working definition serve to highlight the differences between spirit possession and spirit mediumship. Although Crapanzano (1977b, Bib. 392, pp. 9–10) points out that the distinction between these two cannot be clearly drawn since they are not analytically separate states, a return to the research on states of consciousness may help elucidate the problem. Spirit possession (Element 4) does not necessarily include the ability to coherently communicate a spoken message, whereas this is the major emphasis in spirit mediumship (Element 5). When the state of possession is studied in one individual over time, development is evident in his or her degree of control over kinetic and verbal behavior. The initial trance state is usually characterized by wild, frenetic actions and complete loss of mental control. Interpreted in another way, this initial state, usually accompanied by fear, may be termed loss of ego control or ego-death. Over time, as the individual is trained and initiated by a specialist (as frequently occurs in possession or spirit cults), the onset of the trance state becomes more controlled, and if desired, the individual learns to become a medium for the spirits. This learning process leads to an ability of cult leaders, who have practiced the trance state, to be possessed by a spirit which speaks through them and at the same time to be aware of the possession, though this awareness does not seem to negate the validity of the possession experience. Because of this, we feel that the theoretical distinction between spirit possession and spirit mediumship is useful, although in need of further analysis.

B (4). Religion and possession. The view that spirit possession and mediumship are forms of *religious* experience has received less attention than other approaches. Crapanzano, who does not discuss this dimension, states that "the spirit idiom serves to synthesize the psychological and the sociological aspects of human nature" (1977b, Bib. 392, p. 19). It appears to us that this is also the role of a religious system within a culture. In many cultures, entering into and practicing a trance state is frequently couched in terms of religious experience. One might say, therefore, that religion may be defined, at least in the case of spirit possession and mediumship, as the knowledge obtained through the use of a set of techniques facilitating the transcendence of one's ego-identified consciousness and the communication with nonordinary beings. Thus, spirit possession and spirit mediumship are together to be considered as only one aspect of religious behavior found in many different types of ritual and ceremonial activities.

In some societies, trance behavior is supported by beliefs in spirit possession; however, in other societies these phenomena do not necessarily occur together. As indicated in the work of Erika Bourguignon (Bib. 234-250), the complexity of the social organization of a society determines in part the relationship of these phenomena to each other.

This line of research generates many new questions concerning the distribution and use of altered states of consciousness in communities and religions around the world. One hypothesis is that a general psychophysiological "hyperaroused" trance state, which may be achieved through specific inductive techniques, is elaborated in various ways from one culture to another as emphasis is placed on different mental abilities available in the trance state. Thus, glossolalia and possession and mediumship trances may be of a similar psychological nature to healing trances (as practiced by the !Kung Bushmen), shamanism, vision quests and techniques of visualization in meditative practices. The cultural belief systems determine which aspects of the trance state will be considered valid and valuable religious experience. But common to all these elaborations is use of dissociation and communication with the spirits for religious and curing purposes.

B (5). New research approaches and orientations. Many of the most recent developments in the study of spirit possession and mediumship have been mentioned above. These avenues of research have been opened up by the new groups of scholars beginning to take an interest in these phenomena. One important group are the African social scientists trained in African universities. They bring their own perspectives to African materials, previously analyzed solely by Europeans and Americans. Another group of scholars who are increasingly becoming interested in spirit possession, especially in Africa, are Western-trained psychiatrists and psychologists tackling the thorny problems of cross-cultural translation and interpretation. One of the major psychiatric contributions so far has been the study of folk beliefs and healing methods as compared with the prevalent Western therapeutic techniques; in addition, the theoretical importance of the psychological study of states of consciousness has been emphasized above. A final group of scholars who have begun to study spirit possession and mediumship are social scientists drawn from fields other than anthropology, such as historians, demographers and ecologists. With their specialized training, they bring to light new areas of research and contribute further to our understanding of these complex phenomena.

C. Organization of the Bibliography

Differences of style between the 1966 publication of the *Bibliography on Spirit Possession and Spirit Mediumship* and the present compilation have been resolved whenever possible. All the citations of the 1966 bibliography have been combined with the additional entries and renumbered.

C (1). **Authors.** The bibliography is organized alphabetically by author. In most cases, the form in which the author's name appears has been determined by its appearance on the title page of the original text, thus accounting for the variations of a name such as J. Beattie, J.H.M. Beattie, John Beattie, John H.M. Beattie. For compound names such as Wim M.J. van Binsbergen, the reference is listed under the first letter of the final name (in this case, "B"). There are, however, exceptions to this rule according to accepted library conventions for citations. One author listed here has published under two names, and the entries are cross-referenced (i.e., Sister Mary Aquina, O.P., and A.K.H. Weinrich). Also listed alphabetically are "*A*nonymous" entries; ones published by the "*C*atholic Church"; specific colloquia and conferences such as "*C*olloque de Cotonou" and "*P*an-African Psychiatric Conference, 1st" and "*E*ncyclopedia." All names beginning with "Mc-" are listed together with "Mac-"; these entries have been placed alphabetically between "Mab-" and "Mad-."

C (2). Citation Style. The references conform to the following conventions:

> vol. = volume
> no. = number
> pt. = part
> p. = page
> pp. = pages
> Ill. = illustrated
> 5, no. 3: 51–62 = volume 5, number 3, pages 51–62
> 12:124–26 = volume 12, pages 124–126
> pp. 45 ff. = page 47 and following pages

The spelling of the place of publication follows that of the original text (e.g., Bruxelles, not Brussels). The place of publication of journals is included only if the journal is not well-known or if there are several publications with the same name but originating in different places.

When two or more articles from an edited collection of essays appear as separate entries, the edited volume itself is listed in the following form:

450. Dickson, Kwesi A., and   *Biblical Revelation and Afri-*
      Paul Ellingworth, eds.   *can Beliefs.* Maryknoll, N.Y.:
      1969   Orbis Books.

Includes in this bibliography:

12	E.A. Adeolu Adegbola (1969)
[bibliography 1250	V. Mulago (1969b) [second ar-
numbers]	ticle alphabetically published
	by author in same year]
1615	S. Sidhom (1969)

References for the individual articles refer back to the edited volume and are listed as follows:

12. Adegbola, E.A. Adeolu   "The Theological Basis of
       1969   Ethics." In *Biblical Revelation*
                              and African Beliefs, edited by
                              K.A. Dickson and P. El-
                              lingworth, pp. 116–36.
                              (Bib. 450.)

Although spirit possession is not explicitly labelled, the Yoruba oracles and the belief that spirits can "catch" people are discussed (pp. 120 ff.).

C (3). Annotations. The annotation includes whenever possible (a) ethnic group and its location; (b) source of information if relevant or necessary; (c) date of observation if available; and (d) description of the general content and location of the material in the text. Because only the major issues the author has dealt with in relation to spirit possession and mediumship have been annotated, the scholar should not be dissuaded from investigating the text if his particular area of interest has not been mentioned.

All spellings of foreign words, of ethnic groups and of cults appear as in the original text. Therefore, for instance, the variations of the term "voodoo" appear as vaudou, vodoun, vodun, voudou, and so on. Capitalization generally follows the author's original text. However, we have underlined consistently all foreign words except proper names (including names of individuals, countries, ethnic groups, places and churches).

C (4). Texts unavailable for annotation. Some texts were unavailable for annotation but have been cited since there is sufficient evidence that they contain information relevant to the topic of spirit possession and mediumship in Africa and Afro-America.

C (5). Portuguese citations from Brazil. At the end of the bibliography, a list of unannotated Brazilian publications appears (Bib. 1936 through 2054). These books, written in Portuguese, contain extremely detailed information on the social organization, the rituals and the religio-philosophical underpinnings of the

Brazilian spirit possession and spirit mediumship cults of Candomblé, Kardecism, Macumba, Quimbanda and Umbanda. It was impossible to annotate each book, since the material is so germane, comprehensive, detailed and repetitive. The scholar will wish to explore these texts according to his own particular field of research. (These works are listed in Index 6.)

C (6). Bibliographies. Three bibliographies are listed in this compilation, all having to do with the contemporary religious movements in Africa: Bib. 658, Geuns, André (1973), "Bibliographie commentée du prophétisme kongo"; Bib. 1218, Mitchell, Robert Cameron, and Harold W. Turner, eds. (1966), *A Bibliography of Modern African Religious Movements*; and Bib. 1766, Turner, Harold W. (1968/70), "Bibliography of Modern African Religious Movements—Supplement." The last two bibliographies were extensively used as source material in this compilation.

A recent bibliography by Stephen D. Glazier, *Bibliography: Spirit Mediumship and Possession to 1975*, has provided a valuable cross-check for sources cited here.

This bibliography does not purport to list all the major works in such areas as altered states of consciousness research, glossolalia, art and music. If interested, the scholar may refer to other bibliographies. For instance, there is an excellent bibliography on altered states of consciousness research in the *International Journal of Clinical and Experimental Hypnosis*: Daniel P. Brown and Erika Fromm, "Selected Bibliography of Readings in Altered States of Consciousness in Normal Individuals" (vol. 25, no. 4, October 1977). For further study of the Pentecostal use of glossolalia, the Charismatic Christianity Bibliography in the *Journal of Theology for Southern Africa* (Cape Town), no. 7, 1974, pp. 66–67, gives a good selection of major works.

C (7). Journals, Newsletters, Periodicals. The lists of journals, newsletters and periodicals supplied at the end of this volume are organized into three groups: (1) those which were extensively searched and were found to contain relevant material; (2) those which were on peripheral subjects and were used only when a reference to an article in a particular issue was found; and (3) those which were found to contain no relevant information on the topics of spirit possession and mediumship in Africa and Afro-America. We have listed them in order to help the scholar avoid duplicating our research.

   C (8). Indices. The eighteen indices, which appear after the main text of the bibliography, have been designed to aid the scholar in his or her research as fully as possible. As a unit and individually, the indices are prefaced by explanatory notes. We suggest that the scholar consult these comments in order to obtain maximum benefit from the indices.

1. Aall-Jilek, Louise M.   "Epilepsy in the Wapogoro Tribe
   1965   in Tanganyika." Acta
                            Psychiatrica Scandinavica
                            (Copenhagen) 41, no. 1: 57-86.

   Spirit possession by evil shetani spirits is considered
by the Wapogoro (Pogoro) of Tanganyika (Tanzania) to be
the cause of epilepsy (p. 64). Case histories and a
discussion of the causes of the disease in Western
psychiatric terms are presented.

2. Abadie, Maurice (Col.)   La Colonie du Niger. Paris:
   1927   Société d'éditions géographiques,
                            maritimes, et coloniales.

   A study of Niger (Niger Colony in 1927) and its people
(Songhai, Zerma, Hausa, and Nomads). The study includes
historical and ethnographic information originally available in unpublished monographs of various administrative areas of the Colony, as well as interesting information on the religious life of the people described.
Abadie was first to indicate the existence of possession
dances among the Songhai and the Zerma, and he lists the
spirits involved in these dances. [This citation appears in Rouch (1954, Bib. 1525). Text and annotation
are in French.]

3. Abd Allah, M. M.   "Siwan Customs." In Harvard
   1917   African Studies, edited by Oric
                            Bates, 1: 1-28. Cambridge,
                            Mass.: Peabody Museum.

   This study contains information for Morocco and Siwan
(upper Egypt). Relevant information on spirit possession appears on page 23, where mention is made of the
Ginns (evil spirits) usually residing in shallow waters.
These spirits may enter the body of a man and obsess
him; consequently they must be exorcised. Exorcism is
performed by a Sheikh. For the duration of the obsession and exorcism the victim remains unconscious.

4. Abdel-Rasoul, Kawthar   "Zar in Egypt." Weiner
   1955   völkerkundliche Mitteilungen
                            3, no. 1: 80-89.

   Describes the Zar cult found in Egypt, Abyssinia
(Ethiopia) and Sudan. The term Zar is applied both to
the possessing spirits and to their exorcism. These
spirits mainly afflict women who become members of the
Zar cult after the curing ceremony. There are mediums
(Kudiya) for the curing ceremony who act as intermediaries between the spirits and those possessed. This
study describes the Zar cult in some detail and comments

1

upon one of its distinguishing characteristics, the Zar language composed of words from Amharic, Galla, and ancient Ethiopian. [For a further summary see African Abstracts, vol. 7, no. 19.]

5. Abraham, D. P.   "Ethno-History of the Empire of
   1964   Mutapa: Problems and Methods."
                     In The Historian in Tropical
                     Africa, edited by J. Vansina, R.
                     Mauny, and L. V. Thomas, pp. 104-
                     26. London: Oxford University
                     Press.

The mhondoro and masvikiro spirit mediums among the Karanga of Rhodesia are discussed on pages 112 ff.

6. Abraham, D. P.   "The Roles of 'Chaminuka' and
   1966   the Mhondoro-Cults in Shona
                     Political History." In The
                     Zambesian Past, edited by E.
                     Stokes and R. Brown, pp. 28-46.
                     (Bib. 1686.)

The role of the mhondoro cults connected with the Chaminuka spirit in the political history of the Shona of Rhodesia is analyzed in depth. The major element of these cults is the communication with the tribal spirits through a spirit medium.

7. Abrahams, R. G.   The Peoples of Greater Unyamwezi,
   1967   Tanzania. Ethnographic Survey
                     of Africa, edited by Daryll
                     Forde. London: International
                     African Institute.

There are several spirit possession societies among the peoples of greater Unyamwezi, Tanzania (Nyamwezi, Sukuma, Sumbwa, Kimbu, Konongo). Among these are the Baswezi and Bamigabo cults. Possession by either spirit, Baswezi or Bamigabo, is cured by being initiated into their cults (pp. 64-65).

8. Ackerknecht, Erwin H.   "Psychopathology, Primitive
   1943   Medicine and Primitive Culture."
                          Bulletin of the History of
                          Medicine (Baltimore) 14:30-67.

Spirit possession in Africa is described in general terms on page 41.

9. Adams, P. C. G.   "Disease Concepts among Africans
   1950   in the Protectorate of Northern
                     Rhodesia." Human Problems in
                     British Central Africa: Rhodes-

2

Livingstone Institute Journal
(Lusaka) 10:14-50.

This article deals with concepts of disease causation
held by the indigenous population of Zambia (Northern
Rhodesia). Disease causality is attributed most often
to sorcery, evil spirits, or taboo violations. The
author interviewed hospital attendants and records their
responses to questions about patients' ethnic origins
and notions of disease causations.

10. Adams, R. F. G.   "OBɛRI ɘKAIME: A New African
       1947   Language and Script." Africa:
                            Journal of the International
                            African Institute (London) 17,
                            no. 1: 24-34.

In 1927 in southeastern Nigeria, there was a Christian-
oriented movement whose members felt themselves either
to be possessed by spirits or actually to be spirits.
In 1931 and 1936 this movement went through a resurgence
when a new language and script, Oberi ɘkaime, were developed, theoretically sent from Sɛminant the "holy
spirit" through some form of divine inspiration.

11. Adedeja, J. A.   "The Place of Drama in Yoruba
       1966   Religious Observance." Odu:
                            University of Ife Journal of
                            African Studies (Ibadan) 3,
                            no. 1: 88-94.

The dramatic quality of Yoruba (Nigeria) religious
rituals is analyzed and included is a discussion of the
ecstatic element of possession by the deities.

12. Adegbola, E. A. Adeolu "The Theological Basis of
       1969   Ethics." In Biblical Revelation
                            and African Beliefs, edited by
                            K. A. Dickson and P. Ellingworth,
                            pp. 116-36. (Bib. 450.)

Although spirit possession is not explicitly labelled,
the Yoruba oracles and the belief that spirits can
"catch" people are discussed (pp. 120 ff.).

13. Aešcoly, A. Z.   "Notices sur les Falacha ou
       1961   Juifs d'Abyssinie, d'après le
                            'Journal de voyage' d'Antoine
                            d'Abbadie." Cahiers d'études
                            africaines (Paris) 2, no. 1:
                            84-147.

Some of the Falacha, or Abyssinian Jews, of Ethiopia
believe in the Zar spirit possession cults (pp. 107,

133).

14. Aguessy, Honorat
1970

"La Divinité Legba et la
dynamique du panthéon vodoun au
Dan-home." Cahiers des
religions africaines (Kinshasa)
4, no. 7: 89-96.

Spirit possession is mentioned in connection with the
god Legba and the Vodoun Panthéon of the Dan-home
(Dahomey, Fon) of Benin (p. 93).

15. Aguessy, Honorat
1972

"Religions africaines comme
effect et source de la
civilisation de l'oralité." In
Les Religions africaines comme
source de valeurs de
civilisation, Colloque de
Cotonou (August 1970), pp. 25-
49. (Bib. 358).

Spirit possession is briefly mentioned on page 43 of
this general theoretical article on the philosophical
and theological foundations of African religions.

16. Akesson, Sam K.
1950

"The Secret of Akom (in
Ashanti)." African Affairs
(London) 49, no. 196: 237-46;
49, no. 197: 325-33.

Study by a Methodist minister in the Gold Coast
(Ghana). Information in the study was given to the
author by a convert to Christianity who had previously
spent a lifetime as a priest of Tanno, an orthodox
obosom in Ashanti. The study deals with spirit possession as the calling of the possessed to the priesthood;
the apprenticeship to the priesthood; the role of the
priest as an intermediary between the possessing spirits
and their victims; spirit possession as it occurs during
dances accompanied by drum music; the fetish fraternity
and various forms of water divination of Nsu-Ayaa; and
finally, the application to the possessed of lotions ex-
tracted from various plants. [Further summary in
African Abstracts, vol. 3, no. 43.]

17. Akstein, David
1974

"Psychosocial Perspectives of
the Application of
Terpsichoretrancetherapy."
Psychopathologie africaine
(Dakar) 10, no. 1: 121-29.

"Terpsichoretrancetherapy," developed by the author
and his associates in Brazil, employs the rhythmic music
found in the Umbanda spirit possession cult seances, and

4

aims to induce a "kinetic" trance as a therapy proce-
dure.

18. Akstein, David   "Les Trances rituelles
    n.d.   brasiliennes et les perspectives
                             de leur application à la
                             psychiatrie et à la médecine
                             psychosomatique." Typescript.
                             15 pp. Rio de Janeiro.

The Umbanda cult of Brazil is discussed in terms of
being therapeutic and prophylactic, particularly with
regards to the ritual trance states practiced in spirit
possession and mediumship. [Cited in Transcultural
Psychiatric Research Review (Bruges) 3 (October 1966):
156-58.]

19. Alagoa, E. J.   "IJO Drumlore." African Notes
    1971   (Ibadan) 6, no. 3: 63-71.

The central position of the drum in African societies
is discussed with particular reference to the Ijọ (Ijaw)
of the Niger Delta (Nigeria). The Kule "constitutes a
literary genre performed and transmitted mainly through
the medium of the drum." The drummer often becomes
possessed when playing the Kule of the gods and spirits.

20. Alapini, M.   "Le Culte de Vodoun et de
    1962   Oricha chez les Fon et les Nago
                           du Dahomey." In Colloque sur
                           les religions (Abidjan, 5-12
                           April 1961), pp. 91-96. Paris:
                           Présence africaine.

Although spirit possession is not explicitly labelled,
it is implied in this article on the Vodoun cult of the
Fon and Nago of Dahomey (Benin).

21. Aldén, Karl   "The Prophet Movement in Congo."
    1936   International Review of Missions
                           25, no. 99: 347-53.

Possession by the Holy Spirit in the Kimbangu movement
of the Congo (Zaire) is described in several case
studies (pp. 348 ff.).

22. Alexander, David, and "Spirit Possession at Chalumbe
    Bill Rau   Primary School." Paper presented
    1972   at the Conference on the History
                           of Central African Religious
                           Systems, Lusaka, 31 August -
                           8 September.

Thirty-eight Ngoni school children in Zambia were

5

possessed frequently for a period of ten days. Local
medium of the Church of the Spirits determined witchcraft as cause. Conversation with medium in possession
trance is included.

23. Alexandre, Pierre, and   Le Groupe dit Pahouin (Fang-
    Jacques Binet   Boulou-Beti). Monographies
    1958   ethnologiques africaines, vol.
                              5. Paris: Institut inter-
                              national africain.

Spirit possession is a cause of illness among the
Pahouin peoples (including the subgroups of the Fang,
Boulou (Bulu), and Beti) located in Cameroon and Spanish
Guinea (Equatorial Guinea) (pp. 116-19).

24. Amara, I. B.   "Possession: Its Nature and
    1964   Some Modes." Sierra Leone
                              Bulletin of Religion (Freetown)
                              6, no. 2: 1-12.

This article examines the connotations of "being possessed" through the ages. The term has varied in
connotation through animism, magic, and religion. An
interpretation is given of the meaning of "being possessed" in association with each of these three terms.
[Cited in African Abstracts, vol. 18, no. 566.]

25. Amara, I.   "Tactile Hallucinations among
    n.d.   Sierra Leoneans." Mimeographed.
                              10 pp.

In discussing the vividness of tactile hallucinations
among Africans (in general), the author mentions spirit
possession to emphasize the importance of the culture-
specificity of personality factors. [Cited in Transcultural Psychiatric Research Review (Bruges), 7 (April
1970): 35-37.]

26. Amato, Francisco   "Les croyances des Ngoros."
    1969   Monde non chrétien (Paris) 22,
                             no. 91: 30-36.

The history of the Ngoro people of Cameroon is presented here along with their religious beliefs concerning Inanga, god of fertility who is their most important
deity. Spirit possession is not explicitly mentioned in
the abstract, but such practices are implied in the
occurrence of verbal communication from Inanga. [Cited
in African Abstracts, vol. 22, no. 4 (October 1971),
no. 810.]

27. Amiel, R.   "Hygiène mentale en Côte
    n.d.   d'Ivoire." World Health Organi-

zation, Expert Report. Mimeo-
graphed. 119 pp.

Because the Ivory Coast remains relatively untouched
by urbanization and industrialization, the mental health
situation, in the hands of traditional healers who
employ spirit possession to cure their patients, is
satisfactory. With increased social change, the amount
and severity of mental disturbances will increase.
[Cited in Transcultural Psychiatric Research Review
(Bruges) 3 (April 1966): 34-35.]

28. Ammar, Sleim   "Médecine psychosomatique en
    1967   Afrique." Médecine et hygiène
                          25:1-15.

In this general theoretical article on Africa, spirit
possession is mentioned as a traditional explanation
for psychosomatic illness. [Cited in Transcultural
Psychiatric Research Review (Bruges) 5 (April 1968):
59-63.]

29. Amon D'Aby, F. J.   Croyances religieuses et
    1960   coutumes juridiques des Agni de
                          la Côte d'Ivoire. Paris:
                          Editions Larose.

Chapter 4 is titled "The Healer, Priests and
Sorcerers." It contains information about the Healers
and their work; the initiation ceremony into the priesthood; spirit possession as an indication of satisfactory
qualification for the priesthood and as an aid to the
priest in his religious duties; the role of the sorcerers
and the secret societies among the Agni (Anyi) people
(Ivory Coast). [Text in French.]

30. Amorin, Deolindo   Africanismo y espiritismo.
    1958   Coleccion siglo espírita, no. 3.
                          Buenos Aires: Editorial Con-
                          stancia.

This volume discusses mediumship and its different
manifestations in both the African-influenced cults and
in Espiritismo, the religious cult based on the philosophy of Allan Kardec, found in Brazil.

31. Anderson, John Q.   "The New Orleans Voodoo Ritual
    1960   Dance and its Twentieth-Century
                          Survivals." Southern Folklore
                          Quarterly 24, no. 2: 135-43.

Traced here is the history of the African-derived
voodoo cult as found in New Orleans.

7

32. Andersson, Efraim   Messianic Popular Movements in
       1958   the Lower Congo. Studia Ethno-
                               graphica Upsaliensia, vol. 14.
                               Uppsala: Almquist & Wiksells.

Andersson, a Swedish missionary, worked in the Congo
(Zaire) between 1929 and 1949. In this study he deals
with several messianic movements of the Congo, one of
which is the Simon Kimbangu movement of the 1920's. The
very early phase of Kimbangu's work involved healing the
sick during prayer meetings. Spirit possession became a
standard part of the religious services; Kimbangu would
become possessed while delivering a sermon, and his
initiates "were seized by 'the Spirit' and began to
quake" (pp. 54-58).

33. Andree, R.   Ethnographische Parallelen.
       1878   Stuttgart.

The Gaila (Galla) people of Ethiopia and the Lango
people of Uganda believe that one of the causes of
disease is spirit intrusion into the body. To cure the
disease the entering spirits must be exorcised. For
information relevant to spirit possession see page 79.

34. Andrews, J. B.   Les Fontaines des génies (Seba
       1903   Aioun), croyances soudanaises
                               à Alger. Alger: A. Jourdan.

A study of possession dances as practiced by the people
of Algeria. Many of the dances were inspired and influenced by the Songhai (Mali, Niger, Sudan) (Songhai
ritual texts). [Cited in Rouch (1954, Bib. 1525).]

35. Anonymous   Zambezi Mission Record. Vol.
       1918   6, no. 82.

Mention is made here of the custom of curing fever by
drum-beating to drive away Masabe spirits. This was introduced by the Karanga (Rhodesia) and spread to nearly
every kraal. [Cited in Jaspan (1953, Bib. 852), p. 68.]

36. Anonymous   Official Year Book of the Colony
       1932   of Southern Rhodesia - 1932.
                               No. 3. Salisbury: Rhodesian
                               Printing and Publishing Co.

Briefly mentioned here are various spirit cults that
use mediumship in Southern Rhodesia (Rhodesia). Included are the following cults: Mwari cult [Vakaranga,
Mambo, Amandebele (Ndebele)]; Karuwa cult [Watawara
(Tawara)]; and Charewa [Babudja (Budya)] (pp. 686-88).

37. Anonymous   "Cherubim and Seraphim."
    1957   Nigeria (Lagos) 53:119-34.   Ill.

This article gives a brief historical account of the
formation of the Cherubim and Seraphim sect in Nigeria,
the derivation of its name and its hierarchical structure. A description follows of the doctrine, tenets of
belief, and places of worship. Spirit possession plays
an important role in prayer meetings. "When a member is
'possessed by the Spirit' he is said to experience a
sort of dizziness and then he relapses into unconsciousness. Suddenly, he is seized by violent convulsions, at
times in phase with the beat of the music. In the end
he recovers and reveals what he has seen. It is said
that a meditative sort of person can be possessed
easily, especially if he prays" (p. 133).

38. Anonymous   "Report: Psychocultural Charac-
    1958   teristics of Africa in Relation
                             to Mental Health." In Mental
                             Disorders and Mental Health in
                             Africa South of the Sahara, pp.
                             84-95. CCTA/CSA-WFMH-WHO, Pub.
                             no. 35. Bukavu.

The "magical practices" of traditional African healers,
which include possession trances, are mentioned as
needing further analysis by psychiatrists.

39. Anonymous   "Kalibari Culture and History."
    1965   African Notes (Ibadan) 2, no. 3:
                             16-17.

A very brief description is offered of the festival
honoring Duminea, the head of the water-spirits among
the Kalabari people of the village of Soku, Nigeria.
Priests officiate and become possessed by Duminea and
other village spirits during the rites.

40. Anonymous   The Man - and His Ways.
    1969   Salisbury: Southern Rhodesia,
                             Ministry of Information.

Spirit possession by Mwari, by various tribal spirits,
and by the shave spirits among the AmaNdebele (Ndebele)
and Mashona (Shona) of Southern Rhodesia (Rhodesia) is
discussed on pages 6-8.

41. Anonymous   "Musique africaine dans
    1973   l'eglise." Flambeau (Yaoundé),
                             no. 37, pp. 37-39.

The role of African music in the Christian church is
discussed, and mention is made of possession by the Holy

Spirit which is facilitated by music.

42. Anyenyola, Jacques-   "Leadership dans les mouvements
    Oscar   prophétiques de la ville de
    1968   Lubumbashi." Problèmes sociaux
                             congolais (Lubumbashi), no. 83,
                             pp. 21-84.

In this detailed analysis of the character of leadership of the prophetic Christian movements in the city of
Lubumbashi, Congo (Zaire), mention is made of three ways
in which the Holy Spirit may be possessed by a believer:
first, it may purify the individual; second, it may
cause the purified person to have thoughts of celestial
things; and third, it may manifest itself through the
person in the performance of miraculous or prophetic
deeds (p. 73).

43. Appolis, Emile   "Une Épidémie de Ramanenjana à
    1964   Madagascar (1863-1864),"
                             Annales de l'université de
                             Madagascar 3:59-63.

Although spirit possession is not explicitly labelled,
in 1863 at Tananarive, Madagascar, a Jesuit father observed and provided a detailed description of an outbreak of ramanenjana, "a kind of hysteria, involving
collective conversion, which has the characteristics of
an epidemic."

Aquina, Sister Mary O. P.   Also publishes under
Weinrich, A. K. H. (Bib. 1848-49b).

44. Aquina, Sister Mary   "Christianity in Rhodesian
    O. P.   Tribal Trust Land." African
    1966   Social Research (Lusaka) 1:1-40.

Proceeding from a general historical account of
Christianity in Rhodesia, a detailed description is given
of the rise of the Zionist Independent African Church in
which spirit possession and exorcism play an important
role.

45. Aquina, Sister Mary   "The People of the Spirit: An
    O. P.   Independent Church in Rhodesia."
    1967   Africa: Journal of the Inter-
                             national African Institute
                             (London) 37, no. 2: 203-19.

Among the Karanga of Rhodesia, an independent African
church, the Apostles, has combined many aspects of both
Christian and local traditional religion. Among the
aspects of traditional Karanga religion which have not
been included in the Christian church is the cult of

Mashave (sing. Shave); the Mashave are spirits of aliens
who have died in Karangaland; they possess people,
making them sick. If the spirit is accepted into the
Karanga tribe in a special initiation ceremony (which is
not described), it confers special skills on its host,
such as healing or hunting. If the host is unwilling to
accept the spirit, it must then be exorcised (p. 204).

46. Aquina, Sister Mary   "A Sociological Interpretation
       O. P.   of Sorcery and Witchcraft Be-
       1968   liefs among the Karanga." Nada
                               (Salisbury) 9, no. 5: 47-53.
                               Bibl.

A theoretical analysis of Karanga (Rhodesia) ideas
about witchcraft and sorcery is presented. Since women
who inherit shave spirits can refuse to be possessed by
them, the term sorcery is determined as being a more
accurate description of their activities than witchcraft.

47. Aquina, Sister Mary   "Zionists in Rhodesia." Africa:
       O. P.   Journal of the International
       1969   African Institute (London) 39,
                               no. 2: 113-36.

The Apostles, a syncretic African Christian church, is
found among the Karanga of Rhodesia. During dances at
church meetings, members often are possessed by the Holy
Spirit. Possession is very rare among men, although one
such incident was witnessed by the author. Mostly
women and persons who have recently joined the church
are possessed. These people hold a very low status in
the church, and it is suggested that possession is the
only avenue through which they can show their participation in the worship (p. 125).

48. Aquina, Sister Mary   "An Aspect of the Development of
       O. P.   the Religious Life in Rhodesia."
       1975   In Themes in the Christian
                               History of Central Africa,
                               edited by T. O. Ranger and J.
                               Weller, pp. 218-37. (Bib. 1449.)

A detailed presentation is given of the role of "women
religious" in the Catholic Church. The position of the
Sisters in Rhodesia is analyzed with particular reference
to traditional Shona customs including those surrounding
the spirit mediums of Shona religion (pp. 229-30, 235).

49. Armstrong, Robert G.   "The Religions of the Idoma."
       1961   Ibadan (Ibadan) 13:5-9.

The Idoma people live in the Benue province of
northern Nigeria. Their religion is composed of a series

11

of cults each having its own beliefs, attitudes, and
practices, and each administered by a particular group.
Trance and spirit possession are rare and never occur in
the presence of a large number of people. Rather, individual women, alone on a path or in a yam patch (but
with a group of people coming into sight), become possessed by the Anjenu spirits or by the yam spirits (if
the woman has offended their taboos). The term Anjenu
may be related to the Arabic term Jinni (evil spirits)
and introduced to the Idoma by the Moslem Kanuri. The
article describes the ceremonies of worship to the
Anjenu spirits and the altars consecrated to them. A
case is reported of a girl acting as a medium for these
spirits. An explanation is offered for the recent popu-
larity of the possession syndrome, particularly as it
affects women (p. 5). [Further summary in African
Abstracts, vol. 14, no. 54.]

50. Armstrong, Robert G.   "African Religion and Cultural
    1975   Renewal." Orita (Ibadan) 9,
                                no. 2: 109-33.

Spirit possession and its use in African traditional
religions are mentioned briefly in this theoretical
essay (p. 113).

51. Arneson, Jeanette   Tradition and Change in Yoruba
    Jensen   Art. Sacramento: E. B.
    1974   Crocker Art Gallery. Ill.

The communication between the deities and man is emphasized in a discussion of Yoruba (Nigeria) use of art
in their religion. Spirit mediumship is implied but not
explicitly labelled (p. 12).

52. Ashton, E. H.   "Medicine, Magic, and Sorcery
    1943   Among the Southern Sotho."
                               Communications from the School
                               of African Studies (Cape Town),
                               n.s., no. 10.

One type of diviner among the Southern Sotho (also
called Basuto) of South Africa acquires his powers from
having been cured of an illness called moteketeke. This
illness is manifested in loss of memory, fainting,
trance, etc., and may eventually develop into spirit
possession (p. 3).

53. Ashton, Hugh   The Basuto. London: Oxford
    1952   University Press.

Among the Basuto of South Africa, a relatively recent
introduction of a type of spiritual illness has many
similarities to spirit possession, although not explicitly

labelled as such. A person so afflicted wanders around
as if in trance, and is visited by spirits in dreams.
Treatment is centered on nightly trance dancing (pp.
283 ff.).

54. Assimeng, Max   "Traditional Religion in Ghana:
    1976   Preliminary Guide to Research."
                         Thought and Practice: Journal
                         of the Philosophical Association
                         of Kenya (Nairobi) 3, no. 1:
                         65-89.

Spirit possession and mediumship are briefly mentioned
as areas for further research in this article on traditional (Akan) religions in Ghana (p. 86).

55. Asuni, Tolani   "Socio-medical Problems of
    1973   Religious Converts." Psycho-
                         pathologie africaine (Dakar) 9,
                         no. 2: 223-36.

Possession by the Holy Spirit is mentioned in this
analysis of the religious converts in five sects (un-
named) in western Nigeria.

56. Atiwiya, G.   "Le 'Zebola': Thérapie
    1971   traditionnelle des maladies
                         mentales dans un cadre urbain."
                         Psychopathologie africaine
                         (Dakar) 7, no. 3: 389-416.

Practiced mainly among those of Mongo and Baenga (Enga)
origin in the Democratic Republic of the Congo, the
Zebola is a traditional healing cult which cures individuals of possession by the bekaji ancestral spirits.
Descriptions of healing practices are included.

57. Aubin, H.   "Introduction à l'étude de la
    1939   psychiatrie chez les Noirs."
                         Annales medico-psychologiques
                         (Paris) 97, pt. 1, no. 2: 181-
                         213.

Spirit possession is analyzed psychologically in a
case study of an African from Senegal (unspecified
ethnic group) (pp. 188-89).

58. Aubin, H.   "Danse mystique, possession,
    1948   psychopathologie." Evolution
                         psychiatrique 4:191-215.

Analysis of the successive phases of the dance of
primitive peoples: preliminary rites, stages and oc-
currences of hysteria, possession, capturing of magical

forces, and break in contact with these forces. [Cited
in Bibliographie ethnographique du Congo belge
(Brussels) 7 (1949): 16.]

59. Aubin, H.   L'Homme et la magie. Paris:
    1952   Desclée de Brouwer & Cie.

    Islamic notions of spirit possession in North Africa
are briefly mentioned in a more general section on possession (pp. 73-78).

60. Augé, Marc, et al.   Prophétisme et thérapeutique:
    1975   Albert Atcho et la communauté
                        de Bregbo. Paris: Hermann.

    Described in detail in a series of essays is the
community of Bregbo (Ivory Coast) which is headed by the
prophet healer Albert Atcho and is a part of the
Harrisist religion, an Independent Black Church. Although spirit possession is not explicitly labelled,
confessions of individuals who say they are attacked by
devils are given throughout this work.

61. Baasher, T. A.   "Observations from the Sudan."
    1961   In First Pan-African Psychiatric
                        Conference - Proceedings, pp.
                        238-40. (Bib. 1344).

    A brief presentation of the Zar spirit possession
healing cult in the Sudan is given, and emphasis is
placed on adapting traditional methods to modern psychiatric therapy.

62. Baasher, T. A.   "Traditional Psychotherapeutic
    n.d.   Practices in the Sudan."
                        Mimeographed. 19 pp.

    Based on fieldwork in the Sudan, detailed discussion
of the Zar healing cult which employs spirit possession
and mediumship is given here. [Cited in Transcultural
Psychiatric Research Review (Bruges) 4 (October 1967):
158-60.]

63. Baëta, C. G.   Prophetism in Ghana. London:
    1962   SCM Press.

    Seven chapters are devoted to the study of nine differ-
ent separatist churches. Some of the descriptions of
the churches concern the role of spirit possession (by
the spirit of the Holy Ghost) in church activities, and
the use of mediums' trances for healing purposes. A
particularly good discussion of spirit possession is
found in chapter 6 (pp. 94-113), dealing with the prayer
and healing group of the Evangelical Presbyterian Church

at Etodome, Ghana. Bibliography but no index of topics.

64. Baëta, C. G.   "Christianity and Healing."
    1967   Orita: Ibadan Journal of
                           Religious Studies (Ibadan) 1,
                           no. 2: 51-61.

    The "healing church" in Ghana combines both Christian
    and indigenous religious elements, including exorcism
    and the use of ecstasy.

65. Baëta, C. G., ed.   Christianity in Tropical Africa.
    1968   London: Oxford University Press.

    Includes in this bibliography:

              289   R. Bureau (1968)
              1063   D. A. Low (1968)

66. Bakaitwako, E.   "Gods and Ancestral Spirits
    1974   among the Bakingwe." Occasional
                           Research Papers in African
                           Traditional Religion and Philo-
                           sophy (Makerere University,
                           Kampala), vol. 20, no. 212.

    The Bakingwe (Kingwe) of Uganda believe in a spirit
    pantheon headed by Nyabingi, the chief spirit of
    emandwa. The spirits can possess people and bring them
    good fortune or illness, and are termed respectively the
    "providing" and "taking away" emandwa. Cases of both
    are given.

67. Balandier, G.   Afrique ambiguë. Paris:
    1937   Librairie Plon.

    Chapter 3 deals with spirit possession and other
    African traditions. The Lebou (Lebu) of Senegal are
    mentioned in particular.

68. Balandier, Georges   "Femmes possédées et leurs
    1948   chants." Présence africaine
                           (Paris) 5: 749-54.

    A study was conducted among the Lébou (Lebu) fishermen
    of Senegal. Spirit possession is part of the traditional
    Lébou religious practices, specifically associated with
    women, of manipulating alien forces for beneficial com-
    munity service. The possession crises recall the old
    matriarchal structure of society which preceded the new
    religion of Moslem origin. This collective and matri-
    archal aspect of possession is revealed by the observed
    ritual: exorcism dances conducted by the "spirit
    mistress," followed by a sacrifice ceremony and a con-

struction of an altar to the spirit. Each possessed
woman remains bound to her spirit and thus becomes an
element of the cosmic order. [Cited in African
Abstracts, vol. 1, no. 198; text and annotation in
French.]

69. Balandier, Georges   "Messianism and Nationalism in
    1965   Black Africa." In Africa:
                             Social Problems of Change and
                             Conflict, edited by Pierre L.
                             van den Berghe, pp. 443-60. San
                             Francisco: Chandler Publishing
                             Co.

   Although spirit possession is not explicitly labelled,
mention is made of the Zionist Churches of Africa and
their use of "fits of seizure" (p. 447) and "sacred
delirium" (p. 445).

70. Balandier, Georges   Daily Life in the Kingdom of
    1968   Kongo. London: George Allen
                             & Unwin.

   The life of the foundress of national religion of the
Kongo (Zaire), Kimpa Vita or Dona Beatriz, is presented
here. Living in the eighteenth century, Dona Beatriz
was said to have been visited by St. Anthony when she
was very ill; she died, and in place of her soul, St.
Anthony possessed her. Comparisons between traditional
African beliefs and the syncretic Christian-oriented
cults such as "Antonianism" are made (pp. 257-61).

71. Balandier, Georges   The Sociology of Black Africa:
    1970   Social Dynamics in Central
                             Africa. New York: Praeger
                             Publishers. (Originally
                             published in French in 1955.)

   Possession by spirits is integral to sorcery practices
among the Fang in Gabon and the Bakongo (Kongo) of
Zaire. The Fang believe that the evur spirits choose
among humans whom they wish to have as their intermediaries, and their power is not considered to be of an
evil nature (pp. 149-50). The Bakongo believe that
those who practice witchcraft to work evil are possessed
by nkundu spirits (pp. 370-71).

72. Balyabuga, M.   "Traditional Religion in
    1974   Buyanja." Occasional Research
                             Papers in African Traditional
                             Religion and Philosophy
                             (Makerere University, Kampala),
                             vol. 17, no. 185.

Among the Nyoro of the Buyanja district of Uganda a
method of spirit exorcism, termed Kubandwa, is practiced.
The author makes an analytical distinction between spirit
possession, spirit mediumship, and shamanism in order to
clarify this practice (pp. 14-15 ff.).

73. Bamunoba, Y. K.   "Diviners for the Abagabe."
    1965   Uganda Journal (Kampala) 29,
                             no. 1: 95-97.

During the reign of Mutambuuka (1852-79), the Abagabe
were on good terms with the Omukama of Bunyoro (Nyoro).
The Omukama sent Mutambuuka a prophetess named
Nyabuzaana. She bewitched Mutambuuka's enemies and performed a ritual at the beginning of his military expe-
ditions in which, assisted by musicians of the Cwezi
cult, she became possessed by Emandwa spirits (Uganda).

74. Bamunoba, Y. K., and   "Emandwa Initiation in Ankole."
    F. B. Welbourn   Uganda Journal (Kampala) 29,
    1965   no. 1: 13-25.

The initiation ceremony into the Cwezi cult is described for the Iru caste of the Ankole (Nkole). Informants are members of the revivalistic Church of
Uganda who had once been initiates of the cult. Although
possession is not a part of the Iru version of the Cwezi
cult--whereas it is for Sumbwa and Nyoro ethnic groups
(Uganda)--initiates are intimately associated with the
spirits.

75. Banda-Mwaka, Justin   "Le Kimbanguisme en tant que
    1971   mouvement prépolitique chez les
                             Kongo." Problèmes sociaux
                             congolais (Lubumbashi), nos. 92-
                             93, pp. 3-54.

The essential element in the conversion experience of
the members of the kimbangu church is the possession
trance occurring as the Holy Spirit enters the individual. The significance of this prophetic movement, with
particular attention paid to the Kongo of Zaire, is
studied here in detail (p. 17).

76. Banton, Michael   "An Independent African Church
    1956   in Sierra Leone." Hibbert
                             Journal (London) 55, no. 216:
                             57-63.

The Church of the Lord, a Nigerian separatist church
with branches in Sierra Leone, conducts church services
in which prophecies and visions are reported by women
members. [Further summary in African Studies, vol. 8,
no. 211.]

17

77. Banton, Michael   "African Prophets." Race 5,
    1963   no. 2: 42-55.

    Although spirit possession is not explicitly labelled,
    the interrelationship between political and religious
    factors in the growth of prophetic cults such as
    Kimbangu is discussed particularly in the context of
    social protest.

78. Barasa, J.   "The Holy Spirit Church of East
    1974   Africa." Occasional Research
                          Papers in African Traditional
                          Religion and Philosophy
                          (Makerere University, Kampala),
                          vol. 21, no. 213.

    The history of the Holy Spirit Church of East Africa,
    located in Uganda, is explored in depth, and reasons
    for its origination are discussed. Possession by the
    Holy Spirit and glossolalia are manifested in the Church.

79. Barclay, Harold B.   Buurri Al Lamaab. Ithaca, New
    1964   York: Cornell University Press.

    The workings of the Zaar spirit possession cult are
    described for the Arab village of Buurri Al Lamaab in
    the Sudan on pp. 196-206, 272.

80. Barker, Anthony   "Physic and Protocol among the
    1972   Zulus." Publication of the
                          Institute for the Study of Man in
                          Africa (Johannesburg), no. 32.

    Spirit possession among the Zulus of South Africa is
    explored, and the Western diagnosis of hysteria is ex-
    plained with ethnographic data (pp. 7 ff.).

81. Barker, Dudley   Swaziland. London: Her
    1965   Majesty's Stationery Office.

    Spirit possession, causing illness and also as a means
    of divination, is discussed for the Swazi of Swaziland
    (pp. 98 ff.).

82. Barrett, David B.   Schism and Renewal in Africa.
    1968   Nairobi: Oxford University Press.

    Six thousand contemporary religious movements in Africa
    are analyzed, and a detailed theoretical framework for
    the rise of the Independent Christian Church is presented
    (see book's index under "Holy Spirit" for page citations
    of spirit possession).

83. Barrett, David B., ed.   African Initiatives in Religion.
    1971   Nairobi: East African Publishing
                              House.

    Includes in this bibliography:
            410   M. L. Daneel (1971b)
            734   M. Hardyman (1971)
            1138   M. L. Martin (1971c)
            1257   M. W. Murphree (1971)

84. Barrett, Leonard   "Portrait of a Jamaican Healer:
    1973   African Medical Lore in the
                             Caribbean." Caribbean Quarterly
                             19, no. 3: 6-19.

    Spirit possession is an integral part of the Jamaican
healers of African descent. No specific African ethnic
group is mentioned, but a list of African "retentions"
in beliefs and rituals is presented.

85. Barrett, Leonard E.   Soul-Force: African Heritage in
    1974   Afro-American Religion. Garden
                             City, N.Y.: Doubleday, Anchor
                             Press.

    The Afro-American religions in the Caribbean, South
America, and the Pentecostal groups (also in North
America) are examined here, and spirit possession in its
various manifestations is discussed throughout (see
book's index under "Possession" for page citations).

86. Bartoli, D., et al.   "Psychopathologie et environne-
    1969   ment familial en Afrique."
                             Psychopathologie africaine
                             (Dakar) 4, no. 2: 173-226.

    Two cases are presented here in order to demonstrate
the relationship between psychopathological disorders
and family environment in Africa. The setting for both
cases is Dakar (Senegal); one patient is of Dahomean
(Benin) background and is a practicing Muslim, while the
other is of the Wolof peoples (Senegal). Possession by
rab ancestor spirits is the traditional explanation
given for both illnesses, and each patient's mother has a
history of being possessed (pp. 200, 213).

87. Bascom, William R.   "The Sociological Role of the
    1944   Yoruba Cult Group." American
                             Anthropological Association
                             Memoirs, vol. 63.

    Considers, in part, the Orisha cults and the spirit
possession ceremonies associated with them among the
Yoruba of Nigeria.

19

88. Bascom, W. R.   "The Focus of Cuban Santería."
    1950   Southwestern Journal of Anthro-
                           pology 6, no. 1: 64-68.

In Cuba the worship of African deities is known as
Santería. Santería practices are characterized by
identification of African deities with names of Catholic
saints and by spirit possession manifested in dances.
The author tries to discover what light Santería sheds
on African religions and what can be learned about the
syncretism of these religions and Catholicism.

89. Bascom, W. R.   "The Yoruba in Cuba." Nigeria
    1951   (Lagos) 37:14-20.

A description of the Afro-Cuban religious ceremonies
as observed by the author in 1948. He lists the African
deities as they are known by their Christian saints'
names and indicates some of their characteristics. The
study shows that African traditions and Yoruba religious
survivals in the New World are not restricted to remote
rural areas, but are strong among the populations of
large urban centers. A description of the Orisha (gods)
worship ceremony includes some details about spirit
possession.

90. Bascom, W. R., and   Continuity and Change in African
    M. J. Herskovits,   Cultures. Chicago: University
    eds.   of Chicago Press.
    1959

     Includes in this bibliography:
               337   J. B. Christensen (1959)
              1180   J. C. Messenger (1959b)

91. Bascom, William   "La Religion africaine au
    1965   Nouveau Monde." In Les Religions
                           africaines traditionnelles,
                           Rencontres internationales de
                           Bouaké (October 1962), pp. 119-
                           37. (Bib. 1466.)

Concentrating mainly on the African influence on
Cuban and Brazilian cults, the author mentions the
phenomenon of spirit possession (see also the Discussion
following the article).

92. Bascom, William   Ifa Divination: Communication
    1969a   Between Gods and Men in West
                           Africa. Bloomington, Ind.:
                           Indiana University Press.

Author includes a discussion of spirit possession in
this volume.

93. Bascom, William   The Yoruba of Southwestern
    1969b   Nigeria. New York: Holt,
                             Rinehart & Winston.

Possession by the Yoruba (Nigeria) gods is described
in detail on pages 78-97.

94. Bascom, William R.   Shango in the New World.
    1972   Occasional Publication, African
                             and Afro-American Research
                             Institute. Austin: The
                             University of Texas at Austin.

Spirit possession and mediumship in the cult of the
Yoruba Thunder-god Shango in Brazil, Trinidad, and Cuba
are outlined.

95. Basset, Henri   Le Culte des Grottes au Maroc.
    1920   Alger: Ancienne Maison Bastide-
                             Jourdan, Jules Carbonel.

Spirit possession is mentioned in connection with the
cult of caves "le culte des grottes" in Morocco (pp.
90 ff.).

96. Bastian, A.   Der Mensch in der Geschichte.
    1860   2:559.

A report on spirit possession as it appeared in
Madagascar. The Saccare were evil demons who possessed
both men and women for a period of from ten to fifteen
days. A description is given of the curing ceremonies,
in the form of dances, offered to the victims. Additional information on spirit possession is also to be
found in Flacourt, Histoire de la grande ile de
Madagascar. [Cited by Oesterreich (1930, Bib. 1301),
p. 138.]

97. Bastide, Roger   "Le Batuque de Porto-Alegre."
    1952   In Acculturation in the
                             Americas, edited by S. Tax, pp.
                             195-206. (Bib. 1715.)

This article discusses the Afro-Brazilian spirit possession cults found in Porto-Alegre.

98. Bastide, R.   "Cavalos dos Santos." In
    1953   Estudos Afro-Brasileiros.
                             Faculdade de filosofia, ciências
                             et letras, ser. 3a, boletim 154.
                             São Paulo: Universidade de São
                             Paulo.

The author draws an analogy between the spirit pos-

21

session phenomenon as it occurs among the Voodooists and the black population of Brazil.

99. Bastide, Roger
    1955

"Le Principe de coupure et le comportement afro-brésilien." Anais do 31 Congresso Internacional de Americanistas (São Paulo) 1: 493-503.

This theoretical article discusses the spirit possession phenomenon in the Afro-Brazilian candomblé cult.

100. Bastide, Roger
     1956

"Immigration et métamorphose d'un dieux." Cahiers internationaux de sociologie (Paris) 20, no. 3: 45-60.

The cult of Exù, known among the Yoruba and the Fon, was brought to the Americas with the slave trade. This study describes the worship of Exù, an intermediary between man and the deities, in Dahomey (Benin) and Nigeria. In Brazil, Exù became identified with the Christian devil, and he is worshipped by the Candomblé cults associated with Macoumba sorcery. Spirit possession is an integral part of these Brazilian religious forms.

101. Bastide, Roger
     1957

Brésil: Terre des contrastes. Paris: Hachette.

Chapter 4 discusses the African influence in Brazil with particular attention paid to religious syncretism. Spirit possession is discussed.

102. Bastide, Roger
     1958a

Le Candomblé de Bahia (rite nago). Paris: Mouton & Co.

Chapter 5, entitled "The Structure of the Ecstasy," deals with the various forms of trances and states of possession as they are found in the Candomblé cults of Bahia (Brazil). An interesting variety of possession, termed éré, is described as an intermediary stage between deep trance and complete recovery. Chapter 6, "Man, Reflection of God," also contains information about spirit possession.

103. Bastide, Roger
     1958b

"Le Messianisme raté." Archives de sociologie des religions, no. 5, pp. 31-37.

The relationship between illness and spirit possession is discussed in the context of Brazilian messianic and spiritualist movements including the Umbanda cult.

104. Bastide, R.   "Psychiatrie, ethnographie et
     1958c   sociologie: Les Maladies
                          mentales et le noir Brésilien."
                          In Mental Disorders and Mental
                          Health in Africa South of the
                          Sahara, pp. 223-30. CCTA/CSA-
                          WFMH-WHO, Pub. no. 35. Bukavu.

     In a comparison between black Brazilian culture and
behavior and that seen in Africa, the point is made
that possession and trance are not pathological but
ritually structured, mystical states.

105. Bastide, Roger   "Réflexions sans titre autour
     1958d   d'une des formes de la
                          spiritualité africaine."
                          Présence africaine (Paris),
                          nos. 18-19, pp. 11-16.

     Spirit possession is briefly mentioned in this
article on African spirituality in general (p. 14).

106. Bastide, R.   "Les Métamorphoses du sacré dans
     1959a   les sociétés en transition."
                          Civilisations (Bruxelles) 9,
                          no. 4: 432-43.

     The author discusses the syncretism of African tradi-
tional religions and Catholicism in the New World, and
the contact situation of the colonial powers and
African belief systems; the author further examines the
lines of development that religion followed in these
instances. The Candomble cults of Brazil were traditionally Yoruba, Fon, or Bantu religious associations,
which have merged and adopted features of Catholicism
and spiritualism. In Nigeria, contact with colonial
powers yielded the Umbanda spiritism. This study
further deals with spirit possession as it is incorpo-
rated in these new syncretic religions. [Further summary
in African Studies, vol. 11, no. 385.]

107. Bastide, Roger   Sociologia do folclore
     1959b   brasileiro. São Paulo: Editôria
                          Anhambi S.A.

     Spirit possession and mediumship in the Candomblé
cult of Brazil are discussed.

108. Bastide, Roger   Les Religions africaines au
     1960   Bresil. Paris: Presses
                          Universitaires de France.

     Not available for annotation.

23

109. Bastide, Roger   "Le Théorie de la réincarnation
     1965   chez les Afro-Américains." In
                        Réincarnation et vie mystique
                        en Afrique noire, Colloque de
                        Strasbourg, pp. 9-29.
                        (Bib. 359.)

     Spirit possession and mediumship among the Afro-
American cults, including Umbanda (Brazil) and Vaudou
(Haiti), are discussed.

110. Bastide, Roger   Les Amériques noires. Paris:
     1967a   Payot.

     This book deals directly with the African influence in
the New World and focuses in large part on the religions
which include the practice of spirit possession.

111. Bastide, Roger   "Le Spiritisme au Brésil."
     1967b   Archives de sociologie des
                        religions, no. 24, pp. 3-16.

     The practices of spiritism including possession and
mediumship in the Afro-Brazilian cults of Umbanda and
Candomble are discussed.

112. Bastide, Roger   "Religions africaines et
     1968a   structures de civilisation."
                        Présence africaine (Paris),
                        no. 66, pp. 98-111.

     Although spirit possession is not explicitly
labelled, mystical trance states and their relationship
to African religions and cultures are discussed on
pages 106-7.

113. Bastide, R.   "Transe mystique, psycho-patho-
     1968b   logie et psychiatrie." In
                        Deuxième Colloque africain de
                        psychiatrie - Proceedings, pp.
                        124-33. (Bib. 1345.)

     This theoretical article discusses in depth the
phenomenon of spirit possession and compares it to
shamanism. Emphasis is placed on the author's opinion
that spirit possession is not an adjunct of mental illness.

114. Bastide, Roger   "Price-Mars et le Vaudou
     1969   haïtien." Présence africaine
                        (Paris), no. 71, pp. 19-23.

     A critique of Jean Price-Mars's work (Bib. 1118-1119)
on the Haitian Vaudou cult is presented; his view of

possession is that it is a "cultural" and not a "pathological" phenomenon (p. 21).

115. Bastide, Roger   African Civilisations in the New
     1971a   World. New York: Harper & Row.

Traced here are the African cultural influences, including the use of spirit possession, on the religions of the New World. Mention is made of the Bush Negroes of Dutch and French Guiana, the Candomblé and Macumba cults of Brazil, the Voodoo cult of Haiti, and various syncretic African and Christian religions (see book's index for page citations).

116. Bastide, Roger   As religiones africanos no
     1971b   Brasil. São Paulo: Pioneira e
                             Universidade de São Paulo.

Not available for annotation.

117. Bastide, Roger   Le Rève, la trance et la folie.
     1972   Paris: Flammarion.

The second section of this book is devoted to possession trance as it occurs both in Africa and Afro-America. No specific group is mentioned in the abstract, and major focus seems to be on the communication between psychiatrists and anthropologists. [Cited in Transcultural Psychiatric Research Review (Montreal) 12 (April 1975): 10-15.]

118. Bastide, Roger   Le Sacré sauvage et autres
     1975   essais. Paris: Payot.

The Umbanda and Candomblé cults of Brazil and the Vodun cult of Haiti, all of which employ spirit possession and mediumship, are discussed in depth in chapters 12 and 13.

119. Bastide, R.   "Les Techniques du repos et de
     n.d.   la relaxation -- étude trans-
                            culturelle." Mimeographed.
                            30 pp.

Spirit possession in the initiation of a "daughter of God" among the Yoruba of Nigeria is mentioned in this general article on transcultural methods of rest and relaxation. [Cited in Transcultural Psychiatric Research Review (Montreal) 10 (October 1973): 103-7.]

120. Bate, H. Maclear   Report from the Rhodesians.
     1953   London: Andrew Melrose.

Although spirit mediumship is not explicitly labelled,

presented here is the incident of the ritual murder performed in 1923 among the Watawara in Rhodesia resulting
from the guilty man having deflowered Nechiskwa, the
"goddess" and wife of the rain spirit (pp. 242-43).

121. Bateson, Gregory   "Some Components of Socializa-
     1975   tion for Trance." Ethos 3, no.
                                2: 143-55.

     Although trance states in Africa are not discussed, an
analysis of possession and mediumship trances is offered
in terms of a theory of socialization and the psychological development of the individual.

122. Baudin, P.   Fetichism and Fetich Worshipers.
     1885   New York: Benziger Bros.

     In this early account written by a missionary among
the Yoruba of Nigeria, Togo and Dahomey (Benin), the
initiation and possession by the "fetich" of a "fetich-
priest" are described on pages 76-79.

123. Baumann, Hermann,   Völkerkunde von Afrika: mit
     Richard Thurnwald,   besonderer Berücksichtigung der
     and Diedrich   kolonialen Aufgabe. Essen:
     Westermann   Essener Verlagsanstalt.
     1940

     Discussion of spirit possession appears on pages 43,
121 ff., 134 ff., 141, 158, 181, 194, 196, 201, and
257. It deals with masks of the Cokwe (Chokwe) peoples
of Angola (p. 141) and others in Central Africa, primarily in Zaire.

124. Baumann, H., and   Les Peuples et les civilisations
     D. Westermann   de l'Afrique. Paris: Payot.
     1967

     The trance state of spirit possession is described for
the following ethnic groups: Tehokwe (Chokwe) and
Rovouma (Angola, p. 57); Chona (Shona)(Rhodesia, p.
144); Ngungela (Angola, p. 159); Swahili (Tanzania, p.
229); and the Nouba (Nuba) (Sudan, p. 304) (see book's
index under "Possession" for further page citations).

125. Baxter, H. C.   "Religious Practices of the Pagan
     1943   Wazigua: The Story of a Dying
                              Creed." Tanganyika Notes and
                              Records (Dar es Salaam) 15:49-57.

     The author focuses on the Zigua (Tanzania) belief in
the spirits of the dead as intermediaries between man
and God and describes the ceremonies devoted to these
spirits. Spirit mediumship is discussed.

26

126. Baxter, P. T. W., and   The Azande and Related Peoples.
     Audrey Butt   Ethnographic Survey of Africa,
     1953   edited by Daryll Forde. London:
                              International African Institute.

There are several types of diviners among the Moru of
the Sudan. One of these, Koyo Yapiri, divines while in
a state of possession. A person must be possessed by
Adro, the earthly aspect of the deity, in order to become a diviner (p. 124).

127. Bazola, Etienne   "Le Kimbanguisme (2)." Cahiers
     1968   des religions africaines
                              (Kinshasa) 2, no. 3: 121-52;
                              2, no. 4: 315-36.

The Kimbangu Christian sect is explored as to its
attitude towards the traditional African religions, its
relationship to mainline Christianity, and its use of
the belief in the Holy Spirit. The Kongo (Zaire)
traditional religion is examined along with spirit possession as an element in it (pp. 318-19). Possession by the
Holy Spirit is discussed on pages 333-36.

128. Bazola, E.   La Çonversion au Kimbanguisme et
     n.d.   ses motifs. Leopoldville:
                             Université Louvanium.

Unavailable for annotation.

129. Beach, D. N.   "Kaguvi and Fort Mhondoro."
     1972   Rhodesiana (Salisbury), no. 27,
                             pp. 29-47.

Kaguvi was the Mhondoro or spirit medium at the time of
the Mashona Rebellion of 1896-97. This article gives
an account first of the importance of the Mhondoros for
the Shona (Rhodesia), and then of the Rebellion itself.

130. Beattie, J. H. M.   "Initiation into the Cwezi Spirit
     1957   Possession Cult in Bunyoro."
                              African Studies (Johannesburg)
                              16, no. 3: 150-61.

The Mbandwa spirit possession cult found among the
Nyoro of Uganda is discussed. The author focusses on a
description of treatment offered to a possessed person;
diagnosis of a person's ills; description of the initiation ceremony into the Mbandwa cult as part of the treatment for spirit possession.

131. Beattie, J. H. M.   "Nyoro Marriage and Affinity."
     1958   Africa: Journal of the Inter-
                             national African Institute

27

(London) 28, no. 1: 1-22.

Among the Nyoro people of western Uganda, the ceremony of z'okubukara is performed before a girl leaves her parents' house to join her husband. She sits on the laps of both her parents, and when she arrives at her husband's home she will sit on his parents' laps. Such a ceremony is also performed upon initiation into the Mbandwa spirit possession cult (p. 8, footnote).

132. Beattie, J. H. M.   "Rituals of Nyoro Kingship."
     1959   Africa: Journal of the Inter-
                            national African Institute
                            (London) 29, no. 2: 134-45.

Among the Nyoro of rural Uganda the title "Mukama" is given to the head of state. The Mukama does not fulfill the role of "a medium for communication with any spiritual power deriving from outside the kingship." This function is reserved for the Babandwa mediums, initiates into the Nyoro possession cult, the traditional religion of the country (pp. 138-39).

133. Beattie, John   Bunyoro: An African Kingdom.
     1960a   New York: Holt, Rinehart &
                           Winston.

General discussion of spirit possession by ghosts and by the Chwezi spirits among the Bunyoro of Uganda; both used in curative treatments for illnesses (pp. 71 ff.).

134. Beattie, J. H. M.   "On the Nyoro Concept of
     1960b   Mahano." African Studies
                            (Johannesburg) 19, no. 3: 145-50.

Among the Nyoro of Uganda, the concept of ritual or magical danger is called Mahano. During initiation into the Cwezi spirit possession cult, novices are considered to be in a state of Mahano. They are freed from this state only by the performing of a ritual act of sexual intercourse with a senior member of the Cwezi cult (p. 148).

135. Beattie, J. H. M.   "Group Aspects of the Nyoro
     1961a   Spirit Mediumship Cult." Human
                            Problems in British Central
                            Africa: Rhodes-Livingstone
                            Journal (Lusaka) 30:11-38.

A description of the Mbandwa cult associated with the pantheon of Cwezi spirits. The article first presents information on spirit mediumship in pre-European times, the traditional relationship between the cults and the local domestic groups forming the elements of Nyoro

(Uganda) community structure. Secondly, the author considers the European influences on mediumship cults; they have become clandestine operations with increased emphasis on the individualistic aspects of spirit possession at the expense of the traditional cult group.

136. Beattie, J. H. M.   "Nyoro Mortuary Rites." Uganda
     1961b   Journal (Kampala) 25, no. 2:
                              171-83.

Following a detailed discussion of the burial customs and attitudes towards death of the Nyoro of Uganda, mention is made of the use of the spirits of the dead by sorcerers (p. 181). Possession is not explicitly labelled but implied.

137. Beattie, J. H. M.   "Twin Ceremonies in Bunyoro."
     1962   Journal of the Royal Anthropo-
                              logical Institute of Great
                              Britain and Ireland 92, pt. 1:
                              1-12.

Spirit mediumship among the Nyoro of Uganda is discussed throughout this article.

138. Beattie, J. H. M.   "A Note on the Connection be-
     1963a   tween Spirit Mediumship and
                              Hunting in Bunyoro, with Special
                              Reference to Possession by
                              Animal Ghosts." Man (London)
                              63, no. 241: 188-89.

The Mbandwa spirit mediumship cult helps the Nyoro (Uganda) people come to terms with natural and other forces around them. Central figures of the cult are Cwezi hero-gods which possess individuals and particularly those who serve as their mediums. However, spirit possession by the ghost of a slain animal may also occur, as evidenced by an account of possession by the ghost of a hippopotamus. Initiation into the spirit possession cult releases the victim from possession and propitiates the possessing spirit. [Further summary in African Abstracts, vol. 15, no. 428.]

139. Beattie, J. H. M.   "Sorcery in Bunyoro." In Witch-
     1963b   craft and Sorcery in East
                              Africa, edited by John Middleton
                              and E. H. Winter. London:
                              Routledge & Kegan Paul.

The author discusses (pp. 32-55) sorcerers as mediums in possession cults; describes Mbandwa ceremonies for curing certain ills; explains advent of new spirits in today's cults as a way of making new forces manageable and comprehensible. Four spirit possession cases are cited as evidence among the Nyoro of Uganda.

140. Beattie, John   "Divination in Bunyoro, Uganda."
     1964a   Sociologus 14, no. 1: 44-62.

Possession by the powerful Chwezi spirits of Bunyoro mediums in Uganda is used as a method of divination. Through participation in the possession rites, interpersonal stresses and strains are alleviated, and they are thus considered primarily to be dramatic and expressive events. [Cited in African Abstracts, vol. 15, no. 4 (October 1964), no. 621.]

141. Beattie, J. H. M.   "The Ghost Cult in Bunyoro."
     1964b   Ethnology 3, no. 2: 127-51.

Among the Nyoro of Uganda, illness can be explained in several ways. Among these is the activity of a ghost. In this case, the Nyoro spirit mediumship cult is called on to induce the spirit to mount the head of its victim. The spirit is then destroyed, driven away, or, under certain conditions, brought into a permanent ritual relationship with its victim.

142. Beattie, J. H. M.   Other Cultures: Aims, Methods
     1964c   and Achievements in Social
                                   Anthropology. London: Cohen &
                                   West.

Chapter 13 discusses spirit possession as a general phenomenon appearing in almost all cultures. Chapter 14 defines possession as ". . . when a person assumes a state of apparent autohypnosis or dissociation and his behavior, which is not that of his ordinary self, is understood to be due to control by some spiritual agent normally outside himself." Nyoro (Uganda) spirit cults have proliferated, and in recent years new spirits have been introduced (e.g., "aeroplane," "Europeanness"); the function of these cults is to translate new and foreign forces into a familiar idiom.

143. Beattie, J. H. M.   "The Story of Mariya and
     1964d   Yozefu: A Case Study from
                                   Bunyoro, Uganda." Africa:
                                   Journal of the International
                                   African Institute (London) 34,
                                   no. 2: 105-15.

In a case of sorcery reported among the Nyoro of western Uganda, reference is made to the Mbandwa spirit mediumship cult. In explaining the conviction of one Yozefu for sorcery, the subcounty chief (who tried the case) states that Yozefu was arrested while on his way

to perform a <u>Mbandwa</u> possession ceremony to cure a man
who was ill (pp. 112-13).

144. Beattie, J. H. M.   "Matiyo and His Two Wives: A
     1965   Further Case Study from
                            Bunyoro." <u>Africa: Journal of</u>
                            <u>the International African</u>
                            <u>Institute</u> (London) 35, no. 3:
                            252-62.

Among the Nyoro of the Kingdom of Bunyoro (Uganda)
some men have made reputations as diviners, usually by
means of spirit mediumship (p. 253). In spite of
European opposition to mediumship and divination, these
practices are not carried on in a clandestine manner.
Several uninvolved people may attend at the same time,
especially when spirit possession is taking place (p.
260).

145. Beattie, J. H. M.   "Consulting a Diviner in
     1966a   Bunyoro: A Text." <u>Ethnology</u>
                            5, no. 2: 202-17.

Spirit possession and mediumship in the <u>Mbandwa</u> cult
are described in this account of a divination séance
among the Nyoro of Uganda. The author recognized the
performance as being artificial, and the medium was un-
impressive in his role as a possessed person.

146. Beattie, John H. M.   "Ritual and Social Change."
     1966b   <u>Man: Journal of the Royal Anthro-</u>
                            <u>pological Institute</u> (London),
                            n.s. 1, no. 1: 60-74.

Among the Nyoro of Uganda, spirit mediums often only
feign possession. The Nyoro, however, consider this to
be of minor importance, since the possession ritual is
often perceived as a drama (pp. 70, 71-72).

147. Beattie, John   "Divination in Bunyoro, Uganda."
     1967   In <u>Magic, Witchcraft, and Curing,</u>
                            edited by John Middleton, pp.
                            211-31. Garden City, N.Y.:
                            Natural History Press.

In Bunyoro, Uganda, there is a traditional cult of
spirit mediumship. This cult used to center on a
pantheon of mythical hero-gods called the <u>Chwezi</u>; now
there are also mediums for a great number of new spirits,
many derived from Bunyoro's Nilotic neighbors to the
north, and, more recently, from the new forces of social
change due to contact with the Western world. All the
spirits may divine through their mediums during a séance.

31

An account is given of a séance with <u>Irungu</u>, a spirit of nilotic origin (pp. 222-25).

148. Beattie, John   "Aspects of Nyoro Symbolism."
     1968   <u>Africa: Journal of the Interna-</u>
                           <u>tional African Institute</u>
                           (London) 38, no. 4: 413-42.

The author challenges the assertion (presented in an article by Needham in <u>Africa</u> vol.37, no. 4 [1967]) that diviners and mediums of the <u>Cwezi</u> spirit mediumship cult of the Nyoro people of Uganda are symbolically associated with women. Although some phases of initiation into the <u>Cwezi</u> cult require the initiate to adopt some female characteristics, the initiate is not perceived to retain any of these characteristics. The author points out that the association of the color white (which is some-times associated with women) with spirit mediums also does not indicate that the medium is perceived to have feminine characteristics, since white is also the color for purification and blessing, one of the functions of the mediums (pp. 418-24).

149. Beattie, John, and   "Introduction." In <u>Spirit</u>
     John Middleton   <u>Mediumship and Society in Africa</u>,
     1969a   edited by J. Beattie and J.
                           Middleton, pp. xvii-xxx.
                           (Bib. 150.)

A general theoretical framework for the study of spirit possession and mediumship in Africa is presented in this introduction.

150. Beattie, John, and   <u>Spirit Mediumship and Society in</u>
     John Middleton, eds. <u>Africa</u>. New York: Africana
     1969b   Publishing Corp.

     Includes in this bibliography:
                 149   J. Beattie and J. Middleton (1969a)
                 151   J. Beattie (1969c)
                 367   E. Colson (1969)
                 570   M. J. Field (1969)
                 573   R. Firth (1969)
                 629   G. K. Garbett (1969)
                 697   R. F. Gray (1969)
                 815   R. Horton (1969)
                 997   S. G. Lee (1969)
                 1037   I. M. Lewis (1969)
                 1204   J. Middleton (1969b)
                 1665   A. Southall (1969)
                 1707   R. E. S. Tanner (1969)
                 1810   P. Verger (1969)
                 1855   F. G. Welbourn (1969)

151. Beattie, John
     1969c

"Spirit Mediumship in Bunyoro."
In Spirit Mediumship and Society
in Africa, edited by J. Beattie
and J. Middleton, pp. 159-70.
(Bib. 150.)

Among the Nyoro of Uganda, there is a traditional
mediumship cult for spirits called Mbandwa. There are
two types of Mbandwa spirits: the Cwezi or "white"
spirits are the spirits of a race of heroes who once
ruled Bunyoro; the "black" Mbandwa spirits are of foreign origin, and some show the impact of Western penetration (e.g., Njungu, the spirit of "Europeanness").
Mediums of both kinds of spirits can act as diviners
and healers.

152. Beattie, John
     1971

The Nyoro State. Oxford:
Clarendon Press.

The mbandwa cult involving spirit mediumship with the
Bacwezi hero-gods among the Nyoro of Uganda is analyzed
politically and historically (pp. 49-51, 81, 264-65).

153. Beattie, John
     1977

"Spirit Mediumship as Theatre."
Royal Anthropological Institute
News, no. 20, pp. 1-6.

Spirit mediumship rituals among the Banyoro of Uganda
are analyzed as being theatrical performances.

154. Becker, Peter
     1962

Path of Blood. London: Longmans.

The Mwari cult among the Matabele (Ndebele) and
Makalanga (Rhodesia) is mentioned on page 187, and the
priests who speak as oracles for the god are called
"masters in the traditional art of ventriloquism."

155. Beckman, D. M.
     1974

"Trance: From Africa to
Pentecostalism." Concordia
Theological Monthly 43:11-26.

Unavailable for annotation.

156. Beckman, D. M.
     1975

Eden Revisited: Spiritual
Churches in Ghana. St. Louis:
Concordia Publishing House.

Unavailable for annotation.

157. Bedri, Ibrahim
     1948

"More Notes on the Padang
Dinka." Sudan Notes and Records
(Khartoum) 29, no. 1: 40-57.

33

The author focuses on aspects of the social structure of the Padang Dinka (Sudan) and notes some of their religious beliefs (e.g., a sky god whose words are spoken through spirit mediums).

158. Beidelman, T. O.   "Kagura Omens." Anthropological
     1963   Quarterly 36, no. 2: 43-59.

Although spirit possession is not explicitly labelled, exorcism of spirits causing deviancy or misfortune among the Kaguru of Tanzania is briefly mentioned on page 45.

159. Beidelman, T. O.   "Swazi Royal Ritual." Africa:
     1966   Journal of the International
                       African Institute (London) 36,
                       no. 4: 373-405.

Spirit possession is briefly mentioned in two contexts in this article on the Swazi of Swaziland: the intro-duction of new types of spirit possession (p. 378); and possession by ancestral spirits, occurring during times of great unrest (p. 388).

160. Beidelman, T. O.   The Kaguru: A Matrilineal People
     1971a   of East Africa. New York: Holt,
                       Rinehart & Winston.

Among the Kaguru of Tanzania, possession by the shetani, evil spirits, who seek recognition and nourish-ment, occurs mainly in women, and dances are held to drum the spirit out of the afflicted (pp. 40-41).

161. Beidelman, T. O.   "Swazi Royal Ritual." In
     1971b   Africa and Change, edited by
                       C. M. Turnbull, pp. 382-421.
                       New York: Alfred A. Knopf.

Spirit possession cults among the Swazi of Swaziland are mentioned on pages 388-89.

162. Beier, H. U.   "The Egungun Cult." Nigeria
     1956   51:380-92. Ill.

Among the Yoruba of Nigeria, members of the Egungun cult wear ancestor masks at the Egungun festival. The wearer of the mask can become possessed by the spirit of the mask and consequently may serve as the ancestor's medium. Pictorial illustrations of possession appear on pages 386-87.

163. Beier, H. U.   "Oshun Festival." Nigeria
     1957a   (Lagos) 53:170-87. Ill.

34

Description of the festival of Oshun, held at Oshogbo, dedicated to the Yoruba (Nigeria) deity of the river. During the festival of the deity Oshun takes possession of the young priestesses who worship him at his temple (illustrations pp. 170-72, 187). [Additional notes in African Abstracts, vol. 9, no. 301.]

164. Beier, H. U.   The Story of Sacred Wood Carving
     1957b   from One Small Yoruba Town.
                           Lagos: Printing Department,
                           Technical Institute, Yaba. Re-
                           printed from Nigeria Magazine
                           (Marina, Lagos).

In the Egungun Secret Society of the Yoruba of Nigeria, dancers are possessed by the ancestor spirit whose mask the dancer wears, and through mediumship, the spirit will speak to his relatives.

165. Beier, H. U.   "The Egungun Cult among the
     1958   Yorubas." Présence africaine
                           (Paris), nos. 18-19, pp. 33-36.

Spirit possession is practiced by the members of the secret society of mask dancers called Egungun among the Yoruba of Nigeria.

166. Beier, H. U.   "Les Anciennes Religions
     1962   africaines et le monde moderne."
                           Présence africaine (Paris), no.
                           41, pp. 128-36.

Trance states and spirit possession are discussed in terms of their use in African traditional religions, and their psychological value for practitioners (pp. 133-34).

167. Beiser, M., J. L.   "Assessing Psychiatric Disorder
     Ravel, H. Collomb,   among the Serer of Senegal."
     and C. Egelhoff   Journal of Nervous and Mental
     1972   Disease 154, no. 2: 141-51.

The ethnopsychiatric classification and terminology of "illnesses of the Spirit" among the Serer of Senegal, which include possession by spirits, are outlined in this article. [Cited in Transcultural Psychiatric Research Review (Montreal) 10 (April 1973): 50-51.]

168. Beiser, Morton, W. A. "Illnesses of the Spirit among
     Burr, J. L. Ravel,   the Serer of Senegal." American
     and H. Collomb   Journal of Psychiatry 130, no.
     1973   8: 881-86.

The types of "illnesses of the spirit" among the Serer

35

of Senegal are presented, along with the native terminologies and diagnoses. These types of illnesses are then contrasted with Western psychiatric terminology.

169. Bell, Hesketh
    1893

    Obeah: Witchcraft in the West Indies. London: Sampson Low, Marston & Co.

    Some description is offered of spirit possession and its relation to the religions of West Africa.

170. Benedict, Ruth
    1934

    Patterns of Culture. Boston: Houghton Mifflin Co.

    Spirit possession of a shaman among the Zulu of South Africa is discussed on pages 268-70, and an example is given of "the neurotic condition of the shaman."

171. Bentley, W. Holman
    1900

    Pioneering on the Congo. New York: Fleming H. Revell Co.

    Demon possession among the peoples of the Congo (Zaire) is discussed on pages 280-81.

172a. Benz, Ernst
    1971

    Neue Religionen. Stuttgart: Klett.

    Within a comparative discussion of new religions around the world, chapter 9 deals with messianic religions in Africa. On page 149, mention is made of the characteristics of spirit possession and exorcism common to messianic religions.

172b. Berger, Iris
    1976

    "Rebels or Status-Seekers? Women as Spirit Mediums in East Africa." In Women in Africa: Studies in Social and Economic Change, edited by Nancy J. Hafkin and Edna G. Bay. Stanford: Stanford University Press.

    A general discussion of spirit possession involving women is found on pages 161-66. A variety of ethnic groups are mentioned including: the Haya (Tanzania), Kiga (Chiga) (Uganda), and Zulu (South Africa).

173. Berglund, A. I.
    n.d.

    Rituals of an African Zionist Church. African Studies Program, University of Witwatersrand, Occasional Paper no. 3. Johannesburg.

    The rituals and symbols of the Zion Jerusalem Church of the Twelve Apostles in South Africa are analyzed.

Both ecstatic trance and exorcism are mentioned.

174. Berlyn, P.   "Traditional Religion of the
     1965   MaShona." Nada (Salisbury) 9,
                                no. 2: 94-96.

Among the MaShona of Rhodesia contact with the supreme
god is made through the spirits who manifest themselves
through hosts or mediums. [Cited in African Abstracts,
vol. 17, no. 108.]

175. Berlyn, Philippa   "The Midzimu Cult." Nada
     1967   (Salisbury) 9, no. 4: 6-9.

Among the MaShona of Rhodesia, ancestor spirits or
midzimu (sing. mudzimu), are worshipped. Midzimu are
incarnate in animals but cannot speak, and seek embodi-
ment in a human medium (svikiro). Mudzimu possession is
usually associated with an unidentifiable illness.
[Cited in African Abstracts, vol. 19, no. 437.]

176. Berlyn, Phillipa   "The Keeper of the Spirit of
     1972   Nehoreka." Nada (Salisbury) 10,
                                no. 4: 55-59.

Spirit mediumship is discussed in connection with the
Mambokadzi, the one chiefdom among the Shona of Rhodesia
which is headed by a woman.

177. Bernus, Suzanne   Particularismes ethniques en
     1969   milieu urbain: L'Example de
                                Niamey. Mémoires de l'Institut
                                d'ethnologie. Paris.

The activities of the possession cults holey and bori
in the town of Niamey in the Republic of Niger are presented and analyzed (pp. 190 ff.).

178. Bertsche, James E.   "Kimbanguism: A Challenge to
     1966   Missionary Statesmanship."
                                Practical Anthropology 13, no.
                                1: 13-33.

In tracing the rise of Kimbanguism, the prophetic
Christian-oriented cult, spirit possession is cited as
becoming important in its later, more nativistic manifestations after the death of Simon Kimbangu (1951).

179. Besmer, Fremont E.   "Avoidance and Joking Relation-
     1973   ships between Hausa Supernatural
                                Spirits." Studies in Nigerian
                                Culture 1, no. 1: 26-51.

The Hausa (Nigeria) boorii spirit possession cult is

discussed in terms of its expression of social attitudes.
[Cited in Abstracts in Anthropology, vol. 5, no. 3
(1974), no. 6050.]

180. Besmer, Fremont   "Initiation into the Bori Cult:
     1977   A Case Study in Ningi Town."
                        Africa: Journal of the Inter-
                        national African Institute
                        (London) 47, no. 1: 1-13.

The Bori spirit possession cult is examined as it
occurs in the Hausa town of Ningi, Nigeria. Case study
and symbolic analyses are presented.

181. Bessell, M. J.   "Nyabingi." Uganda Journal
     1938   (Kampala) 6, no. 2: 73-86.

The origins and development of the Nyabingi cult are
analyzed historically. Originating in the old Kingdom
of Ruanda, it spread into Uganda. Spirit possession and
mediumship are aspects of the cult.

182. Besson, H.   "Notes sur quelques 'possessions'
     1907   en Kabylie." Archives de
                        psychologie (Genève), vol. 6.

A missionary reports cases of spirit possession in
Kabylie (West Africa). Requests other missionaries in
Africa for similar reports if they have come across this
phenomenon (p. 387).

183. Betsch, B. Johnnetta   The Possession Pattern in Tradi-
     1959   tional West African and New
                             World Negro Cultures. Master's
                             Thesis, Northwestern University.

Unavailable for annotation.

184. Beyerhaus, P.   "What is Our Answer to Sects?"
     1961   Ministry (Morija, Basutoland) 1,
                        no. 4: 4-13.

The differences between the African Ethiopian and
Zionist churches are discussed, and then the latter is
focussed upon. The Zionist practices of ecstatic trance
and glossolalia are mentioned on page 9.

185. Beyerhaus, Peter   "The Christian Approach to An-
     1966   cestor Worship." Ministry
                        (Morija, Basutoland) 6, no. 4:
                        137-45.

Spirit possession as a traditional practice in worshipping the ancestors in Africa is dealt with in terms

38

of its significance for Christianity.

186. Beyerhaus, P. "An Approach to the African In-
     1969   dependent Church Movement."
                      Ministry (Morija, Lesotho) 9,
                      no. 2: 74-80.

The relationship is outlined between the traditional
African use of spirit possession and possession by the
Holy Spirit in the African Independent Church Movement.

187. Bhebe, N. M. B. "The Ndebele and Mwari before
     1972   1893: A Religious Conquest of
                      the Conquerors by the Van-
                      quished." Paper presented at
                      the Conference on the History of
                      Central African Religious Sys-
                      tems, Lusaka, 31 August - 8
                      September.

Unfamiliar with the new Rhodesian lands they had con-
quered, the Ndebele before 1893 turned to the native
Shona for ways to make rain and solve other problems.
Over time, the Shona high god, Mwari, was adopted by the
Ndebele, and this religious development is described in
detail. Possession is briefly mentioned.

188. Biebuyck, D. "La Société kumu face au
     1957   Kitawala." Zaïre (Bruxelles) 11,
                    no. 1: 7-40.

Describes the belief system and religious ceremonies of
the Kumu people of Zaïre. Includes consideration of the
prophetic and mystic elements of Kitawala and how they
fit into the Kumu belief system.

189. Biebuyck, D. "Kongolese Dansen." Band
     1958   (Leopoldville) 17, no. 5: 171-81.

Describes various Congolese dances and discusses how
they reflect social organization. These are religious
dances that accompany the ancestor and spirit cults.
Examples are drawn from the Ituri, Kivu, and Maniema
regions, as well as from the northern area of Lake
Tanganyika in Zaire. [Cited in African Abstracts,
vol. 10, no. 374; text in Flemish.]

190. Biesele, Megan "Song Texts by the Master of
     1975   Tricks: Kalahari San Thumb Piano
                      Music." Botswana Notes and Re-
                      cords (Gaborone) 7:171-88.

Among the San (also called Zhŭ/twãsi and Bushmen) of
Botswana, the thumb piano is of relatively recent intro-

duction. An in-depth analysis is given of a San individual who feels himself to be a medium or intermediary
between his people and God when he plays this instru-
ment.

191. Biesheuvel, S.   "Objectives of African Socio-
     1958   logical Research with Special
                             Reference to Mental Health."
                             In Mental Disorders and Mental
                             Health in Africa South of the
                             Sahara, pp. 122-26.
                             CCTA/CSA-WFMH-WHO, Pub. no. 35.
                             Bukavu.

In mental illness research, emphasis should be placed
on the relationship between the African and his sociocultural environment and on the attempt to discover the
actual social importance of such traditional practices
as ritualized spirit possession. Although considered
a mental illness, it may have its use in the release of
emotional tension.

192. Biesheuval, S.   "Synthetic Report: On the Basic
     1959   Psychological Structures of
                             African and Madagascan Popula-
                             tions." In Basic Psychological
                             Structures of African and
                             Madagascan Populations, pp. 1-
                             45. CCTA/CSA, Pub. no. 51
                             (suppl.). Tananarive.

The traditional relationship between spirit possession
and mental illness is mentioned in this general report.

193. Binsbergen, Wim   "Bituma: Preliminary Notes on a
     M. J. van   Healing Movement among the Nyoka
     1972a   of Kaoma District and of Lusaka,
                             Zambia." Paper presented at the
                             Conference on the History of
                             Central African Religious Sys-
                             tems, Lusaka, 31 August - 8⁵
                             September.

The Bituma healing cult is widely practiced among
urban and rural Nkoya of the Kaoma District and in
Lusaka, Zambia. Over time the movement has become more
syncretic, assimilating earlier possession beliefs.
Urban-rural Nkoya relationships are traced through the
growth of the cult.

194. Binsbergen, Wim   "Possession and Mediumship in
     M. J. van   Zambia: Toward a Comparative
     1972b   Approach." Paper presented at
                             the Conference on the History of

40

Central African Religious Systems, Lusaka, 30 August - 8 September.

The author analyzes the heuristic value of various theoretical models about possession currently in use by social scientists, including reinforcement, compensation, and deprivation models. He proposes alternatives in light of general material on possession in Zambia.

195. Bitek, Okot p'   "The Concept of Jok among the
     1963   Acholi and Lango." Uganda
                               Journal (Kampala) 27, no. 1: 15-
                               29.

Among the Acholi and Lango of Uganda, the actions of Jok spirits of both unknown people and of dangerous beasts may cause sickness and misfortune. At spirit possession seances the spirits are induced to voice their demands through a medium (ajwaka). The spirits are then either propitiated by offerings or driven out of the person. Procedures are similar to the Nyoro initiation into the Cwezi cult (pp. 24-27).

196. Bitek, Okot p'   "Acholi Concept of Fate--Woko,
     1965   Wilobo and Ru-piny." Uganda
                               Journal (Kampala) 29, no. 1: 85-
                               93.

An integral part of the world view and religion, which center on spirit possession, of the Acholi of Uganda is a concept of fate variously referred to as woko, wilobo, and ru-piny.

197. Bitek, Okot p'   African Religions in Western
     1970   Scholarship. Kampala: East
                               African Literature Bureau.

In chapter 9, the author presents a detailed analysis of the African word jok used by the Nilotic peoples which denotes more a class of concepts than one particular idea. Individuals possessed by jok may be made ill or may be diviners.

198. Bitek, Okot p'   Religion of the Central Luo.
     1971   Nairobi: East African Literature
                               Bureau.

Spirit possession among the Luo of Kenya is mentioned throughout the book, and chapter 6 deals exclusively with it. Description of a spirit possession ceremony (used to cure a sick individual) is given.

199. Bitek, Okot p'   The Horn of My Love. London:
     1974   Heinemann.

    The songs of the spirit possession dances among the
Acholi of Uganda are presented on pages 79-91.

200. Bjerre, Jens   Kalahari. Translated from Danish
     1960   by Estrid Bannister. London:
                             Michael Joseph.

    The Kalihari Bushman (Botswana) healing dance at the
full moon is described in chapter 23. Trance states
are achieved, although spirit possession is not
mentioned.

201. Blacking, J. A. R.   The Rôle of Music amongst the
     1956/57   Venda of the Northern Transvaal
                             (Union of South Africa).
                             Johannesburg: International
                             Library of African Music.

    Malombo is the general name given to the spirit pos-
session cult found among the Venda people (South
Africa). Possession dances have become an integral part
of Venda culture. The author describes possession by
and exorcism of two categories of spirits: Zwilombo,
malicious spirits, and Malombo, spirits of departed
ancestors. Most of the possession dances have come from
Southern Rhodesia (Rhodesia) via the eastern areas of
Vendaland. The author believes the possession cult
started about 1914; gives reasons for this contention
(chap. 6, pt. 1, pp. 24-28).

202. Blaise, Paul   Le Congo: Histoire -- descrip-
     1892   tion -- moeurs -- et aoutumes.
                             Paris: Lecène, Oudin & Cie.

    The Okanda (Kanda) of Zaire believe that illnesses
are caused by evil spirits possessing people (pp. 196
ff.).

203. Blake-Thompson, J.,   "Mlimo and Mwari: Notes on a
     'and Roger Summers   Native Religion in Southern
     1956   Rhodesia." Nada (Salisbury) 33:
                             53-58.

    Although spirit possession and mediumship are not ex-
plicitly labelled, interaction with the Mwari (Mlimo)
spirit is discussed for the Ndebele of Southern
Rhodesia (Rhodesia).

204. Blakney, Charles P.   "Chipunha, a Rhodesian Cult."
     1969   Practical Anthropology 16, no. 3:
                             98-108.

Among the Shona-speaking vaNdau of Rhodesia, spirit mediumship is practiced in the cult of the chipunha spirits. The trance state is described.

205. Bloomhill, Greta   Witchcraft in Africa. Cape
     1962   Town: Howard Timmins.

Detailed descriptions of spirit-possessed individuals and of spirit mediums are given in this general work on witchcraft in Africa.

206. Boas, F.   "Der Seelenglaube der Vandau."
     1920/21   Zeitschrift für Ethnologie, vol.
                               1.

The Vandau of South Africa maintain that some diseases are caused by spirit intrusion into the body (p. 3).

207. Boccassino, R.   "The Contribution of Old Sources
     1951   on the Religion of the Lotuho,
                               Obbo, Bari, Beri, Dinka, Nuer,
                               and Other People." Annali
                               Lateranensi (Rome) 15:79-128.

Describes the religions of several Upper Nile tribes (Sudan). Gives information based on often overlooked writing of explorers and missionaries. Possession is known for the Nuer and Dinka. [Cited in African Abstracts, vol. 4, no. 235. Text in Italian.]

208. Boccassino, Renato   "Il sacrificio umano practicato
     1966   dagli Acioli dell'Uganda e de
                               altri popoli niloti e nilo-
                               camiti." Anthropos 61, nos.
                               3/6: 637-78.

Among the Paiko lineage of the Acholi (Uganda), an evil spirit, Jok Punn, possessed the body of a certain witch-doctor and demanded the sacrifice of a human child, threatening the safety of the entire lineage if not appeased. Discussion continues of other instances of human sacrifice in various Nilotic ethnic groups.

209. Boghen, Dan, and   "Medical Attitudes, Beliefs and
     Miriam Boghen   Practices in Martinique." Type-
     n.d.   script. 70 pp.

Focussing on the relationship between folk healing and Western medicine on Martinique Island in the Caribbean, description and analysis are given of the procedures used, among which is exorcism of evil spirits. (No mention of African influence is explicitly made.) [Cited in Transcultural Psychiatric Research Review

(Bruges) 3 (April 1966): 47-49.]

210. Bogomos, E. V.   "The Witch-Doctor in Central
     1967   Africa." Nada (Salisbury) 9,
                             no. 4: 44-48.

Spirit possession and mediumship are discussed in relation to the role of the witch-doctor among the Shona
of Rhodesia.

211. Bogomas, E. V.   "Possession by the Spirits in
     1968   Mashonaland." Nada (Salisbury)
                             9, no. 5: 77-80.

The svikiro (spirit medium) of the Mashona of Rhodesia
derives from biblical custom, and is similar also to
classical Greek spirit divination. Accounts of a number
of svikiros who feigned possession to comply with custom. [Cited in African Abstracts, vol. 20, no. 223.]

212. Bohannan, Paul   African and Africans. Garden
     1964   City, N.Y.: Natural History
                             Press.

In this general work on African societies and cultures, possession states in diviners are mentioned on
pages 228 ff.

213. Bond, George   "Minor Prophets and Yombe Cul-
     1975   tural Dynamics." In Colonialism
                             and Change, edited by M. Owusu,
                             pp. 145-62. The Hague: Mouton.

Among the Yombe of Zambia, spirit illnesses caused by
possession by unclean spirits have been dealt with by
various "minor prophets" of Christian persuasion.

214. Bond, John   "Pentecostalism in the Pente-
     1974   costal Church." Journal of
                             Theology for Southern Africa
                             (Cape Town), no. 7, pp. 10-22.

Glossolalia and demon possession are discussed with
regard to the historical development of the Pentecostal
Church. A list of the Pentecostal churches in South
Africa is included.

215. Bonnafe, Pierre   "Un Aspect religieux de
     1969   l'idéologie lignagère. Le Nkira
                             des Kukuya du Congo-Brazzaville."
                             Cahiers des religions africaines
                             (Kinshasa) 3, no. 6: 209-97.

Possession by the nkira spirits among the Kukuya of

44

the People's Republic of the Congo is discussed in detail in the first part of this article (pp. 215-46). Spirit possession is a part of the ancestor cult.

216. Boone, Olga 1951   "Les Tambours du Congo belge et du Ruanda-Urundi." Annales du Musée royal du Congo belge (Turvuren), Sciences de l'homme, n.s. 1:1-121.

Very detailed description is given of the crafting and use of drums in the various ethnic groups of Zaire, Rwanda, and Burundi. Specific mention is made of the use of drums in the spirit possession divination procedures among the Batshioko (Shioko) and the Baluba (Luba) of Zaire (pp. 56, 57).

217. Booth, Newell S. 1937   "The Ministry in Bantu Religion." International Review of Missions 26, no. 103: 334-44.

Ecstasy, trance, and spirit possession are all practiced by Bantu priests in Southern Africa (pp. 337 ff.).

218. Booth, Newell, ed. 1975a   African Religions: A Symposium. New York: Nok Publishers.

Not available for annotation.

219. Booth, Newell S., Jr. 1975b   "Time and Change in African Traditional Thought." Journal of Religion in Africa (Leiden) 7, no. 2: 81-91.

In this philosophical essay, mention is made of the change in the relationship between man and spirit created by spirit possession--the great spirits are brought into closer contact with men. The specific group mentioned is the Baluba of Zaire (p. 89).

220. Bossche, Jean Van den 1954   Sectes et associations secrètes au Congo Belge. Leopoldville.

Not available for annotation.

221. Boston, J. S. 1970   "The Supernatural Aspect of Disease and Therapeutics among the Igala." African Notes (Ibadan) 5, no. 3: 41-56.

The etiology of, symptoms of, and cures for illnesses are given for the Igala-speaking peoples of middle Nigeria. Supernatural causation, spirit-sent sickness,

may be cited when the illness resists treatment or displays unusual features.

222. Botha, C. Graham   General History and Social Life
     1962   of the Cape of Good Hope. Cape
                             Town: C. Struik.

In this account written in the 1800's by a lawyer, the
inhabitants of European ancestry of the Cape of Good
Hope in South Africa are described and are said to be
very pious Christians and to believe that persons (and
places) could be possessed by devils (p. 229).

223. Bouisson, Maurice   Magic: Its History and Principal
     1961   Rites. New York: E. P. Dutton
                             & Co. Ill.

Information for Morocco includes mention of spirit
possession.

224. Boulaga, F. Eboussi   "Christianisme: Comme maladie et
     1973   comme guérison." In Croyance et
                             guérison, edited by M. Hebga,
                             pp. 127-47. (Bib. 752.)

In both the article and the discussion following it,
possession by demons causing illnesses and Christian
exorcism practices are analyzed. No specific ethnic
group is cited.

225. Boulnois, J.   Gnon-Sua: Dieu des Guérés.
     1933   Paris: L. Fournier.

Evil spirits may possess individuals and cause illness
among the Guérés (Ngere) of the Ivory Coast. Sorcerers
also employ a possession trance in their practices, and
can change into various animal forms (pp. 79-80, 94 ff.,
106 ff.).

226. Boulnois, Jean   L'Empire de Gao: Histoire,
     1954   coutumes et magie des Sonraï.
                             Paris: Librairie d'Amérique et
                             d'Orient Adrieu-Maisonneuve.

Analysis of spirit possession occurring among the
Sonraï (Songhai) of Dahomey (Benin) is given in terms of
psychological and psychoneurotic behavior (pp. 77 ff.).

227. Bouquet, Armand   "Féticheurs et médecines
     1969   traditionnelles du Congo
                             (Brazzaville)." Mémoires
                             O.R.S.T.O.M. (Paris), no. 36.

In this general study of traditional medical practices

and practitioners in Zaire, spirit possession is discussed as a cause of disease in chapters 2 and 3 of part
1. Part 2 lists and analyzes the various cures
prescribed by native healers.

228. Bourdillon, M. F. C.   "The Cults of Dzivaguru and
     1972a   Karuva amongst the North-eastern
                             Shona Peoples." Paper presented
                             at the Conference on the History
                             of Central African Religious
                             Systems, Lusaka, 31 August -
                             8 September.

The historical connections between the Dzivaguru and
the Karuva spirit cults are discussed for the Northeastern Shona in the Mount Darwin District of Rhodesia.
Mediums of these autochthonic spirits are said to have
power over all that affects the crops, especially the
rainfall. Their widespread influence is traced to the
social and political changes that have occurred since
the 1800's: the impact of the Korekore invasion and of
European administrative policies.

229. Bourdillion, M. F. C.   "The Manipulation of Myth in a
     1972b   Tavara Chiefdom." Africa:
                             Journal of the International
                             African Institute (London) 42,
                             no. 2: 112-21.

An historical analysis of myths from the Shona-speaking
Korekore and Tavara of northeastern Rhodesia reveals in
passing the origination of the possessing spirits of
these peoples as being those of their great founding
chiefs who first settled the various regions.

230. Bourdillon, M. F. C.   "Spirit Mediums in Shona Belief
     1974   and Practice." Nada (Salisbury)
                             11, no. 1: 30-37.

The various types of spirit possession among the Korekore of Rhodesia are analyzed in detail. Particular
emphasis is placed on the mhondoro, "lion" spirit
mediums, who have lengthy initiations and who, once
accepted, are very influential in the group.

231. Bourdillon, M. F. C.   "Themes in the Understanding of
     1975   Traditional African Religion."
                             Journal of Theology for Southern
                             Africa (Braamfontein, Transvaal),
                             no. 10, pp. 37-50.

Spirit possession and mediumship are mentioned briefly
in various contexts in this theoretical essay on understanding African traditional religions (pp. 46-48).

232. Bourdillon, S. J.   "Peoples of Darwin: An Ethno-
     1970   graphic Survey of the Darwin
                                District." Nada (Salisbury) 10,
                                no. 2: 103-14.

     The Tavara peoples of northeast Rhodesia practice
spirit mediumship by their territorial spirits, an important element in boundary establishment among chiefdoms.

233. Bourgoignie, Georges E.   Les Hommes de l'eau: Ethno-
     1972   écologie du Dahomey lacstre.
                                Paris: Éditions universitaires.

     The vodun possession cult among the Lake Dahomey
(Benin) is discussed in detail (pp. 323-53).

234. Bourguignon, Erika E.   "Dreams and Dream Interpretation
     1954   in Haiti." American Anthropolo-
                                gist 56, no. 2: 262-68.

     The relationship between dream interpretation and
spirit possession among the adherents of the Haitian
vodun cult is outlined.

235. Bourguignon, E., and   "Spirit Possession and Cross-
     L. Pettay   cultural Research." Trans-
     1962   cultural Psychiatric Research
                                2:13-14.

     Not available for annotation.

236. Bourguignon, Erika,   "Spirit Possession, Trance and
     and Louanna Pettay   Cross Cultural Research." In
     1964   Symposium on New Approaches to
                                the Study of Religion, Proceed-
                                ings of the 1964 annual spring
                                meeting of the American Ethno-
                                logical Society. Seattle:
                                University of Washington Press.

     Discusses the difficulty of systematic study of pos-
session because of the character of the literature on
possession and related phenomena; general terminological
difficulty in describing the phenomena; uneven distribution of descriptive materials and biases of observers
focusing on different aspects of the phenomena. Considers different approaches to the study--psychological,
anthropological, etc.--lack of adequate theory to guide
anthropologists in the development of consistent ob-
servational categories. Issues for comparative, cross-
cultural studies are suggested. (The relevant publications on Africa are included in this bibliography.)

237. Bourguignon, Erika   "The Self, the Behavioral En-
     1965   vironment and the Theory of
                                Spirit Possession." In Context
                                and Meaning in Cultural Anthro-
                                pology: Essays in Honour of A.
                                Irving Hallowell, edited by
                                Melford E. Spiro. New York:
                                Free Press.

     The state of spirit possession is spoken of as being
one of discontinuity of personal identity, and not considered to be pathological among the Haitian practitioners of the Voodoo cult.

238. Bourguignon, Erika   Trance Dance. Dance Perspec-
     1968a   tives, no. 35.

     This issue of the journal presents an in-depth study
of trance dancing in religions all over the world including Africa and Afro-America. Spirit possession and
mediumship are discussed.

239. Bourguignon, Erika   "World Distribution and Patterns
     1968b   of Possession States." In
                                Trance and Possession States,
                                edited by R. Prince, pp. 3-34.
                                (Bib. 1421.)

     The distribution of trance and spirit possession in
cultures around the world is presented. Maps are included in the text along with theoretical diagrams of
the trance phenomena.

240. Bourguignon, E.   "Maladie et possession: Elements
     1969   pour une étude comparative."
                                Colloque international sur les
                                cultes de possession (Paris).

     Not available for annotation.

241. Bourguignon, Erika   "Ritual Dissociation and Pos-
     1970   session Belief in Caribbean
                                Negro Religion." In Afro-
                                American Anthropology: Contem-
                                porary Perspectives, edited by
                                Norman E. Whitten, Jr. and John
                                F. Szwed, pp. 87-101. New York:
                                The Free Press.

     Spirit possession beliefs and practices in the
Haitian vodû cult and the St. Vincent Pentecostal group
of the Shakers are described and analyzed.

242. Bourguignon, Erika   "Dreams and Altered States of
     1972   Consciousness in Anthropological
                                Research." In <u>Psychological</u>
                                <u>Anthropology</u>, edited by F. L. K.
                                Hsu, pp. 403-34. Cambridge,
                                Mass.: Schenkman Publishing Co.

     In this general theoretical article, the relationship
between dreams and trance states such as that of spirit
possession is discussed on pages 416-29.

243. Bourguignon, E.   "An Assessment of Some Compari-
     1973a   sons and Implications." In
                               <u>Religion, Altered States of Con-</u>
                               <u>sciousness, and Social Change</u>,
                               edited by E. Bourguignon, pp.
                               321-39. (Bib. 245.)

     This is the conclusion and summary of the findings as
to the nature of trance and spirit possession put forth
by the various authors in the above edited volume.

244. Bourguignon, Erika   "Introduction: A Framework for
     1973b   Comparative Study of Altered
                               States of Consciousness." In
                               <u>Religion, Altered States of Con-</u>
                               <u>sciousness, and Social Change</u>,
                               edited by E. Bourguignon, pp. 3-
                               35. (Bib. 245.)

     General introduction and survey of major literature in
the study of trance, possession trance, altered states
of consciousness, and religion.

245. Bourguignon, Erika, ed. <u>Religion, Altered States of Con-</u>
     1973c   <u>sciousness, and Social Change</u>.
                               Columbus: Ohio State University
                               Press.

          Includes in this bibliography:
                         243   E. Bourguignon (1973a)
                         244   E. Bourguignon (1973b)
                         679   F. D. Goodman (1973a)
                         698   L. Greenbaum (1973a)
                         699   L. Greenbaum (1973b)
                         711   J. Gussler (1973)
                         755   J. Henney (1973)
                        1408   E. Pressel (1973)

246. Bourguignon, Erika   "Spirit Possession Belief and
     1973d   Social Structure." Paper pre-
                                pared for the Ninth International
                                Congress of Anthropological and
                                Ethnological Sciences, Chicago,

August-September.

The distinction between possession belief and possession trance and the differences in the cultures that include one or the other are discussed here.

247. Bourguignon, Erika   "Cross-cultural Perspectives on
     1974a   the Religious Uses of Altered
                           States of Consciousness." In
                           Religious Movements in Contem-
                           porary America, edited by I. I.
                           Zaretsky and M. P. Leone, pp.
                           228-43. (Bib. 1924.)

Beginning with a theoretical distinction between altered states of consciousness and beliefs concerning such states, a summary is presented of the research on the religious use of these states cross-culturally (African and Afro-American cults are mentioned).

248. Bourguignon, Erika   Culture and the Varieties of
     1974b   Consciousness. Addison-Wesley
                           Module in Anthropology, no. 47.
                           Reading, Mass.: Addison-Wesley
                           Publishing Co.

This module focuses on the cross-cultural uses of various types of altered states of consciousness. Given particular emphasis is the relationship between possession trance and the relative complexity of the societies in which it is found (pp. 15-21).

249. Bourguignon, Erika   "The Effectiveness of Religious
     1976a   Healing Movements: A Review of
                           Recent Literature." Transcul-
                           tural Psychiatric Research Re-
                           view (Montreal) 13 (April):
                           5-21.

Following a review of the recent literature on healing movements, including the African ones that employ possession trance--the Spiritual Churches of Ghana, the Akan-Ashanti of Ghana, the Hausa (Nigeria) bori cult, the Moroccan Hamadsha brotherhood, and the Ethiopian Zar cult--the author states that religious healing concentrates more on the life style of the individual and his group, while "scientific medicine" focuses on "symptoms and syndromes, often to the exclusion of the larger picture" (p. 17).

250. Bourguignon, Erika   Possession. San Francisco:
     1976b   Chandler & Sharp.

The phenomenon of spirit possession is explored in

51

great depth, employing data from cultures all over the world. Distinction is drawn between those cultures which have possession beliefs versus those which employ a possession trance.

251. Bradbury, R. E.   The Benin Kingdom and the Edo-
     1957   speaking Peoples of South-
                         western Nigeria. Ethnographic
                         Survey of Africa, edited by
                         Daryll Forde, Western Africa,
                         pt. 13. London: International
                         African Institute.

Among the Urhobo and Isoko of the Niger Delta in Nigeria, "semi-Christian" cults have arisen whose purpose is to "smell out" witches. Spirit possession is an essential part of their rituals (pp. 163-64).

252. Brain, Robert   "Child-Witches." In Witchcraft
     1970   Confessions and Accusations,
                         edited by M. Douglas, pp. 161-
                         79. (Bib. 476.)

Among the Bangwa of Cameroon, children are accused of being witches, and therefore of being possessed by demons. Possession is also used to "smell out" witches (p. 171).

253. Bram, Joseph   "Spirits, Mediums and Believers
     1958   in Contemporary Puerto Rico."
                         Transactions of the New York
                         Academy of Sciences Series II,
                         20, no. 4: 340-47.

After tracing some of the history of spiritualism in Western European thought, attention is turned to contemporary Puerto Rico where spiritualism flourishes on a foundation of African beliefs. A few accounts of possession and mediumship are given.

254. Bramly, Serge   Macumba: forces noires du Brésil:
     1975   Les Enseignements de Maria-José,
                         mère des dieux. Paris: Éditions
                         Seghers.

This book concentrates on the spirit mediumship cult of Macumba of Indian and African origins in Brazil. Descriptions are given of the possessing spirits, of the practitioners, and of the ceremonies.

255. Brand, Roger   "Initiation et consécration de
     1974   deux vodūnɔ dans les cultes
                         Vodú." Journal de la Société
                         des africanistes (Paris) 44, no.
                         1: 71-91.

52

The initiation ceremonies which feature possession by the Vodū spirits (Dahomey) are described in detail for the inhabitants in and around Port Novo, Dahomey (Benin).

256.Brandel-Syrier, Mia   Black Women in Search of God.
     1962   London: Lutterworth Press.

African Christians still hold to the belief in possession by native spirits. The relationship between preaching and spirit possession is discussed (pt. 1, pp. 34-35).

257.Brausch, G. E. J. B.   "La Société N'Kutshu." Bulle-
     1945   tin des juridictions indigènes
                     et du droit coutumier congolais
                     (Elizabethville) 2:29-59; 3:
                     61-89.

Considers cult of diviners among the N'Kutshu (Kutshu) of Zaire, their initiation and methods of divination, and the cult of the magicians (Wetshi), its organization into lodges and grades. Magicians often fall into trances, possessed by the ghost of a dead man. The functions of the magicians (féticheurs) are diagnostic and curative. [Text in French.]

258.Brazier, F. S.   "The Incident at Nyakishenyi,
     1968a   1917." Uganda Journal (Kampala)
                     32, no. 1:17-27.

Spirit possession by the Nyabingi spirit among the Baganda of Uganda is briefly mentioned on the first page of this historical and political study of the Nyabingi cult (p. 17).

259.Brazier, F. S.   "The Nyabingi Cult: Religion and
     1968b   Political Scale in Kigezi 1900-
                     1930." Makerere Institute of
                     Social Research Conference Pa-
                     pers (Kampala), no. 494, pp. 1-
                     17.

Although this study concentrates mainly on the political ramifications of the Nyabingi cult found among the Kiga (Chiga) of Uganda, mention is made of mediumship and possession by the nyabingi spirit (pp. 2, 11).

260.Breidenbach, Paul S.   "Spatial Juxtapositions and Be-
     1975   lief Orientations in a Ritual
                     of a Ghanaian Healing Movement."
                     Journal of Religion in Africa
                     (Leiden) 7, no. 2: 92-110.

Part of the healing ceremony in the Ghanaian Church of the Twelve Apostles, a movement begun by William Wade

Harris, involves the use of a spirit possession trance
during which glossolalia is uttered (pp. 98-101).

261. Breidenbach, Paul S.   "Colour Symbolism and Ideology in
     1976   Ghanaian Healing Movement."
                                  Africa: Journal of the Interna-
                                  tional Africa Institute (London)
                                  46, no. 2: 137-45.

In the edwuma or healing ritual of the Twelve Apostles
Church among the Fante (Fanti) of Ghana, the sunsum
spirits are called to possess the ill person and then in-
terrogated as to their demands; through such revelations,
the person is cured.

262. Brelsford, W. V.   "African Dances of Northern
     1948   Rhodesia." Occasional Papers of
                                the Rhodes-Livingstone Museum
                                (Livingstone), no. 2.

Author includes within the category of "pure convulsive
dance" the demon or spirit possession dances. He claims
these dances are confined to Northern Rhodesia (Zambia),
but cites examples from other authors for Central and
South Africa.

263. Brelsford, W. V.   "Insanity among the Bemba of
     1950   Northern Rhodesia." Africa:
                                Journal of the International
                                African Institute (London) 20,
                                no. 1: 46-54.

Many forms of insanity exist among the Bemba of Northern
Rhodesia (Zambia). One form is hysteria, which may be
caused by spirit possession or by the failure to carry
out some ritual. The Bemba do not class cases of possession as madness, believing it caused by the possession of
the victim's body by the spirit of a dead person. Sometimes during the paroxysm the person will name witches or
give warnings of disaster. Cures of possession are sought
from the Diviner who tries to find out the name of the
possessing spirit (pp. 49, 51).

264. Brewster, Paul G.   "Hantu and Loa: Some Similari-
     1957   ties between Malay Popular Reli-
                                gion and Haitian Vodun." Archivio
                                per L'Antropologia e la Ethno-
                                logia (Firenze) 87:95-108.

Spirit possession beliefs and ceremonies are compared
for the Haitian vodun cult and the Malay popular religion.

265. Brock, Beverly   "The Nyiha of Mbozi." Tanzania
     1966   Notes and Records (Dar es
                                Salaam), no. 65, pp. 1-30.

54

The Nyiha of Tanzania have adopted the muzimu cult,
originally from Nyasaland (Malawi), in which participants are possessed by an ancestor spirit, and are able
to divine (p. 19).

266. Brøgger, Jan   "Spirit Possession and the
     1975   Management of Aggression Among
                          the Sidamo." Ethnos (Stockholm)
                          40:285-90.

The beliefs and ceremonies surrounding possession by
the shetani spirits among the Sidamo of Ethiopia are
described.

267. Brokensha, David   Social Change at Larteh, Ghana.
     1966   Oxford: Clarendon Press.

Spirit possession in the Akan religion of Ghana is
described on page 14 and in chapter 8.

268. Brokensha, David   "Odente: The Nonaccommodating
     1969   God." In Western African His-
                          tory, edited by Daniel F. McCall,
                          Norman R. Bennett, and Jeffrey
                          Butler, pp. 204-13. Boston
                          University Papers on Africa, vol.
                          4. New York: Frederick A.
                          Praeger.

Documentation of a violent episode in 1886-87 during
the process of social change in the town of Lartah,
southern Ghana, where a young girl, possessed by the god
Odente (Akan), demanded a human sacrifice that was sub-
sequently discovered by the British colonial government.

269. Bron, Bernhard   "Zum Phänomen der Besessenheit."
     1975   Confinia Psychiatrica (Basel)
                          18, no. 1: 16-29.

Although Africa is not specifically mentioned, this
general article deals with the psychiatric, psychoanalytic, and theological understandings of spirit
possession.

270. Broster, Joan A.   Red Blanket Valley. Johannes-
     1967   burg: Hugh Keartland Publishers.

A detailed account of the practices and initiation of
a witchdoctor, which include being possessed by and
communicating with animal and ancestral spirits, is
given for the Xhosa-speaking Qaba of the Republic of
South Africa (pp. 46 ff., 83-107). Evil spirits may
cause illness by possessing a person and must be
exorcised by a witchdoctor (pp. 46-56).

271. Broustra-Monfouga,   "Approche ethnopsychiatrique du
     Jacqueline   phénomène de possession: Le Bori
     1973   de Konni (Niger), étude compara-
                             tive." Journal de la Société
                             des africanistes (Paris) 43, no.
                             2: 197-220.

The bori spirit possession cult among the Hausa
of Niger is compared with its manifestation among the
neighboring ethnic group, the Konnawa. The author discusses various structural differences, and after presenting detailed descriptive data gives psychological
analyses.

272. Brown, Daniel   "A Structural Model for States of
     1975   Consciousness, I: The Hyper-
                             aroused States - Trance, Medita-
                             tion and Reverie." Manuscript,
                             University of Chicago.

A structural model of states of consciousness is presented that includes the hyperaroused states of possession trance.

273. Brown, Diana DeGroat   "Umbanda: Politics of an Urban
     1974   Movement." Ph.D. dissertation,
                             Columbia University. Disserta-
                             tion Abstracts International 35,
                             no. 10: 6286A.

The Afro-Brazilian Umbanda cult is extensively explored, including its use of spirit possession.

274. Brown, G. Gordon, and   Anthropology in Action. London:
     A. McD. Bruce Hunt   Oxford University Press.
     1935

Diviners among the Hehe of Tanganyika (Tanzania) employ one of two modes of divination: use of the divining
sticks or direct communication with the spirits. Although the latter method is not termed possession or
mediumship, it occurs in a state of "voluntary or involuntary dissociation" (p. 170).

275. Brown, J. Tom   Among the Bantu Nomads.
     1926   Philadelphia: J. B. Lippincott
                             Co.

The badimo spirits of the dead are generally considered to be evil and to possess individuals among the
Bechuana (Tswana), a Bantu-speaking peoples of South
Africa. Such possession causes madness, and the spirits
must be exorcised (pp. 103, 106 ff., 136).

56

276. Brown, Kenneth I.   "Religion Today: 24 Aladura
     1964   Baptism." Hibbert Journal 62,
                              no. 245: 64-67.

     Discussed is the role of possession by the Holy Spirit
     in the Aladura Church of West Africa.

277. Brown, Kenneth I.   "Worshipping with the African
     1966   Church of the Lord (Aladura)."
                              Practical Anthropology 13, no.
                              2: 59-84.

     The use of possession by the Holy Spirit in the Church
     of the Lord (Aladura) in West Africa is discussed in
     detail.

278. Brown, Kenneth I.   "A Weekend with an African In-
     1971   dependent Church in Natal."
                              Ministry (Maseru, Lesotho) 11,
                              no. 1: 8-16.

     Both glossolalia and possession by the Holy Spirit and
     their use in an African independent church in Natal,
     South Africa, are discussed on pages 13-14.

279. Brown, Kenneth I.   "Forms of Baptism in the African
     1972   Independent Churches of Tropical
                              Africa." Practical Anthropology
                              19, no. 7: 169-82.

     A case of spirit possession is briefly mentioned as
     occurring during a baptismal ceremony in the Cherubim
     and Seraphim independent church of Nigeria (p. 175).

280. Brown, Paula   "The Igbira." In Peoples of the
     1955   Niger-Benue Confluence, edited
                              by D. Forde, pp. 55-74. (Bib.
                              590.)

     Among the Igbira of Nigeria, the bori spirit posses-
     sion cult is practiced (p. 71).

281. Brownlee, Charles   Reminiscences of Kaffir Life and
     1896   History. Lovedale: Lovedale
                              Mission Press.

     Divination among the witch-doctors of the Kaffirs of
     South Africa involves a mediumship trance state (pp. 188
     ff.). An historical account is given of "Cattle-Killing
     Delusion" among the Kaffirs in 1856, instigated by a
     "prophesying medium" (pp. 135-70). The author is a
     missionary.

282. Bryant, Rev. A. T.   "The Zulu Cult of the Dead."
     1917   Man 17, no. 95: 140-45.

   Among the Zulu of South Africa, attendants to the cult
of ancestor spirits are diviners who, after entering a
trance, become the mouthpieces for the possessing
spirits. Two kinds of possessing spirits are described:
(1) the Umbozi speaking spirit, which speaks through the
medium in a form of glossolalia; (2) the Idlozi, a
spirit which inspires the diviner to speak himself. Possession is treated by initiation of the possessed to the
diviner's status.

283. Buakasa, Gérard   "Notes sur le kindoki chez les
     1968   Kongo." Cahiers des religions
                              africaines (Kinshasa) 2, no. 3:
                              153-69.

   Among the Kongo of Zaire, kindoki is the actual power
of the nkisi, dead humans who can act for the good or
evil of the living. Ndoki refers to men who can communicate with and control the nkisi, and also can act
like them. Beliefs, practices, and actual case studies
are given (pp. 160 ff.).

284. Buakasa, Tulu Kia   L'Impense du discours: Kindoki
     Mpansu   et 'nkisi' en pays kongo du
     1973   Zaire. Bruxelles: J. Van
                              Keerberghen & Fils.

   In this complex and detailed analysis of sorcery and
fetishism among the Kongo of Zaire, spirit possession
is described (see pt. 2 especially).

285. Budge, Sir Wallis   Egyptian Magic.   Evanston, Ill.,
     1899   and New York: University Books.
                              Ill.

   Chapter 7 discusses the phenomena of possession and
exorcism in ancient Egypt.

286. Bullock, Charles   Mashona Laws and Customs.
     1913   Salisbury: Argus Publishing Co.

   Shona (Rhodesia) spirit mediumship and possession
practices in their religion are described on pages 66-
83.

287. Bullock, Charles   The Mashona. Johannesburg: Juta
     1927   & Co.

   Chapter 7 describes spirit possession among the Mashona
of Rhodesia by the Mondoro spirits and discusses the
role of priests and mediums in curing ceremonies (par-

ticularly pp. 123-25). Chapter 8 deals with the
Zwirombo and Shawe spirit possession ceremonies.

288. Bullock, Charles   The Mashona and the Matabele.
     1950   Cape Town: Juta & Co.

     In chapter 11, the author discusses the various
hierarchies of spirits and their mediums that comprise
the religion of the Mashona and Matabele of Rhodesia:
from Mwari--the Supreme Being to the various tribal
spirits, to the mudzimu--the personal or familial
spirits.

289. Bureau, R.   "Influence de la christianisa-
     1968   tion sur les institutions
                                traditionneles des ethnies
                                cotieres du Cameroun." In
                                Christianity in Tropical Africa,
                                edited by C. G. Baëta, pp. 165-
                                81. (Bib. 65.)

     Spirit possession is used in the jengu cult of the
water-spirits among the Duala of Cameroon (pp. 170-71).

290. Burke, E. E., ed.   The Journals of Carl Mauch - His
     1969   Travels in the Transvaal and
                                Rhodesia 1869-1872. Salisbury:
                                Mardon Printers, for National
                                Archives of Rhodesia.

     Among the Makalaka of Rhodesia, possession by an evil
ancestor spirit causes illness, misfortune, and death
(pp. 155, 202-3).

291. Burke, E. E.   "Mazoe and the Mashona Rebellion,
     1971   1896-97." Rhodesiana (Salis-
                                bury), no. 25, pp. 1-34.

     Briefly mentioned is the role of the mondoro or spirit
medium of the Mwari cult among the Shona of Rhodesia
during the events which led up to the Mashona Rebellion
of 1896-97 (pp. 1-2).

292. Burssens, H.   Les Peuplades de l'entre Congo-
     1958   Ubangi. Ethnographic Survey of
                                Africa, edited by Daryll Forde,
                                vol. 6, no. 4. London: Inter-
                                national African Institute.

     Spirit possession among the Ngbandi, Ngbaka, Mbandja,
Ngombe, and other peoples of Zaire is discussed on pages
135-52. Spirit mediumship and demonic possession are
both described.

293. Burton, R. F.   A Mission to Gelele, King of
     1864   Dahomey, Vol. 2. London:
                            Tinsley Bros.

     The author does not regard the phenomenon of dancing
mania as peculiar to the African. "Abnormal brain action
is not uncommon amongst the Negro races. During the fit
the subject rushes, as one distracted, to the idol, and
after violent exertions, sinks fainting to the ground.
This ecstasy is the Hal of Arabia, the demoniacal possession of the Days of Ignorance, the 'spirit of
prophecy' among the Camisards or Shakers, the 'spirit'
in Methodism, and the 'jerks' and 'holy laughs' of the
camp meetings" (p. 151). [Cited by Jeffreys (1953, Bib.
853).]

294. Burton, W. F. P.   Luba Religion and Magic in
     1961   Custom and Belief. Annales,
                            Sér. in 8⁰, Sciences humaines,
                            no. 35. Tervuren: Musée royal
                            de l'Afrique centrale.

     Among the Luba of Zaïre, spirit possession may strike
anyone without warning; however, there is also a special
cult of spirit mediums who regularly prophesy for both
individuals and the whole of society (pp. 50-59).

295. Busia, K. A.   "The Ashanti." In African
     1954   Worlds, edited by D. Forde,
                            pp. 190-209. (Bib. 588.)

     The Ashanti (Ghana) God requires a temporary abode and
a priest to serve him. Many priests claim to have been
seized by the spirit of the god they serve. Possession
is diagnosed by a priest, and a cure is offered through
initiation into the priesthood (pp. 193-94).

296. Bustamante, José Angel "Importance of Cultural Patterns
     1961   in Group Psychotherapy and Psycho-
                            drama." Acta Psychotherapeutica
                            et Psychosomatica (Basel) 9,
                            no. 4: 262-76.

     The importance that cultural patterns have for the in-
tegration of the personality is outlined here with
specific emphasis on the Cuban peoples and their religion Santeria. Possession of a medium is mentioned on
page 270.

297. Bustamante, J. A.   "Cultural Factors in Hysterias
     1968   with Schizophrenic Clinical Pic-
                            ture." International Journal of
                            Social Psychiatry (London) 14,
                            no. 2: 113-18.

The occurrence of the "Dissociative Reaction" in various religious groups of the Caribbean Islands, especially that of Santería in Cuba, is discussed here. Possession is not explicitly labelled but implied.

298. Butt, Audrey   The Nilotes of the Ango-Egyptian
     1952   Sudan and Uganda. Ethnographic
                       Survey of Africa, edited by
                       Daryll Forde, vol. 2, no. 4.
                       London: International African
                       Institute.

Description of the cult of Nyikang among the Shilluk of the Sudan and Egypt. Every king at the moment of his installation is possessed by the spirit of Nyikang. Attendants to the shrines of Nyikang are women subject to epileptic fits (held to indicate possession by Nyikang or the spirit of another dead king). The witch-doctors, Ajuago, are often possessed by the spirit of early Shilluk kings. Description of the prophet movements among the Nuer (Sudan), information on possession by Nuer sky spirits (pp. 63-64; 154-55).

299. Byaruhanga-Akiiki,   "Spirit Identity and Their Acti-
     A. B. T.   vities." Occasional Research
     1975   Papers in African Traditional
                          Religion and Philosophy
                          (Makerere University, Kampala),
                          vol. 18, no. 191.

Spirit possession is analyzed in general terms for African religions on pages 7-9.

300. Bylin, Eric   Basakata: Le Peuple du pays en
     1966   l'entre-fleuves Lukenie-Kasai.
                        Studia Ethnographica
                        Upsaliensia, vol. 25. Uppsala.

Possession by the beyi bedi, evil spirits, is spoken of as causing illnesses among the Basakata of the Congo (p. 279).

301. Bynan, G.   "La Trance dans la Candomblé."
     1968   Les Cultes de possession colloque
                        interdie de centre national de
                        recherche scientifique (Paris).

Not available for annotation.

302. Cabrera, Lydia   Yemayá y Ochún. Madrid: Forma
     1974   Gráfica, S.A.

The Lucumí are regarded as the descendents of the Yoruba peoples living in Cuba. Presented in this book is the religion of the Lucumí with its pantheon of deities. Spirit possession is not explicitly labelled but implied.

303. Cabrera, Lydia   El Monte. Miami: Ediciones
     1975   Universal.

Author discusses spirit possession among creoles and blacks in Cuba. Spirit possession is described on pp. 27-38, 199, 205-17, 281, 285 with emphasis on African beliefs brought in by slavery.

304. Calestro, Kenneth M.   "Psychotherapy, Faith-Healing,
     1972   and Suggestion." International
                            Journal of Psychiatry 10, no. 2:
                            83-113.

Beginning with a very brief description of "primitive psychiatry" which includes mention of spirit possession and ritual exorcism on pages 89-90, the author compares the role that therapeutic suggestibility plays in these healing systems with its place in modern psychiatric practices.

305. Callaway, C.   "The Religion of the Amazula."
     1884   Folk-Lore (London), vol. 15

The Zulu of South Africa hold that often disease is caused by spirit intrusion into the body (p. 262).

306. Callaway, H.   The Religious System of the
     1868/70   Amazulu. Springvale, Natal:
                           Blair. (Reissued: London:
                           Folklore Society, 1884.)

Discusses the use of the term "possession." Most Bantu (Southern Africa) tribes say the ancestor spirits accompany a man, control him, and speak through him, but the spirits do not possess a man as does the alien spirit among the Shangana-Tonga. When possession does occur, the spirit departs of its own accord from some people, others have the ghost laid, and in others the disease is allowed to take its course and the possessed become diviners (pp. 185, 289, 348).

307. Callaway, H.   "Divination and Analogous
     1871/72   Phenomena among the Natives of
                           Natal." Journal of the Royal
                           Anthropological Institute of
                           Great Britain and Ireland
                           (London) 1:163-85.

62

Discussion of the mental processes underlying Zulu (South Africa) systems of divination. Describes possession: "the disease consists of a remarkable disturbance of the nervous system, resembling hysteria, and sometimes in certain seasons of the year, can take the form of an epidemic." Compares the latter to Boudah possession found in Abyssinia (Ethiopia) (p. 178).

308. Camargo, Candido   "Aspects socio-culturels du
     Procopio Ferreira de   spiritisms au Bresil." Social
     and J. Labbano   Compass 7, nos. 5-6: 107-30.
     1960

Not available for annotation.

309. Camargo, Candido   Aspectos Sociologicos del
     Procopio   Espiritismo en São Paulo.
     1961a   Friburgo, Suiza and Bogotá,
                               Columbia: Oficina Internacional
                               de Investigaciones, Sociales de
                               Feres.

Based on questionnaires and on participant observation research, the author describes spirit possession in the context of mediumship in chapter 2. Spiritist and Umbanda aspects of spirit possession are described in chapter 3.

310. Camargo, Candido   Kardecismo e Umbanda: Una inter-
     Procopio Ferreira de   pretação sociologia. São Paulo:
     1961b   Livraŕia Pioneira Editôra.

Spirit mediumship and possession in the Kardec and Umbanda cults of Brazil are discussed. African influence is mainly found in the Umbanda practices, and the relationship between spirit possession and socio-cultural values is outlined.

311. Campbell, A. C.   "Chimombe." Southern Rhodesia
     1957   Native Affairs Department Annual
                               (Salisbury) 34:31-37.

Among the Makorekore people (Rhodesia) it is believed that anyone may speak to Chimombe, a native spirit god, but only the Mbayiwa (men possessed of a lion spirit of Mondoro) are able to hear Chimombe and interpret its response.

312. Campbell, A. C.   "A Few Notes on the Gcwi Bushmen
     1964   of the Central Kalahari Desert,
                               Bechuanaland." Nada (Salisbury)
                               9, no. 1: 39-47.

The trance dances among the Gcwi Bushmen of the Central

63

Kalahari Desert in Bechuanaland (Botswana) are described
here. A healing trance is achieved, but spirit possession is not present.

313. Cannon, W. B.   "Voodoo Death." American An-
     1942   thropologist 44:169-81.

The author addresses himself to the source of emotional
states that may lead to death. Descriptions are offered
of experiments with animals and physiological reactions
to certain emotional stimuli. It is suggested that Voodoo death may be real and may be due to emotional stress
or to obvious or repressed terror. (Possible correlation
with spirit possession.)

314. Caplan, Ann Patricia   Choice and Constraint in a
     1975   Swahili Community. London:
                            Oxford University Press.

Spirit possession in the Swahili village of Minazini on
the island of Mafia just off the Tanzanian coast is
discussed in detail in chapter 6. Case studies are presented.

315. Cardinall, A. W.   In Ashanti and Beyond. Philadel-
     1927   phia: J. B. Lippincott Co.

In chapter 14, particularly pages 233-34, the author
reports an Ashanti dance he witnessed in the Gold Coast
(Ghana); he calls the occurrence "Dance of Inspiration"
in which the Ashanti priest became possessed by his god.

316. Carley, Mary Manning   Jamaica: The Old and the New.
     1963   London: George Allen & Unwin.

Description of some of the revivalist and "pacomania"
(a little madness) sects of Jamaica, reflecting certain
West African customs and rites. Author also deals with:
spirit possession by a chosen god; trance phenomenon and
its association with Western revivalism and European
necromancy (chap. 7, pp. 135-36).

317. Carneiro, Edison   Religiões Negras. Rio de
     1936   Janeiro: Civilização Brasileira,
                            S/A.

Spirit possession in the Candomblé cult of Brazil is
examined. The syncretism of African and Christian elements is emphasized.

318. Carneiro, Edison   Negros Bantus. Rio de Janeiro:
     1937   Civilização Brasileira, S/A.

The religion of the peoples of Bahia, Brazil, who are

of African (Bantu) origin is discussed. Spirit possession and mediumship in the Candomble cult are mentioned.

319. Carneiro, Edison   "The Structure of African Cults
     1940   in Bahia." Journal of American
                            Folklore 53, no. 210: 271-78.

     This study deals with the structural aspects of the
Candomble and Caboclo cults, their significance to the
African population of Brazil, and the role of spirit
possession with respect to discipline and authority
within the cults' structure.

320. Carneiro, Edison   Les Cultes d'origine africaine au
     1959   Brésil. Rio de Janeiro:
                            Ministério da Educação e Cul-
                            tura, Biblioteca Nacional.

     Spirit possession in the Candomble and Umbanda cults
of Brazil is described. African origins of these traditions are traced.

321. Carneiro, Edison   Candomblés da Bahia. Rio de
     1961   Janeiro: Conquista.

     The spirit possession trances evident in the African-
influenced Candomblé cults of Bahia, Brazil, are discussed in depth.

322. Carothers, J. C.   The African Mind in Health and
     1953   Disease. WHO Monograph Series,
                            no. 17. Geneva: World Health
                            Organization.

     The native explanation of psychiatric cases of
frenzied anxiety, frequently seen in Africa, has to do
with being possessed by spirits (p. 153).

323. Carothers, John Colin The Mind of Man in Africa.
     1972   London: Tom Stacey.

     Although spirit possession is not explicitly labelled,
the African belief that evil spirits can cause illnesses
is mentioned on page 61.

324. Carr, Andrew T.   "A Rada Community in Trinidad."
     1953   Caribbean Quarterly 3, no. 1:
                            36-54.

     Spirit possession is a major element in the religion
of the peoples of African descent living in Port-of-
Spain, Trinidad. The population is comprised of Rada
(Benin), Ibo, Congo and Mandingo descendents. Detailed
discussion is given of their religious beliefs and

65

ceremonies.

325. Carter, Mary
1972
"Origins and Diffusion of Central African Cults of Affliction." Paper presented at the Conference on the History of Central African Religious Systems, Lusaka, 30 August - 8 September.

The origins and diffusion of the Central African "cults of affliction" are traced; and in addition, information is given about the zar cults of northeastern Africa, the shetani cults from the coastal region, and the cwezi/ryangombe cults from Rwanda. The characteristics of the possession trance are described in general terms for each group.

326. Casalis, E.
1861
The Basutos. London: James Nisbet & Co.

The Barolongs (Rolong) of South Africa (Botswana) give reverence to "deranged" persons who are thought to be directly under the influence of the deities (p. 247). Possession is not explicitly labelled here. Divining doctors among the Basutos (Sotho) of South Africa are able to enter a state of trance and thus become oracles (pp. 284-85).

327. Catholic Church
1969
À la rencontre des religions africaines. Secretariatus pro Non Christianis. Rome: Ed. "Àncora."

In this tract prepared by the Catholic Church for non-Christians, the traditional African religions are discussed separately, and then in relation to Christianity. Spirit possession, with particular emphasis on the Dahomean (Fon) (Benin) beliefs and on the Haitian Voudou cult, is mentioned on pages 67, 80-84.

328. Catholic General
Secretariat
n.d.
Lumpa Church: A Study of the Lenshina Movement 1955-1960.

The spirit of Christ is said to have taken possession of Alice Lenshina, the foundress of the Lumpa Church in Northern Rhodesia (p. 5).

329. Cerulli, E.
1921
"Note sul movimento musulmano nella Somalia." Rivista degli studi orientali (Rome) 10:1-36.

Spirit possession in Somaliland and its relation to the Zar cults of Ethiopia are discussed.

66

330. Cerulli, E.   In Encyclopedia of Islam, 4:
     1929   1217. Leyden: E. J. Brill, Ltd.

     Discussion of the Saar spirit cults; suggestion of
derivations of the term Zar. Ethnographic information
for Abyssinia (Ethiopia), Egypt (Higjaz and Oman), and
Somalia.

331. Cerulli, Ernesta   Peoples of South-West Ethiopia
     1956   and Borderland. Ethnographic
                                 Survey of Africa, edited by
                                 Daryll Forde. London: Inter-
                                 national African Institute.

     The Konso and Gidole of southwestern Ethiopia believe
that devils can cause possession by hitting men with
their spears. Lesser devils can possess not only men
but material objects (p. 66).

332. Chanaiwa, David   The Zimbabwe Controversy: A Case
     1973   of Colonial Historiography.
                                 Syracuse, N.Y.: Eastern African
                                 Studies Program, Syracuse
                                 University.

     The Mwari spirit cult of the Karanga of Rhodesia is
discussed intermittently throughout this historical
study. The relationship between the Mudzima, Mhondoro,
and Mwari spirits and their mediums is discussed
specifically on pages 26-33 ff.

333. Charles-Picard,   Les Religions de l'Afrique
     Gilbert   antique. Paris: Librairie Plon.
     1954

     Around 160 A.D., a writer named Apulée returned to
Greece from what now is Tripoli with the knowledge of
various occult practices, among which was an ability to
sorcerize children into trance and to then act as spirit
mediums (pp. 248-49).

334. Chenet, Gérard   "Haiti et l'héritage africain."
     1961   Recherches africaines (Institut
                                 national de recherches et de
                                 documentation, Conakry, Guinea),
                                 no. 3, pp. 3-23.

     The Haitian elaborations of the vodun cult are dis-
cussed in the more general setting of the African heritage on that island.

335. Choffat, François   "Ait-Baha-ou-Baha. Étude de
     1968   santé publique dans un village
                                 marocain." Psychopathologie

                                67

africaine (Dakar) 4, no. 3: 329-82.

In this detailed study of mental health in a small Moroccan village, traditional beliefs concerning the cause of illnesses, and the treatments which are practiced, are outlined. Possession by djinn spirits is given as the major cause for mental illnesses and epilepsy (pp. 351 ff.).

336. Christensen, James B. 1954 "The Tigari Cult of West Africa." Papers of the Michigan Academy of Science, Arts and Letters 39:389-98.

Description of Tigari shrines in West Africa and the rituals associated with them; ethnographic accounts of spirit possession of Tigari priests and of divination by spirit possession.

337. Christensen, James Boyd 1959 "The Adaptive Functions of Fanti Priesthood." In Continuity and Change in African Cultures, edited by W. Bascom and M. Herskovits, pp. 257-78. (Bib. 90.)

The article is concerned with the Fanti (Ghana) priesthood; spirit possession and mediumship; secular and sacred duties of the priesthood; political and social position of the priest; new cults.

338. Christopher, Robert A. 1955 "The Sacred Waters of Oxalá: An Eerie Pre-dawn Visit to a Brazilian Voodoo Ceremony." Américas 7, no. 1: 23-6.

A description is given of the "Águas de Oxalá" ceremony in the Afro-Brazilian candomblé cult during which the participants, "filhas de santo," become possessed by gods, orixás.

339. Churchill, Rhona 1962 White Man's God. New York: William Morrow & Co.

In this account of her travels in South Africa, the author describes the differing attitudes which prevail among white Christians towards the native African witch-doctors who are able to communicate with the spirits when in trance (pp. 44-9).

340. Clements, Forrest E. 1932 Primitive Concepts of Disease. University of California Publications in American Archeology and

Ethnology, vol. 32, no. 2.
Berkeley: University of California Press.

Classification of concepts of disease, including
spirit possession (pp. 188-90); cross-cultural distribution of spirit possession phenomena (pp. 216-25);
bibliography (relevant sources for Africa included in
this bibliography).

341. Clouzot, Henri-   Le Cheval des dieux.   Paris:
     Georges   Réné Julliard. Ill.
     1951

Discussion of the relationship of the possessed to
his god among Negroes of the New World.

342. Clune, Francis J.   "A Comment on Voodoo Deaths."
     1973   American Anthropologist 75, no.
                         1: 312.

In response to Lester's (1972, Bib. 1025) reformula-
tion of the interpretation of and causes for "voodoo
death," the author emphasizes that poison actually may
be the cause of death in these cases.

343. Coates, Austin   Basutoland. London: Her
     1966   Majesty's Stationery Office.

The great importance that the spirit world has for
the Basotho of South Africa is emphasized. Possession
by ancestor spirits is briefly mentioned (pp. 11-12).

344. Cockcroft, I. G.   "The Mlimo (Mwari) Cult." Nada
     1972   (Salisbury) 10, no. 4: 83-92.

An historical study of the Mlimo or Mwari cult among
the Venda and Kalanga of Rhodesia is presented, and
spirit possession and mediumship are both mentioned as
occurring in the cult.

345. Cohen, Abner   "The Politics of Mysticism in
     1968   Some Local Communities in Newly
                         Independent African States."
                         In Local-Level Politics, edited
                         by Marc J. Swartz, pp. 361-76.
                         Chicago: Aldine Publishing Co.

Sabo, the Hausa quarter in the city of Ibadan, Nigeria,
was the seat of the rise of a mystical Islamic order,
the Tijaniyya, one of whose missions was to crush the
bori spirit possession cult in the early 1950's (pp.
367 ff.).

69

346. Colin, Pierre   Aspects de l'âme malgache.
     1959   Paris: Éditions de l'orante.

     Spirit possession is mentioned in numerous places in
     this general study of Madagascar religion (pp. 15, 59
     ff.).

347. Colldén, Lisa   The Traditional Religion of the
     1971   Sakata. Studia Ethnographica
                         Upsaliensia, no. 34. Uppsala:
                         Institutet för allmän och
                         jämförande Etnografi.

     Spirit possession among the Sakata of Zaire is men-
     tioned in various contexts: possession by the spirit
     Nshu, who signals his desire to possess a person by
     sending illness, and who brings good fortune (pp. 38-
     40); possession by the spirit Mpwo, who brings ecstatic
     revelations (pp. 42-3); possession by dead chiefs
     (p. 43); witches who are possessed by iluo evil spirits
     (chap. 6); and diviners who are possessed (pp. 120 ff.).

348. Colle, A.   "La Notion de l'âme désincarnee
     1929   chez les Bashi." Congo: Revue
                         generale de la colonie belge
                         (Bruxelles) 1, no. 4: 583-97.

     Spirits of the dead can enter and possess the living
     among the Bashi of Zaire; this possession is a devotio-
     nal action, not connected with illness. Description of
     the possession state and accompanying ceremonies is
     given (pp. 590 ff.).

349. Collomb, Henri, et   "Les Migrations au Sénégal:
     Henri Ayats   Étude psychopathologique."
     1962   Cahiers d'études africaines
                         (Paris) 2, no. 4: 570-97.

     The psychological aspects of the migrations of dif-
     ferent peoples in Senegal are analyzed; among these are
     mentioned cases of possession, "les épisodes aigus"
     (p. 592).

350. Collomb, Henri, and "Une Étude psychopathologique
     Henri Ayats   sur les migrants." Afrique
     1963   Documents (Dakar), no. 67, pp.
                         71-95.

     Spirit possession is mentioned on page 91 as being a
     characteristic of mental illness in Africa, specifically
     in relation to the African peoples who have migrated to
     the city in Senegal, including the Wolof, Sérer, Peul
     (Fulani), Toucouleur (Tukulor), Diola, Mandingue

(Malinke), Bambara, Lébou (Lebu) peoples, and others.

351. Collomb, H. and   Psychiatrica in Africa: Clinical
     Zwingelstein, J.   and Social Psychiatry and the
     1964   Problems of Mental Health in
                           Africa. Vancouver.

Not available for annotation.

352. Collomb, H.   "Assistance psychiatrique en
     1965a   Afrique (experience
                          sénégalaise)." Psychopathologie
                          africaine (Dakar) 1, no. 1:
                          11-84.

A holistic view of the position of psychiatric medicine
in Senegal is presented, and includes traditional
African aetiologies of mental illnesses and Western
psychiatric diagnoses. Spirit possession is discussed
from both of these positions: as a social means of
dealing with mental illness (pp. 15-19), and as a
hysteric neurosis (pp. 46-47).

353. Collomb, H.   "Bouffées delirantes en
     1965b   psychiatrie africaine." Psycho-
                          pathologie africaine (Dakar) 1,
                          no. 2: 167-239.

The psychiatric condition termed "Bouffées Délirantes"
is analyzed for various Senegalese peoples such as the
Wolof, Toucouleur (Tukulor), Diola, Sérer, Lébou (Lebu),
Peul (Fulani), and Bambara. Native beliefs concerning
these states which center around ideas of spirit possession are considered to be "distortion factors."
Specific cases are presented in detail throughout the
text (pp. 172, 186 ff.).

354. Collomb, H.,   "Étude d'un cas de
     P. Martino, and   schizophrénie." Psychopathologie
     M. C. Ortigues   africaine (Dakar) 2, no. 1: 9-64.
     1966a

An extensive presentation of a case of a Lebou (Lebu)
man of Senegal who was diagnosed to be schizophrenic by
psychiatrists. His family believed that the ancestral
rab spirits were harming him (pp. 26 ff.), but since the
traditional n'dõp curing ceremony where spirit possession
is induced is no longer practiced, he went to a marabout,
a specialist in the Islamic seytané spirits believed to
send illnesses (pp. 30 ff.). When the man did not get
better, he was taken to a psychiatric hospital.

71

355. Collomb, H.   "Psychiatrie et cultures."
     1966b   Psychopathologie africaine
                          (Dakar) 2, no. 2: 258-73.

In this general essay the interrelationship between
cultural belief systems and psychiatric diagnoses is
explored. The example of possession by rab spirits
among the Wolof and Lebou peoples of Senegal is presented, and termed "bouffée delirante" (pp. 266 ff.)

356. Collomb, H., and   "Ndöp and Psychodrama."
     Chantal de Preneuf   Foreign Psychiatry 1, no. 3:
     1972   299-310.

The Ndöp, a form of traditional African therapy found
among the Wolof and Lebou of Senegal which involves
possession by the rab ancestral spirits, is compared to
psychodrama. Description of the ceremonies are given.
[Cited in Transcultural Psychiatric Research Review
(Montreal) 10 (October 1973): 164-65.]

357. Collomb, Henri   "Psychiatrie moderne et
     1975   therapeutiques traditionnelles."
                         Éthiopiques (Dakar), no. 2,
                         pp. 40-54.

In this general theoretical essay on modern psychiatry
and traditional African therapeutic techniques, spirit
possession as a cause of mental illness is discussed on
pages 44 ff.

358. Colloque de Cotonou   Les Religions africaines comme
     1972   source de valeurs de civilisa-
                           tion. Colloque organisé par la
                           Société africaine de culture,
                           16-22 August 1970. Paris:
                           Présence africaine.

     Includes in this bibliography:
                15   H. Aguessy (1972)
                470   J. E. Dos Santos and D. M.
                          Dos Santos (1972)
                692   H. Gravrand (1972)
                1230   G. Montilus (1972)
                1556   R. Sastre (1972)
                1662   C. Souffrant (1972)
                1811   P. Verger (1972)

359. Colloque de Strasbourg Réincarnation et vie mystique en
     1965   Afrique noire. 16-18 May 1963.
                             Paris: Presses universitaires de
                             France.

Includes in this bibliography:
             109   R. Bastide (1965)
             671   O. Gollnhofer and R. Sillans
                      (1965)
            1357   G. Parrinder (1965)

360. Colson, Elizabeth   "Rain Shrines of the Plateau
         1948   Tonga of Northern Rhodesia."
                              Africa (London) 18, no. 4: 272-
                              83.

     A description of the rain shrines of the Plateau
Tonga of Northern Rhodesia (Zambia) and their social
significance. The rain makers become possessed by the
Basangu spirits, and at their instigation rain shrines
are erected.

361. Colson, Elizabeth   "The Plateau Tonga of Northern
         1951a   Rhodesia." In Seven Tribes of
                              British Central Africa, edited
                              by E. Colson and M. Gluckman,
                              pp. 94-162. (Bib. 362.)

     The rain makers among the Plateau Tonga of Northern
Rhodesia (Zambia) are subject to possession by basangu
spirits, and in such a state they serve as censors of
social behavior (pp. 156 ff.)

362. Colson, Elizabeth, and   Seven Tribes of British Central
     Max Gluckman, eds.   Africa. London: Oxford Univer-
         1951b   sity Press.

     Includes in this bibliography:
             361   E. Colson (1951a)
             666   M. Gluckman (1951)
            1484   A. Richards (1951)

363. Colson, Elizabeth   "Ancestral Spirits among the
         1954   Plateau Tonga." International
                              Archives of Ethnography 47:21-
                              68.

     Details on spirit possession among the Plateau Tonga
of Northern Rhodesia (Zambia) by Masabe and Basangu
spirits and some description of dances associated with
these.

364. Colson, Elizabeth   "Ancestral Spirits among the
         1960a   Plateau Tonga." In Cultures and
                              Societies of Africa, edited by
                              S. and P. Ottenberg, pp. 372-87.
                              (Bib. 1335.)

     Mediumship and possession by the mizimu spirits among

73

the Plateau Tonga of Zambia are discussed in depth here.

365. Colson, Elizabeth 1960b   Social Organization of the Gwembe Tonga. Manchester: Manchester University Press.

Spirit possession is practiced by the prophets of the Gwembe Tonga of Zambia (see book's index under "Prophet" for page citations).

366. Colson, Elizabeth 1962   The Plateau Tonga of Northern Rhodesia. Manchester: Manchester University Press.

Spirit possession among the rain makers and prophets of the Plateau Tonga of Northern Rhodesia (Zambia) is discussed in this work (pp. 92-93, 100).

367. Colson, Elizabeth 1969   "Spirit Possession among the Tonga of Zambia." In Spirit Mediumship and Society in Africa, edited by J. Beattie and J. Middleton, pp. 69-103. (Bib. 150.)

Two types of possession occur among the Tonga of Zambia: Basangu and Masabe. Basangu spirits have mediums who deliver messages of public import while possessed. Masabe spirits may possess people during dances or other ceremonies. Some Masabe spirits are in the forms of agents of social change (e.g., airplane) while others are animals, etc.

368a. Colson, Elizabeth 1971   The Social Consequences of Re-settlement. Manchester: Manchester University Press.

In this study of social change among the Gwembe Tonga of Zambia, the rise and impact of spirit possession cults are discussed on pages 239-244.

368b. Colson, Elizabeth 1977   "A Continuing Dialogue: Prophets and Local Shrines among the Tonga of Zambia." In Regional Cults, edited by R. Werbner, pp. 119-39. (Bib. 1859.)

A review of the development of cults and shrines among the Gwembe and Plateau Tonga (Thonga) of Zambia. Although the author reviews development since the late 19th century, emphasis is placed on data from field research over the past 30 years. Spirit possession is discussed as it relates to various cults and shrines and to processes of social change.

369. Comhaire, Jean L.   "Religious Trends in African and
     1953/54   Afro-American Urban Societies."
                           Anthropological Quarterly 26:
                           95-108.

Although spirit possession is not explicitly labelled,
the Haitian voodoo cult is briefly mentioned on pages
106-7.

370. Comhaire, Jean   "Sociétés secrètes et mouvements
     1955   prophétiques au Congo belge."
                           Africa: Journal of the Inter-
                           national African Institute
                           (London) 25, no. 1: 54-59.

Among the Bakongo of Zaïre indigenous religious cults
have been incorporating Christian names and symbols
into their rituals for a long time. In illustrating
the early date of this incorporation, the author refers
to an early eighteenth century account of an Italian
monk's encounter with a "princess," Dona Beatrice, who
claimed to be possessed by St. Antoine (p. 54).

371. Comhaire-Sylvain,   "La Chanson haitienne." In
     Suzanne   Haiti: Poetes noirs. Presence
     1951   africaine (Paris), no. 12,
                           pp. 61-87.

The songs in the Haitian vodon (voodoo) religion used
in the possession rituals are analyzed.

372. Connor, R. M. B.   "Nyakyusa Pagan Religion."
     1954   International Review of Missions
                           (London) 43, no. 170: 170-72.

Among the Nyakyusa people of Tanzania calamities are
often interpreted as the work of evil spirits whose
activities are set in motion by Kyala (god) at the request of an offended ancestor spirit. Description of
ceremony performed to avert calamity, including prayers
of intercession of priests and mediums. [Cited in
African Abstracts, vol. 6, no. 423.]

373. Consolate, Nassiwa   "African Traditional Religion:
     Mary   Women and the Sacred in Ganda
     1972   Tradition." Occasional Research
                           Papers in African Traditional
                           Religion and Philosophy
                           (Makerere University, Kampala),
                           vol. 7, no. 61.

Spirit mediums among the Ganda of Uganda are the
mouthpieces of the deities and can be either men or

women. If a woman is chosen (through an initial possession), she is considered a wife of the god and must ob-
serve chastity for the rest of her life (pp. 2-3).

374. Cook, Scott   "The Prophets: A Revivalistic
     1965   Folk Religious Movement in
                                 Puerto Rico." Caribbean Studies
                                 (Rio Piedras) 4, no. 4: 20-35.

Among rural Puerto Ricans several revivalistic religious movements flourish. One church of one such movement, the Prophets, is studied. The name of the church,
Cilicia Temple, was revealed to the pastor by a prophet
possessed by the Holy Spirit. A description of an old
woman acting as a medium for the Holy Spirit is given
(pp. 31-33).

375. Coriat, P.   "Gwek, the Witch-Doctor and the
     1939   Pyramid of Denkgur." Sudan Notes
                                and Records (Khartoum) 22:221-
                                37.

Details on the development of the cult of Deng
founded by a Nuer (Sudan) Kujur (witch-doctor) named
Wundeng. Information on how Wundeng and his son Gwek
were seized and possessed by a spirit.

376. Corin, Ellen, and   "De la forme culturelle a vécu
     Gilles Bibeau   des troubles psychiques en
     1975   Afrique." Africa: Journal of
                                the International African
                                Institute (London) 45, no. 3:
                                281-315.

This theoretical article examines closely the relationship between the forms of mental illness found among
various African peoples and their indigenous
aetiologies and therapies, both of which include spirit
possession.

377. Cornet, Joseph   Art from Zaïre. New York:
     1975   African-American Institute. Ill.

In this volume on African art from Zaïre, plate no. 23
shows a diviner's staff, composed of a man's torso and
featuring double pupils, a symbol of the diviner's
clairvoyance and ability to communicate with the
spirits (p. 46).

378. Cory, Hans   "The Ingredients of Magic
     1949   Medicines." Africa (London) 19,
                                no. 1: 13-32.

Mention is made of medicines used to invoke the super-

natural powers for furthering individual or communal
enterprises among the Sukuma people of Tanzania.
(Possible relation to drug-induced possession.)

379. Cory, Hans   "The Buswezi." American Anthro-
     1955   pologist 51, no. 5: 923-52.

Among the Ha and Sumba (Sumbwa) people of Tanganyika
(Tanzania), the Buswezi ritual cult was traditionally an
ancestor worship cult. The article deals with criteria
for admission to the cult and presents a detailed description of the initiation ceremony including drug-
induced possession. The author was initiated to the
Buswezi society in 1932.

380. Cory, Hans   "Religious Beliefs and Practices
     1960   of the Sukuma/Nyamwezi Tribal
                           Group." Tanganyika Notes and
                           Records (Dar es Salaam) 54:
                           14-26.

The Sukuma and Nyamwezi (Tanzania) believe in a variety
of nature spirits which can be induced by magicians to
cause evil; some details on this form of spirit mediumship.

381. Cossard-Binon,   "La fille de saint." Journal
     Giselle   de la Société des américanistes
     1969   (Paris) 58:57-78.

Spirit possession among those of African descent in
Brazil is discussed extensively in this article. The
candomblé cult is focused upon.

382. Coulter, Charles W.   "The Sociological Problem." In
     1933   Modern Industry and the African,
                           edited by J. Merle Davis, pp. 31-
                           127. London: Macmillan & Co.

Speaking of Rhodesian "tribes" in general, the author
mentions spirit possession on page 50.

383. Courlander, Harold   The Drum and the Hoe: Life and
     1960   Lore of the Haitian People.
                           Berkeley: University of
                           California Press.

Chapter 3 deals with spirit possession by the Loas
(gods) and the relationship of the Loas to Catholic
saints in the Haitian Vodun (voodoo) cult. Chapter 4
describes Vodun death rites and the ceremony of dispos-
sessing the Loa from the head of the deceased. Chapter 5
gives information on ritual services to the Loas, and
describes a marriage ceremony for a Loa.

77

384. Courlander, Harold   Negro Folk Music, U.S.A.   New
     1963   York: Columbia University Press.

     Discussed is the importance of music in the generation
     of the ecstatic states during which the practitioner
     "gets" or is possessed by the Spirit in Afro-American
     religions (pp. 7-8, 192-96).

385. Courlander, Harold,   Religion and Politics in Haiti.
     and Remy Bastien   Institute for Cross-cultural
     1966   Research Studies, no. 1.
                                 Washington, D.C.: Institute for
                                 Cross-cultural Research.

     Both of the essays in this book deal with the Vodun
     (voodoo) spirit possession cult in the context of the
     Haitian socio-political structure.

386. Courlander, Harold   Haiti Singing. New York: Cooper
     1973   Square Publishers.

     Originally published in 1939, this volume contains
     detailed description of the spirit possession ceremonies
     in the vodun cult of Haiti (see book's index under
     "Loa" for page citations).

387. Crane, William H.   "Indigenization in the African
     1964   Church." International Review
                                 of Missions 53, no. 212: 408-22.

     "Gifts of the Spirit" including glossolalia and
     healing powers are discussed in the general context of
     the African independent church movements (p. 418).

388. Crapanzano, Vincent   "The Ḥamadsha." Scholars,
     1972   Saints, and Sufis, edited by
                                 Nikki R. Reddie. Berkeley:
                                 University of California Press.

     The possession beliefs of the Moroccan brotherhood,
     the Ḥamadsha, are discussed in this article. Exorcism
     of evil spirits is used as a healing technique. [Cited
     in Transcultural Psychiatric Research Review (Montreal)
     10 (April 1973): 49.]

389. Crapanzano, Vincent   The Ḥamadsha: A Study in
     1973   Moroccan Ethnopsychiatry.
                                 Berkeley: University of
                                 California Press.

     The Ḥamadsha is a religious brotherhood in Morocco
     that practices curing techniques which are largely cen-
     tered around exorcizing the jinn spirits from sick per-
     sons. The author presents and analyzes detailed infor-

mation about spirit possession (see book's index under "Possession" for page citations).

390. Crapanzano, Vincent   "Saints, Jnun and Dreams: An
     1975   Essay in Moroccan Ethnopsycho-
                           logy." Psychiatry 38, no. 2:
                           145-59.

Not available for annotation.

391. Crapanzano, Vincent   Case Studies in Spirit Posses-
     and Vivian Garrison, sion. New York: John Wiley &
     eds.   Sons.
     1977a

     Includes in this bibliography:
                 392   V. Crapanzano (1977b)
                 393   V. Crapanzano (1977c)
                 1238   A. Morton (1977)
                 1410   E. Pressel (1977)
                 1558   L. W. Saunders (1977)
                 1930   A. Zempleni (1977)

392. Crapanzano, Vincent   "Introduction." In Case Studies
     1977b   in Spirit Possession, edited by
                           V. Crapanzano and V. Garrison,
                           pp. 1-40. (Bib. 391.)

     The introduction to this volume of case studies in
spirit possession offers a general theoretical analysis
of this phenomenon.

393. Crapanzano, Vincent   "Mohammed and Dawia: Possession in
     1977c   Morocco." In Case Studies in
                           Spirit Possession, edited by
                           V. Crapanzano and V. Garrison,
                           pp. 141-76. (Bib. 391.)

     The biographies of a northern Moroccan couple, Mohammed
and Dawia, are presented here. Each is possessed by a
jnun (jinn) spirit. Also presented are the practices of
the Ḥamadsha, a cultic group which specializes in curing
illnesses that result from spirit possession.

394. Crawford, J. R.   Witchcraft and Sorcery in
     1967   Rhodesia. London: Oxford Univer-
                          sity Press.

     Among the Shona of Rhodesia, a person may become a
witch either by accepting possession by a spirit or by
the magic of another witch. Becoming a witch may help
to resolve personal problems, for example, barrenness
in women, but it can also cause the person to do evil
(pp. 107-10). Members of the Apostolic Faith Mission of

79

Oregon, an African independent church, believe in the
Baptism of the Holy Ghost, which is evidenced by
"speaking in other tongues as the Spirit gives
utterance" (p. 223).
NOTE: The use of the term "possession" here seems to
differ from the usual definition, as it seems to represent only a special relationship between a person and
a spirit. There is no dissociation, mediumship, etc.

395. Crawford, J. R.   Witchcraft and Sorcery in
     1968   Rhodesia. London: Oxford
                              University Press.

     The Shona and Ndebele of Rhodesia are discussed with
regard to their beliefs in witchcraft and sorcery.
Witches are thought to be women who are possessed by
evil spirits, while sorcery involves the use of
"medicines" to do harm. [Cited in Abstracts in Anthropology, vol. 1, no. 3 (1970), no. 66.]

396. Crawford, J. R.   "The Consequences of Allegation."
     1970   In Witchcraft and Sorcery, edited
                              by Max Marwick, pp. 305-18.
                              Harmondsworth, Middlesex: Pen-
                              guin Books.
     The relationship among witchcraft, witchcraft eradi-
cation movements, the Pentecostal Church, and spirit
possession among the Shona of Rhodesia is explored in
this paper (specifically p. 312).

397. Crocker, H. E.   "Superstition in West Africa."
     1950   West African Review 21, no. 276:
                              1073-75.

     Notes on the superstitions held by Nigerian popula-
tion about sorcerers, "leopard" women, and leopard
associations.

398. Crowley, Daniel J.   "L'Héritage africaine dans les
     1959   Bahamas." Présence africaine
                              (Paris), no. 23, pp. 41-58.

     The African religious influence on Bahamian culture
is described here, and includes the phenomenon of
spirit possession (pp. 45-57).

399. Cunnison, Ian   The Luapula Peoples of Northern
     1959   Rhodesia. Manchester: Man-
                              chester University Press.

     Spirit possession among the Luapula peoples of
Northern Rhodesia (Zambia) is manifested in the priests
or prophets of the ngulu (nature spirits) who send and
forecast misfortune (pp. 220 ff.).

400. Curley, Richard T.   Elders, Shades and Women: Cere-
     1973   monial Change in Lango, Uganda.
                             Berkeley: University of Cali-
                             fornia Press.

Not available for annotation.

401. Cutten, George Barton   The Psychological Phenomena of
     1908   Christianity. New York: Charles
                             Scribner's Sons.

Demoniacal possession and glossolalia are both
examined in depth in this work on Christianity. Africa
is not specifically mentioned.

402. Cutten, George Barton   Speaking with Tongues Histori-
     1927   cally and Psychologically Con-
                             sidered. New Haven, Conn.:
                             Yale University Press.

Although Africa is not mentioned, the phenomenon of
speaking with tongues (glossolalia) within the Christian
tradition is examined both historically and psychologically.

403. Da Cruz, Clément   "Les Instruments de musique dans
     1954   la Bas-Dahomeny." Études
                             dahoméennes (Porto Novo) 12:
                             11-79.

Description of different orchestras, their instruments,
players, and function in the Dahomean (Fon) community
(Benin). Religious communities have their own
orchestras, which are often used for divination ceremonies or in scenes of possession. [Text in French.]

404. Dada, T. O.   "Epilepsy in Lagos, Nigeria."
     1970   African Journal of Medical
                             Sciences (Oxford) 1, no. 2:
                             161-84.

The African traditional belief that epilepsy is caused
by possession by evil spirits is mentioned as occurring
in patients seen in Lagos, Nigeria (pp. 161, 166).

405. Dale, Rev. Godfrey   "The Bondei." Journal of the
     1876   Royal Anthropological Institute
                             of Great Britain and Ireland,
                             vol. 25.

Description of devil possession and exorcism by the
devil doctor Mganga wa pepo among the Bondei of Tanzania. The devil is said to mount the women who dance
at the exorcism ceremonies.

406. Dammann, Ernest   Les Religions de l'Afrique.
     1964   Translated by L. Jospin. Paris:
                            Payot.

     Spirit possession is mentioned numerous times in this
theoretical work on African religions. Particularly refer to chapters 2, 3, and 4.

407. Daneel, M. L.   The God of the Matopo Hills.
     1970a   The Hauge: Mouton & Co.

     This account gives a very detailed picture of the
history and present-day sociopolitical activities of
the Mwari cult among the Shona people of Rhodesia.
Possession by the god Mwari through a medium serves as
a means of political and social influence for a very
wide area of this country.

408. Daneel, M. L.   Zionism and Faith-Healing in
     1970b   Rhodesia. The Hague: Mouton.

     Faith-healing in the Zionist movement in Rhodesia
involves glossolalia and exorcism of evil spirits. Detailed descriptions of healing practices are included.

409. Daneel, M. L.   The Background and Rise of
     1971a   Southern Shona Independent
                            Churches. The Hague: Mouton &
                            Co.

     This is an extremely detailed study of the independent
church movements among the Shona and Ndebele-speaking
peoples of Rhodesia. Traditional and syncretic forms
of spirit possession and mediumship are discussed throughout.

410. Daneel, Marthinus L.   "Shona Independent Churches and
     1971b   Ancestor Worship." In African
                            Initiatives in Religion,
                            edited by D. B. Barrett, pp.
                            160-70. (Bib. 83.)

     Possession by the ancestor spirits among the Shona of
Rhodesia is discussed with regard to its role in the
African independent church movements. Healing through
exorcism is also mentioned.

411. Daneel, M. L.   Old and New in Southern Shona
     1974   Independent Churches. 2 vols.
                            The Hague: Mouton & Co.

     Spirit possession, mediumship, glossolalia, and ex-
orcism are all mentioned in this analysis of the

African independent churches among the Shona of
Rhodesia.

412. Danielli, M.   "The Witches of Madagascar: A
     1947   Theory of the Function of
                           Witches and of Their Organiza-
                           tion Based on Observation of
                           an Existing Cult." Folklore 58:
                           261-77.

Among the Ambianiandro and Betsileo of Madagascar,
witches are often said to become possessed by gods.

413. D'Anna, Andrea   Da Cristo a Kimbangu. Bologna:
     1964   Editrice Nigrizia.

The major African independent church movements are
discussed, including Ethiopianism, Zionism, Kimbanguism,
Lenshina Church, Harrisism, and others. Exorcism and
possession by the Holy Spirit are mentioned at various
places throughout the text.

414. Dannholz, J. J.   Im Banne des Geisterglaubens,
     1916   Züge des Animistischen bei den
                           Wasu in der deutschen Ost Afrika.
                           Leipzig.

An account of possession among the Wasu in East Africa
by "deceitful" spirits causing the mpepo sickness.
These spirits afflict women particularly, and the malady
they cause is considered noble and distinguished. Includes description of symptoms of possession and curing
ceremonies (p. 23).

415. Davidson, Basil   Black Mother: The Years of the
     1961   African Slave Trade. Boston:
                           Little, Brown & Co.

The oracle of the Aro clan of the Ibo in Nigeria was
very widely respected during the years of the slave
trade, and if one disobeyed the oracle the medium-
priests sold the unfortunate into slavery to the
Europeans (pp. 210-13.).

416. Davidson, Basil   African Kingdoms. New York:
     1966   Time, Inc.

Spirit possession among the Yoruba of Nigeria,
practiced by priests (pp. 124-26), and spirit mediumship as a form of oracular divination among the Zande
(Azande) of the Sudan (p. 128) are mentioned briefly.

417. Davidson, Basil   The African Genius. Boston:
     1969a   Little, Brown & Co.

In this philosophical work on the nature of African culture, references to spirit possession and mediumship may be found throughout part 3.

418. Davidson, Basil   *The Africans*. London: Longmans.
     1969b

     Chapters 16 and 17 present a discussion of spirit possession and mediumship in Africa from the viewpoints of psychology and art.

419. Davidson, Captain S.   "Psychiatric Work among the
     1949   Bemba." *Rhodes-Livingstone*
                             Journal, no. 7, pp. 75-86.

     The explanation commonly given among the Bemba of Northern Rhodesia (Zambia) for the occurrence of lunatics is that they are possessed by evil spirits (pp. 74-75, 78).

420. Davidson, William   "Psychiatric Significance of
     1965   Trance Cults." Paper presented
                            at the annual convention of the
                            American Psychiatric Association,
                            New York.

     Trance is discussed not as a pathological state but as an adaptive mechanism. Fieldwork research among Cubans belonging to the *Babalu* cult, which practices spirit possession, is presented, as is a description of the trance state. Occurring mainly among the socially underprivileged, these cults foster extreme dependence upon a leader. [Cited in *Transcultural Psychiatric Research Review* (Bruges) 3 (April 1966): 45-47.]

421. Davis, J. Merle   *Modern Industry and the African*.
     1967   London: Frank Cass & Co.

     Speaking of the Rhodesian ethnic groups in general, the author briefly mentions spirit possession on pages 49-50.

422. Davis, Martha Ellen   "Afro-Dominican Religious
     1976   Brotherhoods: Structure, Ritual,
                            and Music." Ph.D. dissertation,
                            University of Illinois at Urbana-
                            Champaign. *Dissertation Ab-*
                            stracts International 37, no. 1:
                            421A-22A.

     The religious and musical heritage of Africa in the Dominican Republic is analyzed in a study of the religious brotherhoods in that country. No specific mention is made of spirit possession in the abstract; however,

84

the vodú religious organization is discussed.

423. Dawson, John   "Urbanization and Mental
     1964   Health in a West African Com-
                           munity." In Magic, Faith and
                           Healing, edited by A. Kiev, pp.
                           305-41. (Bib. 902.)

     Among the Temne of Sierra Leone, women members of the
society who control the most powerful of all oaths, the
thunder-and-lightning oath ang-bom, are called ya bai.
Ya bai often enter a state of dissociation or possession when delivering the ang-bom curse. The victims of
the curse suffer fits of spirit possession which can
only be removed by a confession of the crime that had
brought on the curse (pp. 328-29).

424. Debrunner, Rev. H.   Witchcraft in Ghana. Accra:
     1959   Presbyterian Book Depot Ltd.

     Among the Ashanti of Ghana, priests may be possessed
while dancing, or while consulting the spirits. After
such a possession, the priest may deliver oracles from
the spirit (p. 122). The religious services in African
Christian churches in Ghana are often very emotional and
frenzied. Discussion of glossolalia and faith healing
is presented (pp. 151-60).

425. Debrunner, Hans W.   A Church between .Colonial Powers.
     1965a   London: Lutterworth Press.

     The trance state achieved by the priests of the Ewe of
Togo, Ghana, and Dahomey (Benin) is termed by a Christian missionary as devil possession (pp. 69-71).
African Christian prophetic activity of exorcising
devils among these peoples is mentioned on page 281.

426. Debrunner, H.   The Story of Sampson Opong.
     1965b   Accra: Waterville Publishing
                           House.

     The life of the prophet Sampson Opong, who preached
among the Ashanti of Ghana in the 1920's, includes a
brief mention of the traditional Ashanti belief in
spirit possession (p. 10).

427. Decary, Raymond   Moeurs et coutumes des Malagaches.
     1951   Paris: Payot.

     Notes on the Madagascar peoples include spirit posses-
sion by the spirit of a dead king tromba; trance and
glossolalia; description of exorcism ceremonies (chap.
9, p. 225).

428. De Caso, Diosdado,   "Mauvais guérisseur et génie
     et al.   protecteur." Psychopathologie
     1968   africaine (Dakar) 4, no. 3:
                               383-417.

Clinical case report of a young half-caste with a
N'zima (West Africa) mother, who was suffering from
"fits of delirium with systems of anxiety predomina-
ting." Searching for an identity in an acculturation
period, he returned to his traditional N'zima background
and to the possession cults he had been neglecting.
Description of a possession "séance" is given.

429. Decle, Lionel   Three Years in Savage Africa.
     1898   London: Methuen & Co.

Among the Matabele (Ndebele) of Rhodesia possessed
people were considered madmen and were under the protection of the king. Description of ceremony for
smelling out witches in which women doctors danced until
they became possessed, and in that state they pointed
out the witches (chap. 7, p. 154).

430. Decraene, Philippe   "Les Incidences politiques des
     1965   religions syncrétiques et des
                              mouvements messianiques en
                              Afrique noire." Afrique con-
                              temporaire (Paris), no. 17,
                              pp. 19-22.

Trance and possession are briefly mentioned in this
discussion of the modern religious movements in Africa,
particularly Kimbanguism.

431. Degenaar, Johannes   "The Holy Spirit and Communica-
     1976   tion." Journal of Theology for
                              Southern Africa (Braamfontein,
                              Transvaal), no. 14, pp. 17-27.

This work gives a theoretical analysis of the phenomenon of speaking in tongues, glossolalia (occurring
through possession by the Holy Spirit), in Pentecostalism
(Africa is not explicitly mentioned).

432. Deikman, Arthur J.   "Deautomitization and the Mystic
     1969   Experience." In Altered States
                              of Consciousness, edited by C.
                              Tart, pp. 22-46. (Bib. 1710.)

The psychological process by which actions and percep-
tions are reinvested with attention is termed "deautomitization" and is a major element of the mystical experience.

433. Delachaux, Th.   "Méthodes et instruments de di-
     1946   vination en Angola." Acta
                           Tropica (Basel) 3, no. 1: 41-72;
                           3, no. 3: 138-49.

Numerous ethnic groups in Angola are discussed in this
article on the methods and instruments of divination.
Spirit possession is mentioned on pp. 144-45 as
occurring among the Nkouna and Nyaneka.

434. Del Molino, A.   "El mohulá o fuerza espiritual
     1967a   en la religión bubi." Guinea
                          Española (Santa Isabel) 62, no.
                          1596: 266-69; 62, no. 1597: 304-
                          9.

"Mohulá is a Bubi (Equatorial Guinea) word which means
'wind' and 'the breath of the spirit' (like the Latin
spiritus). The average Bubi uses it in the sense of
'blessing' or 'warmth,' but it is also the word used by
the Christians for the Holy Ghost. Kinship (loka) is
the channel of transmission for the spiritual force
(mohulá)." Possession is not explicitly mentioned in
the abstract. [Cited in African Abstracts, vol. 20, no.
3 (July 1969), no. 722.]

435. Del Molino, A.   "El oráculo bubi." Africa
     1967b   (Madrid) 24, no. 312: 628-31.
                          Ill.

The Bubi of Fernando Po (Equatorial Guinea) practice
a form of divination which includes calling down the
spirits with the use of spirit mediumship. The most
important spirits are called batérimos, and the places
where the oracle speaks are rojia.

436. Delobsom, Dim   Les Secrets des sorciers noirs.
     1934   Paris: Librairie Emile Nourry.

Although spirit possession is not explicitly
labelled, communication with the spirits is one method
of divination among the Mossi of Upper Volta (pp. 48-
73).

437. Deluz-Chiva, Ariane "La Société gyé chez les Gouro
     1965   de la république de
                          Côte d'Ivoire." Musées de
                          Genève 55:10-14. Ill.

Description of the Gouro (Guro) (Ivory Coast) ceremonies surrounding the gyé spirits, who are conceived of
as being half man, half animal; these spirits manifest
themselves in dreams, cause illness, demand sacrifices,
and sometimes "affect" the priest of the cult.

438. Dembovitz, N.   In Journal of the Royal Army
     1945   Medical Corps 84:70.

     Reports of episodes characterized as "running amok"
     in West Africa. The symptomatology of this phenomenon
     could allow its classification as spirit possession.

439. Denko, J. D.   "How Preliterate Peoples Explain
     1966   Disturbed Behavior." Archives
                            of General Psychiatry 15, no.
                            4: 398-409.

     Using the Human Relations Area Files, the author ex-
     plores the different explanations or causes of mental
     illnesses that are found among preliterate peoples
     around the world. Spirit possession among the Nuer of
     Sudan is discussed on pages 400-401.

440. Dennis, Benjamin G.   The Gbandes: A People of the
     1972   Liberian Hinterland. Chicago:
                            Nelson-Hall Co.

     Among the Gbande of Liberia, illness is often diag-
     nosed by means of speaking through the patient to those
     ancestor spirits possessing him (pp. 173 ff.).

441. De Plaen, Guy   "Rôle social de la magie et de
     1968   la sorcellerie chez les
                            Bayansi." Cahiers économiques
                            et sociaux (Kinshasa) 6, no. 2:
                            203-35.

     Among the Bayansi (Yanzi) of Zaïre the ndoki are in-
     visible forces that can possess individuals, at times
     against their will, and impart either beneficent or
     evil powers to the possessed (pp. 28-29).

442. Deren, Maya   Divine Horsemen. London:
     1953   Thames & Hudson.

     Spirit possession rituals in Haiti are discussed
     throughout the book. Particularly relevant are chapter
     3, "The Nature of the Loa," and chapter 5, "The Rites."

443. Derose, Rodolphe   Caractère de culture vodou.
     1955   Port-au-Prince: Bibliothèque
                            haitienne.

     Part 2, chapter 2, titled "Demoniacal Possession,"
     describes spirit possession and mediumistic experience
     in Haiti.

444. Dery, P. P.   "Traditional Healing and
     1973   Spiritual Healing in Ghana -
                            Christian Attitude." Ghana
                            Bulletin of Theology (Legon) 4,
                            no. 4: 53-64.

The Christian attitudes both towards traditional
African healing practices, which involve beliefs in
spirit possession and exorcism, and towards spiritual
healing in the Christian tradition are discussed.

445. Desanti, Dominique   Côte d'Ivoire: L'Atlas des
     1962   voyages rencontre. Paris:
                           Éditions rencontre.

The treatments employed by the Harris healer-prophet
Attio Albert in Bregbo, Ivory Coast, are presented
mainly through the recordings of an interview the
author had with him. Mental illnesses are usually
thought of as being caused by a devil, and exorcism is
called for. Cases of treatment are mentioned on pages
79, 81, 84-85.

446. Deschamps, Hubert, and   Les Malagaches du sud-est.
     Suzanne Vianès   Paris: Presses universitaires de
     1959   France.

In a discussion of the religious beliefs of the
Antemoro (Antaimoro) and Antesaka (Antaisaka) peoples of
Madagascar, mention is made of officiants in the ancestor cults who become possessed in order to communicate with the spirit world (pp. 67, 102).

447. Deschamps, Hubert   Histoire de Madagascar. Paris:
     1961   Éditions Berger-Levrault.

In chapter 5 mention is made of nature spirits that
haunt trees, stones, and water in Madagascar. These
spirits can possess people and make them dance (tromba,
bilo). Some comments offered on diviners, healers, and
those who act as intermediaries for the possessing
spirits.

448. Deschamps, Hubert   Les Religions de l'Afrique Noire.
     1970   Paris: Presses universitaires
                           de France.

In this general theoretical work on religion in Africa,
possession is mentioned in several contexts: the
priest, spirit-medium, of the Dahomey (Benin) (pp. 41
ff.); the diviner-curers of the Lobi (Gold Coast, now
Ghana) (pp. 61 ff.); the Islamic marabout (pp. 95 ff.);
and the Christian Zionist churches which emphasize possession by the Holy Spirit (pp. 115 ff.).

449. Dickson, Kwesi A.   Akan Religion and the Chris-
     1965   tian Faith. Accra: Ghana
                                 Universities Press.

     Chapters 6 and 7 deal directly with the traditional
     Akan (Ghana) religion, one element of which is spirit
     possession.

450. Dickson, Kwesi A.,   Biblical Revelation and
     and Paul Ellingworth,   African Beliefs. Maryknoll,
     eds.   N.Y.: Orbis Books.
     1969

          Includes in this bibliography:
                    12   E. A. Adeolu Adegbola (1969)
                    1250   V. Mulago (1969b)
                    1615   S. Sidhom (1969)

451. Dieterlen, G.   "Les Ames de Dogons." Travaux
     1941   et mémoires de l'Institut d'
                               ethnologie (Paris), vol. 40.

     Chapter 7 deals with the cult of Amma (the "creator"),
     who is served by a priestess among the Dogon of Upper
     Volta and Mali. Initiation into the priestly class is
     through spirit possession by the god. Description of
     some religious ceremonies.

452. Dieterlen, G.   Essai sur la Religion Bambara.
     1951   Paris: Presses Universitaires
                               de France.

     Not available for annotation.

453. Diop, M., and H.   "Pratiques mystiques et psycho-
     Collomb   pathologie." Psychopathologie
     1965   africaine (Dakar) 1, no. 2:
                               304-22.

     In Senegal, predominantly an Islamic country, reli-
     gious practitioners who deal with both the evil spirits,
     djinns, and the good spirits, seytanés, are called
     "marabouts." The practices of these individuals, which
     include spirit possession, are discussed in relation-
     ship to a psychiatric case.

454. Diop, M.   "La Dépression chez le noir
     1967a   Africain." Psychopathologie
                               africaine (Dakar) 3, no. 2:
                               123-94.

     In speaking about Africans generally, the author ob-
     serves that the phenomenon of spirit possession may
     not necessarily be a projection of some aspect of an

individual's personality, but instead may point towards
the delusions of persecution accompanying depression
(pp. 190-91).

455. Diop, M., A. Zemplini,   "The Meaning and Values Sur-
P. Martino, and H.   rounding Persecution in African
Collomb   Cultures." In Readings in
1967b   African Psychology, edited by
F. R. Wickert, pp. 357-65.
East Lansing, Mich: African
Studies Center.

Illnesses caused by rab spirit possession among the
Wolof, Lebou (Lebu), Serer, Peul (Fulani) and
Toucouleur (Tukulor) of Senegal are psychiatrically
interpreted as forms of persecution.

456. Dittmer, Kunz   "The Methods of Divination in
1958   the Upper Volta and Its Rela-
tion to the Hunting Culture."
Baessler Archiv (Berlin) n.s. 6,
no. 1: 1-60.

Information is presented here on methods of divination, mediumistic experiences, the role of the diviner
in the community, and his place in the religious belief system of the people of Upper Volta.

457. Doke, C. M.   The Lambas of Northern
1931   Rhodesia. London: Harrop.

Among the Lamba (Northern Rhodesia, now Zambia) Moba
spirit possession was introduced in about 1915; Saybe
possession is the oldest form known (p. 256).

458. Doob, Leonard W.   "Psychology." In The African
1966   World: A Survey of Social Re-
search, edited by Robert A.
Lystad, pp. 373-415. New York:
Frederick A. Praeger.

Zar spirit possession ceremonies are briefly spoken of
as being "group-therapy" practices (p. 398).

459. Dorès, M.   "À propos de l'intervention
1971   d'un médecin au cours d'un
traitement traditionnel à Bangui."
Psychopathologie africaine
(Dakar) 7, no. 1: 101-11.

This article follows the case of an individual, diagnosed as being psychotic, through a traditional healing
treatment involving dancing. Of the M'baka ethnic
group in Bangui, Central African Empire, the individual

was said to be troubled by the water spirits, and within two weeks of the onset of the illness, the patient recovered.

460. Dorès, M., and   "Bilinguisme et psychopatholo-
     M. M'bodj   gie." Psychopathologie
     1972   africaine (Dakar) 8, no. 3:
                            425-41.

Native aetiologies of mental illnesses which include spirit possession among the Wolof of Senegal are mentioned in relationship to the situation of bilingualism in mentally ill patients.

461. Dorjahn, Vernon R.   "The Organization and Functions
     1959   of the Ragbenle Society of the
                            Temne." Africa: Journal of the
                            International African Institute
                            (London) 29, no. 2: 156-70.

The Ragbenle society of the Temne in northern Sierra Leone is composed of both spirit and human members, the former called Maneke, being represented at particular times by masked human members of the society. Through their human vehicles, the Maneke formally identify lovers, thieves, etc. The Maneke may not be seen by women or uncircumcised boys. The blowing of an antelope horn by one of the masked Ragbenle is identified as "the spirit's voice" (pp. 161-62).

462. Dorjahn, Vernon R.   "Some Aspects of Temne Divina-
     1962   tion." Sierra Leone Bulletin
                            of Religion (Freetown) 4, no.
                            1: 1-9.

The various methods of divination among the Temne of Sierra Leone are presented, one of which employs spirit mediumship (p. 7).

463. Dornan, S. S.   Pygmies and Bushmen of the
     1925   Kalahari. London: Seeley,
                            Service & Co.

Although spirit possession is not explicitly labelled, some Bushmen of the Kalahari (Southern Africa) are able, at will, to change into different animals (p. 151). Among the Bechuanas of the Kalahari (South Africa), a person is called by the spirits to be a witch-doctor, and is then able to communicate with them (pp. 293 ff.)

464. Dorsainvil, J. C.   Vodou et névrose. Port-au-
     1931   Prince: Imprimerie la presse.

Discussion of Voodoo in its historical and social
contexts and in its psychological and psychopathological
dimensions. Information on supernatural illnesses (the
Hougan) and a philological explanation of Voodoo.
Possession and mediumship discussed throughout the book.
No index or bibliography.

465. Dorsainvil, J. C.   Psychologie haïtienne: Vodou et
     1937   magie. Port-au-Prince:
                         Imprimerie Nemours Telhomme.

Both the philosophical and psychological aspects of
the Haitian Vodou cult are explored. The phenomenon of
spirit possession and the Vodou pantheon are examined
in detail.

466. Dorsainvil, J. C.   Essais de vulgarisation
     1952   scientifique et questions
                         haïtiennes. Port-au-Prince:
                         Imprimerie Théodore.

Spirit possession in the Haitian vodou cult is mentioned throughout the essays in this volume.

467. Dorsinville, Roger   "Une Clef de l'oralité: La
     1976   Danse." Ethiopiques (Dakar),
                          no. 5, pp. 69-77.

In this theoretical work on African dance, the
phenomenon of spirit possession is discussed on page
74.

468. Dos Santos, Eduardo   "O noroeste Angolano e os movi-
     1964   mentos profético-salvíficos."
                           Ultramar (Lisbon) 5, no. 17:
                           32-73.

Discussion of messianic movements in Angola and their
mixture of traditional African beliefs and religious
doctrines introduced from the West. Included are
Kimbanguism, Lassyism, the Watch Tower Movement, and
Baha'ism. Spirit possession is discussed.

469. Dos Santos, Juana   "Ancestor Worship in Bahia: The
     Elbein, and   Egun-cult." Journal de la
     Deoscoredes M.   Société des Américanistes
     Dos Santos   (Paris) 58:79-108.
     1969

Extensive discussion of the religious beliefs and
ceremonies is given for those Brazilians of African
(mainly Yoruba) descent. Spirit possession and mediumship are integral elements in the ceremonies concerned

with ancestor worship.

470. Dos Santos, Juana E.,   "La Religion nago génératrice
     and Deoscoredes M.   et reserve de valeurs cultu-
     Dos Santos   relles au Brésil." In Les
     1972   Religions africaines comme
                                     source de valeurs de civilisa-
                                     tion, Colloque de Cotonou,
                                     (August 1970), pp. 156-71.
                                     (Bib. 358.)

     The African influence on Brazilian religious move-
ments is discussed here particularly with regard to the
Yoruba culture (called Nago in Brazil). Spirit possession is described on pages 162 ff.

471. Dotson, Floyd, and   The Indian Minority of Zambia,
     Lillian O. Dotson   Rhodesia and Malawi. New Haven,
     1968   Conn.: Yale University Press.

     The manner in which ghosts are exorcised from people
whose illness they caused is described for the Hindu
Indians of Zambia, Rhodesia, and Malawi on page 90.

472. Douglas, Mary   "The Lele of Kasai." In
     1954   African Worlds: Studies in the
                                     Cosmological Ideas and Social
                                     Values of African Peoples,
                                     edited by D. Forde. (Bib. 588.)

     In discussing the cult groups among the Lele of Zaïre,
the author describes the cult of the diviners. Initiation into this guild depends on a person's being called
to this status by spirit possession or by a dream
summons (p. 24).

473. Douglas, Mary   The Lele of Kasai. London:
     1963   Oxford University Press.

     The Lele of Zaïre commune directly with the spirit in
the Bukang cults, in which diviners become possessed.
Description of possession states is given on pages 210
ff.

474. Douglas, Mary   "Witch Beliefs in Central
     1967   Africa." Africa: Journal of
                                     the International African
                                     Institute (London) 37, no. 1:
                                     72-80.

     Theoretical discussion of the sociological distinc-
tions between witchcraft and sorcery in Central Africa,
in which spirit possession and its relationship to
these phenomena are mentioned. Societies discussed are

94

the Luvale, Cewa (Chewa), Lele, Yao, Ndembu, Plateau
Tonga, and Azande.

475. Douglas, Mary, and   Man in Africa. London: Tavistock
     Phyllis Kaberry, eds. Publications.
     1969

     Includes in this bibliography:
                    1203   J. Middleton (1969)
                    1300   C. Odugbesan (1969)
                    1315   M. Onwuejeogwu (1969)

476. Douglas, Mary, ed.   Witchcraft Confessions and Ac-
     1970   cusations. London: Tavistock
                               Publications.

     Includes in this bibliography:
                    252   R. Brain (1970)
                    861   G. I. Jones (1970)
                    1038   I. M. Lewis (1970)
                    1463   A. Redmayne (1970)
                    1880   R. G. Willis (1970)

477. Douglas, Mary   Implicit Meanings. London:
     1975   Routledge and Kegan Paul.

     In this theoretical work, spirit possession among
the Lele of Zaire is discussed in Chapter 2.

478. Doutreloux, A.   "Prophetisme et culture." In
     1965   African Systems of Thought,
                               edited by M. Fortes and G.
                               Dieterlen, pp. 224-39.
                               (Bib. 597.)

     In this general theoretical essay, the curing
practices of the prophet Simon Kimbangu are described
as being exorcisms; spirit possession is not explicitly
labelled (p. 235).

479. Doutte, E.   Magic et religion dans
     1909   l'Afrique du Nord. Alger:
                              Jourdan.

     Not available for annotation.

480. Douyon, E.   "Trance in Haitian Voodoo."
     1965   Transcultural Psychiatric Re-
                              search Review 2:155-59.

     Not available for annotation.

481. Douyon, Emerson   "L'Examen au Rorschach des
     1968   vaudouisants haitiens." In

Trance and Possession States,
edited by R. Prince, pp. 97-
119. (Bib. 1421.)

This is a study of Rorschach tests taken from a
sample of Haitians participating in the vaudon (voodoo)
spirit possession ceremonies.

482. Doyle, Arthur Conan   *Our African Winter.* London:
     1929   John Murray.

With an interest in psychic phenomena, the author
cites several cases of spirit mediumship; particularly
of interest is that of a South African (white) medium
who is possessed by the spirit of an African girl,
speaking a click language (p. 46); and also an account
of a Zulu woman who practices mediumship (pp. 94-95).

483. Drague, Georges   "A propos des Aisaoua." *Afrique*
     1960   *et l'Asie* (Paris) 51:3-12.

The Aisaoua of Morocco, a religious society, got its
start at the end of the fifteenth century. Some of its
rituals involve possession dances. Although the society
is being persecuted by the government, it is still
active in Algeria, Morocco, and Tunis.

484. Dubb, Allie   *Community of the Saved: An*
     1976   *African Revivalist Church in*
                     the East Cape. Johannesburg:
                     Witwatersrand University Press.

Although unavailable for annotation, this volume has
useful information on the use of glossolalia in the
African independent churches of South Africa.

485. Duerden, Dennis   *African Art: An Introduction.*
     1974   London: Hamlyn. Ill.

In this volume on African art, the Yoruba spirit
possession cults (Nigeria), the Haitian Voodoo, the
Brazilian Candomble, and the Cuban Bembe cults are all
discussed, and spirit possession is implied but not
explicitly labelled (pp. 53-54).

486. Du Moulin, John   "The Participative Art of the
     1962   Afrocuban Religions."
                        Abhandlungen und Berichte des
                        Staatlichen Museums für
                        Völkerkunde (Dresden) 21:63-77.

The feeling of social participation and integration
is very central to membership in Afrocuban religions.
The three whose history are traced here are: Palo Monte,

from the Bantu region of South and Central Africa; the
Ocha or Santería, from Yoruba territory; and the
Abakuá, said to originate in Calabar. Spirit posses-
ion is discussed.

487. Dunbar, A. R.   A History of Bunyoro-Kitara.
     1965   Nairobi: Oxford University
                            Press.

Among the Nyoro of Uganda, spirits called Embandwa
are worshipped through a spirit mediumship cult. There
are two classes of these spirits. The "white" Bachwezi
spirits represent a group of demigods who once ruled
Bunyoro; their worship has declined recently. The
"black" embandwa spirits are recent arrivals, some of
which represent elements of European influence (e.g.,
Ndege--the spirit of the airplane). Spirit mediums
perform curing and divination rituals (pp. 214-16).

488. Dupré, Marie-Claude   "Les Femmes mukisi des Teke
     1974   Tsaayi: Ritual de possession et
                            culte anti-sorcier." Journal de
                            la Société des africanistes
                            (Paris) 44, no. 1: 53-69.

The women of the Teke Tsaayi (Teke) in Zaïre have a
socially inferior status to that of the men, and the
author states that membership in the mukisi spirit possession cult is a means of dealing with and altering
this situation. Description of the possession trance
is given.

489. Dupré, Marie-Claude   "Le Système des forces nkisi
     1975   chez les Kongo d'après le
                            troisième volume de K. Laman."
                            Africa: Journal of the Inter-
                            national African Institute
                            (London) 45, no. 1: 12-28.

An in-depth analysis is given of the Kongo (Zaïre)
belief in the nkisi spirit forces which can possess
those persons who are called nganga, intermediaries between men and the spirits.

490. Dutel, R.   "L'Animisme de populations
     n.d. (1946?)   islamisées du moyen Niger
                            (Songhay et Zerma)." Mémoires
                            du Centre des hautes études
                            d'administration musulmane,
                            vol. 146.

A very detailed study of spirit possession dances a-
mong the Zerma, and of certain manifestations of magic
among the Songhay (Songhai) of Niger. Results of re-

search done in the region of Niamey, Tera, Dori, between
1941 and 1946. [Cited by Rouch (1954, Bib. 1525).]

491.Dutton, E. A. T.   The Basuto of Basutoland.
    1923   London: Jonathan Cape.

    Among the Basuto (Sotho) of South Africa, if an enemy
has the right recipe, he can cause a snake to enter into
a man, thereby possessing him and making him ill (p. 91).

492.Duval, Alain   "L'Intronisation d'un jeune
    1947   sorcier." Chine, Madagascar
                            (Lille), n.s. 7:18-19.

    Short but important note on the initiation of a
Batsileo (Betsileo) magician in Batsileoland,
Madagascar, through the ritual of spirit possession.
Offers a comparison of spirit possession in various
rites. [Cited in African Abstracts, vol. 12, no. 444.
Text and annotation in French.]

493.Duvignaud, Jean   "Existence et possession."
    1959   Critique (Paris) 15, no. 142:
                            253-63.

    This article reviews and criticizes the following
authors on their presentations and analyses of spirit
possession phenomena: Alfred Metraux, 1959 (Bib. 1191),
Roger Bastide, 1958 (Bib. 102), and Michel Leiris, 1958
(Bib. 1012).

494.Earthy, E. Dora   "The Vandu of Sofala." Africa
    1931   (London) 4, no. 2: 222-30.

    Among the Vandau of South Africa, spirit possession
and illnesses are attributed to the Mutupo (a ghost, or
that part of a man that never dies). Includes lists of
ritual activities that appease the Mutupo and a discussion of drug-induced possession (p. 226).

495. Earthy, E. Dora   Valenge Women. London: Oxford
     1933   University Press. Ill.

    Chapter 15 deals with: spirit possession by Ndau
(Central Africa) and Ngoni (Southern Africa) spirits;
mediumship cults engaged in spiritualistic seances;
testimony of a woman who had been possessed (pp. 182-
225). No bibliography.

496.Eberhardt, Jacqueline   "Note sur l'acculturation et
    1957   culte de possession malombo
                            chez les Bantous du sud-est."
                            Monde non chrétien (Paris)
                            43/44:218-24.

Description of spirit possession by Shilombo, spirit
of the dead, and its exorcism ritual by a dance among
the Bantu peoples of southeast Africa. The Christian
Bantu equates Malombo with a biblical demon. The
exorcised are considered as children of the exorcist
and form a cult which is quite different from the ancestor cult and shows a certain disintegration of Bantu
society. The significance of this cult to Bantu society
is discussed. [Cited in African Abstracts, vol. 11, no.
81.]

497. Edel, May Mandelbaum   The Chiga of Western Uganda.
     1957   New York: Oxford University
                               Press.

     For the Chiga of Uganda, the author discusses a ghost
that establishes contact with a living relative through
the mediumship of a diviner, spirit possession by
Embandwa spirits, symptoms of possession, its diagnosis
and cure, the cult of Nyabingi, the role of women as
priestesses. Ethnographic accounts are presented of the
frequency of cults similar to Embanda and Nyabingi in
neighboring areas to the Chiga (pp. 138-62).

498. Edgerton, Robert B.   "Conceptions of Psychosis in
     1966   Four East African Societies."
                               American Anthropologist 68,
                               no. 2: 408-25.

     Indigenous aetiological explanations for psychosis,
among which is spirit possession, are given for the
Sebei (southeast Uganda): Pokot (Suk) (northwest Kenya);
Kamba (south central Kenya); and Hehe (southwest
Tanganyika, now Tanzania).

499. Eduardo, Octavio da   The Negro in Northern Brazil:
     Costa   A Study in Acculturation.
     1948   Monographs of the American
                               Ethnological Society, no. 15
                               (Reprint 1966). Seattle:
                               University of Washington Press.

     Not available for annotation.

500. Edwards, A. C.   Review of Carlos Estermann,
     1963   Etnografia do sudoeste de
                               Angola: Junta de investigacóes
                               do ultramar (Mémórias, no. 30),
                               vol. 3 (1961). Africa (London),
                               vol. 33, no. 1.

     The third volume of Father Estermann's trilogy deals
with Angola. Ethnographic accounts on the Herero include consideration of the influences of spirit-posses-

sion cults from other tribes in southwest Angola.

501. Egerton, F. C. C.   African Majesty. London:
     1938   Routledge.

Report on a magician's being possessed among the
Bameleke (Bamileke) of Cameroon (p. 229).

502. Eiselen, W. M., and "Religious Beliefs and Prac-
     I. Schapera   tices." In The Bantu Speaking
     1937   Tribes of South Africa, edited
                          by I. Schapera. (Bib. 1563.)

Chapter 11 contains a general survey of beliefs held
by the Bantus of South Africa about the spirits of the
dead, manifestation of these spirits, worship of ancestors, and rain making.

503. Ekejiuka, Felicia   "Aro World View: An Analysis of
     1970   the Cosmological Ideas of
                          Arochukwa People of Eastern
                          Nigeria." West African Religion
                          (University of Nigeria, Nsukka),
                          no. 8, pp. 1-11.

Sickness, both mental and physical, may be caused by
bad spirits possessing an individual among the
Arochukwa (Ibo) people of eastern Nigeria.

504. Elder, J. D.   "The Yoruba Ancestor Cult in
     1970   Gasparillo." Caribbean Quarter-
                         ly (Kingston) 16, no. 3: 5-20.

The African influence, particularly that of the Yoruba
ethnic group, in the village of Gasparillo in South
Trinidad is discussed mainly with regard to ancestor
worship. Spirit possession by the Orishas or "powers"
is mentioned on page 13.

505. Eliade, M.   Le Chamanisme et les techniques
     1951   archaïques de l'extase. Paris:
                         Payot. English translation:
                         1964.

General discussion of shamanism; some examples throughout the book refer to African material concerning spirit
possession.

506. Ellenberger, D. F., History of the Basuto Ancient
     and J. C. MacGregor and Modern. London: Caxton
     1912   Publishing Co.

Among the Basuto (Sotho) of South Africa, evil spirits
are thought to cause illness by possessing people.

Treatment by exorcism is performed by witch-doctors
(pp. 248-49).

507. Ellenberger, H. F.   "Aspects ethno-psychiatriques de
     1968a   l'hystérie." Confrontations
                                 psychiatriques, no. 1.

     Spirit possession by the djin spirits in Muslem coun-
tries is mentioned in this general theoretical article
on hysteria and its treatment cross-culturally. [Cited
in Transcultural Psychiatric Research Review (Bruges) 6
(October 1969): 121-24.]

508. Ellenberger, H. F.   "Impressions psychiatriques
     1968b   d'un séjour à Dakar." Psycho-
                                 logie africaine (Dakar) 4, no.
                                 3: 469-80.

     Conclusions reached at the Second Pan-African
Colloquium on psychiatry held in Dakar, Senegal, in
1968 centered mainly on the theme that psychopathological
illnesses are similar for peoples from all cultures, but
each culture has its own interpretation of the illnesses
and these must be closely examined. Cases are presented
from Senegal of "bouffées délirantes" (fits of delirium),
and of a child thought to be possessed by a spirit but
classified clinically as "infantile autism."

509. Ellenberger, Victor   Afrique: Avec cette peur venue
     1958   du fond des âges. Paris: Livre
                                 contemporain - Amiot-Dumont.

     Writing on Africa in general, the author mentions
spirit possession and mediumship in a discussion of the
"voyant" or seer who can enter trance and then prophesy (pp. 74 ff.); and in a specific chapter on possession and exorcism (pp. 184-98).

510. Elliott, A. D.   "Witchcraft in the Lowveld."
     1966   Nada (Salisbury) 9, no. 3: 5-9.

     Account of the measures that the Venda of the Lowveld
(South Africa) took to counteract the drought of 1963.
Witchcraft was cited as the cause, and various spirit
mediums were summoned to uncover the evil-doer and
placate Mlimo (God).

511. Ellis, A. B.   The Land of Fetish. London:
     1883   Chapman & Hall.

     Although neither spirit possession nor mediumship is
explicitly labelled, both are implied in a brief description of the "fetish fit" in which Dahomean (Fon)

priests speak "the holy fetish word" and act in any manner that they wish (West Africa) (pp. 52-53).

512. Ellis, A. B.   The Tshi-speaking People of the
     1887   Gold Coast of West Africa.
                      London: Chapman & Hall.

Information for the Tshi-speaking peoples (Akan) of the Gold Coast (Ghana) on disease due to spirit intrusion; possession as the calling to the priesthood; possession dances; priests and priestesses, their appearance, initiation ceremony, and communication with the spirits; functions of the priest within the community (p. 148 and chap. 10).

513. Ellis, A. B.   The Ewe Speaking Peoples of the
     1890   Slave Coast of West Africa.
                      London: Chapman & Hall.

Among the Ewe-speaking peoples of West Africa the deity Legba is a phallic divinity. Sexual desire is attributed to possession by this god (similar to Yoruba god Egbe) (chap. 3, p. 41). Chapter 9 discusses recruitment, training, spirit possession during dances and ordination ceremony of the priests; priests absolved of crimes committed while possessed; role of spirit possession for communication with the deities (p. 143); disease caused by spirit intrusion (p. 96).

514. Ellis, A. B.   The Yoruba-speaking Peoples of
     1894   the Slave Coast of West Africa.
                      London: Chapman & Hall.

The religion of the Yoruba of Dahomey (Benin) and Nigeria is discussed in detail, and spirit possession is mentioned (pp. 112 ff.).

515. Elmslie, W. A.   Among the Wild Ngoni. London:
     1970   Frank Cass & Co.

Written by a missionary and originally published in 1899, this work discusses the Ngoni of South Africa, and describes spirit possession of witch-doctors on pp. 66 ff.

516. Elserrag, M. E.   "Psychiatry in the Northern
     1968   Sudan: A Study in Comparative
                      Psychiatry." British Journal
                      of Psychiatry 114, no. 513: 945-
                      48.

Brief mention is made of zar spirit possession in cults in this general discussion of the major psychiatric problems in the northern Sudan (p. 945).

102

517. Emin, Pasha   *Emin Pasha in Central Africa*.
     1888   Edited by Schweinfurth et al.
                            London: Philip.

     Emin Pasha recorded his impression of the Mbandwa
     mediums at the headquarters of the Bito (Nyoro) (Uganda)
     princes whom he visited. Description is given of women
     mediums and of spirit possession (p. 285). [Cited in
     Beattie (1961a, Bib. 135), p. 20.]

518. Enang, K. N.   "The Holy Spirit in the Nigerian
     1976   Independent Churches." *Africana
                           Marburgensia* 9, no. 2: 3-31.

     Possession by the Holy Spirit is examined in great
     detail in this article; data are collected from the
     Nigerian independent African churches.

519. Encyclopedia   *Encyclopédie du Congo belge*.
     n.d. (1950?)   Vol. 1. Bruxelles: Éditions
                           Bieleveld.

     In a theoretical discussion of religion in Zaïre, men-
     tion is made of spirit possession as being an essential
     ingredient of mediumship (p. 118).

520. Enem, Edith   "Nigerian Dances." *Nigeria
     1975   Magazine* (Marina Lagos), nos.
                           115-16, pp. 68-103. Ill.

     In this descriptive essay on dance in Nigeria, ritual
     possession dances are mentioned mainly in connection with
     the Hausa **bori** cult (pp. 70, 90, 96-98).

521. Engelvin, A.   "The Beliefs and Ritual Prac-
     1941   tices of the Vezi of Madagascar."
                           Missioni cattoliche (Milano),
                           pp. 231-32, 246-47.

     The Vezi (Madagascar) believe evil spirits cause ill-
     ness. The supreme spirit *Zanahary* is appealed to
     through the mediumship of the sorcerer (*Ombiasa*). This
     appeal is made on the occasions of marriage or illness.
     [Cited in *African Abstracts*, vol. 9, no. 593.]

522. Epega, Rev. D. Onadele   *The Mystery of Yoruba Gods*.
     1931   Lagos: Hope Rising Press.

     Although spirit possession is not explicitly labelled,
     this book deals with the Yoruba Ifa religion in Nigeria,
     and gives the characteristics of the various gods.

523. Epega, D. Qlarimwa   *The Basis of Yoruba Religion*.
     1971   Abeokuta: Ijamido Printers.

Although spirit possession is not explicitly labelled, this work discusses the characteristics of the major Yoruba deities (Nigeria).

524. Epelle, E. M. T.   "Development of the Sects in
     1972   Eastern Nigeria." West African
                          Religion (University of Nigeria,
                          Nsukka), nos. 13-14, pp. 40-51.

The roles of trance, glossolalia, and spirit possession in the new African sects based on Christianity in eastern Nigeria are mentioned on page 49.

525. Erivwo, S. U.   "The Holy Ghost Devotees and
     1974   Demonday's Ministry - an Evalua-
                          tion." West African Religion
                          (Nsukka), no. 15, pp. 19-31.

Possession by the Holy Spirit and Christian healing practices employing exorcism of evil spirits are dis-cussed for Nigeria. The healer-minister, Monday Uzoechi, or Demonday, is profiled.

526. Erny, Pierre   "Phénomènes de possession entre
     1971   Congo et Zambèze. A propos du
                          livre de Beatrix Heintze."
                          Problèmes Sociaux Congolais,
                          (Bruxelles/Lubumbashi), nos.
                          92-93, pp. 115-17.

This long review article of Beatrix Heintze's Besessen-heits -- Phanomene in mittleren Bantu-Gebiet (Franz Steiner Verlag, Wiesbaden 1970, 288 pp., 6 maps) (Bib. 753), presents the major points and discusses some of her concepts. Six ethnic-groups are covered, including: Nyaneka-Humbi (Angola), Tchokwe (Chokwe, Angola), Baluba (Luba, Zaire), Balamba (Lamba, Zambia), Shona (Rhodesia), and Swahili (Tanzania).

527. Erny, Pierre   "Images de la folie et de la
     1972   possession sondage au pres
                          d'étudiants zairois." Problèmes
                          sociaux zaïrois. (Lubumbashi),
                          nos. 98-99, pp. 73-80.

The differences and similarities between madness ("la folie") and possession are explored for various ethnic groups in Zaire, including: Baluba (Luba), Bakongo (Kongo), Bayanzi (Yanzi), Lulua, Bambala (Mbala), Batetela (Tetela), Bapende (Pende), Alur, Basakata (Sakata), and Bilumbu (Lumbu).

528. Estermann, Charles   "Cultes d'esprits   et magie
       1954   chez les Bantous de sud-ouest
                                de l'Angola." Anthropos 49,
                                nos. 1-2: 1-26.

Spirit possession is prevalent in the spirit cult of
the Ambo and Nyaneka-Humbe peoples of Angola. Ancestor
spirits possess their descendants, who become healers and
diviners. Possession by the Onondele spirits requires
dances as means of cure. Since 1944, a new class of
Onondele spirits is on the rise; description of these
follows (pp. 1-17). Illustration page 16.

529. Estermann, Charles   "Zum umbandu-Kult in Brasilien."
       1964   Anthropos 59, nos. 5-6: 935.

The origin of the term umbandu is traced to the Bantu
languages, where it is used to describe an "initiation
ceremony" in which the candidate is possessed by a spirit
and thus obtains divine or healing powers.

530. Estermann, Carlos   "O Tocoísmo como fenómeno
       1965   religioso. Tocoísm as a reli-
                                gious phenomenon." Garcia de
                                Orta (Lisbon) 13, no. 3: 325-42.

The "Church of Our Lord Jesus Christ," founded by
Simon Toco in Angola, is examined. One instance of an
African ritual in the church is that of the integration
of the neophyte into the church, which is considered to
occur when a spirit takes possession of him, and not by
baptism. [Cited in African Abstracts, vol. 19, no. 608.]

531a. Estermann, Carlos   "Inovações recentes no culto dos
       1966   espíritos no sul de Angola."
                                Ultramar (Lisbon) 23:12-24.

Discussion of the relatively recent (turn of the century) introduction of a spirit cult of foreign origin
into the Nhaneka-Humba (Nyaneka) culture of South
Angola, and its impact upon the traditional ancestor-
oriented religion. Spirit possession is discussed.

531b. Estermann, Carlos   The Ethnography of Southwestern
       1976   Angola: The Non-Bantu Peoples,
                                the Ambo Ethnic Group. (Edited
                                by Gordon D. Gibson.) New York:
                                Africana Publishing Company.

Spirit possession is discussed in connection with the
occupation of the hunter. Apprenticeship in hunting
demands spiritual initiation involving possession (p.
144).

532. Etienne, Ignace (Abbé)   "Le Fétichisme des Nègres du
     1908   Brésil." Anthropos (Vienne) 3:
                                 881-904.

     Spirit possession by Orisha gods in Brazil is dis-
     cussed.

533. Etienne, Pierre   "Phénomenes religieux et
     1966   facteurs socio-économiques dans
                                 un village de la région de
                                 Baoulé." Cahiers d'études
                                 africaines (Paris) 6, no. 3:
                                 367-401.

     The two modern cults of Tɛtɛ-Kpã and Tigali among the
Baoulé of the Ivory Coast are discussed with emphasis on
their religious beliefs (which includes spirit possession, pp. 379 ff.) and on their socioeconomic factors.

534. Euchu   "The Concept of Sickness and
     1967   Death among the Kumam People
                                 of Uganda." Occasional Research
                                 Papers in African Traditional
                                 Religion and Philosophy
                                 (Makerere University, Kampala),
                                 vol. 7, no. 66.

     Spirit possession by the evil jwogi spirits is a major
cause of illness among the Kumam of Uganda.

535. Evans, C. C., and   "An Experiment in the Electro-
     Edward Osborn   encephalography of Mediumistic
     1951   Trance." Journal of the Society
                                 for Psychical Research 36:588-
                                 96.

     Data from an experiment with a British medium shows no
significant changes in the normal EEG patterns when the
medium is in trance.

536. Evans-Pritchard, E. E.   "The Nuer: Tribe and Clan."
     1935   Sudan Notes and Records
                                 (Khartoum) 18:37-87.

     Discussion of spirit possession among the Nuer
(Sudan). The deity Deng possessed Gwek, who became a
prophet. Possession can proceed in a hereditary line,
but the man wishing to be possessed by the spirit of his
father must exert effort toward this (pp. 60-61).

537. Evans-Pritchard, E. E.   Witchcraft, Oracles and Magic
     1937   among the Azande. Oxford:
                                 Clarendon Press.

Although spirit possession, mediumship, or trance is
not explicitly labelled for the Azande of the Sudan, in
part 2, chapter 1, the witch-doctor's séance is described in which he communicates with the spirits while
"intoxicated" by the drum music.

538. Evans-Pritchard, E. E.   The Nuer. London: Oxford
     1940   University Press.

     Nuer prophets are often possessed by sky-gods. The
author gives a history of the first prophet to gain great
influence and analyzes why prophets arose and their
political function among the Nuer. Spirit possession is
claimed to have existed among the Nuer since the 1880's
(pp. 184-91).

539. Evans-Pritchard, E. E.   The Divine Kingship of the
     1948   Shilluk of the Nilotic Sudan.
                               Cambridge: Cambridge University
                               Press.

     Among the Shilluk of the Sudan, the king-elect and
his wife become possessed in the investiture ceremonies
by the spirit Nyikang, the original founder of the
Shilluk Kingdom (pp. 27 ff.).

540. Evans-Pritchard, E. E.   "A Note on Ghostly Vengeance
     1953   (Acieni) among the Annuak."
                               Man 53, no. 3: 6-7.

     Illness among the Annuak (Anuak)(Sudan) resulting
from ghostly vengeance is treated by a woman healer
(ajua). The treatment involves dancing and is described
as similar to possession and mediumship trances,
especially the role of the healer.

541. Evans-Pritchard, E. E.   "A Problem in Nuer Religious
     1954   Thought." Sociologus (Berlin)
                               4, no. 1: 23-41.

     Examines Nuer notions of spirit and their manifesta-
tions.

542. Evans-Pritchard, E. E.   "A Seance among the Azande."
     1957   Tomorrow (New York) 5, no. 4:
                               11-26.

     Witch doctors among the Azande of the Sudan divine
the individuals practicing witchcraft by dancing and
entering into an ecstatic trance state. Possession is
not explicitly mentioned.

543. Evans-Pritchard, E. E.   Nuer Religion. Oxford: Claren-
     1962   don Press.

Among the Nuer of the Sudan, the spirits of the air may possess individuals, either through inheritance or by way of an illness sent by the spirits. Such a person is referred to as a prophet (pp. 33 ff., 303 ff.; see also book's index under "Spirits" for further page citations).

544. Evans-Pritchard, E. E.   "Zande Notions about Death,
     1969   Soul and Ghost." Sudan Notes
                               and Records (Khartoum) 50: 41-
                               52.

A collection of statements about death, the soul, and ghosts by Zande (Azande) informants is presented; illness occurs when evil spirits "seize" people during sleep. Possession is not explicitly labelled but implied.

545. Ezeh, Innocent   "Children of Satan Confess."
     1976   Drum (Lagos), June, pp. 16-17.

Communication with the spirit realms is emphasized in the Ogbanje cult (Nigeria), whose leader is named Satan. Personal accounts of individuals involved in this cult are given.

546. Fabiyi, T. F., and   "The Sense of 'Concreteness' in
     Harry Sawyerr   Yoruba Worship." Sierra Leone
     1965   Bulletin of Religion (Freetown)
                            7, no. 1: 13-22.

Possession of priestesses by the orisha deities among the Yoruba of Nigeria is mentioned on pages 16-21.

547. Fabunmi, Chief M. A.   Ife Shrines. Ife: University
     1969   of Ife Press.

Although spirit possession is not explicitly labelled, the various Yoruba shrines for their gods found in Ife, Nigeria, are discussed in this book.

548. Fadipe, N. A.   The Sociology of the Yoruba.
     1970   Ibadan: Ibadan University
                            Press.

Chapter 8 deals with the religion of the Yoruba of Nigeria, and briefly mentions spirit possession (p. 287).

549. Fakhouri, Hani   "The Zar Cult in an Egyptian
     1968   Village." Anthropological
                           Quarterly 41, no. 2: 49-56.

The Zar cult is practiced in many rural areas of Egypt. People troubled with chronic illness may have their problem diagnosed as possession by a spirit.

108

Through ceremonies in which the victim becomes possessed, the spirit is praised and flattered so that it is transformed from an evil spirit to a guardian spirit.

550. Falcon, R. P. Paul   "Religion du Vodun." Études
     1970   dahoméennes (Porto-Novo), n.s., nos. 18-19.

This is a long (211 pp.) and detailed study of the Yoruban vodun religion in Dahomey (Benin), which involves possession by the gods.

551. Fallers, L. A., and   "Homicide and Suicide in
     M. C. Fallers   Busoga." In African Homicide
     1960   and Suicide, edited by Paul Bohannan, pp. 65-93. Princeton, N.J.: Princeton University Press.

Spirit mediums are briefly mentioned as being one of several types of specialists who deal with the nature spirits and ghosts which cause misfortune for the Basoga (Soga) of southeastern Uganda (p. 70).

552. Fallers, Lloyd A.   Law without Precedent. Chicago:
     1969   University of Chicago Press.

Possession by various types of spirits among the Basoga (Soga) of Uganda is considered as treatment for illnesses sent by them (pp. 47-48).

553. Fallers, Margaret   The Eastern Lacustrine Bantu.
     Clave   Ethnographic Survey of Africa,
     1968   edited by Daryll Forde. London: International African Institute.

The Baganda (Ganda) of Uganda had mediums who were possessed by ancestor spirits called Balubaale. A medium was chosen by being suddenly possessed and then undergoing an elaborate ceremony. Mediums might be consulted by private individuals, but they were also used by Kabaka (king) in matters of public importance (pp. 69-70).

554. Faublée, Jacques   Les Esprits de la vie à
     1954   Madagascar. Paris: Presses universitaires de France.

The religion of the Bara of Madagascar is examined in this book, and spirit possession and mediumship are mentioned throughout (see book's index under "Possédé" and "Possession" for page citations).

555. Faublée, Marcelle, and   "Les Religions malagaches et
     Jacques Faublée   les mysticisme." Présence
     1958   africaine (Paris) 17-18: 37-42.

Among the Bara people of Madagascar, a priest possessed
by a spirit acts as an intermediary between the living
and the ancestor spirit. The societal role of the priest
is discussed.

556. Feci, Damaso   "Vie cachée et vie publique de
     1972   Simon Kimbangu selon la
                                 littérature coloniale et
                                 missionaire Belge." Cahiers du
                                 C.E.D.A.F. (Bruxelles), no.
                                 9-10, pp. 2-84.

The life of the prophet Simon Kimbangu is analyzed
in depth, and mention is made of his communication with
the Holy Spirit, his ability to exorcise evil spirits
possessing people, and the trance states followers enter
when contacted by the Holy Spirit (pp. 31, 33, 44-45).

557. Ferguson, John   Christian Byways: Deviations
     1968   from the Christian Path.
                                 Ibadan: Daystar Press.

The phenomenon of speaking in tongues, possession by
the Holy Spirit, in the separatist African churches of
Nigeria is discussed on pages 19-20.

558. Fernandez, James W.   "Christian Acculturation and
     1961   Fang Witchcraft." Cahiers
                                 d'études africaines (Paris) 2,
                                 no. 2: 244-70.

On the basis of a text written by a Gabonese citizen
of Fang language and tradition, the relationship between
traditional beliefs and Christianity is discussed. The
Fang have notions about witchcraft that center around
the possession of certain spiritual forces called evus.

559. Fernandez, James W.   "Politics and Prophecy: African
     1965   Religious Movements." Practi-
                                 cal Anthropology 12, no. 2:
                                 71-75.

Not available for annotation.

560. Fernandez, James W.   Divinations, Confessions, Testi-
     1967   monies: Zulu Confrontation with
                                 the Social Structure. Institute
                                 for Social Research, Occasional
                                 Paper no. 9. Durban: University
                                 of Natal.

110

A comparison is drawn between the Zulu divination cult of Emakhehleni and the Zionist Church, both located in and around Durban, South Africa. The divination cult employs spirit possession (pp. 11 ff.), and Zionism is concerned, among other things, with exorcism of evil spirits (p. 26).

561. Fernandez, J. W. "Independent African Christia-
     1969a   nity: Its Study and Its Future."
                        Journal of Asian and African
                        Studies (Leiden) 4, no. 2: 132-
                        47.

In this theoretical article on the African independent churches and their relationship to mainline Christianity, the phenomena of glossolalia and ecstatic dancing are mentioned (pp. 134-35, 143).

562. Fernandez, James W. Microcosmogony and Moderniza-
     1969b   tion in African Religious Move-
                          ments. McGill University
                          Occasional Paper Series, no. 3.
                          Montreal.

Although spirit possession and mediumship are not explicitly labelled, a state of ecstasy is mentioned as being attained in the Bwiti cult rituals of Gabon (p. 13); and communication with spirits of the dead, especially with that of the founder of Amakheleni cult (Durban, Natal, South Africa), is spoken of on page 17.

563. Fernandez, James W. "Zulu Zionism." Journal of
     1971   American Museum of Natural
                          History 80, no. 6: 45-51.

Both possession and glossolalia, inspired by the Holy Spirit, are features of the Zulu Zionists of South Africa, a cult which has its origins in the work of some evangelists who came to Africa from Zion City, Illinois. [Cited in Transcultural Psychiatric Research Review (Bruges) 9 (April 1972): 51-53.]

564. Field, M. J. Social Organization of the Gã
     1940a   People. London: Crown Agents
                    for the Colonies.

Among the Gã of Ghana, the Wɔyei are mouthpieces for the gods. They are chosen through possession by the gods to fulfill this role (p. 58). Further description of the possession trance is recorded on pages 94-95.

565. Field, M. J. "Some New Shrines of the Gold
     1940b   Coast and Their Significance."
                    Africa (London) 13, no. 2:

111

138-49.

The author discusses the different kinds of shrines in the Gold Coast (Ghana), the treatments they offer, the government's attitude toward the shrines, spirit possession by women attendants of the shrines.

566. Field, M. J.   "Ashanti and Hebrew Shamanism."
     1958a   Man 58, no. 7: 14.

The author discusses the similarity of Ashanti (Ghana) to Hebrew shamanism, and how the former is illuminated by the latter. The Ashanti shaman (okomfo) starts his career usually on the occasion of public religious ritual, when he suddenly becomes possessed by an obosom and rushes off to the bush, often reporting auditory or visual hallucinations. The usual bush sojourn is forty days (similar to Jesus' ministry). Additional ethnographic material is presented.

567. Field, M. J.   "Mental Disorder in Rural
     1958b   Ghana." Journal of Mental
                      Science (London) 104, no. 437:
                      1043-51.

This article deals with religious shrines and their work. Spirit possession is described for the Ashanti priests and Ga women (Ghana). Description is given of spirit possession of certain mediums. Very detailed, very useful for information on symptoms of possession.

568. Field, M. J.   Search for Security: An Ethno-
     1960   psychiatric Study on Rural
                      Ghana. London: Faber & Faber.

Chapter 3 deals with the nature of spirit possession, associated hysterical stigmata, spirit possession and the priesthood, the role of dissociation, Ashanti (Ghana) and Hebrew spirit possession; suggests that such mental states might be important to social institutions and belief systems.

569. Field, M. J.   Religion and Medicine of the Gã
     1961   People. London: Oxford Univer-
                      sity Press.

The author describes public religious worship among the Gã of Ghana in seven different communities, principles and practices of medicine and magic, spirit possession and mediumship séances as they occur in different communities.

112

570. Field, M. J.   "Spirit Possession in Ghana."
     1969   In Spirit Mediumship and
                      Society in Africa, edited by J.
                      Beattie and J. Middleton, pp.
                      3-13. (Bib. 150.)

     ˷Descriptions of spirit possession and mediumship among
     Ga, Adangme, Ashanti, and other peoples of southern
     Ghana. Spirit possession (by the "Holy Ghost") among
     African Christians is also described.

571. Field, M. J.   Akim-Kotoku. Westport, Conn.:
     1970 (1948)   Negro Universities Press.

     Among the Akim-Kotoku of the Gold Coast (Ghana), the
     traditional spirit mediumship cults are declining in
     importance as the rate of social change increases (pp.
     153, 172).

572. Figge, Horst H.   Geisterkult, Besessenheit und
     1973   Magie in der Umbanda Religion
                      Brasiliens. Freiburg/Muenchen:
                      Verlag Karl Alber.

     A detailed ethnographic and analytic study is pre-
     sented for the syncretic Umbanda cult of Rio de Janeiro,
     Brazil, which has African origins (mainly Yoruba) and
     utilizes spirit possession.

573. Firth, Raymond   "Foreword." In Spirit Medium-
     1969   ship and Society in Africa,
                      edited by J. Beattie and J.
                      Middleton, pp. ix-xiv.
                      (Bib. 150.)

     In the foreword to this volume of essays on spirit
     possession and mediumship in Africa, the author empha-
     sizes the importance of communication and control in
     these phenomena.

574. Fischer, P. J.   "Cultural Aspects of Bantu
     1962   Psychiatry." South African
                      Medical Journal (Cape Town) 36,
                      no. 8: 133-38.

     A detailed study is made of the southern Bantu-
     speaking peoples of South Africa, with particular em-
     phasis upon their cultural beliefs and practices.
     Spirit possession of mediums and as a cause of illness is
     mentioned.

575. Fischer, Roland   "A Cartography of the Ecstatic
     1971   and Meditative States." Science
                      174, no. 4012: 879-904.

A theoretical framework for the meditative and
ecstatic states of consciousness is presented in terms
of level of psychophysiological arousal.

576. Fischer, W. Singleton   "Kumaleli, le royaume des
     1951   esprits, source de terreur en
                         Afrique." Congo Mission News
                         (Leopoldville) 156:12-13.

This volume has been cited as having information on
possession and mediumship, but was not available for
annotation.

577. Fisher, Mrs. A. B.   Twilight Tales of the Black
     1911   Baganda. London: Marshall.

Information on spirit possession by Mbandwa spirits
among the Baganda (Ganda) (Uganda) and the relation of
possession to clan membership (pp. 99-101). [Cited by
Beattie (1961a, Bib. 135.), p. 15.]

578. Fitzgerald, Dale   "Prophetic Speech in Gã Spirit
     1970   Mediumship." Working Paper No.
                         30: Language-Behavior Research
                         Laboratory. Berkeley: Univer-
                         sity of California.

Based on field work among the Gã peoples of Ghana, the
author discusses the prophetic speech of Gã spirit
mediums in terms of the linguistic style and the socio-
religious functions of such speech events. Prophetic
speech is described as having two major characteristics,
glossolalic style and prophetic message content. A
detailed analysis of the speech event is included in this
paper.

579. Flasche, Rainer   Geschichteund Typologie
     1973   Afrikanisches Religiositat in
                         Brasilien. Marburg an der Lahu:
                         Marburger Studien zur Afrika und
                         Asien Kunde.

Not available for annotation.

580. Fleming, C. J. W.   "Systems of Land Tenure." Nada
     1974   (Salisbury) 11, no. 1: 53-63.

Among the Shona-speaking peoples in Rhodesia, the role
of the chief as a medium through whom the ancestral
spirits may be contacted, especially when rain is needed
in times of drought, is mentioned on pages 58-59.

581. Fletcher, Harold   Psychic Episodes of Great
     Clarkson   Zimbabwe. Cape Town: Cape
     1941   Times Ltd.

     The author and a medium, both British, went to the
     ruins of Zimbabwe, South Africa, and through the spirits
     who possessed the medium, the history of the civiliza-
     tion that built those monuments was revealed.

582. Fodeba, Keïta   "La Danse africaine et la
     1957   scène." Présence africaine
                               (Paris), nos. 14-15, pp. 202-9.

     Both spirit possession and exorcism are mentioned in
     this general article on African dance.

583. Fodor, Nandor   "Medicine Man Psychoanalyzed."
     1957   Tomorrow (New York) 5, no. 4:
                               77-83.

     Spirit mediumship used by a diviner to find the cause
     of drought is presented here in a case of a man from an
     unspecified ethnic group in Southern Rhodesia (Rhodesia).

584. Foli, B.   "African Explains Witchcraft."
     1935   Africa (London) 8, no. 4: 504-
                               59.

     Description of mediumship trances in relation to witch-
     craft for the Xhosa (South Africa) people. An account
     of possession of a witch among the Ewe (Dahomey, now
     Benin) people (p. 550). Text appears in the ethnic
     vernacular and also translated into English.

585. Fontaine, Pierre   La Magie chez les Noirs. Paris:
     1949   Dervy.

     In this general work on magic among the peoples of
     Africa, spirit possession, mediumship, and ecstatic
     trance dancing are discussed (especially pp. 110 ff.).

586. Fontanelle, Alvizeo   A Umbando Attaves dos Seculos.
     1953   Rio de Janeiro: Organizacao
                               Sinoes.

     Not available for annotation.

587. Foran, W. R.   "Black Magic in Africa: Belief
     1946   in Witchcraft Is Not on the
                               Decline." African World, July,
                               pp. 18-21.

     The author argues that the diviners in Africa earn
     their livelihood by treating those people who pretend to

115

be possessed by evil spirits, by healing the sick, and
by preparing different sorts of charms. Deals with
Zaïre.

588. Forde, Daryll, ed.   African Worlds: Studies in the
     1954   Cosmological Ideas and Social
                               Values of African Peoples.
                               London: Oxford University Press.

     Includes in this bibliography:
                   295   K. A. Busia (1954)
                   472   M. Douglas (1954)
                   933   J. D. Krige and E. J. Krige
                               (1954)
                   1045   G. Lienhardt (1954)
                   1115   J. J. Maquet (1954)
                   1174   P. Mercier (1954)
                   1827   G. Wagner (1954)

589. Forde, Daryll   "The Nupe." In Peoples of the
     1955a   Niger-Benue Confluence, edited
                              by D. Forde, pp. 17-52.
                              (Bib. 590.)

     The Nupe of Nigeria believe that certain individuals
are possessed by a supernatural power which they can
use for evil purposes such as practicing witchcraft
(p. 48).

590. Forde, Daryll, ed.   Peoples of the Niger-Benue Con-
     1955b   fluence. Ethnographic Survey
                              of Africa, pt. 10. London: In-
                              ternational African Institute.

     Includes in this bibliography:
                   280   P. Brown (1955)
                   589   D. Forde (1955a)

591. Forde, Daryll   "Spirits, Witches, and Sorcerers
     1958   in the Supernatural Economy of
                              the Yakö." Journal of the Royal
                              Anthropological Institute of
                              Great Britain and Ireland 88,
                              pt. 2: 164-78.

     Although spirit possession is not explicitly labelled,
the diviners among the Yako of Nigeria receive a "calling" from Obasi, the creator, in the form of a temporary
illness (p. 175).

592. Forde, Daryll, and   West African Kingdoms in the
     P. M. Kaberry, eds.   Nineteenth Century. London:
     1967   Oxford University Press, for the
                              International African Institute.

Includes in this bibliography:
1242   P. Morton-Williams (1967)
1657   M. G. Smith (1967)

593. Forster, E. F. B.   "A Short Psychiatric Review
     1958   from Ghana." In Mental Dis-
                             orders and Mental Health in
                             Africa South of the Sahara, pp.
                             37-41. CCTA/CSA-WFMH-WHO,
                             Pub. no. 35. Bukavu.

The prevailing beliefs in Ghana about spirit possession
causing illness and the efficacy of cures by "fetish
doctors" are discussed in their relationship to the
growth in the number of individuals who seek psychiatric
help. The new stresses from rapid social change are
given as the cause for an increase in the number of the
mentally ill.

594. Forster, E. F. B.   "Treatment of the African Men-
     1961   tal Patient." In First Pan-
                             African Psychiatric Conference -
                             Proceedings, pp. 276-79.
                             (Bib. 1344.)

Although spirit possession is not explicity labelled,
spirits are said to be a "strong aetiological factor" in
the African's explanation of mental illness in Ghana,
along with witchcraft, "juju," the ancestors, the gods,
the evil eye, etc. (p. 277).

595. Forster, E. B.   "The Theory and Practice of
     1962   Psychiatry in Ghana." American
                             Journal of Psychotherapy 16;
                             no. 1: 7-51.

African beliefs in spirit possession are discussed in
several contexts throughout this article. Zar possession cults of Ethiopia are mentioned in the context of
the history and development of this phenomenon (p. 11).
The possession by evil spirits that is the trademark of
a witch is discussed for the Ashanti of Ghana (p. 20).
Possession by the Holy Spirit in Christian churches may
lead to an intense awareness of sin and guilt (p. 24).
Finally, the author discusses the general belief in
juju or supernatural causation of mental illnesses, which
includes spirit possession (pp. 38 ff.).

596. Forster, Edward B.   "A Short Ethnopsychiatric Study
     1974   of Swaziland." Psychopathologie
                             africaine (Dakar) 10, no. 2:
                             211-27.

Spirit possession is considered to be a cause of mental

illness among the Bantu-speaking Swazi of Swaziland.

597. Fortes, M., and African Systems of Thought.
     G. Dieterlen, eds. London: Oxford University Press.
     1965

     Includes in this bibliography:
               478   A. Doutreloux (1965)
               647   M. Gelfand (1965b)

598. Fortes, M., and "Psychoses and Social Change
     D. Y. Mayer among the Tallensi of Northern
     1966 Ghana." Cahiers d'etudes
               africaines 6, no. 21: 5-40.

The point is made that the Tallensi of northern Ghana do not have spirit possession of any sort (as compared with the mediumistic divination of the Ashanti in southern Ghana). [Cited in Transcultural Psychiatric Research Review and Newsletter (Bruges) 3 (October 1966): 144-49.]

599. Fortier, Joseph Le Mythe et les Contes de sou
     1967 en pays mbaï-moïssala. Paris:
               Julliard.

Among the Mbaï people of the Sara ethnic group in Uganda, Kadò is a spirit force that possesses individuals and is the cause of all misfortune (p. 29).

600. Fortune, G. "Who Was Mwari?" Rhodesian
     1973 History (Salisbury) 4:1-20.

The identity and theological characteristics of the Supreme Being, Mwari, in Rhodesia are explored extensively in this article. Mention is made of his oracle throughout, and the ethnic groups cited are the following: Shona, Zezuru, Venda, Rozvi (Rozwi), Kalanga, Ngona, Mbedzi, Karanga, Mbire, Hera, Korekore, Pedi, Tswana, Torwa, and Tavara (Tawara).

601. Fourche, J. A. Tiarko, "Les Communications des indi-
     and H. Morlighem genes du Kasai avec les âmes
     1939 des morts." Mémoires de
               l'Institut royal colonial belge
               (Bruxelles) 9, no. 2: 1-78.

The various methods employed by the peoples of the Kasai region in Zaire to contact the spirits of the dead are described, and include spirit possession and mediumship.

602. Fox, Renée C., Willy   "'The Second Independence': A
     De Craemer, and   Case Study of the Kwilu Rebel-
     Jean-Marie   lion." Comparative Studies in
     Ribeaucourt   Society and History 8, no. 1:
     1965   78-109.

     In 1932 in the Kwilu Rebellion of Zaïre, there arose
the "talking serpent" or "snake-man" sect which held that
the serpent would appoint prophets to fight against the
white masters. Spirit mediumship is implied (p. 85).

603. Fraenkel, Merran   Tribe and Class in Monrovia.
     1964   London: Oxford University Press.

     Chapter 5 deals with the significance of the Pente-
costal Churches in Liberia; there is a discussion of
spirit possession as it occurs within the church to allow
self-expression and identification with the rest of the
congregation (pp. 162-71).

604. Frankenberg, Ronald   "Man, Society and Health: Towards
     1969   the Definition of the Role of
                            Sociology in the Development of
                            Zambian Medicine." African
                            Social Research (Lusaka),
                            no. 8, pp. 573-87.

     In a general discussion of the role of sociology in the
study of medicine and the training of doctors, spirit
possession is mentioned as a traditional means of curing
the sick.

605. Fraser, Donald   Winning a Primitive People: Six-
     1914   teen Years Work among the War-
                            like Tribes of the Ngoni and the
                            Senga and Tumbuka Peoples of
                            Central Africa. London: Seeley
                            Service & Co.

     Discusses exorcism of spirit possession through a
poison ordeal among the Ngoni, Senga (Nsenga), and
Tumbuka peoples of Central Africa (p. 115). [Cited by
Willoughby (1932, Bib. 1885), p. 30.]

606. Fraser, Donald   African Idylls. New York:
     1923   Fleming H. Revell Co.

     The exorcism practices performed by a witch-doctor (of
unspecified ethnic group) in Nyasaland (Tanzania) are recorded, as observed by the author, a missionary. An evil
spirit had possessed the patient and was coaxed out of
her by steam and by music (pp. 190-94).

607. Fraser, Donald   The New African. London:
     1927   Edinburgh House Press.

     Spirit mediumship among African medicine men is men-
     tioned on page 45. Communication for healing purposes is
     established through dancing and drumming.

608. Fraser, Donald   The Future of Africa. Westport,
     1970 (1911)   Conn.: Negro Universities Press.

     In this account, written at the turn of the century by
     a missionary, African witch-doctors in general are spoken
     of as having the ability to speak with the spirits (pp.
     119, 123-24).

609. Frazer, J. G.   The Magic Art and the Evolution
     1911   of Kings. (Part 1 of The Golden
                                   Bough, a Study in Magic and Re-
                                   ligion.) London: Macmillan &
                                   Co.

     The Maraves (Maravi) of Malawi have a spiritual head
     called Chissumpe who is believed to have spiritual
     powers. He is believed to be invisible and immortal,
     making himself known through a hereditary official called
     Fumo-a-Chissumpe, that is, by an intimate of Chissumpe.
     The official is revered exactly as Chissumpe (p. 393).
     The Baganda of Uganda believed in a god of Lake Nyanza
     who sometimes took up his abode in a man or woman. When
     the god possessed a person, that person was called
     Lubare. The god would speak through this medium, per-
     forming religious rituals at each new moon, and would act
     as an oracle for the king (p. 395).

610. Frazer, J. G.   Adonis, Attis, Osiris: Studies
     1927   in the History of Oriental Re-
                                   ligions. Vol. 1. London:
                                   Macmillan & Co.

     In West Africa, future priests undergo three years'
     novitiate after which, proof of acceptance by the god is
     manifested through spirit possession (convulsions,
     frenzied dancing, foaming at the mouth) (p. 68). [Cited
     by Jeffreys (1953, Bib. 853).]

611. Frazer, James George   Aftermath: A Supplement to the
     1936   Golden Bough. London:
                                   Macmillan & Co.

     Among the Barundi (Rundi), a tribe of Burundi to the
     west of Lake Victoria-Nyanza, each of the gods has his
     own form of worship and his own priest, whom he possesses
     and through whose mouth he gives oracles. The priest-
     hood is generally hereditary, but the priest of the great

god, Kiranga, is selected by a sign of the god's power, for example, by being struck, but not killed, by lightning (p. 119).

612. Frazier, E. Franklin   "The Negro Family in Bahia,
     1942   Brazil." American Sociological
                               Review 7, no. 4: 465-78.

Discussion of the Candomblé and Caboclo spirit cults in Brazil. Account of a woman possessed by an Indian spirit (p. 473).

613. Frink, Maurice, Jr.   "The Airplane Becomes an African
     1946   God." Travel (New York) 86,
                              no. 3: 29-32.

The author watched tribal dances in Accra, Ghana. One of these dances was a spirit possession dance by the airplane spirit; some explanation is offered for the dance, reflecting the construction of air bases by Pan American Airways.

614. Frobenius, Leo   Und Afrika sprach. Vol. 2.
     1912   Berlin. [The Voice of Africa.
                              London: Hutchinson & Co., 1913]

Collection of documents relating to spirit possession in Central Africa and Abyssinia (Ethiopia). These documents describe induced and spontaneous possession, possession as a sort of epileptic state, exorcism of spirits (chap. 11). [Cited in Oesterreich (1930, Bib. 1301), p. 133.]

615. Froelich, Jean-Claude,   Les Populations du Nord-Togo.
     Pierre Alexandre, and   Monographies ethnologiques
     Robert Cornevin   africaines, vol. 9. Paris:
     1963   Institut international africain.

Among the Kabrè and Lamba of north Togo, it is believed that infants can become possessed by evil spirits, emozea, and must be exorcised. "Voyants" or seers are possessed of a different spirit, alewu, and are able to divine while in trance (pp. 115-17). Among the Konkomba, the Moba, and the Dyé, spirit possession is a way of communicating with the spirits, but also may cause illness and the spirits must be exorcised (pp. 156-57).

616. Froelich, Jean-Claude   Animismes: Les Religions
     1964   païenne de l'Afrique de
                              l'ouest. Paris: Éditions
                              l'orante.

The traditional African religions of Western Africa are the subject of this book, and spirit possession is mentioned in various places, including pages 85 ff. and chapters 5 and 6.

617. Froelich, J. C.   "Sorciers et magiciens, question
     1968   de mots." Afrique et l'Asie
                            (Paris), nos. 83-84, pp. 74-79.

An examination is made of the definitions of various terms such as "sorcerer," "witch," "magician," etc., to clarify their various uses in the literature on African cultures. Possession by and communication with the spirits are mentioned.

618. Froelich, Jean-Claude   Les Nouveaux Dieux d'Afrique.
     1969   Paris: Éditions de l'orante.

In this general work on African religions, spirit possession is discussed several times. It is the author's opinion that this state is not a pathological but a mystical phenomenon (pp. 25 ff., 30-31, 58, 86-87).

619. Fromm, Erika   "An Ego-psychological Theory for
     1977   Altered States of Conscious-
                           ness." International Journal of
                           Clinical Experimental Hypnosis,
                           vol. 25, no. 4.

Altered states of consciousness are discussed in terms of an ego-psychological model, employing the concepts of ego activity, ego passivity, and ego receptivity.

620. Fry, Peter   Spirits of Protest. Cambridge:
     1976   Cambridge University Press.

Spirit possession and mediumship among the Zezuru and Korekore of Rhodesia are examined in terms of the social structure of these peoples and the process of social change.

621. Fuchs, Peter   "The Maragai Cult of the
     1960   Hadjerai." Mitteilungen der
                           Anthropologischen Gesellschaft
                           in Wien 90:85-97.

Among the Hadjerai (Chad), the cult of Maragai, the nature spirits, represents the prevailing religion. The Maragais' wishes must be fulfilled and they are revealed only by oracles through women mediums. Description is given of the priesthood and of Maragai altars. [Cited in African Abstracts, vol. 13, no. 86.]

622. Fuller, Charles Edward "An Ethnohistoric Study of Con-
     1955   tinuity and Change in Gwambe
                             Culture." Ph.D. dissertation,

Northwestern University,
Evanston, Ill.

Among the Gwambe of South Africa, spirit possession by
foreign spirits causes illness and misfortune. If suc-
cessfully cured, the individual may become a professional medium and practice divination and healing (pp. 130
ff., 137 ff., 200-204).

623. Funkhouser, W. D.   Primitive Magic. Lexington, Ky.
      1946

A "study" of magic and the primitive mind of the
savage. Description of a ceremony in the voodoo cult of
the West Indies (Haiti) and West Africa; the ceremony includes a state which may be characterized as possession.
"The delirium increased and is further aroused by the
use of spirituous liquors. Fainting spells follow for
some, and a kind of madness for others, but with them all
there is a nervous trembling which they seem unable to
control" (pp. 13-14).

624. Gamble, David P.   The Wolof of Senegambia.
      1959   Ethnographic Survey of Africa,
                             edited by Daryll Forde.
                             London: International African
                             Institute.

The use of spirit possession among the Wolof, Lebu, and
Serer of Senegal and Gambia is discussed on pages 70 ff.,
94 ff., 102 ff.

625. Gann, L. H.   A History of Southern Rhodesia -
      1965   Early Days to 1934. London:
                            Chatto & Windus.

The "inspired" spirit mediums of the Mlimo cult among
the Mashona (Shona) and the role they played in the early
history of Southern Rhodesia (Rhodesia) are presented on
pages 128-29, 135-36. Also mentioned are the "inspired"
medicine-men of the Shona capable of curing and hunting
out witches (pp. 334-35).

626. Gann, Lewis H.   Central Africa: The Former
      1971   British States. Englewood
                            Cliffs, N.J.: Prentice-Hall,
                            Inc.

Brief mention is made of the Shona (Rhodesia) belief in
Mwari, the Supreme Being, and in spirit mediums who are
his intermediaries with man (pp. 46, 53).

627. Garbett, G. Kingsley   "Religious Aspects of Political
      1966   Succession among the Valley
                            Korekore (N. Shona)." In

The Zambesian Past, edited by
E. Stokes and R. Brown, pp. 137-
70. (Bib. 1686.)

The spirit mediums among the Valley Korekore, a
northern Shona people in Rhodesia, are discussed in detail here. Their specific political influences are emphasized, particularly with regard to disputes dealing
with political succession.

628. Garbett, G. Kingsley   "Prestige, Status, and Power in
     1967   a Modern Valley Korekore Chief-
                               dom, Rhodesia." Africa:
                               Journal of the International
                               African Institute (London) 37,
                               no. 3: 307-26.

In a theoretical and ethnographic discussion of power
and status among the Valley Korekore of Rhodesia, the
importance of spirit mediumship and possession in the
Masowe Separatist Church is outlined.

629. Garbett, G. Kingsley   "Spirit Mediums as Mediators in
     1969   Korekore Society." In Spirit
                               Mediumship and Society in Africa,
                               edited by J. Beattie and J.
                               Middleton, pp. 104-27.
                               (Bib. 150.)

Among the Korekore of the Zambezi Valley there is a
cult of spirit mediums. They are organized into a
spiritual hierarchy and have specific territories for
which they are responsible. When possessed, the mediums
may be called on to settle disputes in society, and
since the possessing spirit is from outside of the
society, it is granted great respect.

630. Garbutt, H. W.   "Native Witchcraft and Super-
     1909   stition in South Africa."
                               Journal of the Royal Anthropo-
                               logical Institute of Great
                               Britain and Ireland 39:530-58.

In South Africa, I-shumba spirits are said to inhabit
the air and to await a favorable opportunity to enter the
living body of one of their descendants. The possessed
are treated by female mediums. If a boy is possessed,
the spirit must be transferred to a girl; however, if a
girl is possessed, she is cured by becoming a priestess
for the I-shumba. Description is given of curing ceremonies involving possession dances (pp. 553-55).

631. Gardenier, William J. G. "Witchcraft and Sorcery in a
     1976   Pastoral Society: The Central

Sakalava of West Madagascar."
Ph.D. dissertation, Rice
University. Dissertation Abstracts International (October
1976) 37, no. 4: 2273A.

Spirit possession among the Sakalava of Madagascar allows an individual to speak his mind without taking responsibility for it, a useful response in this society
which has strong beliefs in witchcraft and sorcery.

632. Gass, P. Michel   "Croyances, magie et super-
      1973   stitions des Bagwe ou Basukuma
                                établis au sud du lac Victoria-
                                Nyanza (1919)." Annali
                                Lateranensi (Vatican City) 37:
                                385-459.

The Bagwe (Guha), located on the southern shores of Lake
Victoria-Nyasa (Lake Malawi) in Malawi, practice a form
of spirit possession which is not to be considered as a
pathological illness, and the possessed speak in unknown
tongues (p. 411).

633. Gastaut, H., J. Roger,   "Editorial." Colloque de
      and C. A. Tassinari   l'épidémiologie de l'épilepsie en
      1970   Afrique, Marseille, 3 September
                                1968. African Journal of
                                Medical Sciences (Oxford) 1, no.
                                2: 115-23.

In this general resumé of the research on epilepsy in
Africa, native beliefs of its cause being spirit possession are mentioned on page 115.

634. Geerling, R.   "Some Thoughts on Religion and
      1963   the Community." South African
                                Medical Journal (Cape Town) 37,
                                no. 18: 490-93.

Shona mediums (Rhodesia) are mentioned in this general
article on the relationship between religion and the
sociocultural domain.

635. Gelfand, Michael   "Chikwambo (Runhare)." Nada
      1954   (Salisbury) 31:59-61.

Among the Shona (Rhodesia), a person possessed by
Chikwambo is both a Nganga (doctor) and a Muroi (witch).
Possession seems to involve males. Description of possession by Mudzimu and Shawe spirits and of the séance between the Nganga and his client.

636. Gelfand, Michael   Medicine and Magic of the
     1956a   Mashona. Cape Town: Juta & Co.

     Discussed in great detail are the Shona (Rhodesia) be-
     liefs in and uses of spirit possession and mediumship in
     religious and medical practices.

637. Gelfand, Michael   "The Religion of the Mashona."
     1956b   Nada (Salisbury) 33:27-31.

     Discussion of the domain of influence of the Vadzimu
     (ancestral) spirits and the Mhondoro (tribal) spirits
     among the Mashona (Rhodesia); these spirits are approached
     only through their mediums.

638. Gelfand, Michael   "Christina." Nada (Salisbury)
     1957   34:6-7.

     Christina is a wandering spirit who seeks to find a
     medium among the Shona (Rhodesia). Some people call pos-
     session by this spirit a state of bad luck. No cere-
     monies are given to this spirit, as they are to Shawe or
     Mudzimu spirits. Description of cures offered for pos-
     session by the Nganga (diviner).

639. Gelfand, Michael   "The Mhondoro-Chaminuka." Nada
     1959a   (Salisbury) 36:6-10.

     History of the spirit Chaminuka, the different abodes
     of this tribal spirit; examples of possession by this
     spirit (Shona, Rhodesia).

640. Gelfand, Michael   Shona Ritual. Cape Town: Juta
     1959b   & Co. Ill.

     Spirit possession is described in different parts of
     this volume on Shona (Rhodesia) ritual. Chapter 5 deals
     with the cult of Chaminuka, giving instances of posses-
     sion and mediumship trances. No bibliography.

641. Gelfand, Michael   "The Totem of the Tutelary
     1961   Spirit (Mhondoro) and That of
                             the Clan of the Sokoto District."
                             African Studies (Johannesburg)
                             30, no. 4: 214-16.

     Among the Korekore group of the Shona people of
     Southern Rhodesia (Rhodesia), the tribal spirit of a clan
     speaks through a spirit medium. The story of one such
     medium is given. A childhood illness was diagnosed as
     spirit possession. Several years later the child became
     possessed, journeyed to a distant district, and claimed
     to be the medium of the local tribal spirit. He proved
     himself by being possessed in public and by having the

126

spirit reveal through him details of the history and geography of the region.

642. Gelfand, Michael   Shona Religion. Cape Town:
         1962   Juta & Co.

Chapter 10 deals with different forms of spirit possession among the Shona of Rhodesia.

643. Gelfand, Michael   Medicine and Customs in Africa.
         1964a   London: E. & S. Livingstone.
                             Ill.

Chapter 2 discusses spirit possession among the Shona (Rhodesia) as a means of communication with the spirits; some detail on the Mhondoro and Chikwambo spirits. Chapter 3 deals with the magician's use of spirit possession (pp. 31-35). Illustrations (pp. 18-25).

644. Gelfand, Michael   "Psychiatric Disorders as Re-
         1964b   cognized by the Shona." In
                             Magic, Faith and Healing, edited
                             by A. Kiev, pp. 156-73.
                             (Bib. 902)

Mental disorders among the Shona (Rhodesia) are often regarded as due to spirit possession. Description of native cures for possession, including comments on role of spirit mediumship, are part of the treatment.

645. Gelfand, Michael   Witch Doctor: Traditional Medi-
         1964c   cine Man of Rhodesia. New York:
                             Frederick A. Praeger.

Among the Shona of Rhodesia, witch-doctors are called Nganga. Nganga are sometimes "called" to their profession by being possessed by ancestor spirits. They sometimes divine by undergoing possession by these spirits. Possession also sometimes exists among dancers.

646. Gelfand, Michael   African Background: The Tradi-
         1965a   tional Culture of the Shona-
                             speaking People. Cape Town:
                             Juta & Co.

Among the Shona of Rhodesia, each clan has its own tribal spirit (Mhondoro) which comes through its human host, or medium (Svikiro), and speaks to the tribesmen seated around him. They listen carefully to the man so possessed, revealing the causes of the drought, or who should be the next chief, and so on (p. 5).

647. Gelfand, M.   "The Mhondoro Cult of the Shona
         1956b   Peoples of Southern Rhodesia."

In *African Systems of Thought*,
edited by M. Fortes and G.
Dieterlen, pp. 341-50.
(Bib. 597.)

Spirit possession and mediumship in the Mhondoro cult
of the Shona (Rhodesia) are not only induced by the
medium during ceremonies through dancing and music, but
may also occur in the early hours of the morning.

648. Gelfand, Michael   "The Normal Man, a New Concept
     1965c   of Shona Philosophy." Nada
                              (Salisbury) 9, no. 3: 78-93.

The relationship between the spirit and the living is
investigated in this article on the concept of normalcy
among the Shona of Rhodesia. Spirit mediumship is discussed.

649. Gelfand, Michael   An African's Religion, the Spirit
     1966a   of Nyajena. Cape Town: Juta
                              & Co.

A case study of the spirit mediums, masvikiro, of the
Vakaranga peoples of Rhodesia is presented.

650. Gelfand, Michael   "The Great Muzukuru: His Role in
     1966b   the Shona Clan." Nada
                              (Salisbury) 9, no. 3: 38-41.

The role of the muzukuru in the Shona-speaking Chikwaka
of Northern Rhodesia (Zambia), a descendent of the
founding chief's sister, is, among other duties, to determine the succession to the chieftainship--for which
decision he enlists the aid of a spirit medium (sviriko).

651. Gelfand, Michael   The African Witch. London: E.
     1967a   S. Livingstone, Ltd.

Among the Shona of Rhodesia, the spirits may reveal themselves by possessing living people. If a person is possessed by a good spirit he may become a Nganga witch-
doctor and act as a diviner, herbalist, and witch finder.
If a person is possessed by an evil spirit he may become
a muroyi, a witch. Muroyi will kill others, either
through the actions of their spirit or through poisons.

652. Gelfand, Michael   "Psychiatric Disorders as Re-
     1967b   cognized by the Shona." Central
                              African Journal of Medicine
                              (Salisbury) 13, no. 2: 39-46.

Outlined in detail are the traditional descriptions of
and treatments for the various mental disorders found

128

among the Shona of Rhodesia. Spirit possession is of
two major types: possession by an angered spirit,
causing mental illnesses, and possession by an ancestor
spirit, creating, through mediumship, a means of caring
for the well-being of an entire community.

653. Gelfand, Michael   "The Shona Religion." Zambezia
     1969   (Salisbury) 1, no. 1: 37-45.
                             Ill.

In order to approach the Creator, Mwari, the Shona
(Rhodesia) communicate with the lesser spirits through
possession. Each of the five categories of spirit has
its appropriate medium. Owing perhaps to the profound
personal satisfaction its members receive from participation, the religion does not lose its hold on them in
the urban environment.

654. Gelfand, Michael   "Medicine and Magic." Central
     1970   African Journal of Medicine
                             (Salisbury) 16, no. 2: 45-48.

The ability to perform remarkable cures comes to the
African witch-doctor through being possessed by a
spirit - usually by the spirit of a former witch-doctor.
The successes and limitations of this traditional practice are discussed.

655. Gelfand, Michael   "A Nganga Who Has Adopted Two
     1971   Faiths." Nada (Salisbury) 10,
                             no. 3: 73-76.

Biography of a Shona man in Rhodesia who has adopted
Christianity while retaining his traditional Shona beliefs. Possession by the Holy Spirit is mentioned (p.
73).

656. Gelfand, Michael   "The Egalitarian Shona." Nada
     1972   (Salisbury) 10, no. 4: 51-54.

Spirit possession and mediumship among the Shona of
Rhodesia are mentioned briefly on page 51.

657a.Gelfand, Michael   "The Mhondoro Cult among the
     1974   Manyika Peoples of the Eastern
                             Region of Mashonaland." Nada
                             (Salisbury) 11, no. 1: 64-95.

Given here are detailed descriptions, based on the
author's field studies, of the ceremonies witnessed
among the Shona-speaking Manyika peoples of Rhodesia
which comprise the spirit possession Mhondoro cult.
The article also compares the Manyika version of this
cult with those of the MaZezuru (Zezuru), VaKaranga
(Karanga), and Korekore.

129

657b. Gerlach, Luther G.   "Pentecostalism: Revolution or
      1974   Counter-Revolution?" In Reli-
                                  gious Movement in Contemporary
                                  America, edited by Irving I.
                                  Zaretsky and Mark P. Leone.
                                  (Bib. 1924.)

     Based on research on spirit possession among the Digo
of East Africa, the author does a comparative study of
Pentecostals in the United States and the Caribbean.

658. Geuns, André   "Bibliographie commentée du
     1973   prophétisme kongo." Cahiers du
                                  C.E.D.A.F. (Bruxelles), no. 7.
                                  Index.

     This bibliography is a useful reference for the pro-
phetic movements, including spirit possession phenomena,
in the Congo.

659. Giel, R., Y. Gezahegan,   "Faith-Healing and Spirit-Pos-
     and J. N. van Luijk   session in Ghion, Ethiopia."
     n.d.   Mimeographed. 14 pp.

     The practices of a well-known faith-healing Orthodox
priest of Ghion, Ethiopia, who professes to have cured
more than one million persons in fourteen years, are
examined. A very common treatment for illness is
exorcism of possessing spirits. Theoretical analysis of
spirit possession follows case studies. [Cited in
Transcultural Psychiatric Research Review (Bruges) 5
(April 1968): 64-67.]

660. Gilsenan, Michael   "Myth and the History of African
     1972   Religion." In The Historical
                                  Study of African Religion, edited
                                  by T. O. Ranger and I. N.
                                  Kimambo, pp. 50-70. (Bib. 1442.)

     Spirit possession in the Kubandwa cult in Central
Africa is briefly mentioned in this theoretical essay on
the study of myths.

661. Girard, Jean   Déima: Prophètes paysans de
     1974   l'environnement noir. 2 vols.
                                  Grenoble: Presses universi-
                                  taires.

     In this extensive work the Déima religion of the Ivory
Coast, an Independent African Christian Church with over
400,000 members in 1970, is presented. The background
of traditional religious beliefs among the Godié (Godye),
Guéré (Ngere) and Bété peoples is given and includes the
spirit possession cult of Gle (pp. 17-22).

130

662. Glenday, David K.   "Acholi Ancestor-Veneration and
     1976   the Communion of Saints."
                                 Afer: African Ecclesiastical Re-
                                 view (Eldoret) 18, no. 4: 224-
                                 32.

     Among the Acholi of Uganda the ajwaka spirit-priest
goes into trance and becomes the medium for the ancestral
saints (p. 226).

663. Gloyne, H. F.   "Tarantism, Mass Hysterical Re-
     1950   action to Spider Bite in the
                                Middle Ages." American Image
                                (Boston) 7:29-42.

     Information from this article can be compared with
dancing mania reported in African materials.

664. Gluckman, M.   "Zulu Women in Hoecultural
     1935   Ritual." Bantu Studies 9:255-
                               71.

     Discussion of the Nomtubulwana ceremonies and their
significance to Zulu (South Africa) women; description
of the women's disease ceremony held in December, when
fever is rife, to exorcise the fever demon; spirit possession as a means for women to gain prestige outside the
family circle (p. 261).

665. Gluckman, M.   "Notes on the Social Background
     1949   of Barotse Music." In African
                               Music in Northern Rhodesia and
                               Other Places, edited by A. M.
                               Jones. Occasional Papers of
                               the Rhodes-Livingstone Museum,
                               No. 4. Livingstone.

     Lists of curative songs and dances of the Barotse
(Lozi) (Zambia); illness due to possession and cured
during possession dances; description of diviner's role
in these dances (appendix 2).

666. Gluckman, Max   "The Lozi of Barotseland in
     1951   Northwestern Rhodesia." In
                               Seven Tribes of British Central
                               Africa, edited by E. Colson and
                               M. Gluckmann, pp. 4-93.
                               (Bib. 362.)

     Brief mention is made of the healing ceremonies in-
volving a possession trance among the Lozi of Barotseland (Zambia) (p. 85).

667. Gluckman, Max   <u>Rituals of Rebellion in South-</u>
     1952   <u>east Africa</u>. Manchester:
                         Manchester University Press.

     In discussing the position of women in Zulu society
(Southeast Africa), one path of ritual action mentioned
as being open to them is that of becoming possessed by
spirits and thus becoming diviners. This possession and
initiation are an extremely painful and long process
(p. 7).

668. Gluckman, Max   "Accused of Witchcraft."
     1957   <u>Tomorrow</u> (New York) 5, no. 4:
                         100-103.

     Among the Zulu of South Africa, witchcraft may be the
cause behind a person's being possessed by an evil spirit.

669. Gluckman, M.   <u>Order and Rebellion in Tribal</u>
     1963   <u>Africa</u>. London: Cohen & West.

     The ritual action open to women, among the Zulu (South
Africa), is divination and healing through spirit possession; description of initiation to the diviner's
status (pp. 115-17).

670. Goldney, K. M., and   "An Examination into Physio-
     S. G. Soal   logical Changes Alleged to Take
     1938   Place during the Trance State."
                         <u>Proceeding of the Society for</u>
                         <u>Psychic Research</u> (London) 45:
                         43-87.

     In this early study of a British medium, the psycho-
physiological correlates of the mediumship trance are
examined.

671. Gollnhofer, Otto, and "Recherche sur le mysticisme des
     Roger Sillans   Mitsogo." In <u>Reincarnation et</u>
     1965   <u>vie mystique en Afrique noire</u>,
                         Colloque de Strasbourg, pp. 143-
                         73. (Bib. 359.)

     Among the Mitsogo of Gabon, spirit possession and
mediumship are practiced in the <u>Bwiti</u> cult.

672. Gollnhofer, Otto, and "Phénoménologie de la possession
     Roger Sillans   chez les Mitsogho: Aspects
     1974   psycho-sociaux." <u>Psychopatho-</u>
                         <u>logie africaine</u> (Dakar) 10, no.
                         2: 187-209.

     Among the Mitsogho (Mitsogo) of south Gabon, spirit

possession occurs mainly among women in a highly
structured society, the Ombudi. Details of the society's
activities are given, and emphasis is placed on the
authors' opinion that spirit possession in this case is
not pathological.

673. Gomm, Richard   "Bargaining from Weakness:
     1975   Spirit Possession on the South
                            Kenya Coast." Man (London),
                            n.s. 10, no. 4: 530-43.

Spirit possession among the Digo of the south Kenya
coast predominantly occurs in women who are inferior in
social status to men. The possession illnesses and
exorcism ceremonies not only call attention to the interests of women, but, it is argued, also reinforce the
hierarchical social system.

674. Gonzalez Echegaray,   "Comment on prépare une Ivanga."
     Carlos   Africa (Madrid) 151:11-15.
     1954

Description of the Ivanga dance and its origin in Gabon
and Spanish Guinea (Equatorial Guinea); the participation
of singers and musicians. Comments on the dance's participants, chorus of singers, and musicians. (Although
the author does not characterize the dance as a spirit
possession dance, the description is very symptomatic
of spirit possession material and merits investigation in
that area.) [Cited in African Abstracts, vol. 6, no.
409.]

675. Gonzáles-Wippler,   Santería. New York: Julian
     Migene   Press.
     1973

The Santería cult of the Caribbean and South America is
discussed in detail. Santería, literally meaning the
worship of saints, is a mixture of Catholic and Yoruba
traditions and involves spirit possession (mentioned
throughout).

676. Goode, William J.   Religion among the Primitives.
     1959   Glencoe, Ill. Free Press.

Among Dahomeans (Fon) (Benin), a spirit mediumship
cult is used to bless and open markets and new villages.
For a market to be open, an intermediate member of the
cult must become possessed by a spirit (pp. 90-91).

677. Goodman, Felicitas D. "Glossolalia: Speaking in Tongues
     1969   in Four Cultural Settings."
                            Confinia Psychiatrica (Basel)
                            12, no. 2: 113-29.

The phenomenon of glossolalia, ascribed to possession
by the Holy Spirit, is examined in detail, employing
data from the Streams of Power movement on St. Vincent
Island in the Caribbean; a Midwestern tent revival
meeting in the United States; a mainline Protestant
church in Texas; and a Pentecostal church in Mexico.

678. Goodman, Felicitas D.   Speaking in Tongues. Chicago:
     1972   University of Chicago Press.

Employing data collected from an Apostolic Church in
the Yucatán, Mexico (that does not have African cultural
elements), the author presents a detailed analysis of the
phenomenon of glossolalia and of the hyperaroused trance
state.

679. Goodman, Felicitas D.   "Apostolics of Yucatán: A Case
     1973a   Study of a Religious Movement."
                              In Religion, Altered States of
                              Consciousness, and Social Change,
                              edited by E. Bourguignon, pp.
                              178-218. (Bib. 245.)

Detailed description of the evolution of a Pentecostal
Church in the Yucatán, Mexico. Of interest here is the
theoretical work on hyperaroused trance and glossolalia.

680. Goodman, Felicitas D.   "Glossolalia and Hallucination in
     1973b   Pentecostal Congregations."
                              Psychiatria Clinica (Basel) 6,
                              no. 2: 97-103.

Proposed here is a three-stage sequence, lasting
thirty-five to fifty-seven days, to the occurrence of
visionary hallucinations in clinically normal individuals: a blinding white light, a dreamlike sequence, and
superimposition of hallucinated objects onto tangible
ones. Glossolalia and kinetic behavior such as shaking
are also evident. Data are based mainly on field experience among a Pentecostal congregation in Yucatan,
Mexico.

681. Goodman, Felicitas D.   "Disturbances in the Apostolic
     1974a   Church: A Trance-based Upheaval
                              in Yucatán." In Trance, Healing
                              and Hallucination, edited by
                              F. D. Goodman, J. H. Henney, and
                              E. Pressel, pp. 227-364.
                              (Bib. 683.)

This article presents a very detailed account of
trance, possession by the Holy Spirit, and glossolalia in
an Apostolic Church in the Yucatán, Mexico. Although
African cultural elements are not present, this work is

included owing to its presentation and analysis of the
trance states.

682. Goodman, Felicitas D.   "Prognosis: A New Religion?" In
     1974b   Religious Movements in Contem-
                                porary America, edited by I. I.
                                Zaretsky and M. P. Leone, pp.
                                244-54. (Bib. 1924.)

Although African cultural elements are not evident,
this work gives a short account of the occurrence of
glossolalia and of possession by the Holy Spirit in an
Apostolic Church in the Yucatán, Mexico.

683. Goodman, Felicitas D.,   Trance, Healing and Hallucina-
     Jeannette H. Henney,   tion: Three Field Studies in
     and Easter Pressel,   Religious Experience. New York:
     eds.   John Wiley & Sons.
     1974c

     Includes in this bibliography:
               681   F. D. Goodman (1974a)
               756   J. H. Henney (1974)
              1409   E. Pressel (1974)

684. Goodman, Felicitas D.   "The Effect of Trance on Memory
     1975   Content." Psychiatria Clinica
                                (Basel) 8, no. 5: 243-49.

Beginning with a survey of some of the psychological
literature on trance, dreams, and EEG research, the
author discusses the relationship between memory and
glossolalia and possession trances in a Pentecostal congregation in Yucatán, Mexico.

685. Gorer, Geoffrey   African Dances. New York:
     1935   Alfred A. Knopf.

Possession dances are performed by members of the cult
of Legba, the phallic devil among the Heviosso (Dahomey,
now Benin). Also, description of the dancers of Sagbata
(.smallpox), mostly women, who perform dances that can be
characterized as possession dances (pp. 211-13).

686. Goriawala, Mu'izz   "Maguzawa." Orita: Ibadan
     1977   Journal of Religious Studies
                                (Ibadan) 4, no. 2: 115-23.

The Maguzawa, a political and demographic minority in
Nigeria, share with the Hausa Muslems a common culture
and language. Although increasingly influenced by Islam,
of immediate concern are the iskookii (spirits) of the
boorii (spirit possession cult). Description of possession is given.

135

687. Gouldsbury, Cullen,   The Great Plateau of Northern
     and Hubert Sheane   Rhodesia. London: Edward
     1911   Arnold.

The various forms of spirit possession practiced among
the Wembe of the plateau region of Northern Rhodesia
(Zambia) are discussed in chapter 6.

688. Grant, Cyril Fletcher, African Shores of the
     and L. Grant   Mediterranean. New York:
     1912   McBride, Nast & Co.

Information about the Aïssaoua, nominally a Moslem
sect, retaining certain pagan ceremonies. Authors describe a prayer meeting they attended; details on prayer
forms that are strikingly similar to spirit possession
descriptions (information for Tunis) (chap. 10, pp. 431-
35).

689. Grant, J. A.   A Walk across Africa. London:
     1864   Blackwood.

A report by one of the first two Europeans to visit
Bunyoro (Nyoro) (Uganda) about 100 years ago. Description of Bandwa mendicants allied with the Wichwezee
spirits. [Cited in Beattie (1961a, Bib. 135.), p. 19.]

690. Gravrand, H.   "Le Lup sérèr: Phénoménologie de
     1966   l'empire des Pangols et psycho-
                             thérapie de 'possédés.'"
                             Psychopathologie africaine
                             (Dakar) 2, no. 2: 195-226.

Among the Sérèr of Senegal, possession by the pangol
spirits can occur through inheritance, as punishment, as
part of an agreement, or by free choice and is an important part of their religious life. Therapeutic aspects
of the ritual treatment of the possessed (Lup) are discussed.

691. Gravrand, R. P.   "Le 'Lup' sérèr comparé au
     Henri   'ndoep' des Lébou." In Congrès
     1972a   international des africanistes
                             (Dakar), 2e session, 11-20
                             December 1967, pp. 237-42.
                             Paris: Présence africaine.

The possession trance ceremonies among the Sérèr, the
lup cult, and among the Lébou (Lebu), the ndoep cult, in
Senegal are analyzed from a psychological approach, and
descriptions of the various stages of these cults are
given.

692. Gravrand, Henri
     1972b

"Les Religions africaines traditionnelles source de civilisation spirituelle." In Les Religions africaines comme source de
valeurs de civilisation, Colloque de Cotonou (August 1970),
pp. 88-114. (Bib. 358.)

Basing most of his theory on the Sérèr of Senegal, the
author discusses the spiritual element in African religions, and includes the phenomenon of spirit possession
(pp. 92 ff.).

693. Gravrand, R. P. Henri
     1973

"Le Symbolisme Sérèr." Psychopathologie africaine (Dakar) 9,
no. 2: 237-65.

Possession by the various Sérèr (Senegal) spirits is
mentioned in this detailed theoretical analysis of the
use of symbolism in Serer thought.

694. Gravrand, R. P. Henri
     1975

"'Naq' et sorcellerie dans les
conceptions sereer." Psychopathologie africaine (Dakar) 11,
no. 2: 179-216.

The characteristics of the invisible psychic worlds explored and manipulated by the Sereer (Serer) sorcerer and
his own psychological and psychic makeup are outlined.
Although neither spirit possession nor mediumship is explicitly mentioned, communication with the spirits is
discussed.

695. Gray, Sir John
     1955

"Nairuzi or Siku Ya Mwaka."
Tanganyika Notes and Records
(Dar-es-Salaam) 38:1-22.

Description of Pemba (Tanzania) ceremonies associated
with the yearly calendar. Many ceremonies involve
mediums who intervene for the resident spirits of different localities.

696. Gray, Robert F.
     1957

"Exorcising Demons on the
Swahili Coast." Tomorrow
(New York) 5, no. 4: 43-48.

Given here is a case of an exorcism of a shetani spirit
which had suddenly attacked and mentally disoriented a
woman of the Segeju people on the Tanganyikan (Tanzania)
coast.

697. Gray, Robert F.
     1969

"The Shetani Cult among the
Segeju of Tanzania." In Spirit
Mediumship and Society in Africa,
edited by J. Beattie and J. M.

Middleton, pp. 171-87.
(Bib. 150.)

Among the Segeju of Tanzania, diseases are often blamed on possession by spirits called <u>Shetani</u>. If divination indicates <u>Shetani</u> possession as the cause of an illness, the spirit must be exorcised, usually by a ritual dance. Members of the <u>Shetani</u> cult, consisting of former victims of the disease, may become temporarily possessed during this dance.

698. Greenbaum, Lenora   "Possession Trance in Sub-
     1973a   Saharan Africa: A Descriptive
                       Analysis of Fourteen Societies."
In <u>Religion, Altered States of Consciousness, and Social Change</u>, edited by E. Bourguignon, pp. 58-87. (Bib. 245.)

An extension of Greenbaum (1973b), this work investigates in great depth the relationship between social structure and possession trance in Africa. Ethnic groups mentioned are: Ashanti (Ghana), Ganda (Uganda), Mende (Sierra Leone), Nyoro (Uganda), Hehe (Tanzania), Chiga (Uganda), Nyima (Sudan), Tallensi (Ghana), Zulu (South Africa), Nuer (Sudan), Amba (Uganda), Kikuyu (Kenya), Kung (Bushmen) (Southwest Africa), and Turkana (Kenya).

699. Greenbaum, Lenora   "Societal Correlates of Posses-
     1973b   sion Trance in Sub-Saharan
Africa." In <u>Religion, Altered States of Consciousness, and Social Change</u>, edited by E. Bourguignon, pp. 39-57. (Bib. 245.)

Employing statistical analyses of African Sub-Saharan societies, the author finds the possession trance is more likely to occur in societies with "fixed internal status distinctions and differentiations" (p. 54).

700. Greenberg, J.   <u>The Influence of Islam on</u>
     1946   <u>Sudanese Religion</u>. American Ethnological Society, Monograph no. 10. New York: J. J. Augustin.

Ethnography of the pagan Hausa (Maguzawa) of Kano, Nigeria, tied into careful documentary and field studies of the Moslem Hausa cult of spirit possession, sheds light on pre-Islamic religious practices among Hausa and certain conditions of Islamic conversion. [Cited in M. G. Smith (1965, Bib. 1656), p. 153.]

138

701. Greschat, Hans Jürgen   "Legend? Fraud? Reality? Alice
      1968   Lenshina's Prophetic Experience:
                               Notes from Some Sources."
                               Africana Marburgensia (Marburg)
                               1, no. 1: 8-13.

     Analysis of seven sources written on the experiences of
     the prophetess Alice Lenshina in September 1953 shows
     that these experiences were definitely not "possession"
     but perhaps "dream" or "inspiration."

702. Grey-Jackson, J.   An Account of Timbuktoo and
      1820   Hausa Territories in the In-
                               terior of Africa, by El Haje
                               Abd Salam Shabeeny. London:
                               Longman, Hurster, Rees, Orme,
                               Brown.

     An account of a North African voyage of a young man
     from Tetouan (Morocco) traveling to Timbuktoo (Mali) in
     the year 1787. The author interviewed this person and
     records information on spirit possession dances present
     in eighteenth-century Timbuktoo. [Cited in Rouch (1954,
     Bib. 1525).]

703. Griaule, Marcel   "Le Livre de recettes d'un
      1930   dąbtara abyssin. Travaux et
                               mémoires de l'institut
                               d'ethnologie (Paris), vol. 12.

     Information was collected from Ethiopians available in
     the Paris area. Informants tell of spirit possession by
     the Zar spirits and others (appendix, pp. 129-51).

704. Grimley, John B., and   Church Growth in Central and
      Gordon E. Robinson   Southern Nigeria. Grand Rapids,
      1966   Michigan: William B. Eerdmans
                               Publishing Company.

     Although glossolalia is not specifically mentioned,
     chapter 4, part 2, deals with the rise of prophetic
     African independent churches in Nigeria which employ
     faith healing, drumming, dancing, whirling, and other
     trance-related activities.

705. Grismondi, G.   "The Magician and the 'Rain
      1942   Spirit' in Bahr et Ghazal."
                               Nigrizia (Verona), pp. 68-70.

     Among the Dinka (Sudan) rain is summoned through me-
     diumship trances of a magician, with repeated sacrifices
     of cattle. [Cited in African Abstracts, vol. 9, no.
     567.]

706. Grottanelli, Vinigi L.   "Asonu Worship among the Nzema:
     1961   A Study in Akan Art and Reli-
                                 gion." Africa: Journal of the
                                 International African Institute
                                 (London) 31, no. 1: 46-60.

Among the Nzema of southwestern Ghana, spirits called
Asonu, usually represented by small clay figurines, are
worshipped. The Asonu spirits are believed to cause
death in young children. If, however, the action of an
Asonu can be detected in time, the victim can placate
the spirit through sacrifices. The Asonu would then protect his former victim from the evil acts of others. On
occasion, the Asonu are apt to possess priests and
priestesses during dances, when they reach a condition
of trance. (Little detail on this aspect of Asonu worship is provided.) The author witnessed a woman dancer
who was so possessed (pp. 55-57).

707. Grottanelli, Vinigi L.   "Gods and Mortality in Nzema."
     1969   Ethnology 8, no. 4: 370-405.

Spirit possession is practiced as part of the religion
of the Akan-speaking Nzema of Ghana (p. 378).

708. Guena, P., Ch. de   "Aspects psychopathologiques de
     Preneuf, and   la grossesse au Senegal."
     Ch. Reboul   Psychopathologie africaine
     1970   (Dakar) 6, no. 2: 111-46.

Detailed case studies of the relationship between illnesses contracted during pregnancy and traditional beliefs concerning their cause, which center mainly around
possession by spirits, and are termed clinically as
"bouffee delirante." Peoples of Senegal included in this
study are: Wolof, Toucouleur (Tukulur), Serer, Diola,
Lebou (Lebu), Peul (Fulani) and Bambara.

709. Guenther, Mathias G.   "The Trance Dancer as an Agent of
     1975   Social Change among the Farm
                                 Bushmen of the Ghanzi District."
                                 Botswana Notes and Records
                                 (Gaborone) 7:161-66.

The recent socioeconomic changes occurring in Bushmen
culture in Botswana due to outside influences have led
to a change in these peoples' self-image. Traditional
trance healers have emerged as leaders of this social
change.

710. Guillebaud, Rosemary   "The Doctrine of God in Ruanda-
     1950   Urundi." In African Ideas of
                                 God: A Symposium, edited by E.
                                 W. Smith. (Bib. 1654.)

140

Information on the cult of Ryangombe (Ruanda-Urundi,
now Rwanda and Burundi), including invisible spirits that
are malevolent in the main. Initiates into the cult become possessed by these spirits (pp. 181-82).

711. Gussler, Judith D.   "Social Change, Ecology, and
     1973   Spirit Possession among the South
                            African Nguni." In Religion,
                            Altered States of Consciousness,
                            and Social Change, edited by E.
                            Bourguignon, pp. 88-126.
                            (Bib. 245.)

A biological and nutritional explanation for the illness
said to be caused by spirit possession and a description
of the trance behavior itself are presented for the
Nguni Bantu of South Africa.

712. Gwassa, G. C. K.   "Kinjikitile and the Ideology of
     1972   Maji Maji." In The Historical
                            Study of African Religion,
                            edited by T. O. Ranger and I. N.
                            Kimambo, pp. 202-17.
                            (Bib. 1442.)

The practice of spirit possession in the Maji Maji
mass movement against German colonial rule in Tanzania at
the turn of the century is analyzed historically (pp.
204 ff.).

713. Haberland, Eike   "Possession Cults in Southern
     1960   Ethiopia." Paideuma (Frankfurt)
                            7, no. 3: 142-50.

Zar cults were introduced to southern Ethiopia about
1910 by Christian and Moslem Ethiopians. The author
discusses why the southern Ethiopians were receptive to
these cults, as, for example, due to contact with new
cultural communities. [Cited in African Abstracts, vol.
12, no. 21.]

714. Hagenbucher-Sacripanti, "Les Fondements spirituels du
     Frank   pouvoir au royaume de Loango."
     1973   Mémoires O.R.S.T.O.M. (Paris),
                               no. 67.

In this complex and detailed presentation, the funda-
mental elements of sorcery in the Loango Empire of the
Republic of Congo are described and analyzed. Possession
by different spirits is mentioned throughout the work,
specifically with regard to causing certain illnesses.

715. Hahn, C. H. L., H.   The Native Tribes of South West
     Vedder, and L.   Africa. New York: Barnes &
     Fourie, eds.   Noble.
     1966a

141

Includes in this bibliography:
716   C. H. L. Hahn (1966b)
1801   H. Vedder (1966a)

716. Hahn, C. H. L.   "The Ovambo." In The Native
     1966b   Tribes of South West Africa,
                             edited by C. H. L. Hahn, H.
                             Vedder, and L. Fourie, pp. 1-
                             36. (Bib. 715.)

     Among the Ovambo (Ambo) of Angola, illness is sent by
the spirit of a deceased person through a medium to the
sick individual. Healing ceremony is staged to rid both
the sick and the medium of the troublesome spirit (p. 5).

717. Haile Maskal, Fisseha   "Atete." Bulletin of the Uni-
     1959   versity College of Addis Ababa
                             Ethnological Society 9:45-51.

     The ceremony of the cult of Atete in Ethiopia described.

718. Hall, R. N., and   The Ancient Ruins of Rhodesia.
     W. G. Neal   New York: Negro Universities
     1969 (1904)   Press.

     The authors present a lengthy quotation written by a
missionary on the nature of the "Mñwali" cult which includes spirit mediumship, among the Makalanga of Matabeleland in Rhodesia (pp. 135-36).

719. Hallpike, C. R.   The Konso of Ethiopia. Oxford:
     1972   Clarendon Press.

     The use of spirit possession in divination rituals a-
mong the Konso of Ethiopia seems to be of relatively
recent introduction. Detailed personal observations of
several trances are presented (pp. 315-21).

720. Hama, Boubou   "Note sur les Holé." Éducation
     1941/43   africaine (Dakar).

     A detailed study of possession dances among the Zerma
and Songhai people of Niger; classification of spirits,
dance rituals, and kinds of initiations of the possessed.
[Cited in Rouch (1954, Bib. 1525).]

721. Hambly, Wilfrid   Serpent Worship in Africa.
     1931   Field Museum of Natural History,
                             pub. no. 289, Anthropological
                             Series, vol. 21, no. 1. Chicago.

     Possession of priests and priestesses by the python
spirit in Dahomey (Fon) (Benin) is mentioned on pages 11,
14, 16.

722. Hambly, Wilfrid   The Ovimbundu of Angola. Field
     1934   Museum of Natural History, pub.
                              no. 329, Anthropological Series,
                              vol. 21, no. 2. Chicago.

     Although spirit possession is not explicitly labelled,
the medicine men among the Ovimbundu of Angola have a
"peculiar neurotic temperament" described as having
"spirit in the head" (p. 273). Various types of healing
practices also seem to use a variety of spirit possession
trances (pp. 278 ff.).

723. Hambly, Wilfrid   Culture Areas of Nigeria. Field
     1935   Museum of Natural History, pub.
                              no. 346, Anthropological Series,
                              vol. 21, no. 3. Chicago.

     Spirit mediumship among the medicine men of the Bantu-
speaking peoples of Nigeria is mentioned on page 458.

724. Hamer, John, and   "Spirit Possession and Its
     Irene Hamer   Sociopsychological Implication
     1966   among the Sidamo of Southwest
                              Ethiopia." Ethnology 5, no. 4:
                              392-408.

     Among the Sidamo of Ethiopia, illness is sent by a
spirit seeking to possess the individual. Curative
treatment is to consult the Kolica, the specialist in
healing, who will determine the song used to summon the
spirit to full possession of the patient. [Cited in
Transcultural Psychiatric Research Review (Bruges) 4
(April 1967): 39-42.]

725. Hammond-Tooke, W. D.   "The Initiation of a Bhaca
     1955   Isangoma Diviner." African
                              Studies (Johannesburg) 14, no.
                              1: 16-22.

     Description of initiation ritual of a Bhaca (South
Africa) diviner; before initiation is complete, the
future diviner must become possessed by a spirit.

726. Hammond-Tooke, W. D.   The Tribes of King William's
     1958   Town District. South Africa,
                              Native Affairs Department Ethno-
                              logical Publications, no. 41.
                              Pretoria.

     General comments about native beliefs found among the
Pretoria imiDushane (Dushane), imiQhayi (Qhayi) and
amaNtinde (Ntinde) of South Africa include a reference
to the notion that witches are persons who are possessed
by "mythical" beings who are able to send illnesses to
others (p. 59).

727. Hammond-Tooke, W. D.   "Some Bhaca Religious Cate-
     1960   gories." African Studies
                                (Johannesburg) 19, no. 1: 1-13.

     Discussion of traditional religion of the Bhaca people
     (South Africa), especially as it concerns the belief in
     the ancestral shade who, upon death, would leave the body
     it occupied and continue to be concerned with its descen-
     dants, whom it may visit in dreams. Further discussion
     of spirit possession, mediumship, and ethical and
     sociological implications of Bhaca religion. [For addi-
     tional information see African Abstracts, vol. 13/14,
     no. 130.]

728. Hammond-Tooke, W. D.   Bhaca Society: A People of the
     1962   Transkeian Upland, South Africa.
                                London: Oxford University Press.

     Chapter 10, titled "Dependence on the Supernatural,"
     deals with spirit possession among the Bhaca of South
     Africa. Dances serve as part of the cure prescribed by
     a diviner for possession cases, while initiation into the
     diviner class is another outlet for the possessed (pp.
     258-59).

729. Hammond-Tooke, W. D.,   The Bantu-Speaking Peoples of
     ed.   Southern Africa. London:
     1974a   Routledge & Kegan Paul.

     Includes in this bibliography:
                    730   W. D. Hammond-Tooke (1974b)
                    731   W. D. Hammond-Tooke (1974c)
                    1367   B. A. Pauw (1974b)

730. Hammond-Tooke, W. D.   "World-View I: A System of Be-
     1974b   liefs." In The Bantu-Speaking
                                Peoples of Southern Africa,
                                edited by W. D. Hammond-Tooke,
                                pp. 318-43. (Bib. 729.)

     Among the Bantu-speaking Nguni of Southern Africa,
     possession by one's maternal ancestral spirits is in-
     terpreted as a calling to the divination profession
     (p. 335).

731. Hammond-Tooke, W. D.   "World-View II: A System of
     1974c   Action." In The Bantu-Speaking
                                Peoples of Southern Africa,
                                edited by W. D. Hammond-Tooke,
                                pp. 344-63. (Bib. 729.)

     Among the Bantu-speaking peoples of Southern Africa,
     the role of the diviner includes the ability to communi-
     cate with the ancestral spirits. Specific peoples men-

tioned are: Nguni, Zulu, Xhosa (Xosa), Tsonga, South Sotho, Pedi, Pondo, and Venda (pp. 348-50).

732. Hammond-Tooke, W. D.   "African World-View and Its Rele-
     1975   vance for Psychiatry."
                             Psychologia Africana 16, no. 1:
                             25-32.

Spirit mediumship and trance states are described in their context among Nguni diviners of South Africa (p. 30).

733. Hanna, William J., and   "The Social Significance of
     Judith L. Hanna   Dance in Black Africa."
     1971   Civilisations (Bruxelles) 21,
                              nos. 2-3: 238-42.

Spirit possession dances among the Gã of Ghana are conducted as an annual ritual asking for supernatural help for the coming year (p. 240).

734. Hardyman, Marjorie   "The Church and Sorcery in
     1971   Madagascar." In African Initia-
                             tives in Religion, edited by
                             D. B. Barrett, pp. 208-21.
                             (Bib. 83.)

The traditional explanation of a sorcerer among the inhabitants of the Antsihanaka district of Madagascar is that he is possessed by an evil spirit. Exorcism as a healing method for those attacked by sorcery is discussed.

735. Harley, George W.   Native African Medicine.
     1941a   Cambridge, Mass.: Harvard
                             University Press.

Not available for annotation.

736. Harley, George W.   Notes on the Poro in Liberia.
     1941b   Papers of the Peabody Museum of
                             American Archeology and Ethno-
                             logy, Harvard University, vol.
                             19, no. 2. Cambridge, Mass.

An example cited of a man wearing a mask, Zi Ku Ge, and becoming possessed by the spirit of the mask among the Poro cult of Liberia (p. 13).

737. Harley, George W.,   Tribes of the Liberian Hinter-
     ed.   land, by George Schwab. Papers
     1947   of the Peabody Museum of American
                             Archeology and Ethnology, Har-
                             vard University, vol. 31.
                             Cambridge, Mass.

145

Possession by demons is the cause of insanity among
the peoples of southeastern Liberia (unspecified groups)
(p. 336).

738. Harley, George W.   Masks as Agents of Social Con-
     1950   trol in Northeast Liberia.
                           Papers of the Peabody Museum of
                           American Archeology and Ethno-
                           logy, Harvard University, vol.
                           32, no. 2. Cambridge, Mass.

Although neither spirit possession nor mediumship is
explicitly labelled, among the Kra (Kran) peoples of
northeast Liberia the diviner enters into a trance and
becomes an oracle for past, present, and future events
(pp. 34-5).

739. Harris, Grace   "Possession Hysteria in a Kenya
     1957   Tribe." American Anthropolo-
                           gist 59, no. 6: 1046-66.

Spirit possession as it occurs among the Taita (Teita)
of Kenya. Spirit possession when it affects women is
called Saka; description of ceremony and ritual objects
used; analysis of the relationship between men and women
vis à vis rights of land and cattle; Saka ritual is
viewed from the social anthropological perspective rather
than from a psychological one.

740. Harris, P. G.   "Notes on Yauri (Sokoto Pro-
     1930   vince), Nigeria," Journal of
                           the Royal Anthropological In-
                           stitute of Great Britain and
                           Ireland 60:283-334.

The Yan Bori are the devotees of the Bori cult who become possessed by spirits among the Yauri of Sokoto
Province, Nigeria. Their ritual possession ceremonies
are described on pages 305-6, 321-22, 326-34.

741. Harris, W. T., and   The Christian Approach to the
     E. G. Parrinder   Animist. London: Edinburgh
     1960   House Press.

In this short tract stressing the Christian view of
animistic religions, spirit possession and mediumship
are mentioned with regard to the peoples of Dahomey
(Benin) (pp. 42-43).

742. Harris, W. T., and   The Springs of Mende Belief and
     Harry Sawyerr   Conduct. Freetown: Sierra
     1968   Leone University Press.

The Mende, of Sierra Leone, have five different varia-

146

tions of spirit possession: (1) Possession induced by
a diviner into another person in order to make him capable of tracking down social defaulters. (2) A person,
usually a woman and a crank, is accused of ndilei possession and blamed for the deaths of children. (3) A person
may become possessed and claim to have been guilty of
witchcraft. This type of confession is often spontaneous.
(4) Possession which is acknowledged as simple madness.
If the patient can say the name of the invading spirit,
he is automatically cured. (5) Healing-doctors may find
new cures by being possessed by Temuisia spirits (pp.
122-23).

743. Hartwig, Gerald W.   "Long-Distance Trade and the
     1971   Evolution of Sorcery among the
                           Kerebe." African Historical
                           Studies (Boston) 4, no. 3:
                           505-24.

Historical analysis of the relationship between the increase in long-distance trading and the introduction and
growth of sorcery accusations among the Kerebe of Tanzania. As individuals had more access to material possessions, social tensions seem to have increased. Spirit
possession is mentioned as one technique of sorcery.

744. Hastings, J.   Encyclopedia of Religion and
     1920   Ethics. New York: Charles
                           Scribner's Sons.

Volume 10 contains a discussion of spirit possession:
description of voluntary spirit possession among the
Ba-Thonga (South Africa); exorcism ceremonies, accompanied by drums and rattles, and involving song composition by the possessed. Among the Akikuyu (Kikuyu)
(Kenya) spirit possession is by the ancestor spirits
(pp. 122, 125). Volume 4 includes discussion of spirit
intrusion and disease causation among the Bechuana
(Tswana) and Hottentot (Khoi-Khoi) peoples of South
Africa (pp. 730, 750).

745. Hau, K.   "OBεRI ƆKAIME Script, Texts, and
     1961   Counting System." Bulletin de
                           l'Institut fondamental
                           d'Afrique noire (Dakar), ser. B,
                           23, nos. 1-2: 291-308.

Linguistic and cultural analyses are given for the
Obεri ɔkaime script, which was thought to have been dic-
tated to inspired mediums by Seminant or the Holy Spirit
in southern Nigeria from about 1931 to 1936 (p. 292).

746. Hauenstein, A.   "Les Voyages en caravane des
     1964   Tjiaka." Anthropos 59, nos.
                           5-6: 926-32.

147

Spirit possession trances as a part of healing ceremonies are described for the Ovimbundu of Angola.

747. Hauenstein, Alfred   "Le Roi Pomba Kalukembe et le
     1970   probleme l'ohasa." Anthropos
                               65, nos. 1-2: 154-65.

Article concerns the southeastern Angolan practices of human sacrifice under the reign of Kalukembe. The skull of the victim is thought to hold extraordinary power, and in a ceremony where curses are directed at hostile tribes, the king's specialist woman medium falls into trance.

748. Haumont, Georges   "La Vie religieuse." Paper pre-
     1971   sented at Conference Olivaint de
                               Belgique, "Le Gabon, Afrique de
                               demain?" 15 August -
                               8 September.

Spirit possession and exorcism are mentioned as occurring among the Omiéné of Gabon (p. 239).

749. Hawkesworth, D.   "A Description of a Ceremony by
     1940   which a Nuba Chief Became a
                               Kujur." Sudan Notes and Records
                               (Khartoum) 23, no. 2: 345-47.

Among the Nuba (Sudan) it is believed that a man may be seized by the Kunsi ancestral spirit and rendered possessed. A ceremony may be performed for the possessed which would allow him to become a Kujur or possession priest.

750. Hayes, M. E.   "The WaNyombgwe." Nada (Salis-
     1943   bury), no. 20, pp. 25-26.

The originator of the WaNayombgwe (Nyombgwe) peoples in Rhodesia is traced to Nyanewe, whose spirit upon death became a lion and now occasionally possesses a medium in order to give advice on political matters.

751. Hayley, T. T. S.   The Anatomy of Lango Religions
     1947   and Groups. Cambridge: Cam-
                               bridge University Press.

The Lango of Uganda: their religion, magic, social organization, rites and ceremonies, ancestor cults, and doctors. Some discussion of spirit possession and mediumship experiences.

752. Hebga, M., ed.   Croyance et guérison: Yaoundé:
     1973   Éditions C. L. E.

148

Includes in this bibliography:
    224   F. E. Boulaga (1973)
   1465   A. Renard (1973)
   1513   E. de Rosny (1973)

753. Heintze, Beatrix   Besessenheits - Phänomene im
     1970   mittleren Bantu-Gebiet.
                      Wiesbaden: Frantz Steiner
                      Verlag.

This volume discusses spirit possession and mediumship
among the Nyaneka-Humbi and Cokwe (Chokwe) (Angola),
Luba (Zaire), Lamba (Zambia) and Shona (Rhodesia). The
whole volume is devoted to analysis of both possession
and mediumship.

754. Hellman, Ellen   Handbook on Race Relations in
     1949   South Africa. Cape Town:
                      Oxford University Press.

The close relationship in South Africa between the
faith healing and possession rites (glossolalia being the
voice of the Holy Spirit) in Zionist Churches and traditional African religions is stressed (pp. 567-69).

755. Henney, Jeannette H.   "The Shakers of St. Vincent: A
     1973   Stable Religion." In Religion,
                      Altered States of Consciousness,
                      and Social Change, edited by E.
                      Bourguignon, pp. 219-63.
                      (Bib. 245.)

The Shakers of St. Vincent Island in the Caribbean call
themselves "Spiritual Baptists" and employ both possession by the Holy Spirit, the impetus for glossolalia, and
sensory deprivation techniques in their practices.
African influences are evident.

756. Henney, Jeannette H.   "Spirit-Possession Belief and
     1974   Trance Behavior in Two Fundamen-
                      talist Groups in St. Vincent."
                      In Trance, Healing and Halluci-
                      nations, edited by F. D. Good-
                      man, J. H. Henney, and E.
                      Pressel, pp. 1-111. (Bib. 683.)

The Afro-American cult of the Shakers on St. Vincent
Island in the Caribbean is described in detail in this
study. Possession by the Holy Spirit is an integral part
of the cultic practices and beliefs.

757. Henney, Jeannette   "Trance Behavior among the
     n.d.   Shakers of St. Vincent."
                      Mimeographed. 17 pp.

Three levels are described for the trance caused by possession by the Holy Spirit among the Spiritual Baptists or Shakers of St. Vincent Island in the Caribbean: (1) initial convulsive jerks; (2) synchronized, rhythmic movement; (3) disintegration of level 2 behavior. [Cited in Transcultural Psychiatric Research Review (Bruges) 5 (October 1968): 171-73.]

758. Henry, Frances   "Social Stratification in an
      1965   Afro-American Cult." Anthropo- ·
                      logical Quarterly 38, no. 2: 72-
                      78.

The relationship between social status and spirit possession in the Shango cult on Trinidad in the Caribbean is examined in depth.

759. Hermans, T. J.   "The Exorcism of Evil Spirits or
      1970   Modern Exorcism." Nada (Salis-
                      bury) 10, no. 2: 64-66.

Brief description of the various items used by witches that had been discovered by a well-known healer and exorciser based in Salisbury, Rhodesia.

760. Herskovits, Melville J.   "Some Aspects of Dahomean Ethno-
      1932   logy." Africa: Journal of the
                        International African Institute
                        (London) 5, no. 3: 266-96.

Among the Dahomey (Fon) (most of whom live in Dahomey, now Benin) spirit possession or religious hysteria is little manifested except in disciplined form, spontaneous expression being frowned upon (p. 271). In Dahomey (Benin) a man's best friend plays a leading role in the funeral and other rites involved in ancestor worship. The friend's role is so important that, if the friend should die before the rites are performed, his ghost is called to come and rest on the head of a living being who sacrifices in his place (p. 285).

761. Herskovits, M. J., and   "An Outline of Dahomean Religious
      F. S. Herskovits   Beliefs." Memoirs of the Ameri-
      1933   can Anthropological Association,
                          no. 41.

Vodu ceremonies, including spirit possession, are prevalent in Dahomey (Fon), both in large urban centers and in small rural villages (Benin). However, the possession ceremonies are more "controlled" when compared with the Ashanti variety. Description of vodu priesthood and of a novice becoming possessed or "mounted" by the gods (p. 36).

762. Herskovits, Melville J.,   Rebel Destiny: Among Bush
     and Frances S.   Negroes of Dutch Guiana. New
     Herskovits   York: Whittlesey House, McGraw-
     1934   Hill Book Co.

The Bush Negroes of Dutch Guiana, South America, are
the descendants of runaway African slaves, and they
practice possession by gods (see book's index under
"Possession" for page citations).

763 Herskovits, Melville J.   "African Gods and Catholic
     1937a   Saints in New World Negro Be-
                               lief." American Anthropologist
                               39, no. 4: 635-43.

The relationship between the African gods and the
Christian saints involved in the Haitian vodun and other
Afro-American cults is outlined.

764. Herskovits, M. J.   Life in a Haitian Valley. New
     1937b   York: Alfred A. Knopf.

A very extensive discussion of spirit possession and
religious mediumistic cults. Discussion is primarily
concentrated in part 3, "Haitian Religion," and part 4,
"Haiti, a Cultural Mosaic." Bibliography available.

765. Herskovits, Melville J.   Dahomey: An Ancient West
     1938   African Kingdom. New York: J.
                               J. Augustin, Publisher.

Spirit possession in the ancestor cult of the Dahomey
(Fon) in Benin is discussed in chapter 12.

766. Herskovits, Melville J.   "The Negro in Bahia, Brazil: A
     1943a   Problem in Method." American
                               Sociological Review 8, no. 4:
                               394-404.

This article focuses mainly on the similarities and
differences between traditional African and Afro-
Brazilian social structure, and mention is made of the
possession cults in evidence in Brazil. Spirit possession is not explicitly discussed.

767. Herskovits, M. J.   "The Southernmost Outpost of New
     1943b   World Africanism." American
                              Anthropologist 45, no. 4: 495-
                              510.

Material collected in the city of Porto Alegre, Brazil.
A description of cults having West African origin. Com-
parison of aspects of these cults in southern and northern
Brazil. Possession plays an important role in the cults

since it is "the supreme expression of worship; . . . the god descends to the head of his devotee, replacing him and thus rendering him unconscious of what transpires until the deity departs." Discussion of the semipossessed condition called ere is included (p. 505).

768. Herskovits, Melville J.   "Drums and Drummers in Afro-
     1944   Brazilian Cult Life." The
                                 Musical Quarterly 30, no. 4:
                                 477-92.

Concentrating upon the drummers and their drums of the Afro-Brazilian cults, emphasis is placed on their skill and the rituals surrounding the drums themselves. Although so skillful at inducing trance in the participants of the cults, the drummer never becomes possessed.

769. Herskovits, Melville J., Trinidad Village. New York:
     and Frances S.   Alfred A. Knopf.
     Herskovits
     1947

Spirit possession in the African-influenced Shango and Shouter cults of Trinidad is examined (see book's index under "Possession" for page citations).

770. Herskovits, M. J.   "The Contribution of Afro-Ameri-
     1948a   can Studies to Africanist Re-
                              search." American Anthropolo-
                              gist 50, no. 1: 1-10.

Discussion of éré possession, a transition state between deep trance and complete recovery (pp. 8-9).

771. Herskovits, Melville J. Man and His Works. New York:
     1948b   Alfred A. Knopf.

A general discussion of spirit possession is found on pages 66-68. Possession is termed the supreme expression of religious experience. It is defined as "a psychological state wherein a displacement of personality occurs when the god 'comes to the head' of the worshipper. The individual thereupon is held to be the deity himself."

772. Herskovits, Melville J. "The Social Organization of the
     1955   Candomble." Anais do 31 Con-
                              gresso Internacional de Ameri-
                              canistas (São Paulo) 1:505-32.

In this detailed study of the Afro-Brazilian cult of candomble, emphasis is placed on the African elements evident in it.

152

773. Herskovits, Melville J.   The Myth of the Negro Past.
     1958a   Boston: Beacon Press.

     The African-influenced spirit possession cults of
     Brazil, Trinidad, and Dutch Guiana are discussed (see
     book's index under "Possession" for page citations).

774. Herskovits, M. J.   "Some Economic Aspects of the
     1958b   Afrobahian Candomblé." Octo-
                                genarian Dicata (Universidad
                                Autonova de Mexico) 2:227-47.

     Not available for annotation.

775. Herskovits, Melville J.   "The Panan, an Afrobahian Reli-
     1959   gious Rite of Transition."
                                Caribbean Quarterly (Trinidad)
                                5, no. 4: 276-83.

     Among Yorubas and others of African descent in Brazil,
     the Ketu (a Yoruba town) sect of Afrobahian cult groups
     includes many members. The need for initiation into the
     sect is signalled by the possession of an individual by
     a deity, who "mounts the head" of the one thus marked as
     his devotee. The article is a description of one cere-
     mony in the process of initiation. The ceremony, Panan,
     does not contain spirit possession.

776. Herskovits, Melville J.   Cultural Anthropology. New York:
     1965   Alfred A. Knopf.

     Spirit possession and trance states in African and New
     World Negro religions are mentioned in a discussion of
     the definition of normalcy versus abnormalcy in culture
     (pp. 354-55).

777. d'Hertefelt, Marcel   "Le Rwanda": Les Anciens
     1962   Royaumes de la zone interlacustre
                                méridionale. Ethnographic Sur-
                                vey of Africa, edited by Daryll
                                Forde, vol. 2, no. 14. London:
                                International African Institute.

     Discusses the Nyabingi cult of the Ruanda (Rwanda) and
     spirit possession; possession by the spirits of the dead
     among the Hutu, Tutsi and Twa peoples.

778. Herzog, H.   "The Pentecostal Groups in
     1969   Cameroon: A Challenge to the
                                Churches." Ministry (Morija,
                                Lesotho) 9, no. 4: 147-51.

     Brief descriptions of the Pentecostal Churches in
     Cameroon are given, and mention is made of glossolalia,
     prophecy, and exorcism as forms of faith-healing.

779. Heusch, Luc de   "Cultes de possession et reli-
     1962   gions initiatiques de salut en
                             Afrique." In Religions de
                             Salut, pp. 127-67. Annales du
                             Centre d'études des religions.
                             Bruxelles: Université libre de
                             Bruxelles.

     The article contains a general discussion of spirit
possession in African and Afro-American (Haiti) societies. The article centers on the Voodoo cults of rural
Haiti and the Zima cult of the Fon of Dahomey (Benin),
although other ethnic groups are mentioned. There is
some discussion of the needs possession cults fulfill,
and of the role initiation rites play in shaping and
controlling the actions of possessed persons.

780. Heusch, Luc de   "Possession et chamanisme." In
     1965   Les Religions africaines tradi-
                             tionneles, Rencontres interna-
                             tionales de Bouaké, (October
                             1962), pp. 139-70. (Bib. 1466.)

     The differences and similarities between shamanism and
spirit possession are examined in great detail in this
article (see also the Discussion that follows it).

781. Heusch, Luc de   Le Rwanda et la civilisation in-
     1966   terlacustre. Bruxelles:
                             Université libre de Bruxelles.

Spirit possession among the Rwanda (Ruanda) of Malawi
is described and examples from other African peoples are
discussed, including the Thonga (South Africa), Yoruba
(Nigeria), and Songhay (Songhai) (Niger) (pp. 173-83).

782. Heusch, Luc de   "Le Cru et le cuit dans le
     1968   domaine bantou." Présence
                             africaine (Paris) no. 67, pp.
                             33-48.

Analyses of several Kongo (Zaïre) myths are presented,
and the relationship between spirits and men is explored.
Spirit possession as an illness is mentioned on page 45.

783. Heusch, Luc de   "La Folie des dieux et la raison
     1971a   des hommes." In Pourquoi
                             l'epouser?, by L. de Heusch,
                             245-85. (Bib. 785.)

     Spirit possession, mediumship, and trance states are
discussed from a psychological perspective. Particular
mention is made of the Thonga (South Africa), Kongo
(Zaïre), Sukuma (Tanzania), Lovedu (South Africa), Kuba

154

(Zaïre), Luba (South Africa), Nuba (Sudan), Vandau (South Africa), and Yoruba (Nigeria).

784. Heusch, Luc de   "Myth et société féodale: Le
     1971b   Culte de Kubandwa dans le Rwanda
                         traditionnel." In Pourquoi
                         l'épouser? by L. de Heusch, pp.
                         205-25. (Bib. 785.)

Spirit possession in the Kubandwa cult among the Rwanda (Ruanda) (Rwanda) is discussed on pages 212 ff., 224 ff.

785. Heusch, Luc de   Pourquoi l'épouser? et autre
     1971c   essais. Paris: Éditions
                         Gallimard.

Includes in this bibliography:
       783   L. de Heusch (1971a)
       784   L. de Heusch (1971b)

786. Heusch, Luc de   Le Roi ivre, ou l'origine de
     1972   l'état. Paris: Éditions
                       Gallimard.

Material on the oral traditions of the following Bantu-speaking peoples is presented in this book: the Kuba, Luba, and Lunda of Zaïre, and the Bemba of Zambia. A ritual of exorcism is mentioned on page 75, and spirit mediums are discussed on pages 43, 195-97, 222.

787. Hippler, Arthur E.   "Possession and Trance Cults: A
     n.d.   Cross-cultural Perspective."
                       Typescript. 10 pp.

The necessity of exploring the psychogenesis of the spirit possession phenomenon is emphasized here; examples from the Haitian vodun cult are given, among others. [Cited in Transcultural Psychiatric Research Review (Montreal) 10 (April 1973): 21-23.]

788. Hobley, C. W.   Ethnology of Akamba and Other
     1910   East African Tribes. Cambridge.

Among the Kamba of Kenya, young people are attacked by a form of infectious mania. One of these attacks occurred in Ulu in 1906. The sight of a hat or a cap threw a person into a kind of fit, the whole body but particularly the upper portion would be violently convulsed, and the patient would probably fall down in a semi-insensible state. His condition would continue until the hat was removed. This phenomenon is called Chesu or Ki-Jesu, and some think it is the Kamba pronunciation of Jesus. Other similar possession phenomena are reported (p. 10). [Cited by Jeffreys (1953, Bib. 853).]

789. Hobley, C. W.   Bantu Beliefs and Magic.
     1922   London: H. F. & G. Witherby.

     Discusses notions of possession for various Bantu
     tribes in Kenya, particularly Kikuyu and Kamba. Among
     the Akamba suicide is regarded as due to spirit posses-
     sion. Examples are given of animals becoming possessed
     (chap. 1, p. 29).

790. Hoebel, E. Adamson   Anthropology: The Study of Man.
     1966 (1949)   New York: McGraw-Hill.

     General anthropological text. Chapter 33 deals with
     shamans, priests, and cults. Page 483 has a photograph
     of "a congolese female in a state of spirit possession";
     pages 485-86 include a discussion of Haitian voodoo
     (vodou): "dancers representative of specific gods are
     possessed in turn as each god is called with his drum
     salute."

791. Hoernlé, A. Winifred   "Magic and Medicine." In The
     1937   Bantu Speaking Tribes of South
                                  Africa, edited by I. Schapera.
                                  (Bib. 1564.)

     Comparison of spirit possession as it occurs among the
     Shangana-Tonga and other Bantu tribes in South Africa.
     A diviner is called to his profession by the spirits;
     initiation ceremony described (chap. 10, pp. 230-33).

792. Hoffman, Léon Francois   "The Image of Woman in Haitian
     1960   Poetry." Présence africaine
                                  (English ed.) 6/7, nos. 34-35:
                                  187-213.

     When a poet describes a Voodoo (Haiti) ceremony, the
     usual description is that of a dancing girl. The view
     is one of the girl as a desirable body but also as a
     medium through which the gods can manifest themselves.
     Quotes selections of poetry from several sources. De-
     scribes possession trances as means of perceiving more
     fundamental reality than it is possible to perceive
     through reason (pp. 209-13).

793. Hofstra, Sjored   Differenzierungs Erscheinungen
     1933   einigen afrikanischen Gruppen:
                                  Ein Beitrag zur Frage der
                                  primitiven Individualität.
                                  Amsterdam: Scheltema & Holkema's
                                  Boekhandel.

     In a discussion of prophets and prophetic movements
     among the Bambala, the Basala, the Batwa, and the Baila
     peoples (Ila-speaking peoples of Northern Rhodesia, now

Zambia), mention is made of spirit possession, trance,
and mediumship (pp. 120 ff.). Possession among medicine
men is mentioned on pp. 110 ff.

794. Holas, B.   Les Masques Kono. Paris:
     1952a   Librairie orientaliste, Paul
                           Geuthner S.A.

     Exorcism of evil spirits is cited as a practice of the
Kono of Guinea (pp. 29, 68, 133).

795. Holas, B.   "Practiques divinatoires Kissi."
     1952b   Bulletin de l'Institut français
                           d'Afrique noire (Dakar) 14,
                           no. 1: 272-308.

     Discusses the divinatory practices of the Kissi
(Guinea) people. The Pombo statuettes represent dead
chiefs, who are charged with guiding the life of the
Kissi. For divination purposes, the Pombo statuette is
placed on the head of an individual who enters a trance,
and thus serves as an intermediary for the ancestral
spirits.

796. Holas, B.   "Bref aperçu sur les principaux
     1954   cultes syncrétiques de la basse
                           Côte d'Ivoire." Africa: Journal
                           of the International African
                           Institute (London) 24, no. 1:
                           55-60.

     Brief mention is made of a curer-exorcist named Boto
Adaï among the Dida of the Ivory Coast who acquired a
large reputation for his healing powers (p. 55).

797. Holas, Bohumil   L'Afrique Noire. Paris: Bloud
     1964   & Gay.

     Spirit possession is very briefly mentioned as being
practiced among the Kaffa, a Nilotic group of the Sudan
(p. 34).

798. Holas, Bohumil   Les Dieux d'Afrique Noire. Paris:
     1968   Librairie orientaliste, Paul
                           Geuthner S.A.

     This is a general theoretical analysis of African re-
ligions which includes a section on spirit-possessed
diviners, "chasseurs de sorciers," and healers (pp. 173-
88).

799. Holden, Rev. William C. The Past and Future of the
     1963   Kaffir Races. Cape Town: C.
                             Struik - Africana Specialist &
                             Publisher.

The individual among the Kaffirs of South Africa who
is chosen by supernatural means to become a witch-doctor
dreams about serpents who are said to be possessed by
the spirits of the Kaffir ancestors. His behavior is
distinctively trancelike and frenzied, and he has the
power to speak with the spirits (pp. 285 ff.).

800. Hole, Hugh Marshall   The Making of Rhodesia. London:
     1926   Macmillan & Co.

     The institution of spirit mediumship in connection
with the Mlimo cult among the Matabele (Ndebele) of
Rhodesia is mentioned on page 37.

801. Hole, Hugh Marshall   The Passing of the Black Kings.
     1932   London: Philip Allen.

     Spirit mediumship is briefly mentioned as being prac-
ticed by the Makalanga (Kalanga) "wizards" of South
Africa (p. 23).

802. Holleman, J. F.   "Accommodating the Spirit
     1953   amongst some Northeastern Shona
                                Tribes." Rhodes-Livingstone
                                Institute Papers, no. 22.

     Possession of mediums by the mhondoro ancestral spirits
among the northeastern Shona-speaking peoples of Rhodesia
is described on pages 29 ff.

803. Hollenweger, Walter J.   "Mr. Chips Looks for the Holy
     1975   Spirit in Pentecostal Theology."
                                Journal of Theology for
                                Southern Africa (Braamfontein,
                                Transvaal), no. 12, pp. 39-50.

     Possession by the Holy Spirit and glossolalia in the
Pentecostal movement are examined with regard to: (1)
a charismatic ecclesiology; (2) a charismatic hermeneu-
tic; and (3) a charismatic understanding of para-psycho-
logical phenomena. (African Pentecostal churches are
mentioned.)

804. Hollis, A. C.   The Masai. Oxford: Clarendon
     1905   Press.

     The author describes spirit intrusion among the Masai,
Kenya (p. 308).

805. Hollis, A. C.   The Nandi. Oxford: Clarendon
     1909   Press.

     The author discusses spirit intrusion among the Nandi
(Kenya) (p. 69).

806. Honea, Kenneth   "Buda in Ethiopia." Wiener
     1956   völkerkundliche mitteilungen 4,
                             no. 1: 20-23.

Buda is a term for the evil eye or the force that possesses people in Ethiopia. Little children wear amulets
as protection against being possessed. Description of
curing ceremonies and of the medicine used to induce the
spirit to reveal its name. [Cited in African Abstracts,
vol. 9, no. 136.]

807. Hooker, J. R.   "Witness and Watchtower in the
     1965   Rhodesias and Nyasaland."
                             Journal of African History, vol.
                             6, no. 1.

Brief note on possession in Rhodesia on page 98.

808. Horeis, Martin Werner   "The Afro-Brazilian Candomblé
     1974   Cult: An Anthropological Study
                             of Cultural Performances of
                             Good and Evil." Ph.D. disser-
                             tation, Cornell University.
                             Dissertation Abstracts Inter-
                             national 35, no. 9 (March 1975):
                             5591A.

The spirit possession rituals of the Candomblé cult in
Bahia, Brazil, heavily influenced by Yoruba (Nigeria)
cultural elements, are examined in terms of being cultural performances of good and evil.

809. Horton, Robin   The Gods as Guests: An Aspect of
     1960   Kalabari Religious Life. Lagos:
                             Federal Government Printer.
                             Ill.

Among the Kalabari of eastern Nigeria, masquerades and
dances form a part of many rituals. Both masqueraders
and dancers are susceptible to possession by the spirits
they represent. There are also mediums of water spirits,
hero spirits, and ancestor spirits who regularly become
possessed so that these spirits may play an active role
in social ceremonies. Illustrated with many photographs
of possessed masqueraders and mediums.

810. Horton, Robin   "The Kalabari World-View: An
     1962   Outline and Interpretation."
                             Africa: Journal of the Interna-
                             tional African Institute
                             (London) 32, no. 3: 197-220.

In a detailed theoretical and descriptive account of
the world view of the Kalabari of eastern Nigeria the re-

lationship between the realms of the spirits and of men
is outlined. The phenomenon of possession is spoken of
mainly in philosophical terms.

811. Horton, Robin   "The Kalabari Ekine Society: A
     1963   Borderland of Religion and Art."
                        Africa: Journal of the Interna-
                        tional African Institute (London)
                        33, no. 2: 94-114. Ill.

Among the Kalabari of southeastern Nigeria exists the
Ekine men's society, otherwise known as Sekiapu--the
Dancing People. It is a religious institution for solici-
ting the help of the water spirits; it performs masque-
rade dances in which individual members of the society
adopt mannerisms and speech and don costumes which identify them with particular spirits. The spirits are said
to "walk with" the dancers who represent them, and the
dancers often enter a state where, people say, they have
been possessed. This possession is encouraged and is regarded as the seal of a successful performance (pp. 95-
103).

812. Horton, Robin   "Kalabari Diviners and Oracles."
     1964   Odu (Ibadan) 1, no. 1: 3-16.

Among the Kalabari of Nigeria diviners and oracles are
used to refer particular events in the material world to
particular spiritual forces. Among divination techniques
is the Orukurobo ('Bearer of a spirit') who divines
during possession by a spirit. [Cited in African Abstracts, vol. 1, no. 626.]

813. Horton, Robin   "Duminea: A Festival for the
     1965   Water Spirits in the Niger
                        Delta." Nigeria Magazine
                        (Lagos), no. 86, pp. 187-98.

The Kalabari people of Soku village in the eastern
Niger delta (Nigeria) worship the water spirit Duminea.
During the spirit's festival, offerings are made at a
river shrine, and possession of the priests and priestesses takes place. [Cited in African Abstracts, vol. 17,
no. 639.]

814. Horton, Robin   "African Traditional Thought and
     1967   Western Science." Africa:
                        Journal of the International
                        African Institute (London) 37,
                        no. 1: 50-71; 37, no. 2: 155-87.

A general analysis of the phenomenon of spirit possession is presented. The author believes that spirit possession is one way of establishing ties between men and

160

spirits that would be impossible in the purely human
social field. With spirit possession, people take on
roles that are not available to them as ordinary humans.
Women, for example, in male-dominated societies often
assume roles of male authority figures while in possession, roles that are unavailable to them normally (p.
163).

815. Horton, Robin   "Types of Spirit Possession in
      1969   Kalabari Religion." In Spirit
                              Mediumship and Society in Africa,
                              edited by J. Beattie and J.
                              Middleton, pp. 14-49.
                              (Bib. 150.)

     There are several types of spirit possession among the
Kalabari of Nigeria. People participating in dance ceremonies may be possessed by spirits. There are also
societies of regular mediums who are possessed by hero
spirits and water spirits. Membership in a female spirit
medium cult is related to the efforts of women to experience roles which their social status does not allow
them normally.

816. Horton, Robin   "A Hundred Years of Change in
      1970a   Kalabari Religion." In Black
                              Africa: Its Peoples and Their
                              Cultures Today, edited by J.
                              Middleton, pp. 192-211.
                              (Bib. 1205.)

     The role of spirit possession in Kalabari (Nigeria) re-
ligion and its changes during the last century are discussed.

817. Horton, Robin   "Ikapataka Dogi: A Kalabari
      1970b   Funeral Rite." African Notes 5,
                              no. 3: 57-72.

     The spirit of the dead among the Kalabari of Nigeria
forcefully manifests itself in the Ikapataka Dogi funeral
rites. The body in its coffin, on the shoulders of its
bearers, responds to questions put to it concerning the
cause of death, etc. Analysis and interpretation follow
a detailed description.

818. Horton, Robin   "African Conversion." Africa:
      1971   Journal of the International
                              African Institute (London) 41,
                              no. 2: 85-108.

     Beginning with a detailed presentation of John Peel's
arguments in Aladura: A Religious Movement among the
Yoruba (1968, Bib. 1291), the author analyzes the African

Separatist Churches and their belief in spirits (and in spirit possession).

819. Houser, Tillman
      1972

"The Extent of Karanga Speaking Spirit Possession among the Hlengwe in Rhodesia." Paper presented at the Conference on the History of Central African Religious Systems, Lusaka, 31 August - 8 September.

Descriptive analysis is given of the Hlengwe of Rhodesia who are possessed by Karanga-speaking spirits, after having conquered and settled among the Karanga. Possession trance is demanded to cure various illnesses. Child possession is mentioned.

820. Howell, P. P., and
      W. P. G. Thomson
      1946

"The Death of a Reth of the Shilluk and the Installation of His Successor." Sudan Notes and Records (Khartoum), vol. 27.

The effigy of Nyikang, the first Reth (king) and founder of the royal house of the Shilluk (Sudan), was placed upon the sacred stool and then lifted and carried into the shrine. Then the new Reth was seated in its place. This symbolized the possession of the Reth by the spirit Nyikang.

821. Howell, P. P.
      1953

"Some Observation on 'Earthly Spirits' among the Nuer." Man 53, no. 126: 85-88.

Some of the "earthly spirits" found among the Nuer are said to possess individuals and make their mediums. The discussion of spirit possession is set in context by a summary of some Nuer religious beliefs.

822. Howells, William
      1948

The Heathens: Primitive Man and His Religions. New York: Doubleday & Co.

A general description and discussion of spirit possession and its relation to disease and medicine. Examples drawn from different cultures, for example, Gã people of Ghana. Pictorial illustration of an Ashanti priest possessed (p. 75; chap. 6, pp. 92-96).

823. Howman, E. G.
      1966

"Native Tribes of the South; a Superstitious Race; the Fate of a Rain-Maker." Nada (Salisbury) 9, no. 3: 33-37. (Reprinted from Times (London) 25. May 1914.)

162

The Mashona (Shona), Sangaan (Rozwi), and Matabele
(Ndebele) ethnic groups now living in Zimbabwe but formerly united as the Warozwi (Rozwi) of Rhodesia use
spirit mediums for divination and rain-making purposes.

824. Huber, Hugo   The Krobo: Traditional Social and
       1963   Religious Life of a West African
                           People. Studia Instituti
                           Anthropos, St. Augustin near
                           Bonn, vol. 16. Fribourg: St.
                           Paul's Press.

Among the Krobo of Ghana, priests are chosen by the
deity either by having a specific kind of illness or by
being directly possessed by that deity. Ceremonies surrounding the installation of a priest are recorded (pp.
226 ff.).

825. Huber, Hugo   "Curse and Exorcism: Ideas of
       1969   God among African Peoples." In
                           The Unknown God, edited by
                           István Rácz, pp. 155-85. New
                           York: Sheed & Ward. Ill.

Although possession is not explicitly labelled,
exorcism of spirits is mentioned in this general article
on African religions.

826. Hughes, A. J. B.   "Uzimu: Some Preliminary Notes
       1955   on Vengeance Magic among the
                           Rhodesian Ndebele." Rhodes-
                           Livingstone Journal, no. 19,
                           pp. 27-45.

The use of possession by the spirit of the deceased to
discover the manner by which that spirit may be appeased
is described for the Ndebele of Rhodesia (pp. 38-40).

827. Hugo, Rev. H. C.   "The Mashona Spirits." Nada
       1935   (Salisbury) 13:52-58.

The spirits which possess and speak through the Shona
of Rhodesia include: Mwari--God; Midzimu--the ancestral
spirits; and the Mashavi--alien spirits.

828. Hunter, Monica   "The Effects of Contact with
       1933   Europeans on the Status of
                           Pondo Women." Africa (London),
                           vol. 6, no. 3.

In Zululand (South Africa), Pondo women serve as
mediums for certain spirits, as well as serve as rain-
makers (pp. 268-69).

829. Hutchinson, Harry W.   Village and Plantation Life in
     1957   Northeastern Brazil. Seattle:
                             University of Washington Press.

     Not available for annotation.

830. Huxley, Francis   The Invisibles: Voodoo Gods in
     1969   Haiti. New York: McGraw-Hill
                             Book Co.

     The Haitian Voodoo spirit possession religion is ex-
     tensively examined.

831. Hyppolite, Michelson   Une Étude sur le Folklore
     Paul   Haïtien. Port-au-Prince.
     1953

     In this brief study, the Haïtian vodou cult is ex-
     plored. Details of the various possessing deities, the
     dances, and the musical instruments are given.

832. Ibarrola, R.   "La Musique et la danse dans les
     1953   territoires du golfe de Guinée."
                             Africa (Madrid) 10, no. 142:
                             473-75.

     Description of musical instruments and dances of
     Guinea. The dance, Balele, varies according to its
     theme. There is a Balele for the hunt, work, magic, and
     for spirit possession. Description of dances and their
     accessories; often the possession dance lasts for two to
     three days until the spirit speaks through the mouths of
     the frenzied and convulsed dancers. [Cited in African
     Abstracts, vol. 5, no. 626.]

833. Idowa, E. Bolaji   Olódùmarè: God in Yoruba Belief.
     1962   London: Longmans, Green & Co.

     A discussion of the different Yoruba cults (Nigeria)
     and the priesthood dedicated to their service; medium-
     ship experiences reported (chap. 10, pp. 129-40).

834. Idowa, E. Bolaji   "Religion, Magic and Medicine -
     1967   Special Reference to Africa."
                             Orita (Ibadan) 1, no. 2: 62-77.

     Although spirit possession and mediumship are not ex-
     plicitly labelled, both are implicitly cited among the
     Yoruba of Nigeria (p. 75).

835. Idowa, E. Bolaji   African Traditional Religion.
     1973   Maryknoll, N.Y.: Orbis Books.

In this general theoretical work on African religions, spirit possession is briefly mentioned on pages 177-78.

836. Ige, Oye   "Joseph Babalola--a Twentieth
     1965   Century Prophet." African His-
                       torian (Ibadan) 1, no. 3: 38-42.

Short account of the rise of the Nigerian prophet Joseph Babalola in the early twentieth century. Foretelling and speaking in tongues were the manifestations of the "ecstasy" of "possession" by the Holy Spirit that occurred among his followers.

837. Iliffe, John   "The Organization of the Maji
     1967   Maji Rebellion." Journal of
                       African History 8, no. 3: 495-
                       512.

The Kolelo cult among the Zaramo of German East Africa (Tanzania) is discussed with emphasis on its role in the Maji Maji Rebellion of 1905-7. Spirit mediumship and possession were central features of the cult (pp. 504-5).

838. Ilogu, Edmund   "Christ Healing Church--a Study
     1970   of the Sociology of One Inde-
                       pendent African Church." West
                       African Religion (University of
                       Nigeria, Nsukka), no. 8, pp. 12-
                       19.

The Christ Healing Church in the eastern states of Nigeria practices glossolalia and ecstatic trance, and uses exorcism to cast out evil spirits which cause illness.

839. Ilogu, Edmund   Christianity and the Ibo Cul-
     1974   ture. Leiden: E. J. Brill.

Mention is made of exorcism of evil spirits practiced by Ibo (Nigeria) diviners (p. 53); Pentecostal use of spirit possession (p. 61); and the speaking in tongues and trance states in the Aladura Churches (p. 111).

840. Ilogu, Edmund   "Changing Religious Beliefs in
     1975a   Nigeria." Nigeria Magazine
                       (Marina Lagos), nos. 117-18,
                       pp. 3-20. Ill.

The changing belief systems of Nigerian religious traditions are discussed, and glossolalia and trance states are briefly mentioned on page 7. Islam, Christianity, the African independent churches, and traditional religions are all examined.

841. Ilogu, Edmund   "The Religious Situation in
     1975b   Nigeria Today: A Sociological
                             Analysis." Présence africaine
                             (Paris), no. 96, pp. 504-24.

     A sociological analysis of the interaction between
traditional Nigerian religions, Christianity, and Islam
is given. The African independent church movement,
Aladura, is discussed on page 509, along with its practices of glossolalia and trance states.

842. Imegwu, Chidi   "The Aros and the Oracle."
     1965   African Historian (Ibadan) 1,
                             no. 3: 43-46.

     Although spirit mediumship is not explicitly labelled,
the oracle among the Aros (Igbo) of Nigeria is spoken of
as being a means of direct communication with the god
Tshuku.

843. Ingrams, W. H.   Zanzibar: Its History and Its
     1967   People. London: Frank Cass & Co.

     Many types of spirits in Zanzibar are thought to possess
mainly women. Detailed cases witnessed by the author are
given along with recipes for summoning a "devil" to possess a person and for exorcism. Possession may be a prescribed treatment for spirit-sent illness (pp. 435-39,
453-57).

844. Iwuagwu, A. O.   "Chukwu: Towards a Definition of
     1975   Igbo Traditional Religion."
                             West African Religion (Nsukka),
                             16, no. 1: 26-34.

     The Ala priest in his role of spirit medium among the
Igbo of Nigeria directs sacrifices to the divinities (pp.
28, 32-33).

845. Iyeki, Jean-François   "Essai de psychologie du
     1956   J   primitif." Voix du Congolais,
                             no. 119, pp. 89-93.

     Spirit possession dances in Africa are briefly men-
tioned on page 91.

846. Jackson, Anthony   "Sound and Ritual." Man
     1968   (London), n.s. 3, no. 2: 293-99.

     Spirit mediumship is mentioned in this theoretical
article on the use of sound in ritual contexts. Data
from Africa are cited.

847. Jahn, Janheinz   Muntu. London: Faber & Faber.
     1961   Ill.

Deals primarily with neo-African culture. Chapter 2 deals with the _voodoo_ cults in relation to spirit possession, and chapter 3 describes possession dances. Bibliography.

848. Jahn, Janheinz   _Through African Doors_. New York:
     1962   Grove Press.

Ecstatic trance dancing in the Jehova Witnesses Church of Benin, Nigeria, is described as being due to possession by the Holy Spirit (pp. 225-27).

849. Jambly, W. D.   _Tribal Dancing and Social De-_
     1926   _velopment_. London: H. F. & G.
                           Witherby.

Among Arabs of East and North Africa, as well as other Moslem areas, there are dancing groups called _Dervishes_. _Howling Dervishes_, when in an ecstasy through dancing and drug taking, cut themselves with knives, eat live coals and glass, handle red-hot iron, and swallow snakes. When a _Dervish_ is in a state of ecstasy he is supposed to be unconscious to the actions of his body, for his soul has gone far away to the region of the spirits (p. 210).

850. Janzen, John M., and _An Anthology of Kongo Religion_.
     Wyatt MacGaffey   University of Kansas Publica-
     1974   tions in Anthropology, no. 5.
                           Lawrence, Kans.

This is a collection of primary texts on the various religious movements among the Kongo of lower Zaïre. Possession trance, both as a form of divination or mediumship and as ecstasy (possession by the Holy Spirit), is mentioned in the author's commentaries on these texts (pp. 10, 19, 56-57, 76 ff., 143 ff., 150 ff.).

851. Jarrett-Kerr, Martin _African Pulse_. London: Faith
     1960   Press.

Brief mention is made of spirit mediumship abilities in the African witch-doctor of the Xhosa (Xosa) (South Africa) (pp. 43-44). The main topic of the book is the relationship between Europeans and Africans in South African hospitals.

852. Jaspan, M. A.   _The Ila-Tonga Peoples of North_
     1953   _Western Rhodesia_. Ethnographic
                           Survey of Africa, edited by
                           Daryll Forde, pt. 4. London:
                           International African Institute.

Discussion of religious beliefs and cults found among

the Tonga (Rhodesia). Basangu spirits inhabit the rain shrines, and each shrine has its keeper who may be temporarily possessed by a spirit. Mention is also made of Masabe possession (pp. 60-61).

853. Jeffreys, M. D. W. "African Tarantula or Dancing
     1953   Mania." Eastern Anthropologist
                       6, no. 2: 98-105.

This article is a compilation of reports by several authors about the dancing mania. All of the reports are classified in this bibliography and have been researched separately under the names of the authors: Burton (1864, Bib. 293); Frazer (1927, Bib. 610); Hobley (1910, Bib. 788); Lankester (1914, Bib. 963); Lowie (1929, Bib. 1064); Sibree (1870, Bib. 1613); Swabey (1939, Bib. 1693); Waddell (1863, Bib. 1825); Westgarth (1927, Bib. 1867).

854. Jeffreys, M. D. "The Anam Ofo: A Cult Object
     1956a   among the Ibo." South African
                      Journal of Science (Johannes-
                      burg) 52, no. 10: 227-33.

Among the Ibo, Nigeria, the prayer stick, Ofo, when held in the hand, allows one to get in touch with the spirit world. A comparison is made of the function of this cult object among the Anam Ibo with the attributes of the mummy of Osiris in ancient Egypt. [Cited in African Abstracts, vol. 8, no. 47.]

855. Jeffreys, M. D. W. "The Nyama Society of Ibibio
     1956b   Women." African Studies
                        (Johannesburg) 15, no. 1: 15-29.

Deals with the Ibibio of Nigeria. Not available for annotation.

856. Jenkinson, Thomas B. Amazulu. London: W. H. Allen
     1882   & Co.

Among the Zulus and Kafirs of South Africa, diviners practice spirit possession which gives them extraordinary powers for finding the causes of misfortunes and for healing (pp. 28 ff.).

857. Jilek, W. G., and   "The Problem of Epilepsy in Rural
     L. M. Jilek-Aall   Africa: 'Kifafa' in a Tanzanian
     1968   Tribe." Paper presented at the
                           Colloque d'épidémiologie de
                           l'épilepsie en Afrique, Marseille,
                           3 September. Mimeographed.
                           5 pp.

The epileptic among the Wapogoro of Tanzania is
thought to possess an evil spirit and, when having a
seizure, may not be touched for fear of contracting
that spirit. [Cited in Transcultural Psychiatric Research Review (Bruges) 7 (April 1970): 43-48.]

858. Jilek, Wolfgang G.,   "Transient Psychoses in Afri-
     and Louise Jilek-Aall   cans." Psychiatria Clinica
     1970   (Basel) 3, no. 6: 337-64.

An investigation is conducted into the specific nature
of the transient psychoses or "bouffées délirantes"
commonly found among Africans--attributed to possession
by spirits traditionally--and the conclusion is drawn
that these states are not unique to Africa but are perhaps more prevalent in "tradition-directed cultures or
pre-industrial societies" (p. 359).

859. Johnston, T. F.   "Possession Music of the
     1972   Shangana-Tsonga." African Music
                              5, no. 2: 10-22.

Not available for annotation.

860. Johnston, Thomas F.   "Supernatural Revelation via
     1973   Hallucinogens in Initiation,
                              Spirit-Possession, and Juris-
                              prudence: A South African Prob-
                              lem-Solving Mechanism."
                              Cahiers des religions africaines
                              (Kinshasa) 7, no. 13: 79-112.

Drug use of a species of the Datura family among the
Tsonga of South Africa aids in the exorcism rituals,
mancomane, which are used to get rid of evil foreign
spirits that cause illness (pp. 89 ff.).

861. Jones, G. I.   "A Boundary to Accusations." In
     1970   Witchcraft Confessions and Accu-
                             sations, edited by M. Douglas,
                             pp. 321-32. (Bib. 476.)

Brief mention is made of spirit possession as an element in anti-witchcraft movements among the Ibo of
Nigeria (p. 325).

862. Jules-Rosette,   African Apostles. Ithaca, N.Y.:
     Bennetta   Cornell University Press.
     1975a

In this detailed study of the Apostolic Church of John
Maranke in Zaïre, glossolalia, spirit possession, and
exorcism are all mentioned throughout the text (see
book's index under "Devil Possession," "Exorcism," and
"Glossolalia" for page citations).

169

863. Jules-Rosette,   "Bapostolo Ritual: An African
     Bennetta   Response to Christianity."
     1975b   Canadian Journal of African
                             Studies (Montreal) 9, no. 1:
                             89-102.

The ritual use of ecstatic states of glossolalia and
prophecy are described for the members of the Apostolic
Church of John Maranke called Bapostolo. This African
independent church was founded in Rhodesia and has
spread to Zambia, Malawi, and the Zaire Republic (pp. 97-
98).

864. Jules-Rosette,   "The Conversion Experience: The
     Bennetta   Apostles of John Maranke."
     1975c   Journal of Religion in Africa
                             (Leiden) 7, no. 2: 132-64.

In this general and personal presentation of the conversion experience in the Church of the Apostles of John
Maranke in Zaire, mention is made of illness caused by
demon possession and treatment by means of exorcism
(p. 161).

865. Jules-Rosette,   "Song and Spirit: The Use of
     Bennetta   Song in the Management of Ritual
     1975d   Contexts." Africa: Journal of
                             the International African In-
                             stitute (London) 45, no. 2:
                             150-66.

Members of the Apostolic Church of John Maranke in the
Katanga congregation of the Kasai area of Zaire are said
to be "taken by" the Holy Spirit and to speak in tongues,
prophesy, and cure.

866. Jules-Rosette,   "Grass-Roots Ecumenism: Reli-
     Bennetta   gious and Social Co-operation
     1977   in Two Urban African Churches."
                             African Social Research (Lusaka)
                             no. 23, pp. 185-216.

The interaction between two indigenous African churches,
the Apostolic Church of John Maranke and the Apostolic
Church of John Masowe of Marrapodi, Zambia, is discussed
here, and mention is made of trance states in connection
with the powers of the Holy Spirit and of the healing of
illnesses which occur as a result of possession by evil
spirits.

867. Jumbale, Anderson   "Traditional Religion of the
     1971   Chonyi." Dina na Mila (Kampala)
                             5, no. 2: 29-44.

A practitioner of medicine among the Chonyi of Kenya
has his powers to heal revealed to him through possession
by a divine spirit (p. 39).

868. Junod, Henri A.   "Galagala; Memoir on a Case of
     1896   Possession." Bibliothèque
                              universelle (Switzerland), June.

     A case of possession from Mozambique. [Cited by
     Oesterreich (1930, Bib. 1301), p. 138.]

869. Junod, Henri A.   Les Ba-Ronga, étude ethnographi-
     1898a   que sur les indigènes de la Baie
                              de Delagoa. Neuchâtel.

     First cases of possession appeared among the Zulu (South
     Africa) when young men left to work in the diamond mines
     of Kimberley or the gold mines of Johannesburg and Natal.
     Ba-Ronga (Ronga) travellers passing through Zulu terri-
     tories became possessed by Zulu spirits (pp. 440-41).

870. Junod, H. A.   Bulletin de la Société
     1898b   neuchâteloise de géographie,
                              book 10.

     Possession cases reported for the Ba-Ronga (Ronga)
     (South Africa). Possession by ancestor spirits of the
     Zulu peoples is also discussed (p. 388).

871. Junod, H. A.   The Life of a South African
     1913   Tribe. Vol. 2. Neuchâtel:
                              Imprimerie Attinger frères.

     Among the Thonga (South Africa) people, spirit posses-
     sion is regarded as the "madness of the gods"; the
     spirits causing the illness are called Psikwembu.
     Description of the spirits, diagnosis of the illness, and
     comments upon the following: exorcism, the new condition
     of the exorcised, the society of the exorcised, and
     funeral rites for the exorcised (pp. 344, 434-60). Some
     information also on spirit possession among the Ba-Ronga
     people.

872. Junod, H. P.   "Les Cas de possession et de
     1934   l'exorcisme chez les VaNdau."
                              Africa: Journal of the Interna-
                              tional African Institute
                              (London) 7, no. 3: 270-99.

     Among the VaNdau of Mozambique and South Africa, people
     are possessed by many different ancestral spirits. The
     various categories of possessing spirits are described,
     and the means of exorcising each is given. Initiation
     of exorcised persons into diviner's status is discussed.

171

873. Junod, H. P.   Bantu Heritage. Johannesburg:
     n.d. (1938?)   Hortors Ltd.

     Definition of the terms "spirit possession" and "be-
     witching." Discussion of the similarity of these two
     categories; cites cases of possession and witchcraft to
     support argument. Description of the Ndau medicine bas-
     ket (chap. 6).

874. Kagame, Alexis   "Description du culte rendu aux
     1967   tréspassés du Rwanda." Bulletin
                         de Séances Academie Royal Science
                         Outre-Mer 4:746-79.

     This is a study of the rituals and beliefs surrounding
     the bazimu, spirits of the dead, among the Ruanda
     (Rwanda). Although spirit possession is not explicitly
     mentioned in the abstract, it is implied as occurring
     in the immandwa cult, popular at the end of the sixteenth
     century. [Cited in African Abstracts, vol. 22, no. 1
     (January 1971), no. 170.]

875. Kaggwa, L. B., and "Lubaale Initiation in Buganda."
     F. B. Welbourn   Uganda Journal (Kampala) 28, no.
     1964   2: 218-20.

     When an individual becomes ill among the Baganda
     (Ganda) (Uganda), a diviner is consulted and frequently
     spirits (Lubaale) are said to be the cause. Initiation
     into the cult of these spirits, which includes possession
     by them, may be prescribed as treatment.

876. Kagwa, Benjamin H. "The Problem of Mass Hysteria in
     1964   East Africa." East Africa Medi-
                         cal Journal 41:560-65.

     Reported as occurring mainly among the Bagishu (Gisu)
     ethnic group in and around Mbale, Uganda, a mass hysteri-
     cal epidemic broke out in November 1963. The three
     stages of the illness are described, as well as the
     traditional treatment used by the elders to cure the
     "possessed" through "exorcism." Mention is made of other
     cases of mass hysteria in Africa, but this phenomenon is
     not confined only to that continent. [Cited in Trans-
     cultural Psychiatric Research Review (Bruges) 3 (April
     1966): 35-37.]

877. Kahimbaara, John   "Some Traditional Beliefs of the
     Akiiki   Batooro." Occasional Research
     1974   Papers in African Traditional
                         Religion and Philosophy
                         (Makerere University, Kampala),
                         vol. 29, no. 281.

Among the Batooro (Toro) of Uganda, spirit possession occurs in two instances: (1) the ebigunguza force, which is evil and contagious (pp. 13-15); and (2) possession by the ancestral spirits (pp. 15-18).

878. Kamainda, Thomas   "Le Culte des morts chez les
     1960   Balambo." Anthropos 55, nos.
                        1-2: 145-73.

The Atolo, spirits of the dead among the Balambo (Lambo) (Zaïre), serve as intermediaries between men and god. These spirits will take possession of a descendant who has neglected his obligation toward them, and only propitiation of the spirits will render him unpossessed. Also mentioned are the "nature spirits" who can render people possessed.

879. Kamer, Henri   Haute-Volta. Belgium: Gilbert
     1973   Meirsschaut, Kruishoutem. Ill.

In the introduction of this volume on African art in Upper Volta, the prevalent belief that illnesses are caused by a spirit force having "eaten" one's soul is discussed. Spirit possession is not explicitly labelled, although ritual dances are mentioned (pp. 14-17).

880. Kane, Nora S.   The World's View. London:
     1954   Cassell & Co.

The ceremonies involved in shave spirit possession among the Mashona (Shona) of Rhodesia are outlined on pages 19-21. The Mlimo cult among the Matabele (Ndebele) of Rhodesia is mentioned on pages 27-30.

881. Kaoze, Stephano   "La Psychologie des Bantu: Des
     1910   Beni-Marungu." Revue congolais
                        (Bruxelles), no. 1, pp. 406-35.

Abbé Kaoze writes of the different psychological traits of the Bantu-speaking Beni-Marungu (Lungu) of Zaïre, and mentions spirit possession by the ngulu nature spirits who give revelations and prophecies through their human instruments (pp. 428-30).

882. Karoro, Justin   "A Teacher Who Became a Spirit
     1966   Medium." Nada (Salisbury) 9,
                        no. 3: 72.

The disease of an African teacher named Enoch was diagnosed as being caused by possession by a lion spirit in Rhodesia. Enoch became the official spirit medium of his area, lives as a traditional medium, and denies his literacy. [Cited in African Abstracts, vol. 17, no. 284.]

883. Kasozi, A. B. K.   "Islam and African Institu-
     1975   tions." Makerere Historical
                               Journal (Kampala) 1, no. 1: 33-
                               36.

     In this discussion of the interaction between Islam and
traditional African social institutions, mainly in Uganda,
spirit mediumship is briefly mentioned on page 36.

884. Katz, Richard   "Education for Transcendence:
     1973   Lessons from the !Kung Zhu/-
                              twasi." Journal of Transperson-
                              al Psychology, no. 2, pp. 136-
                              55.

     Discussed from the viewpoint of the psychological
study of altered states of consciousness, material on the
healing of trance dances of the !Kung Zhu/twasi (Bushmen)
of the Kalahari Desert in northwest Botswana is presented
here.

885. Katz, Richard   "Boiling Energy: Community
     1976   Healing among the Kalahari
                              !Kung." Manuscript, Harvard
                              University.

     Very detailed material on the !Kung Bushmen (Botswana)
healing trances is presented. The trance dances are described, and emphasis is placed on the personal experience
of the trance state.

886. Kaufmann, Robert   Millénarisme et acculturation.
     1964   Bruxelles: Institut de socio-
                              logie de l'université libre de
                              Bruxelles.

     The similarities between features of African traditional
religions and the Zionist Churches include spirit possession, discussed on page 63.

887. Keirn, Susan Middleton   "Spirit Mediumship and Status
     1974   Ambiguity: Apartheid and the
                              Urban African Woman." Paper
                              presented at the American Anthro-
                              pological Association Meeting,
                              Mexico City, November. 19 pp.

     The social role of the African woman in the Republic
of South Africa is related to the institution of divination through spirit mediumship (the isangoma diviner).
Spirit possession is also discussed.

174

888. Kennedy, John G.   "Mushahara: A Nubian Concept of
     1967a   Supernatural Danger and the
                             Theory of Taboo." American
                             Anthropologist 69, no. 6: 685-
                             702.

Living in the Aswan region of Egypt, the Nubians, who
are Sunni Moslems, have an elaborate belief structure
built around the Mushahara spirit which causes illness
and misfortune. Discussed here are the ceremonies and
taboos surrounding these beliefs.

889. Kennedy, John G.   "Nubian Zar Ceremonies as Psycho-
     1967b   therapy." Human Organization
                             26, no. 4: 185-94.

The Nubians of the Sudan sometimes attribute psychological disorders to possession of the victim by spirits
called Zar. The purpose of a Zar ceremony is to cure
mental illness through contact with the possessing spirits
which cause maladies. This paper analyzes the form and
content of the Zar ceremony in an attempt to account for
its therapeutic effectiveness. [Cited in African Abstracts, vol. 21, no. 554.]

890. Kennett, B. L. A.   "The Afoshi Dancers of Kabba
     1931   Division, Northern Nigeria."
                             Journal of the Royal Anthropolo-
                             gical Institute of Great Britain
                             and Ireland 61:435-42.

Discusses: the Ebora and Egun cults of Nigeria; the
Afoshi dancers, their beginning and development; initiation to the Afoshi through spirit possession; the relation of these cults to the status of women in the
society.

891. Kenyatta, Jomo   "Kikuyu Religion, Ancestor Wor-
     1937   ship and Sacrificial Practices."
                             Africa: Journal of the Interna-
                             tional African Institute (London)
                             10, no. 3: 308-28.

Among the Kikuyu of Kenya, the most solemn religious
service is that of sacrificing to Mwenenyaga (the supreme being, also called Ngai). Elders who perform the
ceremony are held to be in direct communication with
Mwenenyaga, who gives them instructions, generally during
their sleep. Mwenenyaga assists and directs them in exe-
cuting their duty.

892. Kenyatta, Jomo   Facing Mount Kenya: The Tribal
     1962   Life of the Gikuyu. New York:
                             Vintage Books.

Chapter 11 deals with the religious sect Watu Wa Mngu
or people of god among the Gikuyu (Kikuyu) of Kenya.
These people assume the role of holy men and claim to
have direct communication with Mwene-Nyaga or God.
Their religious ceremonies are characterized by possession by the spirit of the Holy Ghost (pp. 263-64). Chapter 12 deals with the magician, his medical role and religious role as the medium for the ancestral spirits; the
reaction of Europeans to the medical practice of the
magician (pp. 270-96).

893. Kerboull, Jean   Le Vaudoo - magie ou religion?
     1973   Paris: Éditions Robert Laffont.

     This book focusses on the Haitian Vaudou (voodoo)
spirit possession cult and presents both descriptive data
and theoretical analyses.

894. Kerharo, J., and   Sorciers, féticheurs et
     A. Bouquet   guérisseurs de la Côte d'Ivoire-
     1950   Haute Volta. Paris: Vigot
                          frères.

     Discussing the peoples of the Ivory Coast and Upper
Volta, the first part of the book deals with: sorcerers,
healers, and diviners; religious beliefs on disease
causation; magic and exorcism practices. Part 2 deals
with the pharmacological aspects of disease.

895. Kerharo, J., and   "La Médecine traditionnelle des
     L. V. Thomas   Diola de Basse-Casamance."
     1963   Afrique Documents (Dakar), nos.
                          70-71, pp. 167-79.

     Spirit possession by an evil spirit is often cited as
the cause of illness among the Diola of Senegal (p. 172).

896. Kerharo, J.   "Le Facteur magico-religieux
     1969   dans l'exercice de la médecine
                          traditionnelle en milieu
                          sénégalais." Psychopathologie
                          africaine (Dakar) 5, no. 2: 269-
                          84.

     The Islamic curer, marabout, who has the ability to
communicate with spirits and to exorcise evil ones from
ill persons, the traditional curing practices of the
Wolof, Sérèr, and Lébou (Lebu) of Senegal, and the mixture
of these curing practices in the spirit possession cult of
ndop are all outlined in this article.

897. Kibirige, F.   "A Report about the Belief of
     1974   the Baganda in Spirits."
                          Occasional Research Papers in

African Traditional Religion and
Philosophy (Makerere University,
Kampala), vol. 19, no. 203.

Possession of mediums by both ancestral spirits (mizimu)
and tribal spirits (lubaale) occurs among the Baganda
(Ganda) of Uganda. Possession state is described (pp.
4-6 ff.). Comparison between these traditional beliefs
in spirits and Christianity is made.

898. Kiev, Ari   "Folk Psychiatry in Haiti."
     1961a   Journal of Nervous and Mental
                       Disease 132:260-65.

Describes: voodoo theory of personality configuration;
causation both natural and supernatural of "folie";
treatment of these "folies." If psychiatry can be defined as "a system of treatment for disorders of
thought, mood and behavior," then voodoo can be classified
as a form of folk psychiatry. Shows how the priest-
patient relationship in voodoo is similar to the Western
doctor-patient relationship.

899. Kiev, Ari   "Spirit Possession in Haiti."
     1961b   American Journal of Psychiatry
                       118, no. 2: 133-38.

Description of Haitian voodoo spirit possession by the
loas is given. The conclusion is drawn that although
becoming possessed is not in itself enough evidence for
the necessity of psychiatric treatment, ritual possession
is termed "an acceptable form of 'going crazy'" (pp. 137-
38).

900. Kiev, Ari   "Brief Note: Primitive Holistic
     1961/62   Medicine." International
                       Journal of Social Psychiatry
                       (London) 8, no. 1: 58-61.

Brief article on the manner in which the Haitian hungan,
voodoo priest, cures by means of spirit possession by the
voodoo spirits, loa.

901. Kiev, Ari   "Psychotherapy in Haitian
     1962   Voodoo." American Journal of
                       Psychotherapy 16, no. 3: 469-76.

The psychotherapeutic practices involved in the Haitian
Voodoo religion, especially those used by the voodoo
priest, are discussed here. A distinction is made between ceremonial possession trance and hysterical or
psychotic behavior, and on the basis of the degree of
success that the voodoo priest has in curing individuals,
the conclusion is drawn that further study of his
methods is needed.

902. Kiev, Ari, ed.   Magic, Faith, and Healing:
     1964a   Studies in Primitive Psychiatry
                             Today. New York: Free Press.

     Includes in this bibliography:
               423   J. Dawson (1964)
               644   M. Gelfand (1964b)
               903   A. Kiev (1964b)
               954   T. A. Lambo (1964)
              1416   R. Prince (1964b)
              1772   V. W. Turner (1964b)
              1869   M. G. Whisson (1964)

903. Kiev, Ari   "The Study of Folk Psychiatry."
     1964b   In Magic, Faith and Healing,
                            edited by A. Kiev, pp. 3-35.
                            (Bib. 902.)

     In this general theoretical article on the study of
folk psychiatry cross-culturally, the phenomenon of
spirit possession is discussed on pages 16, 21.

904. Kiev, Ari   "The Psychotherapeutic Value of
     1968   Spirit-Possession in Haiti."
                            In Trance and Possession States,
                            edited by R. Prince, pp. 143-48.
                            (Bib. 1421.)

     This article on the Haitian voodoo religion emphasizes
the fact that spirit possession is of definite psychotherapeutic value for its practitioners.

905. Kiev, Ari   Transcultural Psychiatry. New
     1972   York: Free Press.

     Spirit possession is discussed from the viewpoint of
psychiatry, and examples are drawn from African cultures
(see book's index under "Possession" for page citations).

906. Kikhela, Nguete, Gilles "La Médecine des guérisseurs
     Bibeau, Ellen Corin,   comme médecine totale." Cul-
     and Matumona-Mvunzi   tures en Zaïre et en Afrique
     1974   (Kinshasa), no. 5, pp. 7-37.

     A detailed outline is given for the study of the tra-
ditional medicines used by healers of various ethnic
groups in Zaïre. Underlying the approach is the
theoretical idea that these healing practices must be
studied as total systems with scientific rigor and
exactness. Questions concerning the nature of spirit
possession are included on pages 18-19.

907. Kilborne, Benjamin   "Symboles oniriques et modèles
     1974   culturels: Le Rêve et son in-
                                  terpretation au Maroc." Ph.D.
                                  dissertation, Universite de
                                  Paris.

     In this study a conclusion is reached that the
"strongest socially negative emotions" tend to be ex-
pressed in Morocco by the cultural themes of jinns
(evil spirits), enemies, and possession (p. 62). [Cited
in Transcultural Psychiatric Research Review (Montreal)
13 (April 1976):62-64.]

908. Kilson, Marion   "Libation in Ga Ritual."
     1969   Journal of Religion in Africa
                                  (Leiden) 2, no. 3: 161-78.

     The role of the Ga priests in southeastern Ghana as
mediums for the gods is examined in relation to the act
of libation in ritual circumstances.

909. Kilson, Marion   "Taxonomy and Form in Ga
     1970   Ritual." Journal of Religion
                                  in Africa (Leiden) 3, no. 1:
                                  44-66.

     The social position of spirit mediums among the Ga of
southeastern Ghana is mentioned in a detailed description
and theoretical analysis of a rite of planting of the
Sakumo cult. However, possession is not mentioned as a
part of this cult.

910. Kilson, Marion   Kpele Lala: Ga Religious Songs
     1971   and Symbols. Cambridge, Mass.:
                                  Harvard University Press.

     The Kpele cult of the Ga of Ghana is presented in de-
tail here. The ritual specialists of this cult include a
male priest and a female medium. The latter is chosen by
the gods to be possessed by them and thus act as a channel
of communication between man and god (see book's index
under "Possession" and "Medium" for page citations).

911. Kilson, Marion   "Ambivalence and Power: Mediums
     1972   in Ga Traditional Religion."
                                  Journal of Religion in Africa
                                  (Leiden) 4, no. 3: 171-77.

     In her analysis of contemporary Ga society in south-
eastern Ghana, the author concludes that "spirit mediumship enables women to resolve various social and psychological conflicts engendered by their sexual, repro-
ductive, and socio-economic statuses" (p. 177).

912. Kilson, Marion   "Twin Beliefs and Ceremony in
     1973   Ga Culture." _Journal of Reli-
                             gion in Africa_ (Leiden) 5, no.
                             3: 171-97.

The medium plays a central role in the twin ceremony
among the Ga people of southeastern Ghana. Theoretical
analysis and detailed description are given for this
ceremony, and mention is made of spirit possession (pp.
178 ff.).

913. Kilson, Marion   "Women in African Traditional
     1977   Religions." _Journal of Reli-
                             gion in Africa_ (Leiden) 8, no.
                             2: 133-43.

The role of spirit mediumship is discussed on pages
137-38 of this analysis of women in African traditional
religions. Ethnic groups mentioned are the Swazi (Swaziland), Yoruba (Nigeria), Bemba (Zambia), Ganda (Uganda),
and Lamba (Zambia).

914. Kilson, Marion   "Possession in Ga-Ritual."
     n.d.   Mimeographed. 3 pp.

Ga (Ghana) spirit possession and mediumship are described for novices and priestesses as being a highly
formalized, learned ritual behavior. [Cited in _Trans-
cultural Psychiatric Research Review_ (Bruges) 5 (April
1968): 67-69.]

915. Kimilu, David N.   "The Separatist Churches." _Dina
     1967   na Mila_ (Kampala) 2, nos. 2-3:
                             11-61.

The various Separatist Churches in Uganda are examined,
most of which practice possession by the Holy Spirit,
glossolalia, and exorcism. Fifty-nine songs are recorded for the "Friends of the Holy Spirit" Church, as
are its rituals.

916. King, Anne   "The Yakan Cult and Lugbara Re-
     1970   sponse to Colonial Rule."
                             Azania (Nairobi), no. 5, pp. 1-
                             24. Maps.

Article traces the interaction between the popular
Yakan or _Allah_ water cult based on spirit possession among
the Lugbara and this people's 1919 uprisings against the
British colonial government in West Nile District, Uganda.

917. King, Noel Quintin   _Religions of Africa_. New York:
     1970   Harper & Row.

180

Spirit mediumship and possession are described for the
Akan (Ghana, Ivory Coast, Togo), the Yoruba (Benin,
Nigeria), the Baganda (Ganda) (Uganda), and the Ankole
(Nkole) (Uganda) (see book's index under "Mediums" for
page citations).

918. Kinuthia, S. M.   "Wangari Margaret: 1974 Pro-
     1974   phetess Who Heard God's Voice,
                              Saw Vision, Acquired Healing
                              Power." Occasional Research
                              Papers in African Traditional
                              Religion and Philosophy
                              (Makerere University, Kampala),
                              vol. 29, no. 275.

The healing of the lunatic Waiya, who had been possessed, by the young healer and prophetess Margaret
Wangari in Kenya is described.

919. Kirk-Greene, A. H. M.   "Festival at Farei." Nigeria
     1954   (Lagos) 45:60-74.

Describes the cult of Nzeanzo found among the Bachama,
Bata, and Mbula peoples of Nigeria. Explains the mythology associated with the cult, and the activities of the
priests as intermediaries between the gods and men.

920. Kitching, Rev. A. L.   On the Backwaters of the Nile.
     1912   London: Fisher Unwin.

Discusses the manifestation of spirit possession and
its cures by a witch-doctor along the Nile in North
Africa. [Cited by Lawrance (1957, Bib. 984.]

921. Klein, Hermanson   "Changing Health Beliefs and
     1976   Practices in an Urban Setting:
                              A Tunisian Example." Ph.D.
                              dissertation, New York Univer-
                              sity. Dissertation Abstracts
                              International 37, no. 3
                              (September 1976): 1656A-57A.

Possession by the jnûn spirits in Tunisia is believed,
in the traditional view of medicine, to cause illness.

922. Kline, Nathan S.   "Applications and Misapplica-
     1961   tions of Pharmaceuticals in the
                              Treatment of West African
                              Psychiatric Disorders." In
                              First Pan-African Psychiatric
                              Conference - Proceedings, pp.
                              101-3. (Bib. 1344.)

181

The skill of "native practitioners" as psychotherapists
is emphasized by an account of an incident during a
Haitian Voo-doo (Voodoo) ceremony where a wife, possessed
by a Loa, scolded her husband for his neglect of her.

923. Klingshirn, A.   "The Trial of a Witch: A Docu-
     1971   ment from Ghana." Africana
                             Marburgensia (Marburg) 4, no. 1:
                             19-23.

The actual dialogue from a witch's confession during
her trial in Ghana in 1930 is given here with the ela-
boration of her deeds and evil spirits she possessed and
controlled.

924. Kloppenburg, Boaventura "Der Brasilianische Spiritismis
     1959   ala Religiose Gefahr." Social
                              Compass 5, nos. 5-6: 237-55.

     Not available for annotation.

925. Knutsson, Karl Eric   "Possession and Extra-institu-
     1975   tional Behavior: An Essay on
                              Anthropological Micro-analysis."
                              Ethnos (Stockholm) 40:244-72.

Following a critique of some of the current theories
on the possession phenomenon, material in the form of a
case study and detailed analysis for the Macha Galla of
Ethiopia is presented.

926. Kohler, M.   The Izangoma Diviners. Trans-
     1941   lated and edited by N. J. Van
                            Warmelo. South Africa Native
                            Affairs Department, Ethnological
                            Publications, vol. 9. Pretoria.

Detailed description of the training and practice of
the izangoma diviners among the Zulu of South Africa.
The ancestor spirits summon an individual in a dream and
then possess him. This possession is an integral element of the izangoma's practice.

927. Kokra, Ch.   "Notions de spiritisme chez les
     1956   Godie de Fresco (Côte
                            d'Ivoire)." Notes africaines
                            de l'Institut français de
                            L'Afrique noire. (Dakar) 70:52-
                            54.

Among the Godie (Godye) of the Ivory Coast particular
importance is attached to the last words uttered by a man
just before his death. If a man dies away from his home,
members of his family will perform a burial ritual where

182

they will substitute a palm branch for the body. A relative of the deceased will invoke the spirit of the dead man to reveal his final words. This invocation is done through spirit possession. [Cited in African Abstracts, vol. 8, no. 16.]

928. Koss, Joan D. "Social Process and Behavior
      1975   Change in Puerto Rican Spiritist
                      Cults." In Caribbean Cults:
                      Individual and Social Change,
                      edited by D. Hogg and J. Koss.
                      San Juan: University of Puerto
                      Rico Press.

Not available for annotation.

929. Krieger, Kurt   "Notizen zur Religion der
      1967   Hausa." Paideuma (Frankfurt)
                      13:96-121. Ill.

This study, focussing on the town of Anka, East Sokoto province of northern Nigeria, describes the various characteristics and activities of isoki spirits which are widely believed in, although most of the Hausa inhabitants confess to being Muslim. Possession cults (bori) and spirit mediums are an important part of religious life.

930. Krige, Eileen Jensen   The Social System of the Zulus.
      1936   London: Longmans, Green & Co.

Diviners among the Zulus of South Africa are thought to be possessed by spirits. Initial calling is sent as an illness by the spirits. Description of the possession state is presented (pp. 299 ff.).

931. Krige, Eileen Jensen   "The Place of the North-eastern
      1938   Transvaal Sotho in the South
                             Bantu Complex." Africa:
                             Journal of the International
                             African Institute (London) 11,
                             no. 3: 265-93.

Among the Sotho of Transvaal, South Africa, some native doctors are associated with a spirit possession cult. There is no special initiation into the cult. People are originally possessed while dancing to the beat of a drum. They are possessed by ancestor spirits, and only those who are possessed by spirits of former native doctors become doctors themselves. They use their spirits to guide them in divination and curing.

932. Krige, J. D., and   Realm of a Rain Queen. London:
      E. J. Krige   Oxford University Press.
      1943

A spirit possession cult was introduced among the
Lovedu people (South Africa) about 1913. Comparison of
spirit possession as it occurs among the Shangana-Tonga
(South Africa) with that of the Lovedu cult; description
of possession dances; a very detailed account of initiation into the cult (chap. 13, pp. 241-47; chap. 12).

933. Krige, J. D., and   "The Lovedu of the Transvaal."
     E. J. Krige   In African Worlds, edited by D.
     1954   Forde. (Bib. 588.)

     One kind of doctor found among the Lovedu (South Africa)
is the Lelopo, directly possessed and guided by an ancestor spirit, who largely confines his activities to
curing possessed people (p. 62).

934. Kronenberg, A.   "Some Notes on the Religion of
     1959   the Nyimang." Kush (Khartoum)
                           7:197-213.

     Concerns the Nyimang (Nyima) of the Nuba Hills (Sudan).
Spirit possession is described. A possessed man may be
initiated into the priesthood and thus gain a great deal
of prestige in the society. [Cited in African Abstracts,
vol. 12, no. 248.]

935. Kudadjie, Joshua N.   "Aspects of Religion and Morality
     1975   in Ghanaian Traditional Society
                           with Particular Reference to the
                           Ga-Adangme." Conch (Buffalo,
                           N.Y.) 7, nos. 1-2: 26-52.

     The Ga of Ghana believe that ancestral spirits may send
illness and misfortune to the living, and, through possessed persons and mediums, the spirits can make their
wishes known (pp. 33-34).

936. Kumwimba, Mwilambwe   Muntu, animisme et possessions.
     Kahoto Wa   Série essais,no. 9.
     1974   Lubumbashi: Editions du Mont
                          Noir.

     A theoretical and philosophical analysis of spirits,
spirit possession, and man's relationship to the spirit
world is presented by the author.

937. Kuntz, Marthe   "Les Rites occultes et la
     1932   sorcellerie sur le Haut-Zambèse."
                          Journal de la Société des
                          africanistes (Paris) 2, no. 1:
                          123-38.

     From observations of the ma-Lozi (Lozi), ma-Kwangwa
(Kwangwa), ma-Mbowe (Mbowe), and ma-Lubale (Lubale) of

184

northwest Rhodesia (Zambia), cases of "man-lions" are mentioned who are possessed by the spirit of an animal and can change their form into lions and other animals, and of diviners who have mediumistic powers and who exorcise evil spirits from people through the use of dance.

938. Kuper, Hilda   "The Swazi Reaction to Missions."
     1946   African Studies (Johannesburg)
                            5, no. 3: 177-88.

     The relationship between the Christian notion of possession by the Holy Spirit and the traditional Swazi (South Africa) practice of possession by ancestral spirits for divination is discussed on pages 187-88.

939. Kuper, Hilda   An African Aristocracy: Rank
     1947a   among the Swazi. London:
                            Oxford University Press.

     Swazi diviners (South Africa) are entered by spirits who give them their skills; the nature of the possessing spirits; treatment of possession; resistance to possession; spirit possession and the role of women in the society (chap. 11, pp. 163-66). Spirit possession as an outlet for the maladjusted in Swazi culture (chap. 14, p. 227).

940. Kuper, Hilda   The Uniform of Colour: A Study
     1947b   of White-Black Relationships in
                            Swaziland. Johannesburg:
                            Witwatersrand University Press.

     Illness and death through being possessed by wild animals are recorded among the Swazi of Swaziland, South Africa (p. 79). The relationship between the missionary and the magician is discussed with regard to being possessed by the Holy Spirit and by ancestral spirits (pp. 126 ff.).

941. Kuper, Hilda, A. J. B.   The Shona and Ndebele of Southern
     Hughes, and J. Van   Rhodesia. Ethnographic Survey
     Velsen   of Africa, edited by Daryll
     1954   Forde, vol. 4. no. 4. London:
                            International African Institute.

     Among the Shona and the Ndebele of Rhodesia, spirit possession plays a role in both divination and spirit propitiation. The members of the Lozwi subtribe sometimes undergo possession while dancing. Possessed persons forget how to speak Ndebele and must be addressed in a Shona dialect. They are addressed by the name of the possessing spirit (p. 106). Among the Zansi and Enhla subtribes divination is carried out by individuals called izangoma

185

who become possessed while dancing, and who can, in this state, "smell out" witches (p. 107). Most diviners are women (p. 94).

942. Kuper, Hilda   "An Ethnographic Description of
      1959   Kavady, a Hindu Ceremony in
                      South Africa." African Studies
                      (Johannesburg) 18, no. 3: 118-
                      32.

Among the Hindu population of South Africa, the god Subrahmanya is worshipped in a ceremony called Kavady. In the ceremony, worshippers who have gained the aid of the deity against sickness pledge themselves to the deity for a period of years. During the ceremonies, these people go into trances which are believed to be caused by the deity entering their bodies. While possessed, these people are believed to have the god's power and wisdom. Several instances of possession are described in detail.

943. Kuper, Hilda   Indian People in Natal. Natal:
      1960   Natal Witness, Ltd., at the
                      University Press.

Chapter 12 gives a detailed analysis of the various features of possession trance states in Hindu religion among the Indians of Natal, South Africa. The possession trance is evaluated as being "good" or "bad" according to the nature of the god possessing the person; if it is an evil god, then exorcism practices must be employed.

944. Kuper, Hilda   The Swazi: A South African King-
      1963   dom. New York: Holt, Rinehart
                      & Winston.

Discusses symptoms of possession among the Swazi (South Africa); frequency of women becoming possessed; prophets of certain Separatist churches who carry on exorcism of possession and are said to be possessed by the spirit of the Holy Ghost (chap. 6, pp. 62-65).

945. La Barre, Weston   "Materials for a History of
      1971   Studies of Crisis Cults: A Bib-
                      liographic Essay." Current
                      Anthropology 12:3-44.

The author discusses on pages 4-5 of the article some of the African crisis cults and movements. Spirit possession is a feature prevalent in many of these cults. The article summarizes materials for other parts of the world as well. This bibliographic essay is useful for cross-cultural research since it offers not only a geographical survey but also topical discussions and considerations of methodology and terminology.

946. Lachatanere, Romulo   Manuel de Santería. La Habana.
     1942   Editorial Caribe.

     Not available for annotation.

947. Lafargue, Fernand   "Le Komyen chez les Baoulé."
     1971   Cahiers des religions africaines
                                (Kinshasa) 5, no. 10: 241-69.

     Spirit possession in the Komyen cult of divination a-
     mong the Akan-speaking Baoulé of Ghana is discussed on
     pages 262 ff.

948. La Fontaine, J. S.   The Gisu of Uganda. Ethno-
     1959   graphic Survey of Africa, edited
                                by Daryll Forde, vol. 2, no. 10.
                                London: International African
                                Institute.

     Deals with circumcision rites among the Gisu of
     Uganda. The skill to circumcise is inherited in certain
     partrilines. A man or woman belonging to a lineage pos-
     sessing the skill can be attacked by a kind of hysteria
     while watching a circumcision; this kind of possession
     syndrome allows the individual to learn the skill. De-
     scription of initiation into the role of circumciser
     (pp. 55-56).

949. Lagae, C. R.   "Les Procédés d'augure et de
     1921   divination chez les Azande."
                                Congo: Revue générale de la
                                colonie belge (Bruxelles), pp.
                                709-30.

     Among the Azande of Zaïre, diviners, through various
     methods such as using divination tools, through drugs,
     and through a trance state (not possession trance), are
     able to discern the bad spirits that are causing illness
     or misfortune by possessing an individual (pp. 723-30).

950. Laguerre, Michel   "Le Tambour et la danse reli-
     1972   gieuse dans la liturgie
                                chrétienne en Haiti." Revue du
                                clergé africain (Inkisi) 27, 6:
                                587-603.

     The great importance of the drum and dance both in the
     Haitian voodoo spirit possession cult and in the Chris-
     tian liturgy of that island is emphasized.

951. Laman, Karl   The Kongo. Vol. 3.
     1962   Studia Ethnographica Upsaliensia,
                                vol. 12. Uppsala.

The Nkisi cult among the Kongo (Zaïre) is dedicated to the spirits of the deceased who wish "to appear . . . in order to be worshipped and invoked." The Nkisi spirits may possess people and the latter may be cured only by becoming priests in service of the former (pp. 67-71; 76 ff., 95 ff., 132).

952. Lambo, L.   "Étude sur les Balala." Bulle-
     1946   tin de juridictions indigènes
                      et du droit coutumier congolais
                      (Elizabethville), 8:231-56; 9:
                      273-300; 10:313-46.

This study includes information on spiritism, spirit possession, and mediumistic experiences among the Balala of Zaïre.

953. Lambo, T. Adeoye   "Further Neuropsychiatric Ob-
     1960   servations in Nigeria."
                        British Medical Journal (London)
                        2:1696-1704.

The major types of mental illnesses found in Nigeria are outlined. Anxiety states among the psychoneuroses include those illnesses considered by traditional cultures to be caused by spirit possession; the author calls these "malignant" anxiety states or "frenzied anxiety" ("bouffée confusionnelle délirante") (p. 1701).

954. Lambo, T. Adeoye   "Patterns of Psychiatric Care in
     1964   Developing African Countries."
                        In Magic, Faith and Healing,
                        edited by A. Kiev, pp. 443-53.
                        (Bib. 902.)
     The paper, first, describes general aspects of African traditional beliefs and customs; second, it examines experiences in Nigeria that have involved integration of modern and traditional methods of psychiatric treatments. Some discussion of spirit possession (pp. 443-53).

955. Landes, Ruth   "A Cult Matriarchate and Male
     1940a   Homosexuality." Journal of Ab-
                       normal and Social Psychology,
                       July.

Discussion of the Candomblé and Caboclo cults of Bahia, Brazil. Analysis of the similarities and differences in the social structure of these cults. Spirit possession is common in both cases. Male homosexuals may become priests of the Caboclo cults.

956. Landes, Ruth   "Fetish Worship in Brazil."
     1940b   Journal of American Folklore 53,
                       no. 210: 261-70.

188

Discusses forms of spirit possession found in Bahia, Brazil, where priestesses of certain cults become possessed by the deities; discusses the structural organization of these cults; compares African influences within the Caribbean areas; observes that possession and mediumship experiences seem to be universal, though in some varying contexts.

957. Lane, Edward William   The Manners and Customs of the
     Before 1928   Modern Egyptians. Everyman's
                            Library, no. 315. London: Dent.

Certain Islamic rites in Egypt are described in which voluntary inducement of epilepsy is practiced (p. 45). [Cited by Willoughby (1928, Bib. 1763), p. 110.]

958. Lane, Eric   "Prophecy and Power in Rwanda
     1972   and Malawi." Paper presented at
                            the Conference on the History
                            of Central African Religious
                            Systems, Lusaka, 30 August -
                            8 September.

The role of the prophetic tradition in relation to sacred kingship is presented for the Rwanda (Ruanda) (Rwanda) and the Basukwa (Sukwa) (Malawi). Possessed prophets have a great deal of social and political power that may supersede the power of the king.

959. Langguth, A. J.   Macumba: White and Black Magic
     1975   in Brazil. New York: Harper
                            & Row.

Author provides a very detailed description of Macumba ceremonies involving spirit possession. The author describes his field research experiences in vivid and personal terms. A list of Afro-Brazilian gods is presented at the end of the volume.

960. Langworthy, H. W.   "The Political and Religious
     1968/69   Elite in the History of Undi's
                            Malawi Empire." In History
                            Papers, University of East
                            Africa Social Sciences Council
                            Conference, pp. 122-37.
                            Kampala: Makerere Institute of
                            Social Research.

Spirit mediumship among the Chewa of Malawi is mentioned on pages 127-28 in this historical study of the origins and growth of the Undi Empire.

961. Langworthy, Harry W.   "Conflict among Rulers in the
     1971   History of Undi's Chewa King-
                              dom." Transafrican Journal of
                              History (Nairobi) 1, no. 1: 1-
                              23.

Spirit mediumship is not explicitly labelled, but its
historical use in the Chewa Kingdom spanning parts of
Zambia, Malawi, and Mozambique is implied on pages 9 ff.

962. Langworthy, Harry W.   "Chewa or Malawi Political Or-
     1972   ganization in the Precolonial
                              Era." In The Early History of
                              Malawi, edited by Bridglal
                              Pachai, pp. 104-22. Evanston,
                              Ill.: Northwestern University
                              Press.

The sociopolitical role of the Chewa (Malawi) spirit
mediums is discussed on pages 111-12.

963. Lankester, Sir Ray   Daily Telegraph (London), April
     1914   23, 1914.

An epidemic of dancing mania was apparently caused
from the bite of a large spider (Lycosta tarantula).
The bite of the spider was supposed to have caused sleepi-
ness which could only be cured by music which set the
bitten one dancing. This phenomenon was deemed an im-
posture by Tarantese peasants. [Cited by Jeffreys (1953,
Bib. 853).]

964. Lanternari, Vittorio   The Religions of the Oppressed.
     1963   New York: Alfred A. Knopf.

Spirit mediumship is used in the Lukusu society among
the Bashilele (Lele) peoples of the Kasai region of
Zaire (p. 10). Spirit possession in the South African
Independent Church movement is discussed on pages 37-44.
Spirit possession is also mentioned on pages 61, 159-65
(the Jamaican revivalist cults) and pages 165-96 (the
Haitian voodoo cult).

965. Lanternari, Vittorio   "Dreams as Charismatic Signifi-
     1975   cants: Their Bearing on the Rise
                              of New Religious Movements."
                              In Psychological Anthropology,
                              edited by T. R. Williams, pp.
                              221-35. The Hague: Mouton.

Spirit possession, glossolalia, and ecstatic trance are
mentioned in the context of the rise of new religious
movements in Africa. The Ghanaian Action Church is
specifically discussed.

966. Lantier, Jacques   La Cité magique. Paris:
     1972   Librairie Arthème Fayard.

     Spirit possession and exorcism are discussed at length
     in chapter 7 for the following ethnic groups: Mora
     (Cameroon), Louba (Luba) (Zaïre), Bénin (Edo) (Togo),
     Kirdi (Nigeria).

967. Lanzas, A., and   "Les Fidèles d'un 'nouvelle
     G. Bernard   église' au Congo." Genève-
     1966   Afrique 5, no. 2:189-216.

     Descriptions of the mediumship and rituals of l'Église
     apostolique africaine, founded in Lusaka (Zambia) in
     1927, are given for Leopoldville, Congo (now Kinshasa,
     Zaire). Its various celebrations and practices, which
     include the laying on of hands and glossolalia, provide
     a substitute for traditional structures for those Luba
     and Lulua who have newly arrived in the urban environ-
     ment.

968. Laoye, H. H.   "Yoruba Drums." Nigeria (Lagos)
     1954   24:4-13.

     Description of different kinds of drums, some used for
     possession ceremonies among the Yoruba of Nigeria.

969. Laroche, Maximilien   "Mythe africaine et mythe
     1975   antillais: Le Personnage du
                              zombi." Canadian Journal of
                              African Studies (Montreal) 9,
                              no. 3: 479-91.

     Although spirit possession is not explicitly discussed,
     this article deals with the African and Caribbean (main-
     ly Haitian) notion of the zombi, the "living dead."

970. La Roche, Robert   La Divination. Washington, D.C.:
     1957   Catholic University of America
                              Press.

     Spirit mediumship and possession are mentioned through-
     out this work on divination and African religious systems.

971. Larson, Thomas J.   "The Spirits of the Ancestors
     1971   and the Mandengure Ceremony of
                              the Hambukushu of Ngamiland."
                              Anthropos 66, nos. 1-2:52-70.
                              Ill.

     When a person is possessed by an ancestor spirit among
     the Hambukushu, a small matrilineal Bantu group of
     Barotseland origin (now in Zambia), a specialist in di-
     vination and medicines is called in. During the course

                                191

of a prolonged ritual, the proper propitiation for the
ancestor and treatment for the patient are specified.

972. Last, Murray   "A Note of Attitudes to the
     1967   Supernatural in the Sokoto
                           Jihad." Journal of the Histori-
                           cal Society of Nigeria 4, no. 1:
                           3-13.

In a historical account of the role the supernatural
played in the Sokoto jihad of Nigeria, mention is made
of possession by several of the many Hausa spirits including the bori.

973. Laszlo, Andreas E.   Doctors, Drums and Dances.
     1955   New York: Hanover House.

The author describes a dance ceremony he witnessed
which was performed as a cure for a possessed woman. In
a very detailed description, he suggests that the kind of
convulsions the possessed woman experienced are symptomatic of epilepsy. Information for Angola (chap. 7).

974. Latere, Ama-Bulie   "Le Devin, le féticheur et le
     1975   sorcier dans le theatre zaïros
                            de langue française." Zaïre-
                            Afrique (Kinshasa), no. 98,
                            pp. 467-83.

After discussing theoretically the diviner,
"féticheur," and sorcerer in African society, the author
pays particular attention to the way in which these
social roles are portrayed in the French-speaking
theater of Zaïre. Mention is made of spirit possession
in these various roles (pp. 468-70).

975. Latham, C. J. K.   "The Social Organization of the
     1974   Mashona." Nada (Salisbury) 11,
                           no. 1: 96-108.

The role of the svikiro spirit mediums in the Mashona
(Shona) (Rhodesia) sociopolitical organization is discussed.

976. Latham, C. J. K.   "Some Notes on the Tribes in
     1975   the Mount Darwin, Rushinga and
                           Centenary Districts." Nada
                           (Salisbury) 11, no. 2: 168-80.

After some introductory remarks about the
"shamanistic" religion found among the Shona-speaking
peoples of Rhodesia and its tradition of spirit-possession, the author presents a summary of the different
chiefdoms in the Mount Darwin, Rishinga, and Centenary
Districts of Rhodesia and specifies the tribal spirits
of each one.

977. Laubscher, B. J. F.   Sex, Custom and Psychopathology.
     1937   London: G. Routledge & Sons.

     An in-depth investigation into the beliefs and prac-
tices of the Tembu group of the Southeastern Cape Bantu
(South Africa) is presented in this work. The specific
focus is on the psychology and psychopathology of these
people with regard to Western psychiatric diagnoses.
Mediumship is mentioned throughout the text, but most
references are to be found in chapter 3.

978. Laurentin, Anne   "Nzakara Women (Central African
     1963   Republic)." In Women of
                               Tropical Africa, edited by
                               Denise Paulme. Berkeley:
                               University of California Press.

     Two accounts of possession: first, description of a
Togbo woman becoming possessed by her Gassuluma; second,
description of the Gambo cult and the priestess who was
possessed by Gambo among the Nzakara (Central African
Empire) (pp. 156-57, 166-67).

979. Laurenty, J. S.   "Les Cordophones du Congo belge
     1960   et du Ruanda-Urundi." Annales
                               du Musée royal du Congo belge
                               (Tervuren), Sciences de l'homme,
                               n.s. 2:1-230.

     In this very detailed description of the stringed in-
struments found in Zaire, in Rwanda, and in Burundi,
brief mention is made of the use of these instruments in
the exorcism of evil spirits among the Hum, Hungana, and
Dikidiki (pp. 177-78).

980. Laurioz, Jacques   "Notes sur les pratiques rela-
     1969   tives aux génies 'zar' en
                               TFAI." Pount (Djibouti) 7:5-12.

     In the French Territory of Afar and Issas (TFAI) (now
Djibouti), the zar cult, imported from Ethiopia, appeals
almost entirely to women, as it gives them rights and
privileges not available to them elsewhere in their
societies. Description is given of the diagnostic and
healing ceremonies, and of the mythological origins of
the zar spirits.

981. Lavignotte, H.   "L'Evur. Croyance des Pahouins
     1947   du Gabon." Paris: Société des
                               missions évangéliques.

     The Evur is an animal that lives in the body of its
possessor among the Pahouins (Fang) of Gabon; it allows
its host to form a spirit personality, and often can

193

leave the host and act in his place. The nature and manifestations of the Evur are described.

982. Lawal, Babatunde   "The Living Dead: Art and Im-
      1977   mortality among the Yoruba of
                           Nigeria." Africa: Journal of
                           the International African
                           Institute (London) 47, no. 1:
                           50-61.

Detailed discussion is given of the "living dead" a-
mong the Yoruba of Nigeria. Although spirit possession
is not explicitly labelled, the forms of reincarnation
involve either an ancestor spirit who is reborn in a
baby, or a spirit child, abiku ("born to die"), who
steals the womb of the expectant mother.

983. Lawrence, Edward   Spiritualism among Civilized and
      1921   Savage Races. London: A. & C.
                           Black. Ill.

Some discussion of mediumship experiences in Africa
(p. 70, illustration of a female medium).

984. Lawrance, J. C. D.   The Iteso. London: Oxford
      1957   University Press.

Among the Teso of East Africa, witch-doctors (mostly
- women) cure those individuals possessed by a spirit.
The doctors serve as mediums to various spirits. Rain-
making ceremonies are described as well as the cult of
witch-doctors. Text of ceremonial songs available (pt.
5, chap. 4, pp. 182-88).

985. Laydevant, F.   "Religious or Sacred Plants of
      1932   Basutoland." Bantu Studies 6:
                           65-69.

Description of the usage of plants to produce states of
intoxication during ceremonies among the Basuto (Sotho)
(South Africa) (a phenomenon related to drug-induced
possession). Also, brief mention of the plants used by
native doctors to cure victims of hysteria (p. 67).

986. Lea, Allen   The Native Separatist Church
      n.d. (1926)   Movement in South Africa. Cape
                           Town: Juta & Co.

Reported in this book are the different Native Separatist Churches to be found in South Africa. Among these
is the sect called the "Resurrectionists," headed by a
woman of the Bantu Presbyterian Church who was divinely
inspired by God. She becomes possessed by an evil spirit
while preaching, a sign of the sins of the people. Her

return to normal consciousness is a sign of resurrection through repentance (pp. 47-48).

987. Leacock, Seth
1964a
"Ceremonial Drinking in an Afro-Brazilian Cult." _American Anthropologist_ 66, no. 2: 344-54.

The relationship between possession by deities and ceremonial drinking is elaborated for the Afro-Brazilian cult of _Batuque_.

988. Leacock, Seth
1964b
"Fun-loving Deities in an Afro-Brazilian Cult." _Anthropological Quarterly_ 37, no. 3: 94-109.

The _Batuque_ cult in the Brazilian Amazon city of Belém is very similar to the _Candomblé_ cult of Bahia (Brazil) and employs spirit possession. The _caboclo_ deities possess individuals mainly to have a good time, and are originally of African origin.

989. Leacock, Seth
1974
"Espiritismo and Dynamic Syncretism in Belém, Brazil." Paper presented at the American Anthropological Association meeting, Mexico City, November 1974. 6 pp.

Although the African influence on the Brazilian _espiritismo_ religions, which involve spirit possession and mediumship, is not explicitly stated, mention is made of the _Umbanda_ cult. Specific data are presented for Belém, Brazil, in the Amazonia region.

990. Leacock, Seth, and
Ruth Leacock
1975
Spirits of the Deep: A Study of an Afro-Brazilian Cult. Garden City, N.Y.: Doubleday & Co., Anchor Press. Ill.

This volume contains an extremely detailed study of the Afro-Brazilian cult of _Batuque_ flourishing in the Amazonian city of Belém. Spirit possession of mediums, discussed throughout, is dealt with specifically in chapter 6.

991. Lebeer, Paul
1956
"Voodoo in the Belgian Congo." _Belgian Congo Today_ (Brussels) 5, no. 3: 111-16.

Among the Lokele of Zaïre, there is a belief that evil sorcerers can remove the soul of an individual and in that way possess them.

992. Lebeuf, Annie   Les Populations du Tchad.
     1959   Monographies ethnologiques
                           africaines, vol. 6. Paris:
                           Institut international
                           africain.

Among the Kotoko of Chad, spirit possession dances are
employed as a healing technique (p. 60).

993. Lebeuf, J. P.   "Santé mentale et 'possession.'"
     1958   In Mental Disorders and Mental
                           Health in Africa South of the
                           Sahara, pp. 164-67.
                           CCTA/CSA-WFMF-WHO, Pub. no. 35.
                           Bukavu.

An argument is presented for the importance of ethnographic data in the research into and treatment of mental
illnesses including spirit possession. The religious
institutionalization of such "psychopathies" as inte-
grative devices is emphasized.

994. Lechaptois, Monseigneur   Aux rives du Tanganyika.
     1932   Maison-Carrée: Imprimerie des
                               Pères Blancs.

Although spirit possession is not explicitly labelled,
the Africans (no specified group) of Tanganyika (now
Tanzania) have rituals of exorcism of evil spirits that
cause illness (pp. 192-93).

995. Lee, Richard B.   "The Sociology of !Kung Bushman
     1968   Trance Performances." In Trance
                           and Possession States, edited
                           by R. Prince, pp. 35-54. (Bib.
                           1421.)

The healing trance dances and the psychological states
achieved in them by the !Kung Bushmen of the Kalahari
Desert of Bechuanaland (Botswana) are described in detail here.

996. Lee, S. G.   "Social Influences in Zulu
     1958   Dreaming." Journal of Social
                           Psychology 47:265-83.

Ukuthwasa possession by the ancestors is briefly mentioned as occurring among the Isangoma diviners of the
Zulu (South Africa) (p. 265). Major focus of the article
is on the use of dreams in this culture.

997. Lee, S. G.   "Spirit Possession among the
     1969   Zulu." In Spirit Mediumship and
                           Society in Africa, edited by

J. Beattie and J. Middleton,
pp. 128-56. (Bib. 150.)

Many forms of possession occur among the Zulus of
South Africa. Amandwa possession is a form of ancestor
possession, and cult members act as diviners and healers.
Ukuthwasa is another form of ancestor possession, and a
similar form of possession exists among members of
Zionist churches. In both cases, this activity is believed to be a therapy for both constitutional neurosis
and immediate social deprivation.

998. Leeson, Joyce, and   "The Patients of Traditional
     Ronald Frankenberg   Doctors in Lusaka." African
     1977   Social Research (Lusaka), no.
                             23, pp. 217-34.

Brief mention is made of spirit possession illnesses on
page 218 of this article on the persistence and use of
traditional doctors, ng'anga, in Lusaka, Zambia.

999. Le Guerinel, N.   "Etude des cas cliniques à
     1968   Bingerville (Côte d'Ivoire)."
                             Psychopathologie africaine
                             (Dakar) 4, no. 1: 7-54.

One of two clinical cases reported from the psychiatric
hospital of Bingerville, Ivory Coast, has to do with a
Dida woman suffering from anxiety neurosis brought on
by being prohibited from giving free verbal and gestural
expression to possession by her dead husband's spirit
during his funeral ceremony.

1000. Lehman, F. Rudolph   "Some Field Notes on the
      1951   Nyakyusa." Sociologus (Berlin),
                             n.s. 1, no. 1:53-68; 1, no. 2:
                             138-48.

An account of the initiation of a medicine man into his
profession among the Nyakyusa (Tanzania).

1001. Lehman, J. P.   "Quelques aspects des thérapeuti-
      1968   ques traditionneles." In
                             Deuxieme Colloque africain de
                             psychiatrie - Proceedings, pp.
                             96-103. (Bib. 1345.)

The role of spirit possession in both causing and curing
illness is examined in this article. No specific ethnic
group is discussed in detail, although most information
seems to come from Abidjan, Ivory Coast.

1002. Lehman, Jean-Pierre   "La Fonction thérapeutique du
      1972a   discours prophétique." Psycho-
                             pathologie africaine (Dakar) 8,

197

no. 3: 355-82.

Although spirit possession is not explicitly labelled
as a cause of disease, this article is directly concerned with healers, prophets, medicine men, and
shamans who use spiritual sources to cure illnesses.

1003. Lehman, J. P.   "Le Vécu corporel et ses inter-
      1972b   pretations en pathologie
                             africaine. A propos de inhibi-
                             tions corporelles en milieu
                             scholaire." Revue de médecine
                             psychosomatique 14:43-67.

Written about African peoples in general, the ideas of
the body with regard to spirit possession are examined.
Possession comes as punishment for or protection from
sin and guilt. [Cited in Transcultural Psychiatric Research Review (Montreal) 10 (April 1973): 53-57.]

1004. Leighton, A. H., and   "Yoruba Concepts of Psychiatric
      J. M. Hughes   Disorder." In First Pan-African
      1961   Psychiatric Conference - Pro-
                             ceedings, pp. 138-41.
                             (Bib. 1344.)

Although spirit possession is not explicitly labelled,
mention is made of the Yoruba (Nigeria) belief that all
mental illnesses are "the result of magic or the work of
spirits" (p. 141).

1005. Leighton, A. H., et al. Psychiatric Disorder among the
      1963   Yoruba. Ithaca, N.Y.: Cornell
                               University Press.

A report on psychic disorders among Yoruba near
Abeokuta, Nigeria. The case of a woman with symptoms of
schizophrenia is discussed. The woman, a member of an
African-Christian sect, claimed that St. Michael had possessed her thirty years previously. She claimed to have
had regular contact with St. Michael since that time
(pp. 119-20).

1006. Leiris, Michel   "Le Taureau de SeyFu Tchenger
      1933   (Zar)." Minotaure (Paris), no.
                            2, pp. 75-82.

Among Ethiopians, most diseases are blamed on spirits
called Zar. Zar-created illnesses are cured by inducing
the spirit to possess its victim. It is then induced to
become benevolent. Description of such a ceremony.

1007. Leiris, Michel   "Le Culte des Zars à Gondar."
      1934   Aethiopica (New York) 2, no. 3:
                            96-103.

198

Among Ethiopians, many illnesses are attributed to
possession by Zar spirits. To cure victims of the
spirits, the Zar are induced to possess their victims and
speak through them. Various rites are then used to placate the spirit and then make it benevolent.

1008. Leiris, Michel　　　　　"Une Rite médico-magique
　　　　1935　　　　　　　　éthiopien." Aethiopica (New
　　　　　　　　　　　　　　York) 3, no. 2: 61-74.

Among Ethiopians, many illnesses are attributed to possession by Zar spirits. In order to cure the possessed
person, the spirit is not exorcised, but, rather, it is
transformed into a benevolent spirit.

1009. Leiris, Michel　　　　　"La Croyance aux génies 'zar' en
　　　　1938　　　　　　　　Étiopie du nord." Journal de la
　　　　　　　　　　　　　　psychologie normale et patholo-
　　　　　　　　　　　　　　gique 35:108-25.

Psychological interpretations of the phenomenon of Zar
spirit possession as it occurs in Ethiopia.

1010. Leiris, Michel　　　　　La Langue secrète des Dogons de
　　　　1948　　　　　　　　Sanga. Travaux et mémoires de
　　　　　　　　　　　　　　l'Institut d'ethnologie, vol.
　　　　　　　　　　　　　　50. Paris: Université de Paris.

Spirit possession among the Dogon of Mali is discussed
in various contexts but is mainly used in religious contexts (see book's index under "Possession" for page
citations).

1011. Leiris, Michel　　　　　"Sacrifice d'un taureau chez le
　　　　1950　　　　　　　　Houngan Jo Pierre-Gilles."
　　　　　　　　　　　　　　Haïti: Poètes noirs. Présence
　　　　　　　　　　　　　　africaine (Paris), no. 12, pp.
　　　　　　　　　　　　　　22-36.

The possession trances and rituals surrounding the
sacrifice of a bull are described for the Haitian vodou
religion.

1012. Leiris, Michel　　　　　La Possession et ses aspects
　　　　1958a　　　　　　　théâtraux chez les Étiopiens de
　　　　　　　　　　　　　　Gondar. Paris: Librairie Plon.

The entire book is devoted to the study of spirit possession as it occurs in the Zar cults of Ethiopia. The
author examines possession as it functions for the individual and the community as a whole.

1013. Leiris, M.   "La Possession par le Zar chez
      1958b   les chrétiens du nord de
                                l'Etiopie." In Mental Disorders
                                and Mental Health in Africa South
                                of the Sahara, pp. 168-75.
                                CCTA/CSA-WFMF-WHO, Pub. no. 35.
                                Bukavu.

Discussion of possession; self-inflicted injuries
during states of possession having a penitential value
for the possessed in the Zar cult of Ethiopia.

1014. Lem, F. H.   "Le Culte des arbres et des
      1948   génies protecteurs du sol au
                                Soudan français." Bulletin de
                                l'Institut français de
                                l'Afrique noire 10:539-59.

Discussion of the Da Siri Dugu, or protecting spirit
of a village in the Sudan, and description of a cult devoted to this spirit. Author gives some of the religious and social beliefs of the cult members. Mediumship
experiences reported.

1015. Lembezat, Bertrand   Les Populations païennes du
      1961   Nord-Cameroun et de l'Adamaou.
                                Monographies ethnologiques
                                africaines, vol. 7. Paris:
                                Institut international africain.

In north Cameroon the Toupouri (Tuburi) and the Massa
(Masa) believe that an individual may become spirit possessed. Sometimes this possession may give the person
psychic powers and the gift of prophecy; at other times
ceremonial dances are held to exorcise the demons which
are causing illness and misfortune (pp. 104-5).

1016. Leonard, Arthur Glyn   The Lower Niger and Its Tribes.
      1906   London: Macmillan & Co.

Discussion of spirit possession with ethnographic accounts from the Niger Delta, Nigeria. Also, description
of exorcism of spirit possession (sec. 5, chaps. 1-5, pp.
227-71).

1017. Lepage, André   "L'Organisation du prophétisme
      n.d.   kongo." Cultures et développe-
                                ment (Louvain) 2, no. 2: 407-25.

A theoretical analysis of the phenomenon of prophetism
in Zaire is presented, and possession by the Holy Spirit
and by evil spirits is discussed (pp. 410 ff.).

200

1018. Leroux, H.   "Animisme et Islam dans la sub-
      1948   division de Maradi (Niger)."
                                   Bulletin de l'Institut Français
                                   de l'Afrique Noire 10:595-697.

      Religious beliefs of the Datwenawa and Goberawa (Hausa)
      people of Niger; mediumship experiences of diviners re-
      ported.

1019. Le Roy, Alexander   The Religion of the Primitives.
      1922   New York: Macmillian Co.

      A missionary account based on travels in South Africa,
      Cameroon, Congo, and Gabon and dealing mainly with Bantu
      religion. One manifestation of the world of spirits is
      possession. Spirit possession can sometimes cause ill-
      ness. In such cases a sorcerer induces the spirit to pos-
      sess the patient and speak through him. The sorcerer
      asks the spirit who he is, why he entered the body, what
      he requires, etc. (pp. 228-29).

1020. Lerrigo, P. H. J.   "The 'Prophet Movement' in
      1922   Congo." International Review of
                                   Missions 10, no. 42: 270-77.

      The rise of the Kimbangu Movement in Zaïre is dis-
      cussed and mention is made of the "shaking" manifested
      by its followers (p. 274). Possession by the Holy Spirit
      is not explicitly labelled.

1021. Leslau, Wolf   "An Ethiopian Argot of People
      1949   Possessed by a Spirit." Africa:
                                   Journal of the International
                                   African Institute (London) 30,
                                   no. 3: 204-12.

      The Zar possession cult of Ethiopia is said to have
      been invented by women in order to gain increased liberty.
      Members of the cult had frequent opportunities to be a-
      way from their families at night. Description of cere-
      monies to control Zar spirits is given. The language
      used during possession is analyzed.

1022. Leslau, W.   Ethiopia Documents: Gurage. New
      1950   York.

      Discussion of Zitänï possession among the Gurage people
      of Ethiopia. This form of possession is a ritual curse
      by a deity, in this case the deity Damwamwit (p. 58).

1023. Leslau, Wolf   "Ethiopia's Language of the Pos-
      1957   sessed." Tomorrow (New York)
                                   5, no. 4: 84-88.

The Ethiopian Zar spirit possession cult is discussed here with special emphasis placed on its use of distinctive languages.

1024. Leslie, David   Among the Zulus and Amatongas.
      1875   Edited by W. H. Drummond.
                             Edinburgh: Edmonston & Douglas.

After a general description of Kaffir "doctors" in South Africa, the author proceeds to relate two incidents where these "doctors" were able to foretell events that actually came true for the author. This knowledge was gained through communication with spirit familiars (pp. 41-57).

1025. Lester, David   "Voodoo Death: Some New Thoughts
      1972   on an Old Phenomenon." American
                             Anthropologist 74, no. 3: 386-
                             90.

The importance of social support or lack of support for an individual who has been "hexed" in the manner of the voodoo death phenomenon is emphasized above physiological explanations. The article is a response to Cannon's work on Voodoo death in 1942 (Bib. 313.)

1026. Lestrade, A.   "La Médecine indigène au Ruanda
      1955   et lexique des termes médicaux
                             français-urunyarwanda."
                             Mémoires de l'Académie royale
                             des sciences coloniales d'outre-
                             mer (Bruxelles) 8, no. 1: 1-277.

Listed as an illness, the symptoms and treatment (exorcism) of possession by spirits are described for the people of Ruanda (pp. 199-212).

1027. Lestrange, M. de   "Génies de l'eau et de la brousse
      1950   en Guinée française." Études
                             guinéennes (Conakry), no. 4,
                             pp. 1-24.

Although spirit mediumship is not explicitly labelled, communication with python spirits of the water and of the bush of French Guinea (Guinea) is discussed.

1028. Lewicki, Tadeusz   "Prophètes, devins, et magiciens
      1965   chez les Berbères medievaux."
                             Folia Orientalia (Cracow) 7:3-27.

According to medieval Berber writers, prophets in North Africa arose from time to time who had special skills such as telling the future and the past, making rain, and finding hidden objects, by, among other methods, becoming possessed.

1029. Lewis, B. A.   "Nuer Spokesmen: A Note on the
      1951   Institution of the Ruic."
                            Sudan Notes and Records, vol.
                            32, pt. 1.

Discusses the role of the Ruic, a person who can synthesize public opinion at a general meeting, in Nuer
(Sudan) society. Some Ruics become possessed by the sky
spirits; cases of such occurrence are reported.

1030. Lewis, B. A.   The Murle: Red Chiefs and Black
      1972   Commoners. Oxford: Clarendon
                            Press.

Witch-doctors among the Murle of the southern Sudan
possess in their heads the kwolo, mythical insects which
impart to them supernatural powers (pp. 137 ff.).
Spirit possession is not explicitly labelled.

1031. Lewis, Herbert S.   "Wealth, Influence, and Prestige
      1970   among the Shoa Galla." In
                            Social Stratification in Africa,
                            edited by A. Tuden and L.
                            Plotnicov, pp. 163-86.
                            (Bib. 1760.)

The K'allu, spirit mediums among the Shoa Galla of
Ethiopia, are discussed as to their social position in
that society (pp. 174-79).

1032. Lewis, I. M.   "Sufism in Somaliland: A Study
      1955/1956   in Tribal Islam." Bulletin of
                            the School of Oriental and
                            African Studies 17, no. 3: 581-
                            602; 18, no. 1: 146-60.

Discussion of the Saar (Zar) cults, description of the
spread of these cults outside the Horn of Africa (18:
147).

1033. Lewis, I. M.   A Pastoral Democracy. London:
      1961   Oxford University Press.

Chapter 8 deals with various forms of spirit possession. Discusses Zar possession and its spread from
Ethiopia to Somaliland (Somalia) among the Dulbahente
(Dolbohanta) people; Wadaaddo possession and its cure by
the Wadaad or men of religion. The jobs of these priests
are described, and their function in the community is
analyzed (pp. 260-65).

1034. Lewis, I. M.   "Introduction." In Islam in
      1966a   Tropical Africa, edited by I. M.
                            Lewis, pp. 4-96. (Bib. 1035.)

The Islam-influenced spirit possession cults of the
Hausa (Nigeria), Songhay (Songhai) (Niger), and Mossi
(Upper Volta) are mentioned along with the Ethiopian zar
cult (p. 64).

1035. Lewis, I. M., ed.   Islam in Tropical Africa.
      1966b   London: Oxford University Press.

      Includes in this bibliography:
                  1034   I. M. Lewis (1966a)
                  1490   P. J. A. Rigby (1966)
                  1684   R. C. Stevenson (1966)

1036. Lewis, I. M.   "Spirit Possession and Depriva-
      1966c   tion Cults." Malinowski Memorial
                            Lecture. Man (London) 1, no. 3:
                            307-29.

      Among the Somali of Somaliland (Somalia) and Ethiopia,
spirit possession fulfills several sociological functions
which can be related to deprivation. Frustrated lovers,
isolated camel herders, and women in a male-dominated
society are discussed as examples. The article also includes a discussion of the general phenomenon of spirit
possession and of different types of possession cults.
Also mentioned are the Valley Tonga (Thonga) of Zambia.
[Cited in African Abstracts, vol. 19, no. 61.]

1037. Lewis, I. M.   "Spirit Possession in Northern
      1969   Somaliland." In Spirit Medium-
                            ship and Society in Africa,
                            edited by J. Beattie and J.
                            Middleton, pp. 188-219.
                            (Bib. 150.)

      Among Somalis (Somaliland, now Somalia), people who are
in physical or mental distress and who are deprived of
a secular means of easing that distress may become possessed by Saar spirits; in this way they obtain attention
and sympathy not otherwise available. Cases of frustrated
lovers, lonely camel herders, and women in a male-dominated society are given.

1038. Lewis, I. M.   "A Structural Approach to Witch-
      1970   craft and Spirit-Possession."
                            In Witchcraft Confessions and Ac-
                            cusations, edited by M. Douglas,
                            pp. 293-309. (Bib. 476.)

      In this theoretical article on spirit possession and its
role in the social structure, mention is made of the following ethnic groups: BaVenda (Venda) (South Africa),
Gurage (Ethiopia), Nuba (Sudan), Lugbara (Zaïre, Uganda),
Banyoro (Nyoro) (Uganda), Lenje (Lenge) (Kenya),

BaThonga (Thonga) (Mozambique), Akamba (Kamba) (Kenya),
Taita (Teita) (Kenya), Zulu (South Africa), Luo (Kenya),
and Pondo (South Africa).

1039. Lewis, I. M.   Ecstatic Religion. Harmonds-
      1971   worth, Middlesex: Penguin Books.

      This volume is devoted to an anthropological study of
      spirit possession with extensive material on many Afri-
      can ethnic groups. Key concepts such as "peripheral
      cults," "deprivation," and the social status of women are
      discussed in great depth regarding their applicability to
      spirit possession religions in Africa.

1040. Lex, Barbara W.   "Voodoo Death: New Thoughts on
      1974   an Old Explanation." American
                            Anthropologist 76, no. 4: 818-
                            23.

      Discusses the research to date on the phenomenon of
      "voodoo death" and introduces new physiological data of
      a more sophisticated nature than previous research.

1041. Lex, Barbara W.   "Hallucination, Healing and
      1975   Trance." Reviews in Anthropo-
                            logy 2, no. 4: 473-8.

      This review of F. D. Goodman, J. H. Henney and E.
      Pressel, 1974, Trance, Healing and Hallucination: Three
      Field Studies in Religious Experience (Bib. 683) con-
      centrates largely upon their handling of the psycho-
      physiological aspects of the spirit possession trance.

1042. Leyburn, James G.   The Haitian People. New Haven,
      1941   Conn.: Yale University Press.

      The Haitian vodun spirit possession religion is ex-
      amined in chapter 7 of this volume.

1043. Lhermitte, Jean   "Essai sur les phénomènes de
      1946-47   possession demoniaque."
                            L'Encéphale (Paris) 36, no. 10:
                            261-82.

      Although African material is not discussed, this
      article deals in a general manner with demoniacal posses-
      sion and includes a review of some of the more well-known
      literature written up to that time.

1044. Lhote, H.   Le Niger en Kayak. Paris: J.
      1943   Susse.

      Reports cases of spirit possession in Niger. [Cited by
      Rouch (1954, Bib. 1525).]

205

1045. Lienhardt, Godfrey   "The Shilluk of the Upper Nile."
      1954   In African Worlds, edited by D.
                               Forde. (Bib. 588.)

The Shilluk (Sudan) king must be possessed by or identified with Nyikang, founder of the royal line. Description of hysterical possession as manifestation of communication with superior powers (pp. 152, 160).

1046. Lienhardt, Godfrey   Divinity and Experience: The
      1961   Religion of the Dinka. London:
                               Oxford University Press.

Discussion of possession and mediumship among the Dinka
of the Sudan on pages 57-64, 70-72.

1047. Lindblom, Gerhard   The Akamba in British East
      1920   Africa. 2d ed. Uppsala: K. W.
                               Appleberg. Ill.

Several cases among the Akamba (Kamba) of Kenya are
cited of Aimu possession, afflicting both men and women,
and Mbatho possession, afflicting only women; causes for
spirit possession are explained and description is given
of the kinds of exorcism used for different forms of possession. Insanity and temporary possession are cured in
very similar ways (pp. 229-40, 264-65). Illustrated
(pp. 231, 232, 265).

1048. Linden, Ian   "'Mwali' and the Luba Origin of
      1972a   the Chewa: Some Tentative Sug-
                               gestions." Society of Malawi
                               Journal (Zamba) 25, no. 1: 11-
                               19.

Mention is made of the spirit mediums among the Chewa
of Malawi who are thought to be married to a snake or
python at the shrines of Salima and Makewana (p. 12).
Also described are various other spirit possession cults
including that of the mashave spirits (p. 14).

1049. Linden, Ian   "The Shrine of the Karongas at
      1972b   Mankhamba: Some Problems in the
                               Religious History of Central
                               Malawi." Paper presented at the
                               Conference on the History of
                               Central African Religious Sys-
                               tems, Lusaka, 30 August - 8
                               September.

The history of the major shrine of the Karonga
(Karanga) in Central Malawi is traced, and descriptions
of possession, mainly by snake spirits, are presented in
detail.

1050. Linden, Ian   "Chewa Initiation Rites and Nyau
       1975   Societies: The Use of Religious
                        Institutions in Local Politics
                        at Mua." In Themes in the Chris-
                        tian History of Central Africa,
                        edited by T. O. Ranger and J.
                        Weller, pp. 30-44. (Bib. 1449.)

     Brief mention is made of the fact that among the Chewa
of Malawi the men's secret societies (nyau) are connected with spirit possession mainly by treating people who
are repeatedly bothered by ancestors appearing in dreams
(p. 32).

1051. Lipsky, George A.   Ethiopia: Its People, Its
       1962   Society, Its Culture. New Haven,
                        Conn.: HRAF Press.

     Members of the Zar cults in Amhara areas of Ethiopia
are mostly women, since mainly it is they who are affected
by the Zar spirits. In Moslem areas, both men and women
are members of the cult. Much government hostility to
these cults is causing them to operate undercover in
Amhara areas, but with more freedom in Moslem areas
(chap. 7, pp. 100-120).

1052. Little, K. L.   "The Role of the Secret Society
       1949   in Cultural Specialization."
                        American Anthropologist 51:199-
                        212.

     Discussion of various dances and rituals devoted to
various Mende spirits. (Reference is here being made to
the Mende of Sierra Leone.)

1053. Little, Kenneth   "The Political Function of the
       1965   Poro (Part 1)." Africa: Journal
                        of the International African In-
                        stitute (London) 35, no. 4: 349-
                        65.

     Among the Mende, Mano, Gbunde (Gbundi), and other
ethnic groups of rural Sierra Leone and Liberia, the
Poro secret society fulfills many religious and political
functions. The supernatural power of the Poro is often
manifested in the form of the "spirits" of the society;
in fact, officials wearing masks and capes, etc., are
addressed as being the particular spirits that their
costumes indicate. Among the Mano of Liberia these masked
spirits are identified as the ancestors of the current
members of the cult (pp. 354-60).

1054. Littlewood, Margaret   Peoples of the Central Came-
       1954   roons: The Bamileke. Ethno-

graphic Survey of Africa, edited
by Daryll Forde, vol. 1, no. 9.
London: International African
Institute.

A discussion of magic among the Bamileke (Cameroon).
Information on magicians and medicine men and their
sphere of operations. The Minnyi, a medicine man, is
subject to spirit possession, and especially during his
two years novitiate training (pp. 128-29).

1055. Lombard, J.   "Les Cultes de possession en
      1967   Afrique noire et le bori Hausa."
                             Psychopathologie africaine
                             (Dakar) 3, no. 3: 419-39.

After briefly discussing spirit possession cults among
the Yoruba of Dahomey (Benin) and in Brazil, Haiti
(voodoo), Ethiopia (zar), and Senegal (rab), the author
describes the Hausa bori cult in Dahomey (Benin). The
practices and beliefs surrounding the bori spirits are
analyzed.

1056. Lonfernini, Bruno   "Stregoni si nasce."
      1969   Nigrizia (Verona) 87, no. 9:
                             12-17. Ill.

Although spirit possession is not explicitly labelled,
diviners among the Sidamo of Ethiopia may take up this
trade by personal impulse or by training, and description of a diviner's séance with Sidamo beliefs about
the shetana demons is presented.

1057. Long, Joseph K.   "Medical Anthropology, Dance and
      1972   Trance in Jamaica." Bulletin of
                             the International Committee on
                             Urgent Anthropological and Ethno-
                             logical Research, no. 14, pp.
                             17-24.

Although spirit possession is not explicitly mentioned
in the abstract, the Kumina cult and the "Pocomania"
religious cult, among others occurring in Jamaica, are
mentioned. [Cited in Abstracts in Anthropology, vol. 5,
no. 3 (1974), no. 6071.]

1058. Longmore, L.   "Medicine, Magic and Witchcraft
      1958   among Urban Africans on the
                             Witwatersrand." Central African
                             Journal of Medicine (Salisbury)
                             4, no. 6: 242-49.

The traditional practices of medical and religious
practitioners have continued to exert their influences on

Christian Africans living in urban areas in South Africa.
Medicine and magic have been areas where traditional beliefs are most strongly guarded. Some discussion of
spirit possession.

1059. Loran, Erle, Thomas K.   African and Ancient Mexican Art:
      Seligman, Jane P.   The Loran Collection. San
      Dwyer, and Edward B.   Francisco: Fine Arts Museum of
      Dwyer   San Francisco. Ill.
      1974

Although not explicitly labelled, spirit mediumship is
implied in a discussion of man's communication with the
spirit worlds with regard to African art (pp. 16-17).

1060. Loudon, J. B.   "Psychogenic Disorder and Social
      1959   Conflict among the Zulu." In
                                 Culture and Mental Health Cross
                                 Cultural Studies, edited by
                                 Marvin K. Opler. New York:
                                 Macmillan Co.

Discusses the relation between certain kinds of rituals
and certain forms of psychogenic disorder occurring
among the Zulu of South Africa. The ritual discussed is
that of Nomkubulwana, a ceremony to ensure the fertility
of crops. One of the questions asked is, what is the relation of the ritual to conversion hysteria and spirit
possession to which Zulu women are particularly liable.
A discussion follows of possible answers to this question.

1061. Loudon, J. B.   "Social Aspects of Ideas about
      1965   Treatment." In Transcultural
                                 Psychiatry, edited by A. V. S.
                                 de Reuck and Ruth Porter, pp.
                                 137-61. Boston: Little, Brown
                                 & Co.

Healing practices of the Bantu of Southern Africa are
discussed in terms of the concept of power which the
healer is said to obtain through spirit possession
(p. 143).

1062a. Louis-Jean, Antoine   La Crise de possession et la
       1970   possession dramatique. Ottawa:
                                 Les Editions Lemeac.

Not available for annotation.

1062b. Lovekin, Adams and   "Religious Glossolalia: A Lon-
       H. Newton Malony   gitudinal Study of Personality
       1977   Changes." Journal for the
                                 Scientific Study of Religion 16,
                                 no. 4: 383-93.

209

This article presents the results of a longitudinal
study of glossolalia (as it occurred in North American
Pentecostal groups) and the personality changes which
tend to be manifested over time.

1063. Low, D. A.   "Converts and Martyrs in
      1968   Buganda." In Christianity in
                                Tropical Africa, edited by C. G.
                                Baëta, pp. 150-64. (Bib. 65.)

    Mediumship among the priests of the Buganda Kingdom
(Ganda) (Uganda) is mentioned in this historical account
of the introduction of Christianity (pp. 152, 154).

1064. Lowie, R. H.   Nigerian Annual Report. Lagos,
      1929   1929.

    Report of "spirit movement." Eleven "spirit" people
convicted on murder charges and executed in Nigeria.
[Cited by Jeffreys (1953, Bib. 853).]

1065. Lucas, J. O.   "The Cult of the 'Adamu
      1943   Orisha.'" Nigerian Field 11:
                              184-96.

    Discusses a cult, associated with funeral ceremonies
and spirit possession, found among the coastal Awori of
Nigeria.

1066. Lucas, J. Olumide   The Religion of the Yorubas.
      1948   Lagos: C. M. S. Bookshop.

    A general review of all the deities and spirits wor-
shipped by the Yoruba of western Nigeria. Abiku are
spirits who possess the bodies of unborn children and
cause them to die as infants. These spirits may thus
be born and die several times unless they are propitiated,
driven away, or convinced to stay (p. 149). Eluku is a
deified spirit of an ancestor. Members of his cult assist
in funeral rituals. When the spirit of the deceased is
invoked, he is heard to "respond in the loud cries of
the Eluku" (i.e., through the mouths of Eluku cult members, pp. 128-29). The Egungun cult also plays a role in
funeral ceremonies. Egungun are the spirits of the ancestors of the community, represented by costumed members
of the cult at many social rituals. In funeral ceremonies
the spirit of the deceased is represented by an Egungun;
the spirit may speak to his descendents through the
Egungun (pp. 136, 144, 230, 231).

1067. Lucas, J. Olumide   Religions in West Africa and
      n.d. [1970?]   Ancient Egypt. Apapa: Nigerian
                              National Press.

210

Dealing with West African data from Ghana, Togoland, Dahomey, and southern Nigeria, the author compares the religious elements found there with those from ancient Egyptian culture. Spirit possession and mediumship are mentioned throughout the work.

1068. Lucena, Jose   "Aspcctos culturals na patho-
      1969   logia mental em certos grupos
                             humanos brasileiros." Revista
                             brasileira de psiquiatria 3,
                             no. 1: 7-30.

In this survey of psychiatric studies of the different ethnic groups in Brazil, mention is made of the spirit possession cult, Candomble, of African origins. [Cited in Transcultural Psychiatric Research Review (Bruges) 7 (October 1970): 180-84.]

1069. Ludlow, Captain W. R.   Zululand and Cetewayo. London:
      1882   Simpkin, Marshall, & Co.

Chapter 9 includes several accounts of the activities of "witch-doctors" divining the causes of illnesses and misfortunes among the Zulu of South Africa. The witch-doctors are thought to be spirit mediums, communing with the ancestor spirits.

1070. Ludwig, Arnold   "Altered States of Conscious-
      1969   ness." In Altered States of
                             Consciousness, edited by C.
                             Tart, pp. 11-24. (Bib. 1710.)

Altered states of consciousness are defined and classified according to how they are produced, their general characteristics, and their functions.

1071. Lufuluambo, Francois-   "Mentalité religieuse africaine
      Marie   J   ct Christianisme." Revue du
      1967   clergé africain (Inkisi) 22, no.
                             3: 318-41.

Spirit mediumship is implied but not explicitly labelled in this article, which discusses the role of the African diviner, the "féticheur," and the "médecin" in African thought and in Christianity (p. 322).

1072. Lugira, A.   "The Concept of Katonda." In
      1968/69   Religious Studies Papers,
                             University of East Africa Social
                             Sciences Council Conference,
                             pp. 23-35. Kampala: Makerere
                             Institute of Social Research.

Both possession and mediumship are mentioned in this

analysis of the Buganda (Ganda) (Uganda) concept of their deities and especially of their high god, Katonda.

1073. Lugira, A. M.   "African Traditional Religion
      1970a   vis-à-vis Christianity." Dina
                         na Mila (Kampala) 4, no. 2: 23-
                         34.

Spirit mediumship among the traditional African religions of Uganda is briefly mentioned on page 26.

1074. Lugira, A. M.   Ganda Art. Kampala: Osasa
      1970b   Publication.

Spirit mediums and their role in Ganda (Uganda) religion are discussed on pages 23-24.

1075. Lukwiyangom, G.   "Ajwagi of Patiko Clan - Their
      1975   Work in Connection with Jok."
                         Occasional Research Papers in
                         African Traditional Religion and
                         Philosophy (Makerere University,
                         Kampala), vol. 27, no. 257.

An in-depth analysis is presented of the Ajwagi, a type of healer-diviner who is said to be possessed by Jok, a spirit force of an ambiguous nature among the peoples of the Patiko region of Uganda.

1076. Lussy, Kunibert, and "Opinions et coutumes religieuses
      Aquilin Engelberger   des Wapogoro." Anthropos 49,
      1954   nos. 1-2: 103-22; 49, nos. 1-2:
                         605-26.

Among the Wapogoro (Pogoro) of Tanganyika (Tanzania), the family elders and diviners act as intermediaries between the world of spirits and that of men. A description of the religious practices associated with the spirit world is included. [Text in German.] [Cited in African Abstracts, vol. 6, no. 586.]

1077. Lutatenekwa, F.   "The Bachwezi: Ancient Kings or
      1972   Living Spirits?" Kale (Dar es
                         Salaam), no. 1, pp. 1-6.

The bachwezi are spirits who possess priests in the Kiziba (Haya) Kingdom of Kenya. Discussion centers around question of whether these spirits were originally living kings as is claimed by the Kiziba.

1078. Lwakale, Celestin   Initiation africaine et initia-
      Mubengayi   tion chrétienne. Léopoldville:
      1966   Éditions du C.E.P.

In this philosophical work analyzing the relationship
between Christian and African beliefs, exorcism of evil
spirits (Satan) is mentioned on pages 4, 57-59.

1079. Lystad, Robert   The Ashanti: A Proud People.
      1958   New Brunswick, N.J.: Rutgers
                            University Press. Ill.

The village of Goaso in Ashanti, Ghana, has two patron
gods, Nentiga and Bonsam. Every ninth day the priest of
Bonsam is possessed by his god. On these occasions the
god speaks through the priest's body, using a special
language, said to be an archaic Twi dialect. He gives
cures, advice and protection to people of the town who
request aid (pp. 166-77).

1080. M., D. W.   "Oshogbo Celebrates Festival of
      1953   Shango." Nigeria (Lagos) 40:
                            298-313. Ill.

Possession ceremonies described; traditional forms of
worship of the festival of Shango among the Yoruba
(Nigeria) have given way to new religious forms.

1081. Mabona, Antoine   "Éléments de culture africaine."
      1962   Présence africaine (Paris), no.
                            41, pp. 144-50.

This general philosophical article on African culture
mentions possession by deities on page 148.

1082. McAll, R. K.   "Demonosis or the Possession
      1971   Syndrome." International
                            Journal of Social Psychiatry
                            (London), no. 2, pp. 150-58.

Brief mention is made of the general phenomenon of the
African "witch-doctor" who treats cases of illness caused
by spirit possession (p. 153). Main emphasis of the
article is on the Western interpretations given for possession based on the Christian idea of Satanic possession.

1083. MacAlpine, A. G.   "Tonga Religious Beliefs and
      1906   Customs." Journal of the Afri-
                            can Society (London) 5, no. 19:
                            257-68.

Among the Tonga (Thonga) of Northern Rhodesia (Zambia),
intercourse between the living and the dead was believed
possible to a very considerable extent, as far, indeed,
as "possession" in certain individuals by the spirit of
some dead friend or acquaintance. The soothsayer was
believed to receive his message from the spirits, and his

213

word was seldom called into question. Soothsayers sometimes gave the people advice and warnings while in a
trance, addressing themselves as the spirit by whom they
were possessed (pp. 263-65).

1084. McCallum, Frances   "African Ideas and the Old Testa-
      V. I.   ment." Nada (Salisbury) 10, no.
      1970   2: 3-11.

Spirit mediumship in Africa is discussed in relation
to the Old Testament, particularly Deuteronomy 18:10-
11. The cattle-killing "delusion" among the Gcaleka
peoples (Rhodesia) in 1856, which was perpetrated by the
spirit medium Nongquase, is related.

1085. McClean, David M., and "Divination among the Bena
      Ted J. Solomon   Lulua." Journal of Religion in
      1971   Africa (Leiden) 4, no. 1: 25-44.

Spirit possession and mediumship are two of several
techniques..of divination among the Bena Lulua of south
central Zaire. The ancestors are called by the diviner
so that by means of possession they may tell of the
cause of misfortune or of illness and the curative treatment necessary (pp. 29, 34-38).

1086. McCulloch, M.   The Peoples of Sierra Leone Pro-
      1950   tectorate. Ethnographic Survey
                              of Africa, edited by Daryll
                              Forde, pt. 2. London: Inter-
                              national African Institute.

Spirit possession and its role in the religions of the
Mende and Lokko (Loko) of Sierra Leone are discussed on
pages 39 ff.

1087. McCulloch, Merran   The Southern Lunda and Related
      1951   People. Ethnographic Survey of
                              Africa, edited by Daryll Forde,
                              vol. 3, no. 1. London: Inter-
                              national African Institute.

The Mahamba spirits are ancestral spirits that possess
their descendants among the Lunda of Zambia. The spirits
must be exorcised before a cure for the victim can be
effected. Description of the new kinds of Mahamba found
today. The diviner who cures spirit possession is called
to his profession by having been possessed by the Ngombo
demon; description of exorcism and apprenticeship of the
diviner (pp. 76-83).

1088. McCulloch, Merran   The Ovimbundu of Angola. Ethno-
      1952   graphic Survey of Africa, edited

by Daryll Forde, vol. 3, no. 2.
London: International African
Institute.

Description of divination techniques among the
Ovimbundu of Angola, often involving spirit possession.
Describes illness caused by spirit possession and the
necessary ceremonies for a cure (pp. 35-40).

1089. MacDonald, Rev. James   Religion and Myth. New York:
      1969   Negro Universities Press.

This study, written by a missionary around 1892, deals
with African religions in general. "God-possession" is
mentioned on pages 65, 121; chapter 7 deals with exorcism
of evil spirits; and chapter 9 is concerned with prophecy and mediumship with the spirits.

1090. MacGaffey, Wyatt, and   Cuba: Its People, Its Society,
      Clifford R. Barnett   Its Culture. New Haven, Conn.:
      1962   HRAF Press.

The Afro-Cuban religions which practice spirit possession, including Santería and Abakua, are described on
pages 205-10.

1091. MacGaffey, Wyatt   "Autobiography of a Prophet."
      1966   Cahiers économiques et sociaux
                               (Kinshasa) 4, no. 2: 231-35.

Presented here is the autobiography of the prophet
Mabwaaka Mpaka Gabriel, better known as Ngunza, the
prophet in Zaïre. Mabwaaka was ordained by the prophet
Simon Kimbangu to carry on the latter's work of healing
and speaking the word of God, a message which was con-
veyed by Kimbangu after he returned from the dead.
Glossolalia is cited on page 232.

1092. MacGaffey, Wyatt   "The Religious Commissions of
      1970   the Bakongo." Man (London),
                               n.s. 5, no. 1: 27-38.

The Bakongo (Kongo) (Zaïre) distinguish between the
roles of magician and of prophet, both of whom are said
to be spirit possessed. The sociological distinctions
between these and other specialists, such as the chief
and the witch, are examined in detail.

1093. MacGaffey, Wyatt   "Comparative Analysis of Central
      1972   African Religions." Africa:
                               Journal of the International
                               African Institute (London) 42,
                               no. 1: 21-31.

In a comparative analysis of Central African religions, focussing on the distinction between witchcraft, magic, and prophecy among the Kongo (Zaire) and Nyakyusa (Tanzania), the author traces the development of spirit possession and its religious institutionalization from the earth-spirit cults to the prophets of more recent origin.

1094a. MacGaffey, Wyatt   "Oral Tradition in Central
       1975   Africa." International Journal
                                  of African Historical Studies
                                  7, no. 3: 417-26.

Spirit possession among the Bakongo (Kongo) of Central Africa is mentioned in an analysis of their oral tradition (pp. 424-26).

1094b. MacGaffey, Wyatt   "Cultural Roots of Kongo Prophe-
       1977   tism." History of Religion 17,
                                  no. 2: 177-93.

This article deals with the religious movements of Antonism and Kimbanguism among the Bakongo (Kongo) of Zaire. Mention is made of possession by the Holy Spirit on p. 179.

1095. McGrath, Damien   "The Catholic Charismatic Re-
      1974   newal." Journal of Theology for
                                  Southern Africa (Cape Town),
                                  no. 7, pp. 30-40.

Africa is included in this analysis of the international growth of the Catholic charismatic movement.

1096. MacKenzie, D. R.   The Spirit Ridden Konde. London:
      1925   Seeley, Service & Co.

Description of spirit trances, ecstasies, and posses-sion for the Konde (Ngondi) people of the Lake Nyasa region (Malawi) (pp. 185; 222-23). Description of the role of the chief as the "man who speaks with God" (p. 196). Possession by evil spirits is discussed (p. 224).

1097. McKenzie, P. R.   "Sango - A Traditional Yoruba
      1976   Cult-Group." Africana
                                  Marburgensia 9, no. 1: 3-33.

The Sàngó cult among the Yoruba of Nigeria practices spirit possession by the Sàngó òrîsà, this being an act of devotion towards the god (pp. 17 ff.).

1098. Maclean, Colonel   A Compendium of Kafir Laws and
      1968   Customs. London: Frank Cass &
                                  Co.

216

Originally published in 1858, this work is a collection of customs and laws of the Kafir peoples of South Africa. Mention is made of the seizure of an individual by the ghosts of the dead; the resultant illness is called ukutwasa and is a sign of priestly calling. This illness is marked by mental and physical suffering, excitement, and utterance of "unintelligible jargon" (pp. 82 ff.).

1099. Maclean, Una   Magical Medicine: A Nigerian
      1971   Case-Study. London: Allen
                          Lane, Penguin Press.

Trance and spirit possession are mentioned in various places in this study of traditional Yoruba medicine in Nigeria (pp. 32, 58-60, 72). Case descriptions of Ibadan healers and their practices are given.

1100. Maclure, H. L.   "Religion and Disease in Sierra
      1962   Leone." Sierra Leone Bulletin
                          of Religion (Freetown) 4, no.
                          1: 29-34.

The activities of spirits among the Temne of Sierra Leone are said to be a major cause of disease; a skin rash is the result of a spirit having "borrowed" the person's body to go hunting (p. 32).

1101. McMahon, E. O.   Christian Missions in
      (Archdeacon)   Madagascar. (Publisher unknown).
      1914

Spirit possession by the ghosts of the dead among the peoples of Madagascar (pp. 52-53).

1102. Madziyire, Rev.   "An Obstacle Race towards under-
      Salathiel   standing Bernard Mizeki Martyr's
      1972   Life." Paper presented at the
                          Conference on the History of
                          Central African Religious Sys-
                          tems, Lusaka, 31 August -
                          8 September.

Amidst a detailed account of the author's lifelong search for an understanding of Bernard Mizeki Martyr's life in Rhodesia and Zambia lies a very rich account of his Shona father, who was the only man in the first half of the twentieth century to be possessed by the Mhondoro tribal spirit Kasosa. Because of the ability to foretell the future, to make rain, to dream, and to cast lots, this man had wide-reaching political and social importance. Fasting and sonic driving are inductive techniques used, and an interesting relationship with snakes and with submersion under water is mentioned. Interchange between father and Christian son is described—father being converted to Christianity on his deathbed.

217

1103. Madziyire, Salathiel K.   "Heathen Practices in the Urban
      1975   and Rural Marandellas Area and
                                 Their Effects upon Christia-
                                 nity." In Themes in the Chris-
                                 tian History of Central Africa,
                                 edited by T. O. Ranger and J.
                                 Weller, pp. 76-82. (Bib. 1449.)

      Detailed description is given of the spirit possession
and mediumship cults among the present-day rural and urban Shona-speaking peoples around the Marandellas area
of Rhodesia. Reports of interviews with spirit mediums
show that the traditional attitude towards Christianity
is one of respect, an attitude not often reciprocated.

1104. Magomi, A.   "Funeral Rites of the First Born
      1974   Child and of a Mbuyi (Old Man-
                               High Priest-Diviner) among the
                               Wapogoro." Occasional Research
                               Papers in African Traditional
                               Religion and Philosophy
                               (Makerere University, Kampala),
                               vol. 27, no. 280.

      Among the Pagoro (Pogoro) of Uganda the mbuyi, the
oldest man in the clan, is responsible for leading the
spirit possession ceremonies practiced by these people
(p. 12). Funeral ceremonies following the death of a
mbuyi are described.

1105. Mair, Lucy   New Nations. Chicago: Univer-
      1963   sity of Chicago Press.

      A discussion of spirit mediumship in Ashanti (Ghana)
as reported by Margaret Field and compared with spirit
cults and mediums as they are known in Singapore and
China (chap. 6, pp. 188-89).

1106. Mair, L. P.   An African People in the
      1965a   Twentieth Century. New York:
                               Russell & Russell.

      Possession of prophets by the ancestor spirits,
mizimu, of ordinary people and by the gods, lubale,
occurs frequently among the Buganda (Ganda) of Uganda,
and is used for cures of illnesses, oracles, and divination (pp. 223 ff.).

1107. Mair, Lucy   An Introduction to Social Anthro-
      1965b   pology. Oxford: Clarendon Press.

      Spirit possession and mediumship are mentioned as oc-
curring among the Azande (Sudan), Lugbara (Uganda), and
Ndembu (Zambia) (pp. 214 ff.).

1108. Mair, Lucy   Witchcraft. New York: McGraw-
      1969   Hill Book Co.

      Spirit mediumship is discussed among the Zande (Azande)
      (Sudan, p. 56); Akan (Ghana, p. 57); and Nyoro (Uganda,
      pp. 81-3, 161, 166 ff.).

1109. Mair, Lucy   African Societies. Cambridge:
      1974   Cambridge University Press.

      Spirit possession is discussed as occurring among the
      Lele of Zaire (pp. 78-79); the Yakö of Nigeria (pp. 108-
      9); the Nuer of the Sudan (p. 128); the Rwanda (Ruanda)
      and Burundi (Rundi) of Rwanda and Burundi (pp. 175-76);
      the Dinka of the Sudan (p. 200); and the Kalabari of
      Nigeria (pp. 212-13).

1110. Makang Ma Mbog,   "Essai de compréhension de la
      Mathias   dynamique des psychothérapies
      1969   africaines traditionelles."
                                Psychopathologie africaine
                                (Dakar) 5, no. 3: 303-54.

      The data for this essay on traditional African healing
      methods were collected from Chad and Cameroon, although
      no specific ethnic groups are mentioned. The use of
      dance and possession trance as psychotherapies is dis-
      cussed on pages 340 ff.

1111. Makang Ma Mbog,   "Confiance et résistances dans
      Mathias   le traitement des maladies en
      1972a   psychopathologie africaine."
                                Psychopathologie africaine
                                (Dakar) 8, no. 3: 419-24.

      The importance of the patient's confidence in or re-
      sistance to the African healer and the relationship of
      these to the patient's belief in spirits and spirit pos-
      session are emphasized in this article.

1112. Makang Ma Mbog,   "Délire hallucinatoire et
      Mathias   société africaine." Psycho-
      1972b   pathologie africaine (Dakar) 8,
                                no. 1: 59-73.

      A theoretical synthesis is presented here, tying to-
      gether the psychotic, the African medicine man, and re-
      ligion: they all have to do with the problem of good
      and evil. Sociological causes of psychoses are not con-
      sidered as important as the anguish that can be found in
      all mentally ill persons.

219

1113. Malefijt, Annemarie   Religion and Culture. New York:
      De Waal   Macmillan Co.
      1968

      Among the Nyoro of Uganda, spirit mediums act as di-
      viners and healers for their patients. When possessed
      by their spirits, diviners may claim to speak a special
      language; but this is really the normal Nyoro language
      with extra sounds added (as in "pig latin") (pp. 206-7,
      225).

1114. Manoukian, Madeline   Akan and Ga-Adangme Peoples of
      1950   the Gold Coast. Ethnographic
                             Survey of Africa, edited by
                             Daryll Forde, vol. 1, no. 1.
                             London: International African
                             Institute.

      Spirit possession and mediumship among the Akan of the
      Gold Coast (Ghana) are incorporated as a major element of
      their religion. Priests are possessed by obosom spirits,
      each of which has its own temple and attendants (pp. 55-
      62). Spirit possession and mediumship are also integral
      to the religion of the Ga peoples of the Gold Coast.
      Here, however, it is not the priests who are possessed
      but the woyei, the official mouthpieces of the gods
      (pp. 94-104).

1115. Maquet, J. J.   "The Kingdom of Ruanda." In
      1954   African Worlds, edited by D.
                             Forde. (Bib. 588.)

      The Banyarwanda (Ruanda) of Rwanda have diviners who
      communicate with the Bazimu, spirits of the dead, through
      spirit possession or through the aid of a female medium
      who is possessed by the Biheko spirit (pp. 172-73).

1116a.Marcelin, Émile   "Les Grands Dieux du vodou
      1947   haïtien." Journal de la
                             Société des américanistes de
                             Paris 35:51-135.

      This article gives a very detailed presentation and
      analysis of the possessing deities in the Haitian vodou
      religion.

1116b.Marks, Morton   "Uncovering Ritual Structures
      1974   in Afro-American Music." In
                             Religious Movements in Contem-
                             porary America, edited by
                             Irving I. Zaretsky and Mark P.
                             Leone, pp. 60-134. (Bib. 1924.)

      A detailed analysis of language and musical structure
      in a variety of groups including Santería cults in Cuba

                             220

and Brazil. Spirit possession and trance behavior are
analyzed in terms of rhythm pattern and music.

1117. Marquard, L., and T. G.   The Southern Bantu. London:
      Standing   Oxford University Press.
      1939

      Among the Bantu of South Africa spirit possession ac-
counts both for the ability of some individuals to
prophesy, becoming the oracles of the gods, and for illnesses. Means of exorcising evil spirits in the case of
illness are outlined (chap. 4).

1118. Mars, Jean Price-   Ainsi parla l'oncle. Port-au-
      1928   Prince.

      The book attempts to examine possible African and
European elements in Haitian folklore. In voodoo ceremonies the voodoo king (le Roi Vaudoux) is often possessed
by voodoo spirits. Chapter 6 describes several such
ceremonies.

1119. Mars, Jean Price-   Une Étape de l'évolution
      1929   haïtienne. Port-au-Prince:
                                Imprimerie la Presse.

      Discussion of the historical aspects of the Voudou
cult of Haiti. [Cited by Simpson (1945, Bib. 1624).]

1120. Mars, Louis   La Crise de possession dans le
      1948a   voudou. Port-au-Prince:
                               Imprimerie de l'État.

      Detailed discussion of spirit possession in Haitian
voudou.

1121. Mars, Louis   "La Psychologie du voudou."
      1948b   Psyché (Paris), nos. 23-24,
                               September - October.

      This article has been cited as having information on
spirit possession and mediumship, but was unavailable for
annotation.

1122. Mars, Louis, and   "Haitian Voodoo and the Rituali-
      George Devereux   zation of the Nightmare."
      1951a   Psychoanalytical Review 38:334.

      Voodoo (Haiti) possession is characterized by the "Loa
(god) riding a horse (the possessed)." Discussion of
the etymology of the terms horse and nightmare, especially
with reference to the consonants 'm, r.' Comparative
data show relation between subjective experience of a
nightmare and the highly ritualized and institutionalized
experience of possession.

221

1123. Mars, Louis   "Nouvelle contribution à
      1951b   l'étude de crise de possession."
                           Psyché (Paris) 60:640-69.

      Baptism of possessing spirits analogous to baptism of
      individuals.

1124. Mars, Louis   "La Psychiatrie au service du
      1966   tiers monde." Psychopathologie
                           africaine (Dakar) 2, no. 2: 227-
                           48.

      The zar possession cult in Ethiopia is cited as an ex-
      ample of psychotherapeutic practices of the traditional
      African cultures (p. 241). The article is a general sur-
      vey of the major issues of practicing psychiatry in the
      "Third World."

1125. Mars, L.   "L'Ethnopsychiatrie et la
      1969   schizophrénie en Haiti." Psy-
                           chopathologie africaine (Dakar)
                           5, no. 2: 235-55.

      After presenting an outline of the Haitian Vodou cult
      and the phenomenon of spirit possession, the author pro-
      ceeds to discuss the relationship between the Vodou be-
      liefs and practices and cases of schizophrenia.

1126. Mars, Louis   "Le Symbolisme dans la religion
      1970   vodouique et les philosophes de
                           l'occident." Psychopathologie
                           africaine (Dakar) 6, no. 1: 67-
                           70.

      The symbol of wind used by the Haitians to describe
      possession by the loa in the Vodun cult is explored and
      related to an experience of the philosopher Rene Des-
      cartes, who was said to have been possessed by an evil
      spirit in a dream.

1127. Marshall, Lorna   "!Kung Bushman Religious Be-
      1962   liefs." Africa: Journal of the
                           International African Institute
                           (London) 32, no. 3: 221-52.

      Among the !Kung Bushmen of NyaeNyae region, Southwest
      Africa, curing dances are performed in which medicine
      men (author's term) go into trances. Although the !Kung
      do not believe divine beings enter into the medicine men
      or speak through them, they do believe that while in a
      trance, a medicine man's spirit leaves his body and goes
      out to meet the Great God (llgquwa) and the spirits of
      the dead (llgauwasi) (pp. 249-50).

222

1128. Marshall, Lorna   "The Medicine Dance of the
      1969   !Kung Bushmen." _Africa: Journal
                                of the International African
                                Institute_ (London) 39, no. 4:
                                347-81.

      Among the !Kung Bushmen of Southwest Africa medicine
dances (N/um Tshxai) are performed. In these dances,
male medicine men (N/um kxao-si or N/um owners) go into
trances in which they try to cure ill people by "drawing
out" the sickness. The dances themselves also provide
an opportunity for recreation.

1129. Martin, Juan Luis   _Ecue, Chango y Yemaya_. Habana:
      1930   Cultural.

      Not available for annotation.

1130. Martin, Marie-Louise   "Face aux mouvements prophétiques
      1962   et messianiques en Afrique
                                méridionale." _Monde non
                                chrétien_ 64:226-55.

      The social and political influence of three types of
religious movements is discussed: (1) the Ethiopian
churches which maintain the teachings of the missions but
have black leaders; (2) the Zionists or prophetic churches
in which possession plays a very large role; and (3) the
messianic movements, similar to the prophetic churches,
but in which the prophet becomes the liberator and
messiah. [Cited in _African Abstracts_, vol. 15, no. 1
(January 1964), no. 119.]

1131. Martin, M. L.   "The Church Facing Prophetic and
      1963   Messianic Movements." _Ministry_
                                (Morija, Basutoland) 3, no. 2:
                                49-61.

      Speaking in tongues and possession by the Holy Spirit
are mentioned throughout this general theoretical article
on the relationship between the mainline Christian Church
and the prophetic and messianic movements.

1132. Martin, Marie-Louise   _The Biblical Concept of
      1964   Messianism and Messianism in
                                Southern Africa_. Morija:
                                Morija Sesuto Book Depot.

      Possession by the Holy Spirit and glossolalia in the
Zionist Church of Southern Africa are analyzed theologically (pp. 110-18).

1133. Martin, Marie-Louise   "Le Messianisme en Afrique."
      1966   _Flambeau_ (Yaoundé) no. 12, pp.
                                201-12.

Possession by the Holy Spirit in the Zionist Churches
of Africa is mentioned on page 206.

1134. Martin, Marie-Louise   Prophetic Christianity in the
      n.d. (1968)   Congo. Johannesburg: Christian
                               Institute of Southern Africa.

The practices of the Church of Christ on Earth through
the Prophet Simon Kimbangu include glossolalia and
ecstatic trance (pp. 4, 12-13).

1135. Martin, M. L.   "Prophetism in the Congo."
      1968   Ministry (Morija, Lesotho) 8,
                               no. 4: 154-63.

The call and communication between the Holy Spirit and
Simon Kimbangu, the prophet in Zaire, are traced on
pages 158-60.

1136. Martin, Marie-Louise   "Les Églises indépendentes
      1971a   d'Afrique et l'Eglise de Jesus-
                               Christ sur la terre par le
                               prophete Simon Kimbangu en
                               particulier." Flambeau
                               (Yaoundé) no. 29, pp. 41-49.

Possession by the Holy Spirit, glossolalia, and
ecstatic trance are all discussed, with particular emphasis on the Church of Jesus Christ on Earth of the
Prophet Simon Kimbangu.

1137. Martin, Marie-Louise   Kirche ohne Weise: Simon Kim-
      1971b   bangu und seine Millionenkirche
                               in Kongo. Basel: Friedrich
                               Reinhardt Verlag.

This volume presents a description and analysis of the
Simon Kimbangu movement in Zaire. Throughout the volume
there are references to spirit possession, such as description of Kimbangu's first calling on page 64.

1138. Martin, Marie-Louise   "The MaiChaza Church in
      1971c   Rhodesia." In African Initia-
                               tives in Religion, edited by D.
                               B. Barrett, pp. 109-21.
                               (Bib. 83.)

The complex relationship between traditional African
beliefs and Christian elements in the African independent
church movements is highlighted by an in-depth discussion
of the MaiChaza Church among the Shona of Rhodesia;
spirit possession and mediumship are both mentioned
throughout the text.

1139. Martin, Marie-Louise   "Un Culte pas comme les autres."
      1975   Flambeau (Yaoundé) no. 48, pp.
                                 219-24.

Presented here is a brief discussion of one of the
African independent churches, the Church of the Lord,
Aladura, based in Nigeria. An ecstatic trance state is
mentioned on page 220.

1140. Marty, Paul   Études sur l'Islam au Sénégal.
      1917   Vol. 2. Les Doctrines et les
                                 institutions. Paris: Maison
                                 Ernest Leroux éditeur.

In section 3 of chapter 5 (pp. 153-83), the beliefs of
Moslems in Senegal concerning the nature of illness are
analyzed. Spirit possession is often cited as a cause of
illness.

1141. Marwick, M. G.   Sorcery in Its Social Setting.
      1965   Manchester: Manchester Univer-
                                 sity Press.

Among the Cewa (Chewa) of Rhodesia and Nyasaland
(Malawi), the mpondolo diviner is believed to be possessed
by a lion spirit (pp. 90 ff.).

1142. Marx, Louise   "Elements of Marina Psycho-
      1959   logy." In Basic Psychological
                                 Structures of African and
                                 Madagascan Populations, pp. 1-
                                 20. CCTA/CSA, Pub. no. 51
                                 (annex 4). Tananarive.

Description of possession trance along with a psychological survey of the Marina personality and culture in
Madagascar.

1143. Masamba ma Mpolo   "Religion et santé mentale."
      1975   Flambeau (Yaoundé) no. 47, pp.
                                 156-70.

The faith-healing techniques of the African Christian
prophets, which include exorcism of spirits possessing
the ill person, are discussed in detail (pp. 162 ff.).

1144. Mason, Philip   The Birth of a Dilemma. London:
      1958   Oxford University Press.

The Shona spirit mediums of Rhodesia are briefly mentioned on pages 290-92.

1145. Massam, J. A.   The Cliff Dwellers of Kenya.
        1968   London: Frank Cass & Co.

    The spirits of the dead can seize the living and make
    them do their bidding among the Elgeyo (Keyu) of Kenya.
    A mild form of possession trance is suggested (pp. 187-
    98).

1146. Masters, Henry, and   In Wild Rhodesia. London:
        Walter E. Masters   Francis Griffiths.
        1920

    The Bantu-speaking peoples of Rhodesia are discussed in
    general in this report by missionaries. The institution
    of spirit mediumship in connection with the tribal spirits
    is presented on pages 142 ff.

1147. Matthews, J. B.   "The Mhondoro of Mutota and His
        1960   Village." Southern Rhodesia
                                     Native Affairs Department
                                     Annual 37:66-74.

    Description of Shona spirit mediumship connected
    with the Mhondoro spirit in Rhodesia. Details on healers
    and rain makers as these become spirit possessed. Some
    information on the history of the Mhondoro spirit.

1148. Matthews, J. Brian   "One Account of the History of
        1966   the Vatande." Nada (Salisbury)
                                     9, no. 3: 31-32.

    Original ownership of the land they now occupy is
    claimed by Chief Matsivo of the Vatande (Tande)
    (Rhodesia), tracing his lineage back to Bangomwe, the son
    of the founding chief who upon death became a Mhondoro
    spirit. Spirit mediumship is not explicitly labelled
    but implied.

1149. Mauchamp, Émile   La Sorcellerie au Maroc. Paris:
        n.d.   Dorbon-Ainé.

    Moroccan beliefs in spirits and spirit possession are
    discussed in various places, but especially in chapter 5
    of this book written by a French doctor who lived in
    Marrakech around the turn of the century.

1150. Mawanda, J. M.   "The Baganda Conception of the
        1974   Ancestors." Occasional Research
                                     Papers in African Traditional
                                     Religion and Philosophy
                                     (Makerere University, Kampala),
                                     vol. 19, no. 198.

    The ancestral spirits among the Baganda (Ganda)

of Uganda, termed mizimu, are venerated, and those of
kings and culture heroes may have their own priests and
mediums.

1151. Maxmilien, Louis   Le Vodou haitien. Port-au-
       1945   Prince: Imprimerie de l'Etat.

    A discussion of spirit possession in the vodou cult of
Haiti is found throughout the book.

1152. May, L. C.   "A Survey of Glossolalia and Re-
       1956   lated Phenomena in Non-Chris-
                              tian Religions." American An-
                              thropologist 58, no. 1: 75-96.

    Discussion of the phenomena of speaking in tongues.
Gives different categories for classifying the information on glossolalia. Some ethnographic information for
various parts of Africa.

1153. Mayer, Philip   Townsmen or Tribesmen. Vol. 2.
       1961   Cape Town: Oxford University
                              Press.

    Chapter 9 discusses the diviner's role among the
Xhosa (Xosa) of South Africa as being the communicator
between the spirits and man. Spirit mediumship is implied.

1154. Mayson, John Schofield The Malays of Cape Town.
       1861   Manchester: J. Galt & Co.

    The trances that are a part of the Mahometan (Moslem)
religious festivals of the Malay-speaking peoples of
South Africa are described on pages 19 ff.

1155. Mbiti, John S.   African Religions and Philosophy.
       1969   New York: Frederick A. Praeger.

    Both spirit possession and mediumship are discussed in
this general theoretical work on African religions (see
book's index under "Mediums" and "Possession" for page
citations). "Spirit possession occurs in one form or
another in practically every African society" (p. 81).

1156. Mbiti, John S.   Concepts of God in Africa.
       1970   New York: Praeger Publishers.

    In this general theoretical work, spirit possession is
mentioned for the following ethnic groups: Dinka, Sudan
(p. 17); Darasa, Ethiopia (p. 127); Lugbara, Zaire (p.
223); Moru, Sudan (p. 226); Ndebele, Rhodesia (pp. 226-
27). Spirit mediumship is cited for the following
groups: Bamum (Mum), Cameroon (p. 105); Ganda, Uganda

227

(p. 119); Gikuyu (Kikuyu), Kenya (p. 222); Lango, Uganda
(p. 223); Turkana, Kenya (p. 223); Twana (Tswana),
Botswana (p. 223); Meru, Kenya (p. 223). Also see pages
226-27.

1157. Mbiti, John S.   Introduction to African Reli-
      1975a   gion. London: Heinemann.

Spirit possession and mediumship are discussed in terms
of their roles in African religions in general (pp. 120
ff., 154 ff., 170).

1158. Mbiti, John S.   The Prayers of African Religion.
      1975b   London: S.P.C.K.

Although spirit possession is not explicitly labelled
in this general work on African religions, exorcism is
mentioned on several occasions, mainly in connection with
spirits which cause illness (pp. 10, 39 ff., 101 ff.).

1159. Meek, C. K.   "A Religious Festival in
      1930   Northern Nigeria." Africa:
                           Journal of the International
                           African Institute (London) 3,
                           no. 3: 323-46.

The Bachama, one of the Bata peoples of northern
Nigeria, worship a hero-god named Nzeanzo. The
priestess of Mbamto of Nzeanzo is regarded as a medium
between the god and the people. She is not, however,
subject to possession by the god; the hysterical symptoms
that would normally be regarded as a sign of possession
would, in her case, be regarded as a rejection by the god
(pp. 327-29).

1160. Meek, C. K.   A Sudanese Kingdom. London:
      1931a   Kegan Paul, Trench, Trubner &
                           Co.

Description of the cult of Mam and aspects of spirit
possession among the Jukun people (Nigeria) (chap. 4,
p. 197; chap. 6, pp. 277-93).

1161. Meek, C. K.   Tribal Studies in Northern
      1931b   Nigeria. Vols. 1 and 2.
                           London: Kegan Paul, Trench,
                           Trubner & Co.

The Nzeanzo cult and its priestesses are described
(vol. 1, chap. 1). Description of a professional class
of shamans among the Ngizim people (Nigeria); discussion
of spirit possession (vol. 2, pp. 236, 261, 521).

1162. Meek, C. K.   "The Kulŭ of Northern Nigeria."
      1934   Africa: Journal of the Interna-
                           tional African Institute
                           (London) 7, no. 3: 257-69.

   Among the Kulŭ of northern Nigeria the Mam arm-slashing
cult is a fairly recent introduction. Novices in the cult
spend the night before their initiation in a hut where
they may not eat, but where large amounts of beer are
consumed. The next day, the novices participate in
dances with other members of the cult. Dancers often
enter a state of dissociation or hysteria. In this
state, they stab themselves in the arm with an iron
spear. They are said to be possessed by the spirit of
Mam (pp. 263-64).

1163. Meek, C. K.   "The Religions of Nigeria."
      1943   Africa: Journal of the Interna-
                           tional African Institute
                           (London) 14, no. 3: 106-17.

   Spirit possession exists in many Nigerian tribes.
Among the Muslem Hausa the practice of Bori is widespread.
People become possessed through drumming or other
stimuli; some are capable of becoming possessed at any
time; priests of the cult come from this group. Among
the Yoruba, the Alifan (king) of Oyo defers only to a
special class of shamans when they are possessed by the
spirits of former kings. Among the tribes of the Benue,
possession centers around the cult of Mam. An outbreak
of possession occurred among Christians in Nigeria in
1927. Description of cures for possession (pp. 115-16).

1164. Meer, Fatima   Portrait of Indian South
      1969   Africans. Durban: Avon House.

   Both Hindu (pp. 153 ff.) and Muslim (pp. 184 ff.)
rituals involving possession are discussed in the context of the Indians residing in South Africa. Among the
Hindu, the God "Mother Draupadi" possesses the devotee,
while among the Muslem, djinns, spirits of fire, are
capable of possessing individuals. Also mentioned are
the "unorthodox" Islamic cults where devotees are infused
with divine power (pp. 201 ff.).

1165. Meldon, J. A.   "Notes on the Sudanese in
      1908   Uganda." Journal of the African
                           Society (London) 7, no. 26: 123-
                           46.

   Among the Lur (Alur) of Uganda, illness is sometimes
attributed to the possession of a person by an evil
spirit, called a Shaitan. The spirit is induced to leave
the ill person's body by a ritual cleansing (pp. 127,
135-36).

229

1166. Melland, F. H., and   Through the Heart of Africa.
      E. H. Cholmeley   Boston: Houghton Mifflin Co.
      1912

An account of possession in the Malesa cult of the
Wakuluwe (Kuluwe) people of the Lake Nyasa (Malawi) area.
Consumption of narcotics is described as aiding states of
trance (p. 20).

1167. Melland, Frank H.   In Witch Bound Africa. London:
      1923   Seeley, Service & Co.

The religion of the Lunda tribe (Zambia) is described
by J. L. Keith. Description of spirit possession by the
Chihamba tribal spirit (pp. 162-75).

1168. Mendonsa, Eugene L.   "The Soul and Sacrifice amongst
      1976   the Sisala." Journal of Reli-
                                gion in Africa (Leiden) 8, no.
                                1: 52-68.

Among the Sisala (Isala) of northern Ghana, the diviners are able to communicate with the spirits and thus
provide the link between the human and spirit realms.
When illnesses do not respond to "natural causal" treatments, the advice of a diviner is sought to discover from
which spirit the affliction has been sent (pp. 58-59).

1169. Mennesson-Rigaud, O.   "The Feasting of the Gods in
      1946   Haitian Vodou." Primitive Man
                                19:1-2.

Describes voodoo ceremonies involving spirit possession
(Haiti).

1170. Mennesson-Rigaud, O.   "Noël vodou en Haïti." Haïti:
      1951   Poètes noirs. Présence
                                africaine (Paris), no. 12, pp.
                                37-60.

The Christmas celebration in the Haitian vodou religion
is described and includes spirit possession trances.

1171. Mennesson-Rigaud, O.   "Étude sur le culte des Marassas
      1952   en Haiti." Zaire: Belgian
                                African Review (Bruxelles) 6,
                                no. 5: 597-621.

Detailed description is given of the cult of the
Marassas or Twins in Haiti. Possession by the (various)
Marassas nanchons (nations) is rare these days; however,
given in the text of this article is the description of
a possession by the Manger-Marassas (pp. 612 ff.).

230

1172. Mennesson-Rigaud,   "Le Role du vaudou dans
      Odette   l'indépendance d'Haïti."
      1958   Présence africaine, nos. 18-19,
                             pp. 43-67.

The African-influenced vaudou cult in Haïti is examined historically as to its role in Haitian independence. Spirit possession is mentioned on pages 49 ff.

1173. Mercier, P.   "Un Initiation au 'Bori' chez
      1951   les Zerma de Natitingou."
                             Notes africaines de l'Institut
                             francais de l'Afrique noire, no.
                             51, pp. 83-84.

Initiates to the Bori cult of the Zerma (Dahomey, now
Benin) are possessed by various kinds of spirits.

1174. Mercier, P.   "The Fon of Dahomey."   In
      1954   African Worlds, edited by D.
                             Forde. (Bib. 588.)

Description of the Vodu cults among the Fon (Dahomey,
now Benin) and spirit possession. "The gods intervene
in daily life, to reward or to punish, to exalt the man
who has been initiated by entering his head and possessing him" (p. 229).

1175. Meredith, L. C.   "Melsetter District - History of
      1976   Native Tribes and Chiefs." Nada
                             (Salisbury) 11, no. 3: 338-44.

This is the first publication of information supplied
to the South African Native Affairs Commission in 1903
by L. C. Meredith, the Native Commissioner of the
Melsetter District (Rhodesia) from 1895 to 1909. Several
ethnic groups are mentioned, among which the Wadondo
(Danda) are documented as having rain medicine connected
with a rain spirit (pp. 340-41). Mediumship is not explicitly labelled.

1176. Merriam, Alan P.   "Music--Bridge to the Superna-
      1957a   tural."   Tomorrow (New York) 5,
                             no. 4: 61-67.

The use of the drum in African possession trance ceremonies is outlined. Specific mention is made of the
Dahomey (Fon) (Dahomey, now Benin).

1177. Merriam, Alan P.   "Songs of the Ketu Cult of
      1957b   Bahia, Brazil." African Music
                             (Johannesburg) 1, no. 3: 53-67;
                             1, no. 4: 73-80.

The ceremonies of the Ketu cult (Brazil) are derived
from Yoruba religious practices; possession dances are
performed and are accompanied by percussion instruments.

1178. Merwe, Rev. W. J.   The Shona Idea of God. Fort
      van der   Victoria: Morgenter Mission
      1957   Press. [Reprinted from NADA,
                               no. 34 (1957).]

Spirit possession and mediumship are discussed throughout this short tract dealing with the Shona (Rhodesia)
idea of God, commonly called Mwari.

1179. Messenger, John C., Jr.   "The Christian Concept of For-
      1959a   giveness and Anang Morality."
                                 Practical Anthropology 6:97-103.

Among the Anang (Ibibio) of southeastern Nigeria, possession by the Holy Spirit and glossolalia are practiced
in the nativist Christian denominations (p. 101).

1180. Messenger, John C., Jr.   "Religious Acculturation among
      1959b   the Anang Ibibio." In Continu-
                                 ity and Change in African Cul-
                                 tures, edited by W. R. Bascom
                                 and M. J. Herskovits, pp. 279-
                                 99. (Bib. 90.)

The Anang Ibibio of Nigeria have an annual festival
during which the souls of the ancestors return to be
honored by their patrilineages. Masked dancers are possessed by ancestors or ghosts depending upon the type of
masks they wear (a beautiful mask marks a controlled possession by an ancestor, while an ugly mask marks the wild
possession of a ghost, pp. 281-82). Also discussed is
the practice of possession by the Holy Spirit in the
Ibibio members of Christian churches (pp. 287-89).

1181. Messenger, John C., Jr.   "Reinterpretations of Christian
      1970   and Indigenous Belief in a
                                  Nigerian Nativist Church." In
                                  Black Africa: Its Peoples and
                                  Their Cultures Today, edited by
                                  J. Middleton, pp. 212-21.
                                  (Bib. 1205.)

Glossolalia, possession by the Holy Spirit, and exorcism
practices are all mentioned as occurring among the members of the Christ Army Church, who are mainly of the
Anang (Ibibio) ethnic group in southeastern Nigeria.
[Also in American Anthropologist 62, no. 2 (1960): 268-
78.]

1182. Messing, Simon D.   "Group Therapy and Social Status
      1958   in the Zar Cult of Ethiopia."
                               American Anthropologist 60, no.
                               6: 1120-26.

   Among many Ethiopians of various backgrounds can be
found the Zar spirit possession cult. People possessed
by Zar spirits are cured by a spirit "doctor" inducing
the spirit to publicly possess his victim; the spirit
then is led to reveal his identity and what is required
to propitiate him. Discussion of the membership of Zar
cults, and of the role of the cults in a time of social
change. Also includes a comparison between traditional
and Western modes of group therapy.

1183. Métraux, Alfred   "The Concept of Soul in Haitian
      1946   Vodu." Southwestern Journal of
                               Anthropology 2, no. 1: 84-92.

   After a person dies in Haiti, the Loa (vodu) that used
to possess him must be removed from the head of the deceased by means of a ceremony called Dessonin, which
takes place either immediately after death or sometimes
later, in the cemetery (pp. 89-90).

1184. Métraux, A.   "L'Afrique vivante en Haïti."
      1950   Haïti: Poétes Noirs. Présence
                               africaine (Paris), no. 12, pp.
                               13-21.

   The African influence on the Haitian vodou religion is
discussed, and particular mention is made of the spirit
possession trances.

1185. Métraux, Alfred   "Medecine et vodou en Haïti."
      1953   Acta Tropica (Basel) 10:28-68.

   The traditional Haitian medical practices are discussed
in detail and are intertwined with the vodou spirit possession cult.

1186. Métraux, A.   "Divinités et cultes vodou dans
      1954a   la vallée de Marbial (Haïti)."
                               Zaïre: Belgian African Review
                               (Bruxelles) 8, no. 7: 675-707.

   A very complete description of the Haitian vodou cult
in the Marbial Valley is presented here. Both the
characters of the possessing deities and the ceremonial
activities involved in the cult are outlined.

1187. Métraux, Alfred   "Dramatic Elements in Ritual Pos-
      1954b   session." Diogenes, no. 11, pp.
                               18-36.

The trance state of spirit possession is analyzed in detail from data taken from various African and Afro-American religions including that of the Yoruba (Nigeria), Fon (Dahomey, now Benin), Haitian voodoo, Brazilian macumba and candomblé, and Cuban santería.

1188. Métraux, Alfred   "La Comedie rituelle dans la
      1955   possession." Diogenes. July,
                               pp. 1-24.

Not available for annotation.

1189. Métraux, Alfred   Haiti: La Terre, les hommes, les
      1957a   dieux. Neufchâtel: Baconnière.

Among rural Haitians, the folk religion is called vodou. This religion is derived from a cult in Dahomey, but in Haiti it has become altered by the spread of Catholicism. Vodou spirits are called Loa; they communicate with men by possessing certain of their worshippers and speaking through them. The possessed are called the "god's horse." Possession ceremonies are described in detail (pp. 84-90).

1190. Métraux, Alfred   "Histoire du vodou depuis la
      1957b   Guerre d'Indépendance jusqu'à
                               nos jours." Présence afri-
                               caine (Paris) 16:135-50.

Haitian voodoo (vodou) involves the worship of deities called Loa. During worship rituals the deities communicate with the worshippers by possessing initiates of the cult (called hounsi kanzo). Possessed persons are called the "horses of the Loa" (chevaux des Loa).

1191. Métraux, Alfred   Voodoo in Haiti: New York:
      1972 (1959)   Schocken Books.

Description of cases of possession observed by the author. Possession was known to occur in Haiti as early as the 1760's. Discussion of: history of Voodoo; the social framework of Voodoo; the supernatural world; the ritual; magic and sorcery; Voodoo and Christianity.

1192. Meyerowitz, Eva L. R.   "Notes on the King God Shango
      1946   and His Temple at Ibadan,
                               Southern Nigeria." Man 46, no.
                               27: 25-31.

History of the god Shango, with reference to the Sudanese god Aman; how Shango was introduced to Yoruba (Nigeria) country; description of his temple, with reference to possession; comparison is made with early reports on the subject by Leo Frobenius, 1910-12.

234

1193. Meyerowitz, Eva L. R.   The Sacred State of the Akan.
      1951   London: Faber & Faber.

      Among the Akan of the Gold Coast (Ghana), spirit
      mediumship and possession by the deity Tano of his priests
      are discussed on pages 124 ff.

1194. Meyerowitz, E. L. R.   The Akan of Ghana. London:
      1958   Faber & Faber. Ill.

      Considers the various cults found among the Akan
      (Ghana): moon cult, Venus cult, sun cult, etc. These
      cults have priests and priestesses who fall into trances
      after becoming possessed by spirits. Reference to pos-
      session is made throughout the book.

1195. Meyerowitz, Eva L. R.   At the Court of an African King.
      1962   London: Faber & Faber.

      Detailed description is given of the "birth" of a new
      god through the possession of a priest among the Akan of
      the Gold Coast (Ghana) (pp. 96-106).

1196. Michaux, Didier   "Le Démarche thérapeutique du
      1972   ndöp." Psychopathologie
                                 africaine (Dakar) 8, no. 1: 17-
                                 57.

      After a careful and extensive analysis of the ritual
      practices which are a part of the ndöp spirit possession
      ceremony among the Lebou (Lebu) and Wolof of Senegal,
      the author compares them to the weaning process in these
      cultures, stressing the new social position of the patient
      after the rituals.

1197. Middleton, John   "The Concept of Bewitching in
      1955   Lugbara." Africa: Journal of
                                 the International African In-
                                 stitute (London) 25, no. 3:
                                 252-60.

      The Lugbara (Uganda), who live in the region of the
      Nile-Congo divide, see God as having two aspects,
      Adroa'ba o'bapiri (god in the sky), a transcendent crea-
      tor, and Adro, the earthly aspect, who is terrible and
      greatly feared. The latter sometimes takes possession of
      adolescent girls and gives them the power of divination
      (pp. 256-58).

1198. Middleton, John   The Kikuyu and Kamba of Kenya.
      1958   Ethnographic Survey of Africa,
                                 edited by Daryll Forde. London:
                                 International African Institute.

Among the Kamba of Kenya, states of dissociation and
certain kinds of hysterical fits occur frequently,
especially among women, and are regarded as possession by
a spirit. The ancestor spirits are thought to speak
through a medium, and possession by them is not feared.
It commonly occurs at dances, and the spirit is exorcised
by dancing (p. 95).

1199. Middleton, John   Lugbara Religion. London:
      1960   Oxford University Press.

In the Yakan cult among the Lugbara of Uganda, spirit
possession is a major element of the diviner's role
(pp. 262-64, 269).

1200. Middleton, John   "The Yakan or Allah Water Cult
      1963   among the Lugbara." Journal of
                               Royal Anthropological Institute
                               of Great Britain and Ireland
                               93, pt. 1: 80-108.

Spirit possession is practiced in the Yakan cult
among the Lugbara of Uganda (pp. 96 ff.).

1201. Middleton, John, and   The Central Tribes of the North-
      Greet Kershaw   eastern Bantu. Ethnographic
      1965a   Survey of Africa, edited by
                               Daryll Forde, East Central
                               Africa, part 5. London:
                               International African Institute.

The Kamba of Kenya practice a form of spirit possession induced by dancing and drumming. Ceremonies are
held at important life-cycle transitions (pp. 71, 84, 86).

1202. Middleton, John   The Lugbara of Uganda. New
      1965b   York: Holt, Rinehart & Winston.

Discussion of the Yakan cult among the Lugbara
(Uganda); Yakan is conceived as a power that comes from
the spirit and seizes men and makes them tremble and
speak incoherently. Also, description of spirit possession by the Adro Onzi or evil spirits, possessing young
girls and giving them the power of divination (chap. 6,
pp. 63, 87-88).

1203. Middleton, John   "Oracles and Divination among
      1969a   the Lugbara." In Man in
                               Africa, edited by M. Douglas and
                               P. Kaberry, pp. 261-77.
                               (Bib. 475.)

The diviners of the Lugbara of Uganda are said to be
possessed by a "Spirit" termed Adro. Description of the
possessed state is given (pp. 267 ff.).

236

1204. Middleton, John   "Spirit Possession among the
      1969b   Lugbara." In Spirit Mediumship
                               and Society in Africa, edited
                               by J. Beattie and J. Middleton,
                               pp. 220-31. (Bib. 150.)

    Several forms of spirit possession exist among the
Lugbara (Uganda). Young girls may become possessed by
Adro, the earthly aspect of the deity; the girls then act
as diviners. The Yakan cult was brought to the Lugbara
by a prophet named Rembe. He gave his followers water
to drink that made them possessed and frenzied. Members
of a breakaway church, Balokole (the saved), may enter
into trance and speak in tongues.

1205. Middleton, John, ed.   Black Africa: Its Peoples and
      1970   Their Culture Today. London:
                               Collier-Macmillan Ltd.

    Includes in this bibliography:
              816   R. Horton (1970a)
              1181   J. C. Messenger, Jr. (1970)

1206. Middleton, John   "Secrecy in Lugbara Religion."
      1973a   History of Religions 12, no.
                               4: 229-316.

    Spirit possession in Lugbara (Uganda) religion is dis-
cussed in terms of ritual dangers and the need for
secrecy.

1207. Middleton, John   "Some Categories of Dual Classi-
      1973b   fication among the Lugbara of
                               Uganda." In Right and Left,
                               edited by Rodney Needham, pp.
                               369-90. Chicago: University of
                               Chicago Press.

    The relationship between illness, spirit possession,
and divination among the Lugbara of Uganda is analyzed in
terms of their system of classification.

1208. Milheiros, Mario   "Social and Ethnographic Data
      1953   on the Maiaca Tribe."
                               Mensario administrativo (Luanda)
                               67/68:1-127.

    Discussion of the role of the diviner among the
Maiaca (Yaka) (Angola) spirit world and men. Spirit
possession discussed. Text in Portuguese. [Cited in
African Abstracts, vol. 6, no. 62.]

1209. Miller, Paul M.   "Pastoral Care of 'Demonized'
      1975   Persons." Journal of Theology
                                for Southern Africa (Braam-
                                fontein, Transvaal), no. 12,
                                pp. 51-68.

Although African examples are not explicitly cited,
this article deals with "demonized" or demon-possessed
persons, and the mode of pastoral care they require.

1210. Millingen, J. G.   Curiosities of Medical Experi-
      1839   ence. 2d rev. ed. London: R.
                                Bentley.

Spirit possession cases reported for Africa.

1211. Millot, J., and   "Notes sur la sorcellerie chez
      A. Pascal   les Vezo de la région de
      1952   Morombe." Mémoires de
                                l'Institut scientifique de
                                Madagascar (Tananarive) 1, no.
                                1: 13-28.

Deals with the role of the sorcerer as curer of ills
among the Vezo of Madagascar. The sorcerer becomes possessed in order to communicate with the spirit world.
[Cited in African Abstracts, vol. 5, no. 124.]

1212. Millroth, Berta   Lyuba, Traditional Religion of
      1965   the Sakuma. Uppsala: Almquist
                                & Wiksells.

Among the Sakuma of Tanzania, ancestor spirits, called
masamva, may cause illness if neglected. Medicine men,
called Mfumu, induce the spirit to possess certain receptive individuals, usually women, and tell who they are
and what is troubling them. The Mfumu himself may also
sometimes undergo possession in order to gain guidance
during divination (pp. 117-24).

1213. Miner, Horace   "Culture Change Under Pressure:
      1960   A Hausa Case." Human Organiza-
                                tion 19, no. 3: 164-7.

In documenting the reaction of the Hausa to the British
methods of controlling sleeping sickness in Nigeria, mention is made of the Hausa bori spirit possession cults
(p. 166).

1214. Mischel, Frances   "African 'Powers' in Trinidad:
      1957   The Shango Cult." Anthropologi-
                                cal Quarterly 30, no. 2: 45-59.

Among the Yoruba and others of African descent in rural

238

Trinidad, the Shango cult is widespread. Several acts of spirit possession are described in detail.

1215. Mischel, Frances   "A Shango Religious Group and
      Osterman   the Problem of Prestige in
      1958a   Trinidadian Society." Ph.D.
                                Dissertation, The Ohio State
                                University. Dissertation Ab-
                                stracts 19, no. 12: 3082.

The Afro-American cult of Shango on Trinidad is focussed upon in this study of prestige and religious participation. Spirit possession is discussed in detail.

1216. Mischel, Walter, and   "Psychological Aspects of
      Frances Mischel   Spirit Possession." American
      1958b   Anthropologist 60:249-60.

Very detailed analysis of the possession syndrome.
Offers psychological interpretation of this phenomenon.

1217. Mitchell, Henry H.   Black Belief: Folk Beliefs of
      1975   Blacks in America and West
                               Africa. New York: Harper & Row.

Spirit possession in the Haitian voodoo cult and in
black American Christianity is presented as being not a
pathological phenomenon, but "of the highest order of
religion" (pp. 52-54).

1218. Mitchell, Robert   A Bibliography of Modern Afri-
      Cameron, and Harold   can Religious Movements.
      W. Turner,   Evanston, Ill.: Northwestern
      eds.   University Press.
      1966

This bibliography yields valuable sources on modern
African religious movements, and was used extensively in
the compilation of this bibliography. Supplements I and
II have been published by Harold W. Turner in Journal of
Religion in Africa (Leiden); I--1, no. 3 (1968):173-211;
II--3, no. 3 (1970):161-208 (listed separately in this
bibliography as 1766).

1219. Mitchell, Robert   "Religious Protest and Social
      Cameron   Change: The Origins of the Ala-
      1970   dura Movement in Western
                               Nigeria." In Protest and Power
                               in Black Africa, edited by R. I.
                               Rotberg and A. A. Mazrui, pp.
                               459-96. (Bib. 1520.)

The Aladura Church in Nigeria, which practices possession by the Holy Spirit and glossolalia, is examined
historically.

1220. Mitchell, Robert   "The Place of African Indepen-
      Cameron   dent Churches in the Analysis
      1972   of Religious Change: The Case of
                             the Aladura Churches in Western
                             Nigeria." In Congrès interna-
                             tional des africanistes, 2d
                             session, Dakar, 11-20 December
                             1967, pp. 301-14.

      Detailed presentation of the African Independent Church
of Aladura in western Nigeria, and its development from
1915 onwards. Analysis of its major elements is presented, including the use of an ecstatic state through
possession by the Holy Spirit.

1221. Mohamed, Abbas Ahmed   "Zar Ceremonies among the
      1969   Shaiqiya." Sudan Society
                             (Khartoum), pp. 117-99.

      The Shaiqiya (Arabs) (Sudan) believe that the zar
spirits make demands upon people initially through illness or abnormal behavior. With the assistance of the
Shaikhs of Zar, mainly women of long and wide experience,
the reason for possession is discovered.

1222. Molema, S. M.   The Bantu: Past and Present.
      1920   Edinburgh: W. Green & Son.

      Brief mention is made of a witch-doctor among the Xosa
peoples of South Africa who in 1857 was the "inspired
mouth piece" of the ancestral spirits, and was then moved
to prophesy about various events that would come to pass
for her peoples (pp. 167-68).

1223. Molet, Louis   "Cadres pour une ethnopsychiatrie
      1967   de Madagascar." Homme 7, no.
                            2: 5-29.

      Outlined is the ethnopsychiatric research to be done in
Madagascar, where "people attribute mental troubles to
phantoms, to supernatural beings, or to the activities
of witches." Means of lessening or resolving personal
conflicts are described, including exorcism of possessing
spirits. [Cited in African Abstracts, vol. 20, no. 1
(January 1970), no. 215.]

1224. Mondlane, Eduardo C.   "Guardian Spirits of the Bantu."
      1957   Tomorrow (New York) 5, no. 4:
                             89-94.

      Divination through communication with the ancestor
spirits by means of spirit possession and mediumship is
described for the southeastern Bantu-speaking peoples.

1225. Monfouga-Nicolas,   Ambivalence et culte de posses-
      Jacqueline   sion. Paris: Anthropos.
      1972

      An in-depth ethnographic study of the Hausa bori pos-
      session cult in the Republic of Niger is given here,
      along with hypotheses as to the reason for joining the
      cult.

1226. Mönnig, H. O.   The Pedi. Pretoria: J. L. Van
      1967   Schaik, Ltd.

      Among the Pedi of South Africa, one way that illnesses
      are caused is through spirits, malopo, sent by the an-
      cestor spirits to possess individuals. The healers,
      mapale, of these types of illnesses, badimo, enter into
      a trance state in order to exorcise the evil spirit
      (pp. 87-88).

1227. Monteil, Charles   Une Cité soudanaise: Djénné.
      1932   Paris: Société d'éditions
                            géographiques, maritimes et
                            coloniales.

      Spirit possession causing illness, and exorcism are
      mentioned briefly as occurring among the Bambara of Mali
      (p. 133).

1228. Monteil, Vincent   L'Islam noir. Paris: Éditions
      1964   du seuil.

      Spirit possession among the Muslims of Senegal is con-
      sidered to be a cause of illness. Ethnic groups men-
      tioned are the Sérèr, Dyola (Diola), and Lébou (Lebu).
      Also cited are the Yoruba spirit possession practices in
      Dahomey (Benin) (pp. 24-48).

1229. Monteiro, Duglas   "A Macumba de Vitória." Anais
      Teixeira   do 31 Congresso Internacional de
      1955   Americanistas, São Paulo: vol.
                            1, pp. 464-472.

      A brief description of the beliefs and rituals of a
      Macumba cult. Possession is mentioned in describing
      differences between Macumba and other cults in Brazil.

1230. Montilus, Guérin   "Haïti: Un Cas témoin de la
      1972   vivacité des religions africaines
                            en Amérique et pourquoi?" In
                            Les Religions africains comme
                            source de valeurs de civilisa-
                            tion, Colloque de Cotonou
                            (August 1970), pp. 287-308.
                            (Bib. 358.)

Possession trance is mentioned in this article on the
extent of and the reasons for the influence of African
religions in Haiti.

1231. Moore, Joseph G., and   "A Comparative Study of Accultu-
       George E. Simpson   ration in Morant Bay and West
       1957   Kingston, Jamaica," Zaïre:
                                  Belgian African Review
                                  (Bruxelles) 11, nos. 9-10: 979-
                                  1019. (First part.)

Very detailed description is given of the four major
religious cults found in Morant Bay and West Kingston,
Jamaica. The cults are Cumina, Revival, Pocomania, and
Revival Zion. Specific attention is paid to spirit possession on pages 992-96. Cultic ceremonies are outlined
for each movement (pages 1000 ff.).

1232. Moore, J. G., and   "A Comparative Study of Accultu-
       G. E. Simpson   ration in Morant Bay and West
       1958   Kingston, Jamaica." Zaïre:
                                  Belgian African Review
                                  (Bruxelles) 12, no. 1: 65-87.
                                  (Conclusion.)

In this continuation of their 1957 article, the
authors compare the four cults Cumina, Revival, Pocomania,
and Revival Zion and their various manifestations in the
Morant Bay area and in West Kingston, Jamaica. The
phenomenon of possession is discussed throughout.

1233. Moore, Joseph G.   "Religious Syncretism in
       1965   Jamaica." Practical Anthropology
                                  12, no. 2: 63-70.

Spirit possession trance rituals in the Jamaican syncretic cults of Revival Zionist and Pocomania (or Black
Israelite) are described.

1234. Morkel, E. R.   "Spiritualism among the
       1933   Wabudya." Southern Rhodesia
                                  Native Affairs Department Annual
                                  11:106-16.

Description of ancestral and other classes of spirits
that on occasion possess individuals among the Wabudya
(Budya) (Rhodesia).

1235. Morris, H. S.   The Indians in Uganda. Chicago:
       1968   University of Chicago Press.

Spirit mediums among the Indian settlers in Uganda are
used to discover and placate ghosts who afflict the
household. These mediums can belong to any caste, and
are usually possessed by a mata goddess of the Hindu
pantheon (pp. 58-60).

242

1236. Mors, O.   "Soothsaying among the Bahaya."
      1951   Anthropos 46, nos. 5-6: 825-52.

Among the Bahaya (Haya) people of Malawi, the
Embandwa or soothsayer interprets oracles while falling
in a state of convulsion. Also, information on the work
of the Nyabingi priestess and on spirit mediumship of
those who interpret the wishes of the ancestral spirits.

1237. Morton, Alice L.   "Ethiopian Spirit Possession: An
      1974   Argument for a Theory of Muddling
                          Through." Paper presented at
                          the American Anthropological
                          Association meeting, Mexico
                          City, November. 16 pp.

The disease theory involved in the Ethiopian Zar
spirit possession cult is examined, first in relationship to Western medical diagnoses, and then in terms of
the concept of "incrementalism" or "muddling through" of
planning theory.

1238. Morton, Alice   "Dawit: Competition and Inte-
      1977   gration in an Ethiopian Waqabi
                          Cult Group." In Case Studies
                          in Spirit Possession, edited by
                          V. Crapanzano and V. Garrison,
                          pp. 193-233. (Bib. 391.)

Beginning with the premise that spirit possession af-
fords a method of dealing with personal and interpersonal problems, the author goes on to present a case
study of the activities of the Waqabi (Zar) cult in
Ethiopia.

1239. Morton-Williams, P.   "The Atinga Cult among the
      1956   Southwestern Yoruba: A Socio-
                            logical Analysis of a Witch-
                            Finding Movement." Bulletin de
                            l'Institut français d'Afrique
                            noire (Dakar), ser. B, 18, nos.
                            3-4: 315-34.

Ethnographic description and sociological analysis is
given of the Atinga cult among the Yoruba of Nigeria
that centers on witch finding. By means of possession
by the spirit Tigere, the followers are able to single
out the witches of a community, mainly older women. A
type of divination with chickens is used if further proof
is needed.

1240. Morton-Williams, Peter "Yoruba Responses to the Fear of
      1960   Death." Africa: Journal of the
                               International African Institute
                               (London) 30, no. 1: 34-40.

243

Among the Yoruba of southwestern Nigeria and southern
Dahomey (Benin) the egungun cult is employed as a means
to make visible the ancestral spirits and to give as-
surances of immortality. The egungun are male members of
the cult who wear masks bearing the names of great ancestors and sing the praises of these ancestors. Shortly after the death of an old man, he is represented by
an egungun wearing the old man's clothes and hat who ad-
monishes his family for their shortcomings since his
death, and thus assures them of his continued watchful-
ness and interest. Only men are allowed to be represented by egungun; women are considered to be guaranteed of
immortality through their children (pp. 36-39).

1241. Morton-Williams, Peter   "An Outline of the Cosmology
      1964   and Cult Organization of the
                                  Oyo Yoruba." Africa: Journal
                                  of the International African
                                  Institute (London) 34, no. 3:
                                  243-61.

      Spirit possession is discussed throughout this de-
      tailed analytical article on the Yoruba (Nigeria) Oyo
      cults.

1242. Morton-Williams, Peter   "The Yoruba Kingdom of Oyo." In
      1967   West African Kingdoms in the
                                  Nineteenth Century, edited by
                                  D. Forde and P. M. Kaberry,
                                  pp. 38-69. (Bib. 592.)

      The place of the spirit possession cults and their
      priests in the sociopolitical organization of the Yoruba
      kingdom of Oyo in Nigeria is outlined (pp. 58 ff.).

1243. Moss, Nicola   "The Traditional Installation of
      1976   Raimon Ngaite Ndima (Chief
                                  Ndima)." Nada (Salisbury) 11,
                                  no. 3: 328-32.

      The installation of Chief Ndima among the Shona of
      Rhodesia in 1974 is described here, and mention is made
      of the role played by the svikiro spirit medium, Marira.

1244. Mudenda, E. H. K.   "Some Spiritual Conceptions of
      1948   the Ba-Tonga of Northern
                                  Rhodesia." Makerere (Kampala)
                                  3, no. 1: 20-22.

      Description of a cult whose central characters are the
      spirits of the clan ancestors. Among the Ba-Tonga
      (Thonga) (northern Rhodesia, now Zambia), the diseases
      of Machooba and Izilubi are attributed to spirit posses-
      sion and victims have to be ritually exorcised. Shows

244

the relation between religious beliefs and clan structure. [Cited in African Abstracts, vol. 1, p. 133.]

1245. Mugarura, B.   "Nyabingi Cult in South Kigezi."
      1974   Occasional Research Papers in
                           African Traditional Religion and
                           Philosophy (Makerere University,
                           Kampala), vol. 17, no. 188.

      Although spirit possession and mediumship are not ex-
plicitly labelled, both are implied in this analysis of
the Nyabingi cult among the Bakiga (Chiga) of Uganda.

1246. Mukanga, A.   "The Traditional Belief in
      1973   Balubaale." Occasional Research
                           Papers in African Traditional
                           Religion and Philosophy
                           (Makerere University, Kampala),
                           vol. 15, no. 167.

      The Balubaale cult, in which the lubaale spirits pos-
sess mediums, who are then consulted in matters of personal advice, is analyzed and discussed in relation to
Christianity among the Kiganda (Ganda) of Uganda.

1247. Mulago, Vincent   Un Visage africain du
      1965   Christianisme. Paris: Présence
                           africaine.

      Examining the religions of the Bantu-speaking Bashi,
Rwanda (Ruanda), and Burundi (Rundi) (Rwanda and
Burundi), the author finds spirit possession to be an
aspect of the cult of the ancestors (pp. 97 ff.).

1248. Mulago, V.   "La Conception de Dieu dans la
      1967   tradition bantoue." Revue du
                           clergé africain (Inkisi) 22,
                           no. 3: 272-99.

      Among the Bantu-speaking Bakongo (Kongo) of Angola,
Nzambi, God, is spoken of as possessing them: "Nzambi
nous possède, il nous mange" (p. 274).

1249. Mulago, Vincent   "Le Culte de Lyangombe chez les
      1969a   Bashi et les Banyarwanda."
                           Cahiers des religions africaines
                           (Kinshasa) 3, no. 6: 299-314.

      The cult of the spirit Lyangombe among the Bashi and
Banyarwanda (Ruanda) of Rwanda includes spirit possession
(pp. 312-14).

1250. Mulago, Vincent   "Vital Participation." In
      1969b   Biblical Revelation and African
                             Beliefs, edited by K. A.
                             Dickson and P. Ellingworth,
                             pp. 137-58. (Bib. 450.)

     Bantu religion is discussed in this article, and the
practice of spirit possession among the priests of the
ancestor hero Lyangombe is mentioned on page 155.
Specific Bantu-speaking groups studied are the Bashi of
Zaïre, the Ruanda (Rwanda), and the Barundi (Rundi)
(Burundi).

1251. Mulago gwa Cikala   "Symbolisme dans les religions
      Musharhamina   traditionnelles africaines et
      1972   sacramentalisme." Revue du
                              clerge africain (Inkisi) 27,
                              nos. 4-5: 466-502.

     In speaking of various types of religious ceremonies
among the Bantu-speaking Bakongo (Kongo)(Zaïre, Angola),
Bashi (Zaïre), Banyarwanda (Ruanda) (Zaïre, Rwanda),
Balusa (Lusa) of Kasai (Zaïre), and Mongo (Zaïre), mention is made of the use of spirit possession and mediumship in spirit cults such as that of the secret society
of Lyangombe (pp. 476-78).

1252. Müller, Jac   "Neon-Pentecostalism: A Theolo-
      1974   gical Evaluation of Glossolalia,
                              with Special Reference to the
                              Reformed Churches." Journal of
                              Theology for Southern Africa
                              (Cape Town), no. 7, pp. 41-49.

     The phenomenon of glossolalia is investigated both
psychologically and theologically, and emphasis is
placed on its nonlinguistic (i.e., noncommunicative)
nature and the qualifying remarks made about it in the
New Testament.

1253. Munday, J. T.   "Spirit Names among the Central
      1948   Bantu." African Studies
                             (Johannesburg) 7, no. 1: 39-44.

     Among the Nsenga of Northern Rhodesia (Zambia) for-
gotten ancestral spirits are called cilengwa-lengwa
("created but forgotten"). They are thought sometimes to
take possession of people, driving them mad. Like all
other ancestral spirits, they also can be reincarnated
(p. 42).

1254. Muñoz, Nelida Agosto   "Haitian Voodoo: Social Control
      1972   of the Unconscious." Caribbean
                              Review (San Juan) 4, no. 3:
                              6-10.

A detailed psycho-physiological and sociological analysis of the possession state in the Haitian <u>Voodoo</u> cult is presented.

1255. Muntemba, M.
1972

"Zambia Nzila Sect and Christian Churches in the Livingstone Area." Paper presented at the Conference on the History of Central African Religious Systems, Lusaka, 30 August - 8 September.

The growth of the <u>Nzila Sect</u>--founded in 1926--is traced from both traditional Lozi (Zambia) and Christian roots. Concentrating on healing, membership is obtained through having one's spirit-caused illnesses cured according to the <u>Nzila</u> way. Possession is mentioned as cause and as part of the cure of illness.

1256. Murphree, Marshall W.
1969

<u>Christianity and the Shona</u>.
London: Athlone Press.

Spirit possession and mediumship among the Shona of Rhodesia **are** discussed in terms of their use in the traditional religion and in Christianity (see book's index under "Possession" and "Mediumship" for page citations).

1257. Murphree, Marshall W.
1971

"Religious Interdependence among the Budjga Vapostori." In <u>African Initiatives in Religion</u>, edited by D. B. Barrett, pp. 170-80. (Bib. 83.)

The Vapostori (Apostles) Church among the Shona-speaking Budjga (Budya) of Rhodesia places great emphasis on healing through exorcism techniques and on possession by the Holy Spirit.

1258. Murphy, H. B. M.
1973

"Current Trends in Transcultural Psychiatry." <u>Proceedings of the Royal Society of Medicine</u> 66, no. 7: 711-16.

Although spirit possession is not explicitly labelled in this general article, dissociational trance states are discussed as occurring in many cultures. No specific culture is analyzed, but mention is made of Africa and the Caribbean.

1259. Murray, Colin
1975

"Sex, Smoking and the Shades: A Sotho Symbolic Idiom." In <u>Religion and Social Change in Southern Africa</u>, edited by M. G. Whisson and M. West, pp. 58-77. (Bib. 1870.)

Among the Sotho of South Africa, possession by the
shades causes "madness." Treatment of this illness is
discussed on pages 70-73.

1260. Murray, Jocelyn   "The Kikuyu Spirit Churches."
      1973   Journal of Religion in Africa
                               (Leiden) 5, no. 3: 198-234.

Spirit possession is briefly mentioned in this historical account of the development of Holy Spirit
Churches among the Kikuyu of Kenya (p. 226).

1261. Mwanza, R.   "Mwari: The God of the Karanga."
      1972   Paper presented at the Conference
                              on the History of Central Afri-
                              can Religious Systems, Lusaka,
                              31 August - 8 September.

Tracing of the complex origins of the Mwari, the high
god of the Karanga in Rhodesia, is attempted. Lineages
are given for the high priests at several shrines, as
this is a hereditary position--possession is implied but
not discussed.

1262. Nadel, S. F.   "A Shaman Cult in the Nuba
      1941   Mountains." Sudan Notes and
                              Records (Khartoum) 24:85-112.

Description of the Bayel (Sudan) priest, Bayel being
a term for both the spirit and its human vessel. Description of the role of the priest in the community.

1263. Nadel, S. F.   "The Hill Tribes of Kadero
      1942   (Nuba Mountains)." Sudan Notes
                              and Records (Khartoum) 25, no.
                              1: 37-79.

Discusses the relation between clan structure and
spirit cults in the Sudan. Information on spirit possession and initiation into the priesthood.

1264. Nadel, S. F.   "A Study of Shamanism in the
      1946   Nuba Mountains." Journal of the
                              Royal Anthropological Institute
                              of Great Britain and Ireland 76,
                              no. 1: 25-37.

Description of the kinds of spirits that possess
shamans in the Sudan. Divination practices discussed
and trances described. Epilepsy is not regarded as
symptomatic of spirit possession.

1265. Nadel, S. F.   The Nuba: An Anthropological
      1947   Study of the Hill Tribes in
                              Kordofan. London: Oxford
                              University Press.

248

Consideration of the presence or absence of a spirit
possession cult in the tribes of the Nuba Hills (Sudan).

1266. Nadel, S. F.   Nupe Religion. London:
      1954   Routledge & Kegan Paul.

Chapter 7 deals with the Bori cult among the Hausa
(Nigeria). The idea of spirit possession is revealed in
hysterical or cataleptic fits and in trance states, when
the person so affected is believed to speak with the
voice of a spirit and to behave like one. Description
of the possession cult (p. 209).

1267. Nalder, L. F.   A Tribal Survey of Mongalla Prov-
      1937   ince. London: Oxford Univer-
                            sity Press.

Among the Bari of the Sudan, possession by the wind is
considered to be a cause of illness, and "is often susceptible to cure by modern drugs, strong purges, or
other more humane methods" (p. 133).

1268. Nash, Eleanor S.   "The Psycho-social Context of
      1974   Glossolalia." Journal of
                            Theology of Southern Africa
                            (Cape Town), no. 7, pp. 61-65.

Glossolalia in the Pentecostal Church is examined from
the point of view of research on altered states of consciousness. Particular interpretations of trance
phenomena are culture specific.

1269. Nassau, Rev. R. H.   Fetichism in West Africa. New
      1904   York: Charles Scribner's Sons.

Throughout the book there are discussions of spirit
mediumship in West Africa. Chapter 9 particularly deals
with forms of demoniacal possession.

1270. Ndeti, K.   "The Relevance of African Tra-
      1968/69   ditional Doctor in Scientific
                           Medicine." In Sociology Papers,
                           University of East Africa
                           Social Sciences Council Con-
                           ference, pp. 378-90. Kampala:
                           Makerere Institute of Social
                           Research.

Although spirit possession is not explicitly labelled,
it is implied as a traditional aetiological explanation
of illness in Africa. Comparison is drawn between
African and Western scientific methods and beliefs concerning illness.

1271. Needham, Rodney
      1967a

"Percussion and Transition."
Man (London), n.s. 2, no. 4:
606-14.

The use of percussion instruments to contact and communicate with the spiritual world is explored in this
general theoretical article. Neither Africa nor spirit
possession is explicitly mentioned.

1272. Needham, Rodney
      1967b

"Right and Left in Nyoro Symbolic Classification." Africa:
Journal of the International
African Institute (London) 37,
no. 4: 425-52.

Among the Nyoro of Uganda, the right hand is usually
associated with auspicious events and the left with in-
auspicious ones. To explain the fact that diviners of
the Cwezi spirit mediumship cult use the left hand in
divination, an attempt is made to associate mediums and
diviners with women, with whom the left hand is often
associated. The number three is associated with women,
and the number nine (three times three) plays a role in
the initiations and other rituals of the Cwezi cult.
Furthermore, at the ceremony of initiation in the Cwezi
cult, the novice is given to believe that he must demonstrate his possession by the spirits by becoming a woman.
The initiators, however, do not actually expect him to
do this (pp. 435-38).

1273. Needham, Rodney
      1976

"Nyoro Symbolism: The Ethnographic Record." Africa:
Journal of the International
African Institute (London) 46,
no. 3: 236-46.

The author responds to John Beattie's article on the
Nyoro of Uganda [Africa (1968, Bib. 148)], and discusses
the role of spirit mediums among these people (pp. 239-
40).

1274. Neels, Marcel G.
      1974

"The Relationship between
Priests and Prophets in African
Religious Systems." Cahiers
des religions africaines
(Kinshasa) 8, no. 15: 27-54.

Spirit possession and mediumship are both discussed in
this general theoretical discussion of the relationship
between the roles of the priest and of the prophet in
African religions.

1275. Neher, Andrew
      1961

"Auditory Driving Observed with
Scalp Electrodes in Normal Sub-

jects." Electroencephalography
and Clinical Neurophysiology 13:
449-51.

The "sonic driving" effect produced by drumming is ob-
servable in the EEG brainwave patterns. Psychological
reports by the subjects are included.

1276. Neher, Andrew   "A Physiological Explanation of
      1962   Unusual Behavior in Ceremonies
                             Involving Drums." Human Bio-
                             logy 34, no. 2: 151-61.

Discusses the relation of rhythmic stimulation by
drumming to states of possession. Ethnographic material
from Africa and Haiti. Tests the hypothesis that the
behavior observed in drum ceremonies, that is, spirit
possession, is the result primarily of the effects of
rhythmic drumming on the central nervous system.

1277. Neligan, C. W.   "Kijesu Ceremony." Man, nos.
      1911   34-35. Ill.

The author reports about an Akamba (Kamba) (Kenya)
woman who, after seeing the author's helmet, fell into
a fit. He describes the exorcism ceremonies that followed. Pictorial illustrations are available; they were
taken when the incident happened in 1908.

1278. Nelson, Cynthia   "Self, Spirit Possession and
      1971   World View: An Illustration from
                             Egypt." International Journal
                             of Social Psychiatry (London)
                             17, no. 3: 194-209.

Presented here is a detailed account of the involvement
of Egyptian women in Zar possession cults in Cairo. The
reasons for joining a Zar group, the ceremonies that go
on, and the ramifications of joining in terms of the
position of women in that society are all discussed.

1279. Nelson, Harold D.,   Area Handbook for Southern
      et al.   Rhodesia. Washington, D.C.:
      1975   U.S. Government Printing Office.

The Shona and Ndebele (Rhodesia) beliefs about spirit
possession and mediumship, especially with regard to the
Mwari (Mlimo) cult, the mhondoro tribal ancestor spirits,
the mudzimu ancestor spirits, and the shave spirits, are
presented on pages 95-97. The glossolalia found in the
Zionist church movement is compared with these traditional practices on page 99.

1280. Neveux, M.	Religion des noirs: Fétiches de
1923	la Côte d'Ivoire. Alençon: Im-
	primerie Laverdure.

Among the Gouro (Guro) of the Ivory Coast, the diviners go into a trance state in order to communicate with
their totemic spirits (p. 9).

1281a.Newman, Bernard	South African Journey. Cape
1965	Town: Howard Timmins.

Spirit possession by lion spirits of African witch-
doctors, and exorcism practices employed for healing
illnesses, are both mentioned in a short section of this
travel account (pp. 88-92).

1281b.Ngubane, Harriet	Body and Mind in Zulu Medicine.
1977	London: Academic Press.

The author, a physician, explores the beliefs of her
own people, the Zulu of South Africa. She discusses
notions of evil spirit possession and the relationship
of ancestors to a variety of illnesses.

1282. Nicolaisen, Johannes	"Essai sur la religion et la
1961	magie touaregues." Folk
	(Copenhagen) 3:113-62.

The Tuareg (Mali) believe in spirits, demons, which are
named Kel Asouf. These are considered malevolent spirits
who "enter" an individual and render him ill. The possessed will go into trances during dance ceremonies which
are accompanied by drumming. Description of exorcism
ceremonies. Analysis of the role of the Kel Asouf
spirits in the religious life of the Tuareg. [Cited in
African Abstracts, vols. 13/14, no. 324.]

1283. Nicolas, Jacqueline	"Les Juments des dieux: Rites de
1967	possession et condition féminine
	en pays Hausa." Études
	nigériennes (Paris), no. 21, pp.
	1-142.

A very detailed account of the Hausa women's bori cult
of spirit possession is given here along with an analysis
of the phenomenon of possession itself and the role of
the women in Hausa society (Nigeria).

1284. Nicolas, Jacqueline	"Culpabilité, somatisation et
1970	catharsis au sein d'un culte de
	possession: 'Le Bori hausa.'"
	Psychopathologie africaine
	(Dakar) 6, no. 2: 147-80.

Ideas concerning the cause of illness, reasons for turning to the bori possession cult, and its effectiveness are discussed in detail for the Hausa of Nigeria.

1285. Nida, Eugene A., and William A. Smalley 1959 — *Introducing Animism*. New York: Friendship Press.

In this introductory account of animistic religions, the Haitian Voodoo spirit possession cult is briefly mentioned on page 44.

1286. Nida, Eugene A. 1966 — "African Influence in the Religious Life of Latin America." *Practical Anthropology* 13, no. 4: 133-38.

Despite difficulties arising from the highly divergent and unorganized religions in Latin America, four main religious areas are determined: (1) Cuban Chango rites; (2) Haitian voodoo worship; (3) African healing rituals in Brazil; and (4) a diverse residual group ranging from Caribbean voodoo reinterpretation of Protestantism to Surinam "bush religions."

1287. Nielsen, Peter n.d. (1913) — *The Matabele at Home*. Bulawayo: Davis & Co.

Although spirit possession and mediumship are not explicitly mentioned, the trance behavior among the Matabele (Ndebele) of Rhodesia which is manifested in religious contexts is described on pages 38, 42-43.

1288. Nillroth, L. W., L. Dahlin and K. Dahlin 1964 — *Mass Hysteria in an African Girl's School*. Ndologe.

Not available for annotation.

1289. Nizurugero, Jean 1974 — "La Tradition dans la fête urbaine." *Psychopathologie africaine* (Dakar) 10, no. 3: 353-79.

The role that traditional customs and beliefs play in the urban Senegalese center of Dakar is discussed. Among these traditions are those surrounding spirit possession by the rab ancestor spirits, and the ndep (Lébu), lup (Sérèr), and mbilewu [Tukuler (Tukulor)] ceremonies undertaken to exorcise these spirits (pp. 362-67).

1290. Njaka, Elechukwu N.   "Nigeria's Igbo: Patterns of
      1957   Worship." Tomorrow (New York)
                                  5, no. 4: 95-99.

      Spirit possession and mediumship are practiced among
      the Igbo of Nigeria along with glossolalia and xeno-
      glossia.

1291. Nketia, J. H.   "Possession Dances in African
      1957   Society." Journal of the Inter-
                                  national Folk Music Council
                                  (London) 9:4-9.

      Description of possession dances among the Ga, Akan,
      and Ashanti peoples (Ghana). Description of the pro-
      gression of the dance; possession occurs at the final
      stage when the senior medium becomes possessed. Analy-
      sis is offered of the role of spirit possession in the
      communal life of the peoples described.

1292. Nketia, J. H.   Ghana--Music, Dance and Drama.
      Kwabena   Legon: Institute of African
      1965   Studies, University of Ghana.

      Spirit possession and mediumship, facilitated by
      dancing and drumming, are mentioned as occurring among
      the peoples of Ghana (p. 34).

1293. Noble, D. S.   "Demoniacal Possession among the
      1961   Giriama." Man 61:50-52.

      Spirit possession among the Giriama (Giryama) of
      Kenya. Description of the possessing spirits, some of
      Masai origin; others are said to be European. The
      manifestations of these spirits and curing ceremonies
      for possession are described.

1294. Norbeck, Edward   Religion in Primitive Society.
      1961   New York: Harper & Bros.

      General discussion of primitive religion. Chapter 6
      deals with possession, glossolalia, and other unusual
      psychological states. Among the Amazulu (Zulu) of South
      Africa, a man may interpret a long illness, a lack of
      interest in food, frequent spells of dizziness, posses-
      sion, or some other unusual condition as a sign that he
      should become a diviner (p. 86). Africa is listed as a
      center of glossolalia (speaking in tongues); general dis-
      cussion of glossolalia (p. 91). The Nuba of Sudan use
      deep breathing and a cramped posture as aids to inducing
      a trance seizure (p. 94).

1295. Nsibu, Isaac   "The Ancestral Cult of the
      1968   Baziba." Dina na Mila (Kampala)
                                  3, nos. 2-3: 17-64.

Among the Baziba (Haya) of Uganda spirit possession by
ancestral spirits occurs, and description of the state is
given on pages 42-44.

1296. "Nyangweso"   "The Cult of Mumbo in Central
      1930   and South Kavirondo." Journal
                           of the East Africa and Uganda
                           Natural History Society
                           (Nairobi), nos. 38-29, pp. 13-
                           17.

      This gives a brief sketch of the Mumbo cult among the
Luo of Kenya that arose in 1913. Trance and glossolalia
are cited as elements in being "called" by the Mumbo
Snake spirit.

1297. Nyanzi, E.   "'Dindo': A Traditional Sacred
      1974   Place in Buganda." Occasional
                          Research Papers in African Tra-
                          ditional Religion and Philo-
                          sophy (Makerere University,
                          Kampala), vol. 22, no. 224.

      Dindo is one of the many sacred places in Buganda
(Ganda) land in Uganda, and, like many others, it has
its medium or priest who lives there (p. 12).

1298. Ochieng, William R. "Black Jeremiah." Thought and
      1974   Practice (Nairobi) 1, no. 2:
                          61-74.

      The biography of Sakawa, the famous Gusii (Uganda) di-
viner of the nineteenth century, is recorded here. Known
among many peoples for his healing and prophetic powers,
Sakawa is said to have spoken with and been possessed by
the ancestral spirits.

1299. Ochsner, Knud   "Church, School and the Clash of
      1971   Cultures: Examples from North-
                          west Tanzania." Journal of
                          Religion in Africa (Leiden) 4,
                          no. 2: 97-118.

      In northwest Tanzania, the mixture of thought and be-
liefs by the schoolchildren reflect African traditional
elements along with Christian and Muslim influence. A
fifth of the students studied believe that epilepsy is
caused by spirit possession (p. 108). Ethnic groups included are: Haya, Nyambo, Hangaza, Shubi (Subi), Zinza,
Ha, Sukuma, Sumbwa, Kerewe, Luo, Jita, Ruri, Nyaruanda
(Ruanda), Nyamwezi, Chagga (Chaga), Pare, Nyakyusa, Fipa,
Runga, Makua, and Nyanja.

1300. Odugbesan, Clara   "Femininity in Yoruba Religious
      1969   Art." In Man in Africa, edited
                                      by M. Douglas and P. Kaberry,
                                      pp. 199-211. (Bib. 475.)

      In this analysis of the feminine figure in Yoruba
      (Nigeria) religious art, spirit possession practiced by
      the priests of the Shango cult is discussed on pages 206
      ff.

1301. Oesterreich, T. K.   Possession Demoniacal and Other.
      1930   New York: Richard R. Smith, Inc.

      One of the most often cited books in the literature on
      spirit possession. Very detailed analysis. Chapter 7
      contains ethnographic information for Africa.

1302. Oger, Louis   "Spirit Possession among the
      1972   Bemba: A Linguistic Approach."
                                      Paper presented at the Con-
                                      ference on the History of Cen-
                                      tral African Religious Systems,
                                      Lusaka, 30 August - 8 September.

      A linguistic analysis is given for the Bemba (Northern
      Province, Zambia) possession cults of the ancestors and
      of the ngulu spirits (those of "once-human beings").
      Possession is described from the initial symptoms to its
      full elaboration in healing and divination.

1303. Ogot, B. A.   "British Administration in Cen-
      1963   tral Nyanza District of Kenya,
                                      1900-1960." Journal of African
                                      History (Cambridge), vol. 4,
                                      no. 2.

      Discussion of spirit possession and related phenomena
      (Kenya) (pp. 255-57).

1304. Ogot, Bethwell A.   "On the Making of a Sanctuary:
      1972   Being Some Thoughts on the His-
                                      tory of Religion in Padhola."
                                      In The Historical Study of
                                      African Religion, edited by T.
                                      O. Ranger and I. N. Kimambo,
                                      pp. 122-35. (Bib. 1442.)

      Spirit possession and mediumship in the bura cult
      among the Padhola of Uganda are discussed in detail (pp.
      128 ff.).

1305. O'Hara, Andy   "Donne Zioniste nel Sud-Africa."
      1963   Nigrizia (Verona) 81, no. 10:
                                      18-23. Ill.

                                   256

The practice among the South African Zionist churches
of possession by the Holy Spirit is discussed.

1306. Ojuku, Aloo   "African Thought and the Concept
      1974   of Essence." Thought and Prac-
                               tice (Nairobi) 1, no. 1: 19-26.

      Spirit mediumship and possession are implied but not
explicitly labelled in this philosophical essay on
African thought (p. 21).

1307. Okasha, A.   "A Cultural Psychiatric Study of
      1966   El-Zar Cult in U.A.R."
                               British Journal of Psychiatry
                               112, no. 493: 1217-21.

      An analysis of the Zar cult in the United Arab Republic
is given, and the efficacy of its practices is discussed
with reference to Western psychiatric methodology and
diagnoses.

1308. Okasha, A.   "Psychiatric Observations in
      n.d.   Egypt." Mimeographed. 12 pp.

      The Zar spirit possession healing cult in Cairo, Egypt,
is mentioned in this general survey of the clinical cases
reported in the Ain Shams University Psychiatric Clinic.
[Cited in Transcultural Psychiatric Research Review
(Bruges) 5 (October 1968): 149-51.]

1309. Okumu, pa'Lukobo   "Acholi Dance and Dance Songs."
      1971   Uganda Journal (Kampala) 35,
                               no. 1: 55-61.

      The Jok spirit possession dances of the Acholi of
Uganda are described and the translations of the songs
of several major Jok spirits are given.

1310. Oliver, Roland   "A Question about the Bachwezi."
      1953   Uganda Journal 17, no. 2: 135-
                               37.

      Historical account of the Buchwezi dynasty (Uganda).
The Buchwezi left some notions of a religion which included the belief that the spirits of the dead have the
power to possess the living and thus give oracles through
their mouths.

1311. Omari, C. K.   "The Mganga: A Specialist of His
      1972   Own Kind." Psychopathologie
                               africaine (Dakar) 5, no. 2: 217-
                               31.

      An analysis of the activities required of the mganga,

257

the "medicine man" of Tanzania, is given, and the ethnic
groups mentioned are the Gikuyu (Kikuyu), Akamba (Kamba),
Pare, Ba-Ganda (Ganda), Masai, and Gogo. The spectrum
of roles the mganga plays includes: wiseman, seer, diviner, rain maker, curer, savior, healer, circumciser,
and finally exorcisor of evil spirits that possess
people.

1312. Omoyajowo, Rev. J. A.   Witches? A Study of the Belief
      1965   in Witchcraft and of Its Future
                                 in Modern African Society.
                                 Ibadan: Abiodun Printing Works,
                                 Ltd.

      Written from a Christian viewpoint, this work discusses
the belief in witches prevalent among Africans. Spirit
"familiars" and mediumship are mentioned.

1313. Omoyajowo, J. Akin   "The Cherubim and Seraphim Move-
      1970   ment: A Study in Interaction."
                                 Orita: Ibadan Journal of Reli-
                                 gious Studies 4, no. 2: 124-39.

      The Cherubim and Seraphim Movement in Nigeria grew out
of the activities of the preacher Moses Orimolade
Tunolase from Ikare. Among these was the curing of an
eighteen-year-old girl from a state of prolonged trance.

1314. O'Neil, J.   "Superstitions of the Amakalange
      1906/7   of the Mangwe District."
                                 Zambesi Mission Records 3:146-
                                 49, 185-88, 223-27.

      Some information on spirit reincarnation and rain
making, with relation to mediumistic experience, among
the Amakalanga (Kalanga) of Rhodesia.

1315. Onwuejeogwu, Michael   "The Cult of the Bori Spirits
      1969   among the Hausa." In Man in
                                 Africa, edited by M. Douglas
                                 and P. Kaberry, pp. 279-305.
                                 (Bib. 475.)

      The Bori spirit possession cult of the Hausa of Nigeria
is analyzed, with particular focus on the hierarchies of
the possessing spirits.

1316. Oosthuizen, G. C.   "Independent African Churches.
      1965   Sects or Spontaneous Develop-
                                 ment? A Reply to Dr. J. Alex
                                 van Wyk." Ministry (Morija,
                                 Basutoland) 5, no. 3: 99-107.

      Possession by the Holy Spirit and its role among the
independent African churches are discussed on pages 101-2.

1317. Oosthuizen, G. C.   "Causes of Religious Indepen-
      1968a   dentism in Africa." Fort Hare
                                 Papers 4, no. 2:13-28.

In a detailed and thorough analysis of the African independent churches, ecstatic trance, glossolalia, and
possession by the Holy Spirit are all discussed.

1318. Oosthuizen, G. C.   "Isaiah Shembe and the Zulu
      1968b   World View." History of Reli-
                                 gions 8, no. 1: 1-30.

The uses of possession in traditional Zulu (South
Africa) religion and in the independent Christian move-
ment, the Church of the Nazarites, founded by Isaiah
Shembe, are discussed throughout this article.

1319. Oosthuizen, G. C.   Post-Christianity in Africa.
      1968c   Grand Rapids, Mich.: William B.
                                 Eerdmans Publishing Co.

The role of spirit possession in both traditional
African religions and in Christianity is discussed in
detail in chapter 4.

1320. Oosthuizen, G. C.   "The Independent Religious Move-
      1970   ments versus Orthodoxism."
                                 Afer: African Ecclesiastical
                                 Review (Eldoret) 12, no. 4:
                                 289-300.

In this theoretical analysis of African independent
churches, their emphasis on the Holy Spirit (and possession by the Spirit) is mentioned on page 297.

1321. Oosthuizen, G. C.   "Causes of Religious Independen-
      1971   tism in Africa." Ministry
                                 (Maseru, Lesotho) 11, no. 4:
                                 121-33.

In this theoretical article on the reasons for the rise
and perpetuation of the African independent church movements, the phenomena of ecstasy, glossolalia, and exorcism are mentioned as being frequent characteristics of
them.

1322. Oosthuizen, G. C.   Pentecostal Penetration into the
      1975   Indian Community in Metropolitan
                                 Durban, South Africa. Human
                                 Sciences Research Council
                                 Publication Series, no. 52.
                                 Durban.

Although unavailable for annotation, the material of

259

this volume will likely yield information on the use of
speaking in tongues in the South African pentecostal
churches.

1323. Opler, Marvin K.   "Sociocultural Patterns and
      1971   Types of Schizophrenias."
                                Psychopathologie africaine
                                (Dakar) 7, no. 3: 443-48.

Spirit possession is mentioned in this general article
on the types of schizophrenias found cross-culturally,
as one way of speaking openly and directly about one's
beliefs (p. 444).

1324. Opoku, A. M., and   African Dances: A Ghanaian
      Willis Bell   Profile. Legon: Institute of
      1965   African Studies, University of
                               Ghana. Ill.

Trance dances are mentioned briefly in this pictorial
essay on dance in Ghana. Spirit possession is not explicitly labelled.

1325. Opoku, Kofi Asare   "Training the Priestess at the
      1970   Akonnedi Shrine." Research Re-
                               view (Institute of African
                               Affairs, University of Ghana,
                               Legon) 6, no. 2: 34-50.

The three-year training period of the priestesses at
the traditional shrines of Ghana, which involves learning
to work with possession by a deity and other forms of
divination, is described in detail.

1326. Opoku, Kofi A.   "Aspects of Akan Worship."
      1972   Ghana Bulletin of Theology
                               (Legon) 4, no. 2: 1-13.

The priest or okomfo of the Akan religion (Ghana) becomes possessed by the deities or abosom during public
ceremonies (p. 3).

1327. Orjo de Marchovelette,   "La Divination chez les Baluba
      E. d'   au moyen du 'lubuko' ou du
      1954   'kataloa.'" Zaïre: Belgian
                               African Review (Bruxelles) 8,
                               no. 5: 487-505.

The trance state of a Baluba (Luba) (Zaïre) medium and
the proceedings of a divinatory séance are described.
The spirits of the ancestors and of the most famous
historical figures may be summoned to divine the cause of
illness or misfortune through their human intermediaries.
Exorcism of evil spirits is also performed.

260

1328. Orley, John H.   Culture and Mental Illness: A
      1970   Study from Uganda. East African
                         Studies, no. 36. Nairobi: East
                         African Publishing House.

In general, the Baganda (Ganda) of Uganda believe that
illnesses come either from witchcraft or from spirit possession. Description is given of the different spirits
which cause mental illnesses. Spirit possession is also
a part of the healing ceremonies.

1329. Orr, Kenneth   "Field Notes on Tribal Medical
      1968   Practices in Central Liberia."
                         Liberian Studies Journal
                         (Greencastle, Ind.) 1, no. 1:
                         20-41.

Possession by evil jinni spirits is commonly cited as
a cause of illness among the Kpelle of Liberia. Detailed
case histories are given (pp. 32 ff.).

1330. Ortigues, M. C.,   "Intégration des données cul-
      P. Martino, and   turelles africaines à la psy-
      H. Collomb   chiatrie de l'enfant dans la
      1966a   pratique clinique au Sénégal."
                         Psychopathologie africaine
                         (Dakar) 2, no. 3: 441-50.

The integration of traditional cultural themes within
the psychiatric setting is the major issue of this
article. The case of a Wolof girl in Senegal is given
where she is diagnosed by psychiatrists as showing typical hysteric symptoms. Her mother, however, believes
that she is being possessed by the rab ancestor spirits
as all women in a matrilineage may be.

1331. Ortigues, Marie-Cécile,   Oedipe africain. Paris:
      and Edmond Ortigues   Librairie Plon.
      1966b

Spirit possession ceremonies in Senegal among the
Lébou (Lebu), Wolof, and Sérère (Serer) are analyzed on
pages 153-68.

1332. Ortigues, M. C.,   "L'Utilisation des données cul-
      P. Martino, and   turelles dans un cas de bouffée
      H. Collomb   délirante." Psychopathologie
      1967   africaine (Dakar) 3, no. 1: 121-
                         47.

A detailed account of a psychiatric case of "bouffée
délirante" is presented along with the traditional explanations given for the illness by the patient's Wolof

261

culture in Senegal. According to their beliefs, the
patient is possessed by the rab ancestor spirits. The
article emphasizes the importance of incorporating the
traditional explanations into the psychiatric diagnoses.

1333. Ortiz, Fernando   Los Bailes y el teatro de los
      1951   Negros en el folklore de Cuba.
                             Habana: Ediciones Cardenas y
                             Cia.

      Not available for annotation.

1334. Ortiz, Oderigo, N. R.   "Notes on Afro-Brazilian Ethno-
      1955   graphy: The Candombĺe." Notas
                             e informaciones ciéncias
                             sociales (Washington, D.C.) 6,
                             no. 36: 310-19.

      Discussion of the Candombĺe cult in Bahia, Brazil. De-
      scription of the priestesses of the Orishas (gods) fall-
      ing into possession trances. The Candombĺe cults vary
      in their ritual according to their African origins,
      whether Dahomey (Benin), Angola, Congo, etc. [Cited in
      African Abstracts, vol. 8, no. 318.]

1335. Ottenberg, Simon, and   Cultures and Societies of Africa.
      Ottenberg, Phoebe,   New York: Random House.
      eds.
      1960

      Includes in this bibliography:
              364   E. Colson (1960a)
              1891   G. Wilson (1960)

1336. Ottino, Paul   "Le Tromba (Madagascar)."
      1965   L'Homme 5, no. 1: 84-93.

      The tromba is a particular type of spirit possession
      among the Sakalava of Madagascar which has important
      political and religious consequences. The term refers to
      one who is possessed by the spirit of a dead prince, and
      the beliefs and ceremonies surrounding this phenomenon
      are presented.

1337. Owor, John S.   "African Traditional Religion:
      1972   Lamirok Gi Chowirak." Occasio-
                             nal Research Papers in African
                             Traditional Religion and Philo-
                             sophy (Makerere University,
                             Kampala), vol. 7, no. 58.

      Among the Adhola of Uganda, three types of spirits pos-
      sess people: (1) the ajuoka, who possess diviners acting
      as mediums; (2) the kalumba, who manifest themselves as

lions or leopards in sound and behavior; and (3) the
tida, who possess only women and are violent towards men
(pp. 5-6).

1338. Pagliuchi, Vera Lucia   "Le Spiritisme   d'Umbanda - I.
      Palma   Analyse structurale de la
      1974a   doctrine." Psychopathologie
                               africaine (Dakar) 10, no. 2:
                               229-77.

A detailed structural analysis is conducted of the
Umbanda cult in Brazil which utilizes spirit possession
and mediumship and has African cultural roots. The
spirits and the possession trances are both discussed.

1339. Pagliuchi, Vera Lucia   "Le Spiritisme d'Umbanda - II.
      Palma   Analyse structurale d'une
      1974b   séance." Psychopathologie
                               africaine (Dakar) 10, no. 3:
                               381-422.

Structurally analyzed, the Umbanda spirit possession
ceremony reveals a complex interweaving of Christian and
the Umbandist Afro-American elements. Its syncretic
nature is examined in light of these structural factors.

1340. Painter, John   "Background to 'Charismatic
      1974a   Christianity.'" Journal of
                               Theology for Southern Africa
                               (Cape Town), no. 7, pp. 4-9.

The religious debate between Pentecostals and non-
Pentecostals on the importance of the "gift of tongues"
or glossolalia is outlined.

1341. Painter, John   "The Charismatic Movement and
      1974b   the New Testament." Journal of
                               Theology for Southern Africa
                               (Cape Town), no. 7, pp. 50-60.

Given here is a detailed theological study of the place
of glossolalia and other gifts of the Spirit in the New
Testament, especially in Corinthians. Use of these gifts
in African churches is not explicitly labelled.

1342. Pakenham, R. H. W.   "Two Zanzibar Ngomas."
      1959   Tanganyika Notes and Records 52:
                               11-116.

Discussion of spirit mediumship as it relates to the
activities of the Ngomas, or drums, in Tanzania.

1343. Palmer, Gary   Trance and Dissociation: A
      1966   Cross-Cultural Study in Psycho-
                               physiology. Unpublished M.A.

263

Thesis, University of Minnesota.

The author uses cross-cultural data to discuss the relationship between the physiological state of the brain corresponding to a given psychological or mental state such as trance. The author considers the phenomena of trance, glossolalia and allied possession states.

1344. Pan-African Psychiatric Conference, 1st 1961   First Pan-African Psychiatric Conference - Proceedings, Abeokuta, 1961. Ibadan: Government Printer.

Includes in this bibliography:
61   T. A. Baasher (1961)
594   E. F. B. Forster (1961)
922   N. S. Kline (1961)
1004   A. H. Leighton and J. M. Hughes (1961)
1413   R. Prince (1961)

1345. Pan-African Psychiatric Conference, 2d 1968   Deuxième Colloque africain de psychiatrie - Proceedings, Dakar, 5-9 March 1968. Paris: Association universitaire pour le développement de l'enseignement et de la culture en Afrique et à Madagascar.

Includes in this bibliography:
113   R. Bastide (1968b)
1001   J. P. Lehmann (1968)
1546   E. Sangmuah (1968)

1346. Parkin, David 1970   "Politics of Ritual Syncretism: Islam among the Non-Muslim Giriama of Kenya." Africa: Journal of the International African Institute (London) 40, no. 3: 217-33.

Spirit possession and mediumship, mainly used for divination, are discussed within the broader context of the cultural borrowing of Islamic elements by the Giriama (Giryama) of Kenya. Initial possessions are involuntary, and the spirits may be traditional Giriama, Muslim, or from other tribes. Possession by Muslim spirits may necessitate conversion to Islam, the "therapeutic Muslim," and may result in the waiving of commensual obligations among kin and neighbors.

1347. Parkyns, Mansfield   Life in Abyssinia. London:
       1868   Cass & Co. (1st ed. 1853).

Among peasants in Abyssinia (Ethiopia), blacksmiths are
believed to be sorcerers, called Bouda. Bouda are capable of possessing other people. Possessed persons become ill and often have fits; they must be addressed in
the masculine gender (although most possessed persons are
women), as the Bouda is believed to have displaced the
spirit of his victim. The use of special amulets is required to induce the Bouda to tell his name and leave his
victim (chap. 27).

1348. Parratt, J. K.   "Religious Change in Yoruba
       1969   Society--a Test Case." Journal
                            of Religion in Africa (Leiden)
                            2, no. 2: 113-28.

The effective transition from the traditional Yoruba
(Nigeria) religion to Christian churches, such as the
Aladura (independent) churches, is cited as being due to
the "ethical authority and charismatic appeal" of the
latter, which involves prophecy, glossolalia, and spiritual healing.

1349. Parrinder, G.   West African Psychology.
       1951   London: Lutterworth Press.

Chapter 14 deals with spirit possession, and material is
drawn from Margaret Field's studies (Bib. 564-571) and
from Oesterreich (1930, Bib. 1301).

1350. Parrinder, Geoffrey   Religion in an African City.
       1953   London: Oxford University Press.
                            Ill.

The first two chapters, entitled "The Twilight of the
Gods," discuss traditional religions and Yoruba (Nigeria)
cults in which spirit possession is part of the ritual.

1351. Parrinder, Geoffrey   African Traditional Religion.
       1954   London: Hutchinson's University
                            Library.

General work on African religion. Selection of priests
and mediums by means of possession (among the Dogon
[Upper Volta], p. 37; in Dahomey (Benin) and elsewhere in
West Africa, pp. 100-103). Discussion of training and
initiation of Dahomean (Fon) mediums (pp. 102-3) (Benin).
Many African Christian congregations have broken away
from European churches in order to preserve elements of
traditional African religion, including spirit possession
(pp. 145-46).

1352. Parrinder, E. G.   "Les Sociétés religieuses en
      1958a   Afrique occidentale." Présence
                            africaine (Paris), nos. 18-19,
                            pp. 17-22.

      The spirit possession cults of the Yoruba of Nigeria
      are described here.

1353. Parrinder, Geoffrey   Witchcraft. Harmondsworth,
      1958b   Middlesex: Penguin Books.

      The relationship between spirit possession and witch-
      craft in African religions is discussed. (See book's
      index under "Possession" for page citations.)

1354. Parrinder, E. G.   "The Religious Situation in West
      1960   Africa." African Affairs:
                            Journal of the Royal African
                            Society (London) 59, no. 234:
                            38-42.

      Spirit possession is mentioned in this general theore-
      tical article in connection with the Hausa bori cult in
      Nigeria.

1355. Parrinder, Geoffrey   West African Religion. London:
      1961   Epworth Press.

      Deals with the religious beliefs of the Akan and Ewe
      (Ghana) and Yoruba (Nigeria). Chapters 7-10 discuss:
      temples and forms of worship; priests and devotees;
      spirit possession and mediumship; possession dances.
      Bibliography included.

1356. Parrinder, Geoffrey   Witchcraft: European and Afri-
      1963   can. London: Faber & Faber.

      The relationship between witchcraft and spirit posses-
      sion is discussed for African cultures, in particular
      for the Gã (Ghana) and Azande (Sudan) (pp. 131, 142, 173,
      184).

1357. Parrinder, G.   "Le Mysticisme de médiums en
      1965   Afrique occidentale." In Réin-
                            carnation et vie mystique en
                            Afrique noire, Colloque de
                            Strasbourg, pp. 131-42.
                            (Bib. 359.)

      Spirit mediumship is discussed for the Fon (Dahomey,
      now Benin; Togo), Yoruba (Nigeria), and Gã (Ghana).

1358. Parrinder, Geoffrey   African Mythology. London:
      1967   Paul Hamlyn. Ill.

266

Spirit possession and mediumship are briefly mentioned for the Buganda (Ganda) of Uganda (pp. 79, 89 ff.).

1359. Parrinder, Geoffrey   Religion in Africa. Harmonds-
      1969   worth, Middlesex: Penguin Books.

Spirit possession and mediumship are mentioned in this general theoretical work on pages 74-5, 78. Speaking in tongues and exorcism ceremonies in the Zionist Churches are discussed on page 160.

1360. Parson, Elsie Clews   "Spirit Cult in Hayti."
      1928   Journal de la Societé des
                              Américanistes de Paris 20:157-79.

The study includes some discussion of the spirit cults of Haiti.

1361. Paul, Emmanuel C.   Panorama du folklore haïtien.
      1962   Port-au-Prince: Imprimerie
                              de l'État.

Author discusses Haitian folklore with particular attention to oral literature, music and dance. Chapters 8 through 12 describe the development of voodoo with particular attention to social structure, myth and belief system. Spirit possession is described in the outline of initiation and funerary rituals.

1362. Paulme, Denise   "Un Mouvement féminin en pays
      1950   kissi." Notes africaines de
                              l'Institute français d'Afrique
                              noire (Dakar) 46:43-44.

Discussion of a movement headed by women that took place in 1948 in Kissi country (Guinea). The women offered medical cures and had nightly manifestations of dancing. Possible correlation with possession phenomenon as it is described for other parts of Africa.

1363. Paulme, Denise   Une Société de Côte d'Ivoire
      1962   hier et aujourd'hui: Les Bété.
                              Paris: La Haye.

Among the Bété of the Ivory Coast, spirit mediumship is used as a divinatory technique (p. 167).

1364. Paulme, Denise   "Une Religion syncrétique en
      1963   Côte d'Ivoire: le culte deima."
                              Cahiers d'études africaines
                              (Paris) 3, no. 9: 5-90.

A case of possession by the Holy Spirit in the deima cult, a syncretic mixture of Christian and African traditional elements among the Bété of the Ivory Coast, is described on page 31.

267

1365. Pauw, B. A.   Religion in a Tswana Chiefdom.
      1960   London: Oxford University Press.

      Chapter 6 deals with the rituals of the churches among
      the Tswana (Bechuanaland, now Botswana). Description of
      the Pentecostal services which include healing and spirit
      possession by the spirit of the Holy Ghost (pp. 197-208).

1366. Pauw, B. A.   "Ancestor Beliefs and Rituals
      1974a   among Urban Africans." African
                           Studies 33, no. 2: 99-111.

      Among urban Africans, elements of the traditional be-
      liefs in ancestors have continued, although changed
      slightly. Certain groups of urban dwellers believe that
      deceased overseers and ministers may possess their suc-
      cessors (p. 108).

1367. Pauw, B. A.   "The Influence of Christianity."
      1974b   In The Bantu Speaking Peoples of
                           Southern Africa, edited by W. D.
                           Hammond-Tooke, pp. 415-40.
                           (Bib. 729.)

      Possession by the Holy Spirit, glossolalia, and other
      mystical states are mentioned as occurring in the Zionist
      and Pentecostal Churches among the Bantu-speaking peoples
      of Southern Africa (pp. 432 ff.).

1368. Pauw, B. A.   Christianity and Xhosa Tradi-
      1975   tion. Cape Town: Oxford
                           University Press.

      Amafufunyana is a state of possession by an evil spirit
      which causes mental derangement among the Xhosa (Xosa)
      of South Africa. The relationship between traditional
      beliefs in spirit possession and Christianity is
      stressed (see book's index under "Amafufunyana" for page
      citations).

1369. Pauwels, Marcel   "La Magie au Ruanda." Grands
      1949   lacs (Namur) 65, no. 1: 17-48.

      Deals with sorcery among the Ruanda (Rwanda) and shows
      the distinction between white magic and black magic.
      Also describes divination practices and healing cere-
      monies for possession by evil spirits. [Cited in
      African Abstracts, vol. 1, no. 588.]

1370. Pauwels, Marcel   "Le Culte de Nyabingi (Ruanda)."
      1951   Anthropos (Fribourg) 46, nos.
                           3-4: 337-57.

      This article gives an in-depth historical analysis of

the Nyabingi cult found among the Ruanda peoples of
Rwanda, which practices spirit possession. Possession
trance is described (pp. 345 ff.).

1371. Pauwels, R. P. M.   "Imana et le culte des Manes au
      1958   Ruanda." Mémoires de l'Académie
                            royale des sciences coloniales
                            d'outre-mer (Bruxelles) 17, no.
                            1: 1-263.

      Exorcism of evil spirits who cause illness among the
      Ruanda (Rwanda) is described on pages 166-73.

1372. Pavicevic, Marinko B. "Psychoses in Ethiopia." Addis
      n.d.   Ababa. Typescript. 6 pp.

      The Zar possession cults in Ethiopia are spoken of as
      being "a special form of psychotic disorders," and a mani-
      festation of hysterical dissociation." [Cited in Trans-
      cultural Psychiatric Research Review and Newsletter
      (Bruges) 3 (October 1966): 152-54.]

1373. Pazder, L. H.   "The Attitudes of Catholic Mis-
      1968   sionaries in Eastern Nigeria."
                            In Trance and Possession States,
                            edited by R. Prince, pp. 186-88.
                            (Bib. 1421.)

      Outlined here is the Christian missionary attitude to-
      ward spirit possession in eastern Nigeria.

1374. Pazzi, Roberto   "Culte de mort chez le peuple
      1968   Mina (sud Togo)." Cahiers de
                            religions africaines (Kinshasa)
                            2, no. 4: 249-60.

      Although spirit possession is not explicitly mentioned
      in the abstract, this citation, concerning beliefs
      and rituals surrounding death, may include such material
      for the Mina (Ge) of Togo. [Cited in African Abstracts,
      vol. 22, no. 2 (April 1971), no. 332.]

1375. Peel, J. D. Y.   Aladura: A Religious Movement
      1968a   among the Yoruba. London:
                            Oxford University Press.

      Spirit possession by the Holy Spirit and its role in
      the Aladura Church, an African independent religious
      movement among the Yoruba of Nigeria, are discussed on
      pages 164-65, 284.

1376. Peel, J. D. Y.   "Syncretism and Religious
      1968b   Change." Comparative Studies in
                            Society and History 10, no. 2:
                            121-41.

Spirit possession and glossolalia in both the traditional Yoruba religion and the independent African church movement are mentioned on page 134.

1377. Peel, J. D. Y.   "The Aladura Movement in Western
      1969   Nigeria." Tarikh (London) 3,
                             no. 1: 48-55. Ill.

Discussed here is the rise of the Aladura movement in western Nigeria, including the Christ Apostolic Church, the Cherubim and Seraphim, and the Church of the Lord. Also mentioned is their relationship to the Pentecostal churches that emphasize "speaking in tongues."

1378. Peixe, Júlio dos Santos "Brief Notes on Healing through
      1962   Spirits among the Ba-Tswa
                               People." Boletim da Sociedade
                               de estudos da colónia de
                               Moçambique (Lourenço Marques) 31,
                               no. 130: 5-31.

According to the beliefs of the Ba-Tswa (Mozambique), the nanga is a medium whose function is to put his clients in touch with the supernatural spirits. The mediums claim to be possessed by the spirits of the Va-Nungi invaders, who occupied southern Mozambique in the last century, or by the Va-Ndau spirits. Description of the activities of the ñangas when they fall possessed. Two men and two women reveal how they became ñangas. [Text in Portuguese; cited in African Abstracts, vol. 14, no. 277.]

1379. Pelton, Robert W.   The Complete Book of Voodoo.
      1972   New York: G. P. Putnam's Sons.

The voodoo spirit possession cult in Haiti and in New Orleans is described and analyzed in depth.

1380. Pengo, P.   "Death and After-Life among the
      1974   Fipa." Occasional Research Pa-
                           pers in Traditional African Re-
                           ligion and Philosophy (Makerere
                           University, Kampala), vol. 20,
                           no. 208.

Among the Fipa of Uganda, a person may be possessed by the malicious ingulu spirits or by the mizimu ancestral spirits. The cultural contexts of these two types of possession are discussed.

1381. Perlman, Melvin L.   "The Traditional Systems of
      1970   Stratification among the Ganda
                             and the Nyoro of Uganda." In
                             Social Stratification in Africa,
                             edited by A. Tuden and L.

Plotnicov, pp. 125-61.
(Bib. 1760.)

The political roles of the Ganda and Nyoro priests and
spirit mediums in Uganda are discussed.

1382. Perrin Jassy, Marie-   Basic Community in the African
      France   Churches. Translated by Sister
      1973   Jeanne Marie Lyons. Maryknoll,
                                N.Y.: Orbis Books.

The African independent church movement among the Luo
of Tanzania and Kenya practices a form of trance and
glossolalia (pp. 212-28).

1383. Perrois, Louis   Note sur quelques aspects de la
      1967   circoncision bakota (Gabon).
                                Libreville, Gabon: Office de
                                la recherche scientifique et
                                technique outre-mer.

The role of spirit possession in secret societies is
mentioned on page 90. Discussed in greater detail is the
phenomenon of the "hommes-leopards" men who can change at
will into leopards among the Bakota (Kota) of Gabon
(chap. 5).

1384. Peters, J. R.   "The Fall of Dindikwa." Nada
      1974   (Salisbury) 11, no. 1: 7-10.

The importance of authorization by the swikiro, the
medium of the tribal spirit of the Vagarwe (Garwe) in
Rhodesia, of the man appointed to be chief is greatly
emphasized. The example is given of the difficulties encountered with Chief Dindikwa (1947-73), who did not have
this authorization.

1385. Philippart, L.   Le Bas-Congo: État religieux et
      1929   social. Louvain: Imprimerie
                                Saint-Alphonse.

Spirit mediumship is briefly mentioned on page 41, and
the distinction is made between mediums and "feticheurs"
for the Manianga and Bandibu of the Bas-Congo (Zaïre).

1386. Phillips, C. E. Lucas   The Vision Splendid. London:
      1960   Heinemann.

Among the Bantu-speaking peoples of Northern Rhodesia
(Zambia), witches send illnesses and death by means of
evil spirits who take possession of their victim (pp.
144-47).

271

1387. Philipps, Captain   "The Nabingi." <u>Congo: Revue</u>
     J. E. T.   <u>générale de la colonie belge</u>
     1928   (Bruxelles) 1, no. 1: 310-21.

     The <u>Nabingi</u> cult in British Ruanda (Rwanda) is dis-
cussed historically, and mention is made of possession by
the spirit <u>nabingi</u> among the Banyaruanda (Ruanda).

1388. Philipps, Tracy   "An African Culture of Today in
     1946/1949   the Country between the Bantu
                   Negro and the Semitic Arab."
                   <u>Anthropos</u> 41-44:193-211.

     Description of the malignant spirits that are said to
possess people, among the Azande (Sudan). A footnote
suggests that epileptics are considered as possessed by
demonic spirits (pp. 207-10).

1389. Piault, Colette   "Contribution à l'étude de la
     1963   vie quotidienne de la femme
                   mawri." <u>Etudes nigériennes</u>
                   (Paris), no. 10, pp. 5-133.

     The predominantly female <u>bori</u> possession cult among the
Mawri of Niger is briefly outlined on pages 114-15.

1390. Pidoux, Charles   "Les Rites de possession en pays
     1954   Zerma." <u>Comptes rendus</u>
                   <u>sommaires des séances de</u>
                   <u>l'Institut francais d'anthropo-</u>
                   <u>logie</u> (Paris) 8, nos. 94-100:
                   19-22.

     Among the Zerma (Niger), spirits of the river and the
bush are said to possess individuals. Treatment ceremonies are described.

1391. Pidoux, C.   "Quelques données clinico-cul-
     1958   turelles, en contribution à
                   l'étude psycho-sociologique des
                   rites thérapeutiques de posses-
                   sion chez les populations zerma
                   des environs de Niamey." In
                   <u>Mental Disorders and Mental</u>
                   <u>Health in Africa South of the</u>
                   <u>Sahara</u>, pp. 176-82.
                   CCTA/CSA-WFMH-WHO, Pub. no. 35.
                   Bukavu.

     In support of some therapeutic cooperation between
Western psychiatric principles and traditional cultic
practices of spirit possession, an individual case of
traditional treatment and the activities of the <u>zima</u>,

the "priest-doctors" of the possession cult among the
Zerma of Niger, are discussed.

1392. Pierce, B. E.   "Afro-American and Christian
      1972   Religious Systems of Lower
                             Status Creoles in Paramaribo,
                             Surinam." Paper presented at
                             the meeting of the Northeastern
                             Anthropological Association,
                             Buffalo, N.Y., 21-23 April.

Ethnographic field work among the members of the
nengre cult in Paramaribo, Surinam, yields important
theoretical variations to the way Afro-American religions have been studied. Spirit possession is not explicitly mentioned in the abstract. [Cited in Abstracts
in Anthropology, vol. 3, no. 3 (1972), no. 1135.]

1393. Pierson, Donald   Negroes in Brazil. Chicago:
      1942   University of Chicago Press.

The role of spirit possession in the Afro-Brazilian religious cults, specifically the candomblé cult, is discussed in various contexts (see book's index under "Possession" for page citations).

1394. Pintassilgo, António   "Seitas secretas no Congo."
      Rodrigues   Portugal em Africa (Lisboa) 10,
      1953   no. 60: 361-71.

Discussed here are several religious movements in
Zaïre, including Kimbanguism, Corolário, Nyunza
prophets, and Ngwima féticheurs. Possession and mediumship are briefly mentioned.

1395. Platt, W. J.   An African Prophet. London:
      1934   Student Christian Movement Press.

In discussing the psychology of conversion, the author
classifies the African seer into two types: one who is
possessed by a spirit and one who is inspired through
ecstasy or visions (p. 79). The main topic of the book
is the Prophet Harris and his Ivory Coast movement.

1396. Polanah, Luís   "Possessão e exorcismo em
      1967/68   Moçambique." Memórias do
                             Instituto de investigaçao
                             científica de Moçambique
                             (Lourenço Marques) 9(c):3-45.

"The phenomena of possession and exorcism among the
Africans of Mozambique are compared with those described
for the primitive Jews and Christians. Examples of possession and its psychotherapy among the Tonga, Chopi,

Tswa, Ndau and Cewa (Chewa) groups are given." [Cited in African Abstracts, vol. 22, no. 2 (April 1971), no. 379.]

1397. Pollak-Eltz, Angelina   "El culto de Maria Leonza en
      1967   Venezuela." Caribbean Studies
                                7, no. 4: 47-53.

The cult of Maria Leonza in Venezuela is a syncretic mixture of African traditions and Christianity. Descriptions of the use of spirit mediumship are given.

1398. Pollak-Eltz, Angelina   "The Devil Dances in Venezuela."
      1968   Caribbean Studies 8, no. 2: 65-
                                73.

The Devil Dances in Venezuela, greatly influenced by their African roots, are performed on Corpus Christi day. Although spirit possession is not explicitly labelled, one of the main roles of the Devil Dancers is to exorcise evil spirits.

1399. Pollak-Eltz, Angelina   Afro-amerikaanse Godsdiensten en
      1970a   cultem. Roermond: J. J. Romon
                                und Zoner.

Not available for annotation.

1400. Pollak-Eltz, Angelina   "Des Egugunkalt der Yoruba in
      1970b   Afrika und in Amerika."
                                Zeitschrift fur Ethnologie 95,
                                no. 2: 275-93.

Not available for annotation.

1401. Pollak-Eltz, Angelina   "Shango-Kult und Shouter-Kirche
      1970c   auf Trinidad und Grenada."
                                Anthropos 65:814-32.

The author, following Simpson's research in Trinidad, describes possession by a variety of deities and the ritual similarities to African spirit possession. Comparison is also made with Cuban Santeria and Brazilian Candomble movements.

1402. Pollak-Eltz, Angelina   Vestigios Africanos en la
      1971   Cultura del Pueblo Venezolano.
                                Cuernavaca, Mexico: Central
                                Interculturel de Documentia.

Not available for annotation.

1403. Pollak-Eltz, Angelina   Cultos Afroamericanos. Caracas,
      1977   Venezuela: Universidad
                               Católica Andres Bello.

This text presents a general account of the most influential Afro-American cults and syncretic religious
movements currently extant in South and Central America.

1404. Posnansky, Merrick   "Archeology, Ritual and Reli-
      1972   gion." In The Historical Study
                               of African Religion, edited by
                               T. O. Ranger and I. N. Kimambo,
                               pp. 29-44. (Bib. 1442.)

Archeological findings at Khami in Rhodesia give early
evidence of the mhondoro spirit mediumship cult among
the Shona (p. 36).

1405. Post, Ken   "The Bible as Ideology: Ethio-
      1970   pianism in Jamaica, 1930-38."
                               In African Perspectives, edited
                               by C. Allen and R. W. Johnson,
                               pp. 185-207. Cambridge:
                               Cambridge University Press.

Pocomania and other cults in Jamaica, some of which
have African roots and all of which use spirit possession,
are discussed throughout this article (especially p.
190).

1406. Pouillon, Jean   "Malade et médecin: Le Même
      1970   et/ou l'autre? (remarques
                               ethnologiques)." Nouvelle revue
                               de psychoanalyse 1:77-98.

In this general theoretical article on the relationship between the patient and the healer in traditional
curing practices, the Ndembu of Zambia and the Azande of
the Sudan and Zaire are mentioned. Spirit possession is
contrasted with shamanism as the former emphasizes the
relationship between the sickness and the patient, whereas the latter stresses the importance of the sickness to
the doctor. [Cited in Transcultural Psychiatric Research
Review (Bruges) 7 (October 1970): 118-23.]

1407. Preneuf, Ch. de   "L'Homme qui fait pleurer les
      1969   arbres." Psychopathologie
                               africaine (Dakar) 5, no. 3:
                               395-458.

This is an extensive account of the Senegalese healer
Ousmane N'Dombo, whose practices center around a set of
beliefs in djine, spirits which possess people and thus
cause illness.

275

1408. Pressel, Esther   "Umbanda in São Paulo: Reli-
      1973   gious Innovation in a Develop-
                               ing Society." In Religion,
                               Altered States of Conscious-
                               ness, and Social Change, edited
                               by E. Bourguignon, pp. 264-318.
                               (Bib. 245.)

      Detailed study of the African-influenced Umbanda cult
in São Paulo, Brazil. Sociocultural elements are emphasized.

1409. Pressel, Esther   "Umbanda Trance and Possession
      1974   in São Paulo, Brazil." In
                               Trance, Healing and Hallucina-
                               tion, edited by F. D. Goodman,
                               J. H. Henney, and E. Pressel,
                               pp. 113-225. (Bib. 683.)

      A very detailed description of the practices and mem-
bers of the Umbanda cult in São Paulo, Brazil, is given
here. African cultural elements are evident in the use
of spirit possession and mediumship.

1410. Pressel, Esther   "Negative Spirit Possession in
      1977   Experienced Brazilian Umbanda
                               Spirit Mediums." In Case Studies
                               in Spirit Possession, edited by
                               V. Crapanzano and V. Garrison,
                               pp. 333-64. (Bib. 391.)

      Following a presentation of the practices of the Afro-
Brazilian spirit possession cult of Umbanda, case studies
of several spirit mediums are given emphasizing the way
in which mediumship may be a means of curing illness or
counteracting misfortune.

      Price-Mars, Jean: See Mars, Jean Price-

1411. Price, J. H.   "A Bori Dance in Accra." West
      1957   African Review (Liverpool) 28,
                               no. 352: 20-24.

      Description of the Bori spirit possession cult in
Ghana. This cult might have been a snake cult in pre-
Moslem times. Most of the members are women, and some
men (homosexuals) are also initiated into the cult.

1412. Prince, Raymond   "The Use of Rauwolfia for the
      1960   Treatment of Psychoses by
                               Nigerian Native Doctors."
                               American Journal of Psychiatry
                               117, no. 2: 147-49.

The use of the drug rauwolfia by native Nigerian doctors is discussed, and the symptoms resulting from its administration are compared to those termed "devil possession" both in medieval Europe and in contemporary Nigerian cultures.

1413. Prince, Raymond
1961a

"Some Notes on Yoruba Native Doctors and Their Management of Mental Illness." In First Pan-African Psychiatric Conference - Proceedings, pp. 279-88. (Bib. 1344.)

The role that spirit possession plays in divination among the Yoruba of Nigeria is discussed on pages 281-82.

1414. Prince, Raymond
1961b

"The Yoruba Image of the Witch." Journal of Mental Science [British Journal of Psychiatry] (London) 107, no. 449 (n.s. no. 413): 795-805.

Witches are thought by the Yoruba of Nigeria to "eat" the souls of their victims (p. 800). A case is described of an individual who believed that the Holy Spirit and a witch were fighting inside of him (pp. 802-3).

1415. Prince, R. H., and
E. D. Wittkower
1964a

"The Care of the Mentally Ill in a Changing Culture (Nigeria)." American Journal of Psychotherapy 18, no. 4: 644-48.

Ethnographic material is presented on the treatment of the mentally ill by native doctors among the Yoruba of Nigeria. A major question posed is how the change from the traditional curing practices--based firmly on supernatural causal beliefs and the idea of spirit possession--to Western pragmatically oriented psychiatric methods could be achieved effectively.

1416. Prince, Raymond
1964b

"Indigenous Yoruba Psychiatry." In Magic, Faith and Healing, edited by A. Kiev, pp. 84-120. (Bib. 902.)

Description of spirit possession as it relates to notions of disease and cure of mental illness among the Yoruba (Nigeria) (pp. 84-120).

1417. Prince, Raymond, and
C. Savage
1966

"Mystical States and the Concept of Regression." Psychedelic Review 8:59-74.

Not available for annotation.

277

1418. Prince, Raymond   "Can the EEG Be Used in the
       1968a   Study of Possession States."
                                  In Trance and Possession States,
                                  edited by R. Prince, pp. 121-37.
                                  (Bib. 1421.)

The possibility of employing the EEG to measure the
psychophysiological state of a possessed person is explored here. Psychological analysis of the state is
given.

1419. Prince, Raymond   "Possession Cults and Social
       1968b   Cybernetics." In Trance and
                                  Possession States, edited by
                                  R. Prince, pp. 157-65.
                                  (Bib. 1421.)

The relationship between the spirit possession cults
among the Yoruba of Nigeria and their social structure is
elaborated in this article.

1420. Prince, Raymond   "Psychotherapy without Insight:
       1968c   An Example from the Yoruba of
                                  Nigeria." American Journal of
                                  Psychiatry 124:1171-76.

In the Yoruba (Nigeria) magico-religious healing
techniques, belief and dependency are stressed rather
than insight and independence. Spirit possession as a
cause and cure of illness among the Yoruba is discussed.
[Cited in Transcultural Psychiatric Research Review
(Bruges) 6 (October 1969): 174-75.]

1421. Prince, Raymond, ed.   Trance and Possession States.
       1968d   R. M. Bucke Memorial Society,
                                  Second Annual Conference,
                                  Montreal, 4-6 March 1966.
                                  Imprimerie Electra.

Includes in this bibliography:
                 239   E. Bourguignon (1968b)
                 481   E. Douyon (1968)
                 904   A. Kiev (1968)
                 995   R. B. Lee (1968)
                1373   L. H. Pazder (1968)
                1418   R. Prince (1968a)
                1419   R. Prince (1968b)
                1788   P. H. van der Walde (1968)

1422. Prince, Raymond   "The Problem of 'Spirit Posses-
       1974   sion' as a Treatment for Psy-
                                  chiatric Disorders." Ethos 2,
                                  no. 4: 315-33.

278

Based on extensive research on possession and field-work conducted among the members of the Sopono cult of the Yoruba (Nigeria), the phenomenon of spirit possession is discussed in terms of psychological interpretations.

1423. Prince, Raymond   "Psychotherapy as the Manipula-
         1976   tion of Endogenous Healing
                               Mechanisms: A Transcultural
                               Survey." Transcultural Psy-
                               chiatric Research Review
                               (Montreal) 13 (October): 115-33.

This article gives a general overview of the recent re-search on the many different forms of healing practiced transculturally, including that of spirit possession and mediumship (Africa is mentioned). A conclusion reached is that "Although psychoanalysis may be a superior form of therapy because it brings about more complete integration and understanding of conflicted drives, it is grossly limited in its applicability. Only highly self-aware and Westernized individuals can become signi-ficantly involved in the analytic endeavor. . . . On the other hand, dissociation states, psychoses, and religious exercises are much more universally applicable" (p. 129).

1424. Provansal, Danielle   "Le Phénomène maraboutique au
         1975   Maghreb." Genève-Afrique 14,
                               no. 1: 59-77.

The Islamic healer, the marabout of the Maghreb (Algeria, Morocco, and Tunisia), practices rites of ex-orcism for those who have been made ill by being possessed by a spirit (p. 73).

1425. Quarcoo, A. K.   "The Lakpa: Principal Deity of
         1967   Lubadi." Research Review
                              (Legon) 3, no. 3: 2-43.

Among the Labadi of Ghana the supreme god is believed to be distant from men. The god Lakpa acts as an inter-mediary between the high god and men. The priest of Lakpa is aided by a medium who communicates with Lakpa while in a trance. [Cited in African Abstracts, vol. 21, no. 89.]

1426. Queiroz, Maria Isaura   O Messianismo no Brasil e no
         Pereira de   Mundo. São Paulo: Dominus
         1965   Editôra, Editôra da
                               Universidade de São Paulo.

In part 2 of this volume the author discussed messianic movement in Brazil. A typology of movements is offered and spirit possession appears to play a role in all of them. Author relies on secondary sources for part of the data.

279

1427. Radin, Paul   Primitive Religion: Its Nature
      1937   and Origin. New York: Viking
                                 Press.

Chapter 6 deals with initiation into priest status a-
mong various peoples. An Amazulu (Zulu) of South Africa
who is subject to a prolonged illness, a lack of desire
to eat, dizziness, etc., may be told by an inyanga (diviner) that a spirit is trying to possess him. Once the
spirit succeeds, the man himself becomes an inyanga (pp.
123-26). Among the Ashanti of Ghana, possession by a
spirit is taken as a sign that a person is to undertake
priestly training. The neophyte spends three years with
an experienced priest. After a special ceremony, the
neophyte becomes a full-fledged priest (pp. 126-30).

1428. Radin, Paul   The World of Primitive Man. New
      1953   York: Henry Schuman.

Spirit possession and its religious role among the
Ashanti of Ghana and the Ivory Coast are briefly mentioned on page 83.

1429. Rainaut, Dr. J.   "Un Aspect des psychoses transi-
      1958   toires en milieu africain, la
                                  bouffée aigue confusionnelle et
                                  anxieuse." In Mental Disorders
                                  and Mental Health in Africa
                                  South of the Sahara, pp. 193-
                                  214. CCTA/CSA-WFMH-WHO, Pub.
                                  no. 35. Bukavu.

Presentation of the mental state "la bouffée aigue confusionnelle et anxieuse" typical in most of Africa which,
the author contends, is neither truly psychotic nor
neurotic owing to its limited duration and the sociocultural milieu in which it occurs.

1430. Rakoto, Alexis   "Le Culte d'Andriamosara."
      1947/48   Bulletin de l'Academie
                                  malagache (Tananarive) 28:108-
                                  14.

Some of the information of this study relates to the
healing dances of the cult of Andriamosara in Madagascar.

1431. Ramos, Arthur   "Acculturation among the
      1941   Brazilian Negroes." Journal of
                                  Negro History 26, no. 2: 244-50.

Syncretism of African beliefs and Catholicism in Bahia,
Brazil. Some discussion of the Orishá cults and the role
of spirit possession in their rituals.

1432. Ramos, Arthur   As culturas negras no Novo Mundo.
      1946   2d ed. São Paulo.

      Report of a dance called Mae d'Agua (water mama) per-
      formed in Haiti. In this dance, the dancer becomes pos-
      sessed by the spirits (p. 92).

1433. Randles, W. G. L.   L'Empire du Monomotapa du XVe
      1975   au XIXe siècle. Paris: Mouton.

      The Monomotapa Empire of the Karanga peoples which
      covered a good part of both Zambia and Mozambique in the
      fifteenth through the nineteenth centuries is described
      here. Chapter 7 gives the details of its religion,
      which included spirit mediumship as a part of the Mwari
      cult.

1434. Rangeley, W. H. J.   "Two Nyasaland Rain Shrines.
      1952   Makewana--the Mother of All
                                    People." Nyasaland Journal
                                    (Blantyre) 5, no. 2: 31-50.

      The official rituals and taboos surrounding the rain
      shrine originated by the great prophetess Makawana among
      the Cewa (Chewa) of Nyasaland (Malawi) are described in
      detail. The prophetess and all priestesses of the
      shrines are possessed by spirits.

1435. Rangeley, W. H. J.   "Mbona - the Rain Maker."
      1953   Nyasaland Journal (Blantyre) 6,
                                    no. 1: 8-27.

      The rain shrine named after the historical character
      Mbona is thought to have great power over the rains a-
      mong the Mang'anja (Manganja) people of southern Nyasa-
      land (Malawi). Brief mention is made of the ritual wife
      of Mbona who has the ability to enter trance and utter
      oracles (p. 23).

1436. Ranger, Terence   "The Role of Ndebele and Shona
      1966a   Religious Authorities in the Re-
                                    bellions of 1896 and 1897." In
                                    The Zambezian Past, edited by
                                    E. Stokes and R. Brown, pp. 94-
                                    136. (Bib. 1686.)

      Examined here is the role played by the Ndebele and
      Shona spirit mediums in the Mashona and Matabele Re-
      bellions of 1896 and 1897 in Rhodesia. The mediums were
      intermediaries between Mwari (or Mlimo), the high god,
      and the peoples.

1437. Ranger, Terence   "Traditional Authorities and the
      1966b   Rise of Modern Politics in
                              Southern Rhodesia, 1898-1930."
                              In The Zambezian Past, edited
                              by E. Stokes and R. Brown, pp.
                              171-93. (Bib. 1686.)

      Briefly mentioned is the incident where a medium of the
Nehanda spirit arose after the rebellion of the 1890's
and declared that she was an intermediary between the
government and the Mashona (Shona) peoples in Southern
Rhodesia (p. 173).

1438. Ranger, T. O.   Revolt in Southern Rhodesia
      1967   1896-7. London: Heinemann.

      Great emphasis is placed on the involvement of the
Shona religious beliefs in Mwari, the Supreme Being, and
on the priest-mediums who communicated between the spirit
and men, in the historical background and events leading
up to the 1896-97 revolt by the Shona in Southern
Rhodesia (see book's index under "Mhondoro" and "Mwari,"
etc. for page citations).

1439. Ranger, T. O.   "Connexions between 'Primary
      1968   Resistance' Movement and Modern
                             Mass Nationalism in East and
                             Central Africa. Part I."
                             Journal of African History
                             (Cambridge) 9, no. 3: 437-53.

      In this theoretical essay on nationalism in Africa,
the Shona (Rhodesia) Mwari cult, and the Nyabingi movement, particularly among the Kiga (Chiga) of Zaire, are
discussed, both of which emphasize spirit possession and
mediumship (pp. 449-53).

1440. Ranger, T. O.   The African Churches of Tanzania.
      1969   Historical Association of
                             Tanzania, Paper no. 5. Nairobi:
                             East African Publishing House.

      Emphasis of this article is on the history of the
African independent churches of Tanzania, and mention is
made of their Zionist beliefs in prophecy and possession
by the Holy Spirit (p. 5).

1441. Ranger, T. O.   The African Voice in Southern
      1970   Rhodesia 1898-1930. Evanston,
                             Ill.: Northwestern University
                             Press.

      The roles that various Shona tribal spirits and their

282

mediums played in the sociopolitical history of Southern
Rhodesia at the turn of this century are discussed on
pages 8-11.

1442. Ranger, T. O., and   The Historical Study of African
      I. N. Kamambo, eds.   Religion. Berkeley: University
      1972a   of California Press.

      Includes in this bibliography:
                660   M. Gilsenan (1972)
                712   G. C. K. Gwassa (1972)
               1304   B. A. Ogot (1972)
               1404   M. Posnansky (1972)
               1443   T. O. Ranger and I. N. Kimambo
                                (1972b)
               1444   T. Ranger (1972c)
               1571   M. Schoffeleers (1972b)
               1605   A. Shorter (1972)
               1915   M. Wright (1972)

1443. Ranger, T. O., and   "Introduction." In The His-
      I. N. Kimambo, eds.   torical Study of African Reli-
      1972b   gion, edited by T. O. Ranger
                                 and I. N. Kimambo, pp. 1-26.
                                 (Bib. 1442.)

      In the introductory essay to this volume of historical
studies of religion in Africa, the themes of spirit possession and mediumship are discussed in their various
contextual uses.

1444. Ranger, Terence   "Missionary Adaptation of Afri-
      1972c   can Religious Institutions: The
                                 Masai Case." In The Historical
                                 Study of African Religion,
                                 edited by T. O. Ranger and I. N.
                                 Kimambo, pp. 221-51.
                                 (Bib. 1442.).

      The author emphasizes the historical absence of spirit
mediumship cults among the Masasi of Tanzania during the
period of the introduction of Christianity in the nineteenth and twentieth centuries (p. 223).

1445. Ranger, Terence   "Territorial Cults in the History
      1973   of Central Africa." Journal of
                                 African History (London) 14, no.
                                 4: 581-97.

      The territorial spirit mediumship cults among the
various groups of Shona-speaking peoples of Central
Africa are discussed.

1446. Ranger, T. O.   "The Meaning of Mwari."
        1974   Rhodesian History: Journal of
                               the Central African Historical
                               Association (Salisbury) 5:5-17.

    The word Mwari is traced to its various referential
meanings among the following ethnic groups: Shona and
Kalanga (Rhodesia), Bakongo (Kongo) (Zaïre), Ndembu
(Zambia), Venda (South Africa). Spirit possession and
mediumship are mentioned with regard to the high god
Mwari (Shona).

1447. Ranger, T. O.   Dance and Society in Eastern
        1975a   Africa 1890-1970: The Beni
                               Ngoma. Berkeley: University
                               of California Press.

    Among the Acholi, Luo, and Lango peoples of Uganda and
Kenya, a spirit possession cult formed around the idea
of the colonial military organization at the turn of the
century. People, when possessed, behaved in an "army"
way and wore "army" clothes (pp. 46-47).

1448. Ranger, Terence   "Introduction--Part One." In
        1975b   Themes in the Christian History
                               of Central Africa, edited by
                               T. O. Ranger and J. Weller, pp.
                               3-13. (Bib. 1449.)

    In a general introduction to the relationship between
the traditional Central African religions (mainly of the
Shona-speaking peoples) and Christianity, both historical
and present-day, spirit possession and mediumship are
mentioned with regard to their spheres of influence
(pp. 7, 8, 12, 13).

1449. Ranger, T. O., and   Themes in the Christian History
        John Weller, eds.   of Central Africa. London:
        1975c   Heinemann.

    Includes in this bibliography:
                48   S. M. Aquina (1975)
              1050   I. Linden (1975)
              1103   S. K. Madziyire (1975)
              1448   T. O. Ranger (1975b)
              1574   J. M. Schoffeleers (1975)

1450. Ransford, Oliver   Livingstone's Lake: The Drama of
        1966   Nyasa. London: John Murray.

    "Wizards" (male) and "witches" (female) among the
Amaravi (Maravi) of Nyasaland (Malawi) are thought to be
possessed by "mysterious innate powers which were con-
stantly working to bring disaster to the tribe" (pp. 32-
33).

1451. Ransford, Oliver The Rulers of Rhodesia. London:
      1968   John Murray.

The significance of the Mwari cult and its priest
(spirit mediums) is traced throughout the history of
Rhodesia. The main ethnic groups involved in the cult
are the Karanga, Rozwi, and Shona (pp. 24-25, 77-78, 82,
268-99).

1452. Raponda-Walker, André, Rites et croyances des peuples
      and Roger Sillans   du Gabon. Paris: Présence
      1962   africaine.

In Gabon, illnesses are said to result from being possessed by evil spirits. Rites of exorcism are described
on pages 137-41.

1453. Rattray, R. S. Religion and Art in Ashanti.
      1927   London: Oxford University Press.

The Ashanti (Ghana) doctor (Sumanni) can treat disease
caused by the spirits; he cannot, however, treat cases of
witchcraft. Priests are often possessed by and serve as
mediums for various spirits.

1454. Rattray, R. S. Some Folk-Lore Stories and Songs
      n.d.   in Chinyanja. London: S.P.C.K.

Description of the Kanonomera dance among the Ngoni
(Malawi). Description of curative dances in which spirit
possession occurs. [Cited by Brelsford (1948, Bib. 240),
p. 22.]

1455. Ravenscroft, Kent, Jr. "Voodoo Possession: A Natural
      1965   Experiment in Hypnosis." The
                              International Journal of Clini-
                              cal and Experimental Hypnosis
                              13, no. 3: 157-82.

A detailed discussion of the Haitian voodoo spirit possession phenomenon is presented and analyzed in terms of
the differentiations occurring in the psychological trance
state itself.

1456. Rawcliffe, D. H. The Struggle for Kenya. London:
      1954   Victor Gollancz, Ltd.

The dinis or religious cults of Kenya are mixtures of
Christian elements which include ecstatic trance,
glossolalia, and inscription by the Holy Spirit (pp. 27-
28 ff.). The Mau Mau movement is said to have originally
been of these cults (p. 35).

1457. Ray, Benjamin   "Royal Shrines and Ceremonies of
      1972   Buganda." Uganda Journal
                             (Kampala) 36:35-48.

Spirit mediums become possessed by the spirits of the
Buganda (Ganda) (Uganda) royal ancestors. Requests for
health and fortune and for advice are asked of the
spirits.

1458. Ray, Benjamin C.   African Religions: Symbol,
      1976   Ritual, and Community. Engle-
                             wood Cliffs, N.J.: Prentice-
                             Hall, Inc.

Spirit possession and mediumship in African religions
are discussed in detail in this general theoretical
work (see book's index under "Mediumship" and "Possession" for page citations).

1459. Raymaekers, Paul   "L'Église de Jesus-Christ sur
      1959   la terre par le prophete Simon
                             Kimbangu: Contribution à
                             l'etude des mouvements
                             messianiques dans le bas Kongo."
                             Zaïre 13, no. 7: 675-756.

This article has been cited as having information on
spirit possession and mediumship, but was unavailable
for annotation.

1460. Rayner, William   The Tribe and Its Successors.
      1962   New York: Frederick A.
                             Praeger. Ill.

This study deals with the Mashona (Shona) of Southern
Rhodesia. Chapter 9 deals with the Mhondoro spirits and
their mediums. Discussion of the similarities and differences between the Chaminuka and Mwari spirits. Chapter 11 describes witches being possessed by a ghost of
a dead relative who had been a witch. Chapter 12 discusses the Nganga and his practice. Chapter 13 describes
Shave possession and analyzes why it was adopted by the
Shona.

1461. Read, Carvath   Man and His Superstitions. Cam-
      1925   bridge: Cambridge University
                             Press.

Among the Bokongo (Kongo) (Zaïre) a man may become a
wizard by claiming to be the medium of a dead man. A
medium falls into a frenzy, shouts, trembles all over,
his body undulates, sweat breaks out, etc. He speaks in
an archaic language if he knows one (pp. 140-41).

286

1462. Read, Margaret   The Ngoni of Nyasaland. London:
      1956   Oxford University Press.

      Discussion of the Ngoni (Nyasaland, now Malawi) an-
      cestor spirit cult and the role of the medium in this
      cult. Description of rituals (pp. 157-203).

1463. Redmayne, Alison   "Chikanga: An African Diviner
      1970   with an International Reputa-
                           tion." In Witchcraft Confes-
                           sion and Accusations, edited by
                           M. Douglas, pp. 130-28.
                           (Bib. 476.)

      The activities of Chikanga, a diviner among the Hehe of
      Tanzania, are discussed in the context of the traditio-
      nal beliefs about diviners being possessed by effective
      spirits (p. 117).

1464. Reis, Carlos Santos "The Native 'Art of Healing' in
      1952   the Zavala Territory."
                           Moçambique (Lourenço Marques)
                           71:37-58.

      Discusses folk notions of disease causation and native
      treatment. Spirit possession described briefly among
      the Zavala (Mozambique). [Cited in African Abstracts,
      vol. 5, no. 307.]

1465. Renard, A.   "Jesus guérissant." In
      1973   Croyance et guérison, edited by
                           M. Hebga, pp. 109-27. (Bib.
                           752.)

      In this general article on Africa, the Christian heal-
      ing practice of exorcism of demons is mentioned on page
      112. No specific ethnic group is cited.

1466. Rencontres inter-   Les Religions africaines tradi-
      nationales de Bouaké tionnelles (October 1962).
      1965   Paris: Editions du seuil.

      Includes in this bibliography:
                  91   W. Bascom (1965)
                 780   L. de Heusch (1965)
                1808   P. Verger (1965)

1467. Rennie, J. K.   "Some Revitalization Movements
      1972   among the Ndau and Inhambane
                           Thonga 1915-1935." Paper pre-
                           sented at the Conference on the
                           History of Central African Reli-
                           gious Systems, Lusaka, 30 August-
                           8 September.

287

The interrelationship between the Ndau of Rhodesia and Mozambique and Christian missionaries in terms of revitalization movements is discussed and highlighted by the documented case of the Inhambane Thonga. "The argument of the paper is that missionary penetration in much of the area was slight and that Christian ideas spread as much by the voluntary activities of labor migrants as by deliberate mission propagation" (p. 1).

1468. Retel-Laurentin, Anne, and Robert Bangbanzi 1966
"Les Nzakara et leurs ancêtres." Cahiers d'études africaine (Paris) 6, no. 3: 463-503.

As a part of their ancestor cult, the Nzakara of the Central African Empire practice spirit possession by their ancestors, a phenomenon occurring during the nganga dance (p. 474).

1469. Retel-Laurentin, Anne 1969
Oracles et ordalies chez les Nzakara. Paris: Mouton & Co.

Nzakara of the Central African Empire and of the Congo employ spirit possession as a form of divination. Description is given of the use of language and of the initiation ceremonies that accompany it (pp. 89-99).

1470. Retel-Laurentin, Anne 1974
Sorcellerie et ordalies. Paris: Éditions anthropos.

Spirit possession as a means of divining the practitioner of sorcery among the Nzakara of the Central African Empire is mentioned briefly on pages 33-34.

1471. Reynolds, Barrie 1963a
The African: His Position in a Changing Society. Livingstone: Rhodes-Livingstone Museum.

Many illnesses among the Bantu of South Africa are considered to be the result of spirit possession, and exorcism is used as treatment (p. 28).

1472. Reynolds, Barrie 1963b
Magic, Divination and Witchcraft among the Barotse of Northern Rhodesia. London: Chatto & Windus.

Spirit mediumship and possession among the Barotse (Lozi) of Northern Rhodesia (Zambia) are discussed throughout this volume.

1473. Ribas, Oscar 1958
Ilundo (divindades e ritos angolanos). Luanda: Museu de Angola. Ill.

Describes spirit possession and exorcism rites for Angola.

1474. Ribas, Oscar   "Religiosidade angolana."
      1964   Mensário administrativo
                             (Luanda), nos. 4-6, pp. 51-67.

Angolans retain traditional beliefs and practices along with a predominantly Christian orientation. Among the traditional practitioners are the Kimbanda, the doctor/diviner, and the Kilamba, the interpreter for all water-living creatures who cures illnesses sent by them. [Cited in African Abstracts, vol. 18, no. 1 (January 1967), no. 177; possession is not specifically mentioned in abstract.]

1475. Riberio, Jose   Condomble no Brasil.   Paris:
      1972   Espiritualiste.

Not available for annotation.

1476. Riberio, L., and   O Espiritismo no Brasil.   São
      Murillo de Campos   Paulo: Cia Editoria Nacional.
      1931

Not available for annotation.

1477. Ribeiro, René   "An Experimental Approach to the
      1949a   Study of Spirit Possession "
                            Unpublished Dissertation,
                            Northwestern University.

Not available for annotation.

1478. Ribeiro, René   "The Afrobrazilian Cult Groups
      1949b   of Recife - A Study of Social
                            Adjustment."   M.A. Thesis,
                            Northwestern University.

Not available for annotation.

1479. Ribeiro, René   "Novos Aspectos do Processo de
      1955   Reinterpretacâo nos cultos
                            Afro-Brasileiros do Recife."
                            Anais do 31 Congresso Interna-
                            cional de Americanistas (São
                            Paulo) 1:473-91.

The author provides a detailed description of the ritual ceremonies devoted to a variety of spirits as practiced in Brazil (Recife).   The author builds on Herskovits' work in discussing spirit possession and deals with processes of acculturation and new world influences on spirit cults.

1480.Ribeiro, René   "Analises socio-psicologico de
      1959   la possession en los cultos
                              Afro-Brasilenos." Acta Neuro-
                              psyquiatrica Argentina 5:249-62.

Not available for annotation.

1481.Ribeiro, René   "Male Homosexualism and Afro-
      1969a   Brazilian Religions: A Prelimi-
                              nary Report." In Environmental
                              Influences on Genetic Expres-
                              sion. National Institute of
                              Health, Bethesda.

    Although spirit possession is not explicitly mentioned
in this abstract, the male leaders and members of the
Afro-Brazilian possession cults are discussed with re-
gards to their social and psychosexual adjustments.
[Cited in Transcultural Psychiatric Research Review
(Montreal) 9 (October 1972):148-49.]

1482.Ribeiro, René   "Personality and the Psycho-
      1969b   sexual Adjustment of Afro-
                              Brazilian Cult Members."
                              Journal de la Société des
                              américanistes 58:109-20.

    An in-depth investigation is conducted of the psycho-
logical motivations and sexual orientations of the women
and, most especially, the men involved in the African-derived spirit possession candomblé cult in Brazil.

1483.Richards, Audrey   Land, Labour and Diet in
      1939   Northern Rhodesia. London:
                              Oxford University Press.

    Men or women in Northern Rhodesia (Zambia) believing
themselves possessed by the spirits of dead chiefs start
their vocation by sleeping apart from their community.
Later, when their reputation is assured, their passage
from ordinary life to the trance of spirit possession is
marked by the observation of certain dietary taboos (pp.
47-48).

1484.Richards, Audrey   "The Bemba of North Eastern
      1951   Rhodesia." In Seven Tribes of
                              British Central Africa, edited
                              by E. Colson and M. Gluckman.
                              (Bib. 362.)

    Discussion of Bemba (Northern Rhodesia, now Zambia) re-
ligion and magic; description of spirit possession by the
Ngulu spirits, mythical kings with names and legends attached to them. Also some discussion of drug-induced possession (pp. 184-88).

1485. Richards, Audrey   East African Chiefs. London:
      1959   Faber & Faber.

The Nyabingi spirit possession cult originated in
Ruanda in the previous century. It was opposed by the
Tusi, and many of its priests were driven out of the
country. After the great famine "Rwaranda," the cult
gained support. A discussion of the political ramifications of the cult (p. 287; information for the Kiga
(Chiga) of Uganda).

1486. Richardson, James T.   "Psychological Interpretations
      1973   of Glossolalia: A Reexamination
                               of Research." Journal for the
                               Scientific Study of Religion
                               12, no. 2: 199-207.

The author examines explanatory models for the phenomenon of glossolalia, speaking in tongues, and draws attention to the relationship between psychological and
personality features and glossolalia. Special attention
is paid to the work of Lincoln Vivier. The methodologi-
cal problems in studying glossolalia are analyzed. Most
of the empirical data analyzed was collected from Pente-
costalists in North America.

1487. Richter, C. P.   "On the Phenomenon of Sudden
      1957   Death in Animals and Man."
                              Psychosomatic Medicine 19:191-
                              98.

Relies on Cannon's article "Voodoo Death" (American
Anthropologist 1942, Bib. 313). Experimented with rats
to show that death can occur as a result of emotional
states affecting the parasympathetic nervous system.
Possible relation to effects of possession on the human
organism.

1488. Rigaud, Milo   Secrets of Voodoo. New York:
      1971   Arco.

Detailed study of the Haitian voodoo spirit possession
cult is presented.

1489. Rigaud, Odette   "The Feasting of the Gods in
      1946   Haitian Vodu." Primitive Man
                              19, nos. 1-2: 1-58.

A detailed and rich account is given of the Haitian
vodu ceremony of Mangé loa, the feasting of the gods.
A concentrated study was conducted of one particular
priestess in the cult.

291

1490. Rigby, P. J. A.   "Sociological Factors in the
      1966   Contact of the Gogo of Central
                               Tanzania with Islam." In Islam
                               in Tropical Africa, edited by
                               I. M. Lewis, pp. 268-90.
                               (Bib. 1035.)

    Although not part of the religious structure of the
Gogo of Tanzania, spirit possession and mediumship by
the spirits of the dead do occur (p. 285).

1491. Rigby, Peter, and   "Divination and Healing in Peri-
      Fred Lule   Urban Kampala, Uganda." Paper
      1971   presented at the Nabugabo Con-
                               ference, Makerere Institute of
                               Social Research, Kampala,
                               Uganda. 21-24 March.

    Spirit possession and mediumship are discussed through-
out this essay on the methods of divination and healing
found in the area around the city of Kampala, Uganda.

1492. Ringwald, W.   Religion der Akanstämme und das
      n.d.   Problem ihrer Bekehrung.
                               Stuttgart: Evan. Missionsverlag.

    Study contains some discussion of spirit possession
among the Akan (Ghana). [Cited in Baeta (1962, Bib. 63),
p. 147.]

1493. Rivière, Claude   "Fétichisme et démystification:
      1969   L'Example guinéen." Afrique
                               documents (Dakar), nos. 102-3,
                               pp. 131-68.

    The relationship between modernization and socializa-
tion in Guinea and the traditional African religions is
discussed extensively in this article. Beliefs in
various types of spirits and their influence on the
living are presented, and spirit possession is implied
but not explicitly labelled.

1494. Robert, R. P. J. M.   Croyances et coutumes magico-
      1949   religieuses des Wafipa païens.
                               Tabora: Tanganyika Mission
                               Press.

    Spirit possession and mediumship involving the miao
and mizimu spirits among the Wafipa (Fipa) of Tanganyika
(Tanzania) are examined in great detail throughout this
volume.

1495. Roberts, Andrew D.   "The Lumpa Church of Alice Len-
      1970   shina." In Protest and Power in
                              Black Africa, edited by R. I.
                              Rotberg and A. A. Mazrui, pp.
                              513-68. (Bib. 1520.)

      The traditional beliefs of the Bemba of Zambia include
      that of spirit possession by the ngulu, "chthonic
      deities" of natural features such as caves, waterfalls,
      and rocks (pp. 516 ff.). (The Lumpa Church arose as a
      reform of all traditional religious practices.)

1496. Rodd, F. R.   People of the Veil. London:
      1926   Macmillan & Co.

      Among the Tuareg (Mali), disease is regarded as due to
      spirit intrusion. Description of cases of spirit pos-
      session, time of its usual onset, and methods of curing
      it.

1497. Rodinson, Maxime   "Le Culte des Zar en Egypte."
      1953   Comptes rendus sommaires des
                              séances de l'Institut français
                              d'anthropologie (Paris) 7:21-24.

      Description of the Zar cult of Egypt. The Zar cult is
      calculated to have gained prominence around the 1870's.
      Description of the Kudiya, the cult of the possessed, and
      their curing ceremonies.

1498. Rodinson, Maxime   "Autobiographies de possédées
      1957   égyptiennes." Mélanges Louis
                              Massignon (Damas) 3:259-69.

      Presented here are texts of interviews with three women
      of the zar cult in Egypt; descriptions of spirit posses-
      sion are included.

1499. Rodinson, Maxime   Magie, médecine et possession à
      1967   Gondar. La Haye: Mouton & Co.

      The healers, medicines, ceremonies, and use of spirit
      possession in the zar cult in Gondar are described and
      analyzed. The original text and the French translation
      are given of a 1932 Amharic manuscript from the Mission
      of Dakar-Djibouti containing a list of the healers in
      Gondar along with their specialties, treatment methods,
      and costs. Included also is a lengthy bibliography.

1500. Rodriques, Raymunde   Os Africanos no Brasil. São
      Nina   Paulo: Companhia Editora
      1932   Nacional.

      Not available for annotation.

1501. Roscoe, Rev. J.   "Further Notes on the Manners
      1902   and Customs of the Baganda."
                               Journal of the Royal Anthropo-
                               logical Institute of Great
                               Britain and Ireland 32:42.

      Reports on tobacco being smoked to induce voluntary
possession among the Baganda (Ganda) (Uganda).

1502. Roscoe, Rev. J.   "The Bahima of the Uganda Pro-
      1907   tectorate." Journal of the
                               Royal Anthropological Institute
                               of Great Britain 37:111.

      Description of spirit possession of animals among the
Bahima (Hima) (Uganda). When cattle suffer from an
epidemic, ceremonies are held whereby the disease is
ceremonially transferred to one member of the herd who is
sacrificed as a scapegoat.

1503. Roscoe, Rev. J.   The Northern Bantu. Cambridge:
      1915   Cambridge University Press.

      Discusses spirit possession among the Banyankole
(Nkole), Bagesu (Gisu), Banyoro (Nyoro), and Basoga
(Soga) (Uganda) (pp. 55, 128, 177, 246).

1504. Roscoe, John   Twenty-Five Years in East Africa.
      1921   Cambridge: Cambridge University
                               Press.

      Both spirit mediums who are possessed by the spirit of
the royal ancestors and spirit possession which is a
cause of illness among the Baganda (Ganda) of Uganda are
discussed in chapter 9.

1505. Roscoe, John   The Soul of Central Africa.
      1922   London: Cassell & Co.

      Among the Bunyoro (Nyoro), a Bantu-speaking people of
Central Africa, spirit possession by a ghost may cause
illness and even death if not exorcised (pp. 188-89).

1506. Roscoe, John   The Bakitara or Banyoro.
      1923a   Cambridge: Cambridge University
                               Press.

      Possession by ghosts among the Bakitara or Banyoro
(Nyoro) of Uganda causes illnesses, and a witch-doctor
must be called in to exorcise the ghost (chap. 11).

1507. Roscoe, John   The Banyankole. London: Cam-
      1923b   bridge University Press.

Ghosts can cause illness by possession among the
Banyankole (Nkole) of Uganda, and exorcism is the curative method used (pp. 22-33, 138-40).

1508. Roscoe, Rev. J.   The Bagesu and Other Tribes of
      1924a   the Uganda Protectorate. Cam-
                          bridge: Cambridge University
                          Press.

Among the Bagesu (Gisu) (Uganda) sickness is regarded
as due to ghostly possession, and only propitiation of
the possessing spirits will allow the possessed to be
cured (p. 105).

1509. Roscoe, John   Immigrants and Their Influence in
      1924b   the Lake Region of Central
                          Africa. Frazer Lecture in
                          Social Anthropology - 1923.
                          Cambridge: Cambridge University
                          Press.

The spirit of a dead Buganda (Ganda) (Uganda) king possesses and speaks his will through a medium specifically
designated for that purpose. The medium is particularly
active during the burial ceremonies (pp. 27-28).

1510. Roscoe, John   The Baganda: An Account of Their
      1966 (1911)   Native Customs and Beliefs.
                          New York: Barnes & Noble.

Chapter 9 deals with the Baganda (Ganda) (Uganda)
notions of spirit possession and mediumship in the context of their religion.

1511. Rosen, George   Madness in Society. London:
      1968   Routledge & Kegan Paul.

The history of madness in the Western World is traced
from the Greek and early-Judaic periods through the
Middle Ages up to modern times. The phenomenon of spirit
possession both by gods and by devils is explored extensively throughout. Specific mention is made of the Haiti
vodou cults, and the definition of possession is given on
pages 49-59.

1512. Rosenthal, Eric   They Walk in the Night. London:
      n.d. [1949]   George Allen & Unwin.

After numerous accounts of the appearance of ghosts
among the white people of South Africa, the case of an
exorcism of two demon-possessed girls is given in the
last chapter.

1513. Rosney, Eric de   "Le Jengu de Claire." In
     1973   Croyance et Guérison, edited by
                     M. Hebga, pp. 9-39. (Bib. 752.)

Exorcism and spirit possession are mentioned in the
discussion following this article (p. 35). The ethnic
group cited is the Sara (Chad).

1514. Ross, A. D.   "Epileptiform Attacks Provoked
     1956   by Music." British Journal of
                     Delinquency 7, no. 1: 60-63.

In Somaliland, a case is given of a homicide, the per-
petrator of which was "possessed" by an evil spirit and
would return to such a possession state whenever a certain type of traditional music was played. The author
terms the state "Musiogenic Epilepsy."

1515. Rossini, C. Conti   "Note sugli Agau." Giornale
     1905   della Società asiatica italiana
                     (Florence), vol. 18

Discussion of the Zar cult of Ethiopia with some reference to spirit possession. [Cited by Cerulli, 1929,
Bib. 330.]

1516. Rosy, H.   "Magie, Sorciers, Féticheurs."
     1947   Bulletin militaire 25:59-71.

Spirit possession and its manifestations described for
the Congo.

1517. Rotberg, Robert   "Religious Nationalism: The Len-
     1961   shina Movement of Northern
                     Rhodesia." In Human Problems in
                     British Central Africa. Rhodes-
                     Livingstone Journal, no. 29,
                     pp. 63-78.

Description of the Lenshina movement in Northern
Rhodesia (Zambia), information on its founder, Regina
Mulenga, whose calling came as a result of spirit pos-
session; description of the Lumpa church.

1518. Rotberg, Robert I.   "The Rise of African Nationa-
     1965a   lism: The Case of East and
                     Central Africa." In Modern
                     Africa, edited by Peter J. M.
                     McEwan and Robert B. Sutcliffe,
                     pp. 184-88. New York: Thomas
                     Y. Crowell Co.

The use of glossolalia and spirit mediumship in African chiliastic cults in general is mentioned on pages
186-87.

1519. Rotberg, Robert I.   The Rise of Nationalism in Cen-
      1965b   tral Africa. Cambridge, Mass.:
                                  Harvard University Press.

Although not explicitly labelled, the "frenzied" and
"hysterical" states described by a district commissioner
in Northeastern Rhodesia while trying to disperse Iwa
(Zambia) followers of the Watch Tower Movement appear to
imply a kind of possession-like trance (pp. 137-38).

1520. Rotberg, Robert I.,   Protest and Power in Black
      and Ali A. Mazrui,   Africa. New York: Oxford
      eds.   University Press.
      1970

      Includes in this bibliography:
                1219   R. C. Mitchell (1970)
                1495   A. D. Roberts (1970)
                1904   A. Wipper (1970)

1521. Rouch, Jean   "Aperçu sur l'animisme songhai."
      1943   Notes africaines de l'Institut
                                 Français d'Afrique noire, no.
                                 20, pp. 4-6, 8.

Results of research conducted in 1941/42 among the
Songhai of the Miamey-Tillabery region, Niger. Information on myths and principal rites of several spirit
cults.

1522. Rouch, Jean   "Culte des génies chez les
      1945   Songay." Journal de la Société
                                 des africanistes. (Paris), vol.
                                 15.

Study of rites involving spirit possession dances among
the Songay (Songhai) (Niger).

1523. Rouch, J.   "La Danse." Présence africaine
      1950   8/9:219-26.

Description of various African dances, including
dances of magic and spirit possession.

1524. Rouch, J.   "Rites de pluie chez Songhay."
      1953   Bulletin de l'Institut francais
                                 d'Afrique noire 15, no. 4: 1655-
                                 89.

Forces of nature are contacted through magicians, and
communications are transmitted through possessed persons
among the Songhay (Songhai) (Niger). Rain rites, including possession dances, are described.

297

1525. Rouch, Jean   Les Songhay. Paris: Presses
      1954   universitaires de France.

Some information is available on Songhay (Songhai)
(Niger) cults and the role of possession in the work of
the magicians and in the religious belief system
(chap. 6, pp. 59-63). Bibliography.

1526. Rouch, Jean   La Religion et la magie Songhay.
      1960   Paris: Presses universitaires
                           de France.

A discussion of spirit possession among the Songhay
(Songhai) (Niger) appears on the following pages: 145-47,
175-98, 215-20.

1527. Rouch, J.   "Introduction à l'étude de la
      1963   communauté de Bregbo."
                           Journal de la Société des
                           africanistes (Paris) 33, no. 1:
                           129-202.

The traditional culture of the Akan (Ivory Coast),
which includes beliefs in spirits that "eat" people, and
the rise of the prophet Harris are presented as background for the discussion of Albert Acho, the Harrist
prophet who heads the healing community at Bregbo, Ivory
Coast. Healing techniques include exorcism, among others.

1528. Roumeguère-Eberhardt,   "Pensée et société africaines."
      Jacqueline   Cahiers de l'homme (Paris),
      1963   n.s., no. 3.

Spirit possession and mediumship are mentioned for
various Bantu-speaking peoples of southern Africa in
chapter 5, which focusses on the ritual and mythological
uses of music.

1529. Routledge, W. S., and   With a Prehistoric People: The
      K. Routledge   Akikuyu of British East Africa.
      1910   London: Edward Arnold.

"For the Kikuyu [Kenya], almost every disease is caused
by the action of a dissatisfied or malignant spirit. It
acts from without but can also possess a man. The spirit
of a father . . . who had died in Nairobi might enter
into a child at Nyeri" (p. 240).

1530. Rudner, Jalmar, and   The Hunter and His Art. Cape
      Ione Rudner   Town: C. Struik. Ill.
      1970

In this illustrated work on rock paintings and carvings
in the hunting and gathering societies of Africa, a brief

description is given of the Mlimo rain cult of the
Matabele (Ndebele) of Rhodesia which involves spirit
mediumship (p. 80).

1531. Ruel, M. J.   "Witchcraft Beliefs in an
       1963   African Society." Folklore 74:
                             563-67.

The West African Banyang conceptualize an outer public
and social world, and an internal world of the individual
inhabited by "were-animals" that can be sent out from
the sleeping body of the possessor to his victim, who becomes possessed.

1532. Ruel, Malcolm   "Witchcraft, Morality and
       1965   Doubt." Odu (Ibadan) 2, no. 1:
                             3-27.

Among the Banyang of West Africa, witchcraft is based
on the concept of "were-persons" who possess "were-
animal" counterparts. Such possession is not regarded as
morally bad in and of itself, and it may be used properly
or improperly according to the possessor's discretion.

1533. Ruffin-Pierre, M. P.   "Femmes 'zebola' ou femmes
       1947   hantées par un esprit." Voix du
                             Congolais 14:613-14.

Information on Mongo (Zaïre) women supposed to be
haunted by spirits.

1534. Rusillon, Henry   Un Culte dynastique avec évoca-
       1912   tion des morts chez les Sakalaves
                             de Madagascar, le "Tromba."
                             Paris: Librairie Alphonse Picard
                             & Fils.

The religious beliefs of the Sakalave (Sakalava) of
Madagascar are outlined in detail here. A major element
in the Tromba ancestor cult is spirit possession.

1535. Ryan, C.   "The Role of Spirits of the An-
       1975   cestors in Ugandan Traditional
                             Societies." Occasional Research
                             Papers in African Traditional
                             Religion and Philosophy
                             (Makerere University, Kampala),
                             vol. 18, no. 193.

Spirit possession may be practical both to get advice
and as a means of punishment among Ugandan traditional
societies, in particular the Jonam and the Kuman.

1536. Sachs, Wulf   Black Hamlet. Boston: Little
      1947   Brown.

      Mediumship experiences in South Africa reported on
      pages 15, 196-97.

1537. Sagar, J. W.   "Notes on the History, Religion
      1922   and Customs of the Nuba."
                           Sudan Notes and Records 5, nos.
                           3-4: 137-56.

      According to the religious beliefs of the Dilling Nuba
      (Sudan), the supreme God guides affairs of mortals
      through the aid of lesser spirits, known as Arro. Each
      of these spirits is represented on earth by a priest or
      priestess. Arro may take possession of his priests.
      Description of the duties of the priestly class (pp. 143-
      45).

1538. Salamone, Frank A.   "Further Notes on Hausa Culture
      1969/70   and Personality." International
                           Journal of Social Psychiatry
                           (London) 16, no. 1: 39-44.

      Brief mention is made both of the Hausa (Nigeria) be-
      lief that all mental illnesses are caused by spirit pos-
      session and of the bori possession cult (p. 43).

1539. Salamone, Frank A.   Gods and Goods in Africa. Vols.
      1974   1-2. New Haven, Conn.: Human
                           Relations Area Files, Inc.

      In volume 1, the author discusses the traditional
      Kamberi religious beliefs (Yauri Emirate, Northwestern
      State, Nigeria), which include contact with the spirits
      by the priests (p. 127). Also mentioned is the Hausa
      bori spirit possession cult (pp. 128-29).

1540. Salamone, Frank   "Religion as Play: Bori, a
      1975   Friendly 'Witchdoctor.'"
                           Journal of Religion in Africa
                           (Leiden) 7, no. 3: 201-11.

      Among the Gungawa (Reshe) of northern Nigeria as among
      the Hausa, the word bori refers to spirits. However, the
      Gungawa do not practice spirit possession, favoring a
      direct communication with the spirits through their mani-
      festing their presence by means of sounds and other
      physical phenomena (p. 206).

1541. Samarin, William J. "Sociolinguistic vs. Neurophy-
      1972a   siological Explanations for
                           Glossolalia: Comment on Goodman's
                           Papers." Journal for the Scien-
                           tific Study of Religion 11, no.
                           3: 293-6.

The author comments on the research conducted by
Felicitas Goodman among Pentecostals in North America
and Mexico. He takes issue with the regularity of
glossolalic utterances which F. Goodman (Bib. 667-684)
has found cross-culturally. He offers criticism of the
Goodman data and analysis.

1542. Samarin, William J.   Tongues of Men and Angels.
      1972b   New York: Macmillan Co.

Working with data from several sources including South
African Pentecostal groups, the author defines glossolalia as follows: "A meaningless but phonologically structured human utterance believed by the speaker to be a
real language but bearing no systematic resemblance to
any natural language, living or dead" (p. 2).

1543. Samarin, William J.   "Variations and Variables in
      1972c   Religious Glossolalia."
                              Language in Society 1, no. 1:
                              121-30

Glossolalia is more than just a psychopathological
phenomenon. Within the Pentecostal Church, it is another
"language" manipulated by the speakers. [Cited in Abstracts in Anthropology, vol. 3, no. 4 (1972), no. 1832.]

1544. Samarin, William J.   "Glossolalia as Repressive
      1973   Speech." Language and Speech
                              16:77-89.

Not available for annotation.

1545. Samkange, Stanlake   Origins of Rhodesia. London:
      1968   Heinemann.

The relationship between the land, the territorial
spirits, and the Mwari cult (with its spirit mediums)
among the peoples of Rhodesia is discussed on pages 34-35.

1546. Sangmuah, E.   "The Healing (Spiritual) Therapy
      1968   in Ghana." In Deuxieme Colloque
                              africain de psychiatrie - pro-
                              ceedings, p. 104-8. (Bib. 1345.)

Although not labelled as such, the ceremonies described
as occurring in the Ghana "Spiritual" churches are very
similar to spirit possession rituals. These ceremonies
are investigated for their healing potential and are compared to hypnosis.

1547. Sangree, Walter H.   Age, Prayer, and Politics in
      1966   Tiriki, Kenya. London: Oxford
                              University Press.

Among the Tiriki of Nyanza province, Kenya, spirit possession had been an only occasional occurrence until the coming of the Christian missionaries. Spirit possession is now common in many Pentecostal and independent African churches. Some mission congregations have split over the issue of having spirit possession and "speaking in tongues" in the services. Description of a worship service in an African independent church (the African Church of the Holy Spirit) in which possession is encouraged (pp. 172-89).

1548. Santandrea, Fr. S.   "Evil and Witchcraft among the
      1938   Ndogo Group of Tribes." Africa:
                             Journal of the International Afri-
                             can Institute (London) 11, no. 4:
                             459-81.

Among the Ndogo of the Anglo-Egyptian Sudan (now Sudan) certain individuals, called Mbe-baaci, act as the representative of spirits (including ancestor spirits) called Baaci. The Mbe-baaci are sometimes consulted if a person believes witchcraft is being used against him or if he is ill. The Mbe-baaci are possessed by their Baaci, and give the client exact instruction on how to obtain a cure.

1549. Santo, Eduardo dos   Religiões de Angola. Lisbon:
      1969   Junta de investigacões do
                            ultramar.

On page 433 discussion is presented on the ministers of fetishist cults being able to transform themselves into animals through spirit possession. Influences of the Bakongo (Kongo) (Angola) are stressed, although the discussion centers around religions of Angola in general.

1550. Sargant, William   "Some Cultural Group Abreactive
      1949   Techniques and Their Relation
                            to Modern Treatments." Pro-
                            ceedings of the Royal Society of
                            Medicine (London) 42:367-74.

Spirit possession in the Haitian voodoo cult is discussed from a psychological perspective (pp. 371-72).

1551. Sargant, William   Battle for the Mind. Garden
      1957   City, N.Y.: Doubleday.

The trance state evident in shock or in possession is analyzed in terms of Pavlovian conditioning and the mental collapse coming after intense excitation.

1552. Sargant, William   "Witch Doctoring, Zar and Voo-
      1967   doo: Their Relation to Modern
                              Psychiatric Treatments." Pro-
                              ceedings of the Royal Society of
                              Medicine 60, no. 10: 1055-60.

      Western and traditional methods of dealing with mental
problems are compared, using examples from the Ethiopian
Zar cult, witch-doctors living in Kisumu, Kenya, the
Brazilian Macumba cult, and the Haitian voodoo cult.

1553. Sargant, William   The Mind Possessed. London:
      1973   William Heinemann Ltd.

      Focusing on possession trance, the author discusses its
psychological correlates and likens it to "brainwashing,"
"conversion," and other states of mental dissociation
(p. 31).

1554. Sarpong, P. A.   "Media of Revelation in African
      1975   Traditional Religions." Ghana
                              Bulletin of Theology (Legon) 4,
                              no. 8: 40-47.

      Although not explicitly labelled as such, both spirit
possession and spirit mediumship are implied in this
study of revelation in African traditional religions.

1555. Sastre, Robert   "Spiritualité africaine et
      1957   Christianisme." Presence
                              africaine (Paris), n.s. no. 13,
                              pp. 23-30.

      In this philosophical essay on the differences and
similarities between African traditional concepts of
spirituality and Christianity, spirit possession among
the Yoruba of Dahomey (Benin) and Togo is mentioned
briefly on page 27.

1556. Sastre, Robert   "Les Vodũ dans la vie culturelle,
      1972   sociale et politique du Sud-
                              Dahomey." In Les Religions
                              africaines commes source des
                              valeurs de civilisation, Colloque
                              de Cotonou (August 1970), pp.
                              339-52. (Bib. 358.)

      The spirit possession rites which are a part of the re-
ligious beliefs of various ethnic groups of south Dahomey
(Benin) are discussed. Groups include: Gɛ, Fõ, and
Xwla. (All are influenced by the Yoruba religion.)

303

1557. Saulnier, S. M. A.   "Recherches sur le vodun Dan à
      1975   partir des noms individuels de
                              ses vodunsi." Bulletin de
                              l'Institut fondamental d'Afrique
                              noire (Dakar) 37, no. 2: 358-87.

      Although spirit possession is not explicitly labelled,
this article deals with the vodun deities of southern
Dahomey (Fon), in particular the vodun Dan (Benin).

1558. Saunders, Lucie Wood   "Variants in Zar Experience in
      1977   an Egyptian Village." In Case
                              Studies in Spirit Possession,
                              edited by V. Crapanzano and V.
                              Garrison, pp. 177-91. (Bib.
                              391.)

      General description of the zar possession cult found in
Egypt, the Sudan, Ethiopia, and the Arabian peninsula
precedes the presentation of a case study of the practices of the zar cult in an Egyptian village.

1559. Sawyerr, Harry   "The Dogma of Super-Size-II."
      1963   Sierra Leone Bulletin of Reli-
                              gion (Freetown) 5, no. 1: 1-18.

      An account of spirit possession among the Akan of the
Ivory Coast is given where the possessed woman was
thought to have brought the spirit into being (pp. 3-4).

1560. Sawyerr, Harry   Creative Evangelism: Towards a
      1968   New Christian Encounter with
                              Africa. London: Lutterworth
                              Press.

      Spirit possession and mediumship in traditional African
practices of ancestor worship are mentioned on pages 127-
28, 139.

1561. Sawyerr, Harry   God: Ancestor or Creator? As-
      1970a   pects of Traditional Belief in
                              Ghana, Nigeria and Sierra
                              Leone. London: Longman Group
                              Ltd.

      When discussing the Mende (Sierra Leone) belief in a
supreme deity, mention is briefly made of spirits who can
possess people and do them harm (p. 83).

1562. Sawyerr, Harry   "Quels sont les effects des reli-
      1970b   gions traditionneles sur la foi
                              chrétienne? Quelle doit être la
                              résponse de l'église à cette
                              situation?" Flambeau (Yaoundé),
                              no. 25, pp. 35-46.

Possession by the Holy Spirit and the Christian practice of exorcism are examined in light of traditional
African religious practices (pp. 41-42).

1563. Schapera, I., ed.   The Bantu Speaking Tribes of
      1937   South Africa. London:
                                 Routledge & Kegan Paul.

      Includes in this bibliography:
               502   W. M. Eiselen and I. Schapera
                          (1937)
               791   A. W. Hoernlé (1937)

1564. Schapera, I., ed.   Livingstone's African Journal
      1963   1853-1856. Vols. 1-2.
                                 Berkeley: University of Cali-
                                 fornia Press.

      Spirit possession is briefly mentioned three times in
      Livingstone's journals. He records incidents among the
      Balonda (Londa) (of Angola) (pp. 218-219); the Bakota
      (Kota) (of Rhodesia) (pp. 346-47, 391); and the
      Makololo (Kololo) (of Rhodesia) (p. 391).

1565. Scheerder, Rev. P., and   "Les Wa Lu Guru." Anthropos
      Rev. R. Tastevin   45, nos. 1-3: 241-86.
      1950

      This study deals with the Ulugura (Luguru) people of
      Tanganyika (Tanzania). It describes the cult of ances-
      tor spirits, who may possess individuals. To invoke the
      spirits, one must resort to a Nganga who is the spirits'
      medium. Description of possession dances and ritual
      exorcism (pp. 271-79).

1566. Schenkel, R.   "Le Vécu de la vie sexuelle
      1971   chez les Africains acculturés du
                                Sénégal, a partir des notions
                                d'impuissance et de puissance
                                sexuelle." Psychopathologie
                                africaine (Dakar) 7, no. 3: 313-
                                88.

      In this detailed article on sexual potency and impo-
      tence among acculturated Africans in Dakar, Senegal, men-
      tion is made of the traditional causes of impotence
      which are centered mainly around possession or interfe-
      rence by jealous spirits (pp. 329-30).

1567. Scherer, J. H.   "The Ha of Tanganyika." Anthro-
      1959   pos 54, no. 5/5: 841-904.

      Discusses: the Ha (Tanganyika, now Tanzania) ancestor
      cult; spirit possession by ancestor spirits; exorcism
      ceremonies for the possessed; spirit possession by nature

spirits; spirit possession and divination techniques
(pp. 888-99).

1568. Schlosser, Katesa   Propheten in Afrika.   Braunsch-
       1949   weig: A. Limbach.

      Data on possession in Africa on page 246.

1569. Schoffeleers, J. M.   "Social Functional Aspects of
       1968/69   Spirit Possession in the Lower
                          Shire Valley of Malawi." In
                          Religious Studies Papers, Uni-
                          versity of East Africa Social
                          Sciences Council Conference,
                          pp. 51-61. Kampala: Makerere
                          Institute of Social Research.

      Employing data on spirit possession from the Mang'-
anja (Manganja) and the Sena of the Lower Shire Valley
in Malawi, the author criticizes I. M. Lewis's article
in Man (1966, Bib. 1036) and P. J. Wilson's response in
Man (1967, Bib. 1895). His conclusion as to the nature
of spirit possession and mediumship is that they cannot
be regarded as "uniform phenomen[a] in relationship to
the social system" (p. 60). Descriptions of possession
states are given.

1570. Schoffeleers, J. M.   "The Chisumpi and M'bona Cults
       1972a   in Malawi: A Comparative His-
                          tory."   Paper presented at the
                          Conference on the History of
                          Central African Religious Sys-
                          tems, Lusaka, 30 August -
                          8 September.

      The historical development of the Chisumpi and M'bona
cults in Malawi is traced from the fourteenth century to
the present. In the past, these cults had wide-reaching
social and political influence and their hereditary
priests divined, prophesied, and caused the rains to
come; however, more recently, their structures have
greatly disintegrated.

1571. Schoffeleers, Matthew   "The History and Political Role
       1972b   of the M'Bona Cult among the
                          Mang'anja."   In The Historical
                          Study of African Religion,
                          edited by T. O. Ranger and I. N.
                          Kimambo, pp. 73-94.
                          (Bib. 1442.)

      The historical and political roles of the mediums in
the M'Bona cult among the Mang'anja (Manganja) of
Malawi and Mozambique are discussed in detail.

306

1572. Schoffeleers, Matthew   "Towards the Identification of
      1973   a Proto-Chewa Culture."
                                 Journal of Social Science
                                 (Blantyre, Malawi) 2:47-60.

    The Chisumpi cult of the Chewa (Malawi), which prac-
    tices spirit mediumship, is mentioned in this historical
    analysis of Chewa society (pp. 50 ff.).

1573. Schoffeleers, J. M.   "Crisis, Criticism and Critique:
      1974   An Interpretative Model of Ter-
                                 ritorial Mediumship among the
                                 Chewa." Journal of Social
                                 Science (Blantyre) 3:74-80.

    In Chewa (Malawi) society, territorial spirit mediums
    play a very important part in political crises; indeed,
    the author terms them a "crisis institution." They have
    license to criticize political authority on issues of
    public morality, etc.

1574. Schoffeleers, J. M.   "The Interaction between the
      1975   M'Bona Cult and Christianity,
                                 1859-1963." In Themes in the
                                 Christian History of Central
                                 Africa, edited by T. O. Ranger
                                 and J. Weller, pp. 14-29.
                                 (Bib. 1449.)

    The historical relationship between the traditional
    spirit mediums of the M'Bona cult among the Mang'anja
    (Manganja) people of southern Malawi and adjacent areas of
    Mozambique and the Christian missionaries is traced in
    detail. Particular attention is paid to the shifting
    elements in the central beliefs of the M'Bona cult due to
    Christian influence.

1575. Schumacker, P.   "Au Ruanda. Considérations sur
      1949   la nature de l'homme." Zaire:
                                 Belgian African Review
                                 (Bruxelles) 3, no. 3: 257-78.

    The conversation between the author and four older men
    of the Batutsi (Tutsi) people of Zaire is recorded, the
    topic of which is the nature of the human being. Al-
    though the bazumi, the spirits of the dead, do not
    usually take possession of human beings, when they do
    they cause illnesses (pp. 273-74).

1576. Schurmans, D., M. M.   "Significations psychodynamiques
      Samba Ba, and Ibrahima   et fonctions culturelles des in-
      Tabane   terprétations traditionnelles
      1971   wolof des maladies mentales."
                                 Psychopathologie africaine
                                 (Dakar) 7, no. 1: 57-100.

307

Detailed case studies are presented of mentally ill
patients of Wolof origin in Senegal. The Western psychiatric diagnosis is given for each case, followed by
the traditional explanations of the illness, mainly centered on possession by the various classes of spirits:
rab, djine, and saytaané. The main emphasis of the
article is to demonstrate the logic and rationale behind
the traditional diagnoses and curing practices.

1577. Schurmans, Daniel   "Le Problème de l'Odeipe en
      1972   Afrique." Psychopathologie
                             africaine (Dakar) 8, no. 3:
                             325-53.

After presenting the traditional Wolof and Lébou (Lebu)
(Senegal) explanation of mental illnesses which focus on
possession by various types of spirits, the author goes
on to discuss these beliefs in the context of the
Oedipal relationship in Africa.

1578. Schutte, A. G.   "Dual Religious Orientation in
      1974   an Urban African Church."
                             African Studies (Johannesburg)
                             33, no. 2: 113-20.

The concept of possession by the Holy Spirit is analyzed
for the members of the Dutch Reformed Church located
in Meadowlands, Soweto, South Africa. Practices of the
Zionist prophets are also included.

1579. Schuyler, Philippa   Who Killed the Congo? New York:
      1962   Devin-Adair Co.

A brief description is given of "diabolic possession"
trances practiced among the adherents of the Apostolu
religious movement in the Congo, the main tenet of which
is that God is black (pp. 281-82).

1580. Scott, E. H. M.   "A Study of the Content of
      1967   Delusions and Hallucinations in
                             100 African Female Psychotics."
                             South African Medical Journal
                             (Cape Town) 41, no. 34: 853-56.

This article gives an analysis of the hallucinations of
100 women from the following South African ethnic groups:
Tswana, Zulu, Xhosa (Xosa), Sotho, Swazi (Swaziland),
Pedi, and Shangaan (Thonga). These women are described
as being in an intermediary social position between the
traditional and modern social strata, and their hallucinations consist mainly of hearing voices of God, or of
the spirits speaking to them.

1581. Segy, Ladislas   African Sculpture Speaks. New
      1969   York: Hill & Wang. Ill.

      In this illustrated book on African sculpture, spirit
      possession and exorcism are discussed on pages 17-18.

1582. Seligman, Brenda Z.   "On the Origin of the Egyptian
      1914   Zar." Folklore 25:303-323.

      The origins of the zar cult in Egypt are traced to sub-
      saharan African ethnic groups. Descriptions of posses-
      sion beliefs and ceremonies are given.

1583. Seligman, C. G.   "The Unconscious in Relation to
      1928   Anthropology." British Journal
                            of Psychology, vol. 18, pt. 4.

      Some general discussion of trances and states of dis-
      sociation (p. 375).

1584. Seligman, C. G.   "The Religion of the Pagan
      1931   Tribes of the White Nile."
                            Africa: Journal of the Interna-
                            tional African Institute
                            (London) 4, no. 1: 1-21.

      Among the Dinka of the Anglo-Egyptian Sudan (now Sudan)
      lived a prophet named Wal who was possessed by the spirit
      of Deng, the bringer of rains and an emanation or off-
      spring of the Great God, Nyalie. Wal prophesied a num-
      ber of major events. He also created a number of cere-
      monies that were said to have been demanded by his
      spirit (p. 7). The Dinka are governed by rain makers who
      are regarded as divine rulers. These rulers, called
      Bain, derive their power from having "immanent" in them
      the spirit of a great ancestor (p. 12).

1585. Seligman, C. G., and Pagan Tribes of the Nilotic
      Brenda Z. Seligman   Sudan. London: George Routledge
      1932   & Sons.

      Discussion of spirit possession as it relates to Dinka
      and Nuer medicine men and prophets (Sudan) (pp. 26-27,
      188, 231-32).

1586. Semaine d'études ethno- Dieu, idoles et sorcellerie dans
      pastorales, 2d   la region Kwango/Bas-Kwilu.
      1966   Ser. 1, vol. 2. Bandundu:
                               Centre d'études ethnologiques.

      Although neither spirit possession nor mediumship is
      listed in the index to this conference, useful material
      on the roles of the various types of spirits (causing
      illnesses, part of divination, etc.) is presented through-
      out for the following ethnic groups of Congo-Kinshasa
      (Zaïre): Suku, Yaka, Boma, Yansi (Yanzi), and Mbim.

      309

1587. Semaine d'études ethno-   <u>Mort, funerailles, deuil et</u>
      pastorales, 3d   <u>culte des ancêtres chez les</u>
      1967   <u>populations du Kwango/Bas-</u>
                                <u>Kwilu</u>. Ser. 1, vol. 3.
                                Bandundu: Centre d'études ethno-
                                logiques.

Although neither spirit possession nor mediumship is
listed in the index to this conference, useful material
on the roles that the spirits of the dead play (especially in the ancestor cults) is presented throughout for
the following ethnic groups of Congo-Kinshasa (Zaïre):
Boma, Teke, Yansi, Mbim, Nsala-Mbanda (Yansi), baKeni
(Yansi), and Sakata.

1588. Semi-Bi   "L'Animisme et l'avenir des
      1972   valeurs de la civilisation
                                négro-africaine." <u>Afrique</u>
                                <u>littéraire et artistique</u> (Paris),
                                no. 26, pp. 2-11.

Although spirit possession is not specifically labelled,
the power of the "Esprit" found in the African use of
dance and the trance states obtained thereby is mentioned on page 7. The drum is considered to be the in-
strument of communication between men, both living and
dead.

1589. Sempa, Katende   "Empirical Foundations of the
      1971   Concept of a Soul." <u>Dina na</u>
                                <u>Mila</u> (Kampala) 5, no. 2: 7-28.

The Buganda (Ganda) (Uganda) concepts of spirits are
examined particularly with regard to the philosophical
distinction between mind and body. Both possession and
mediumship are discussed.

1590. Senga, Edward   "Revival Cults in Jamaica:
      n.d.   Notes Toward a Sociology of
                                Religion." <u>Jamaican Journal</u>
                                (Kingston) 3, no. 2: 3-13.

Not available for annotation.

1591. Serpos, Tidani A.   "Rituels." <u>Présence africaine</u>
      1950   (Paris), nos. 8-9, pp. 297-305.

Spirit possession trance among the fetich-priests of
Dahomey (Benin) is described in this case study of their
rituals.

1592. Servier, Jean   <u>L'Homme et l'invisible</u>. Paris:
      1964   Robert Laffont.

310

Spirit possession in the Haitian vaudou and Brazilian candomble cults is discussed on pages 167-68. Particular mention is made of its relation to mental illnesses.

1593. Sévy, Gabriel V.   "Le Wama des Ngbaka de la
      1960   Lobaye." Cahiers des études
                                africaines 3:103-28.

Study of the Ngbaka people (Zaïrc). The Wama, or doctor-diviner, serves as a medium for a variety of spirits. Description of initiation ceremony of the diviner and his function in the community.

1594. Shack, William A.   "Religious Ideas and Social Ac-
      1963   tion in Gurage Bond-Friendship."
                               Africa (London), vol. 33, no. 3.

Discussion of spirit possession among the Gurage of Ethiopia. Possession by evil spirits results in an illness and usually ends in death (p. 204).

1595. Shack, William A.   The Gurage. London: Oxford Uni-
      1966   versity Press.

The zitänä ritual curse among the Gurage of Ethiopia causes an evil spirit possession illness (pp. 167-68, 185 ff.).

1596. Shack, William A.   "Hunger, Anxiety, and Ritual:
      1971   Deprivation and Spirit Posses-
                               sion among the Gurage of
                               Ethiopia." Man (London) n.s. 6,
                               no. 1: 30-43.

The Gurage of Ethiopia live in a climate where food is extremely scarce, and thus hunger is a daily problem for them. Examined here is the relationship between the anxiety of going hungry, illnesses, and the rituals of spirit possession and exorcism.

1597. Sharman, A., and   "Drums in Padhola." Uganda
      L. Anderson   Journal (Kampala) 13, no. 2:
      1967   191-99.

After describing the drums and associated instruments of the Padhola of Uganda, the curing practices are mentioned during which the patient goes into trance to the sound of special drums and rattles.

1598. Sheddick, V. G. J.   The Southern Sotho. Ethno-
      1953   graphic Survey of Africa, edited
                               by Daryll Forde. London: In-
                               ternational African Institute.

Among the Sotho of Southern Africa, spirit possession
is treated by the Mathuela cult, a society of formerly
possessed persons. They require the possessed person to
drink large doses of goat's or sheep's blood and force
her (almost all victims are women) to sing and dance
until completely exhausted. The spirit is then ordered
to quit the body, and the patient becomes a member of the
cult (pp. 68-69).

1599. Shephard, J. B.   Land of the Tikoloshe. London:
      1955   Longmans, Green & Co.

Among the Bantu-speaking peoples inhabiting the
Transkei Region of South Africa, a specific form of mental illness is said to be caused by being possessed by a
spirit called Mamlambo (pp. 84-85). In addition, witches
and female witch-doctors are said to be possessed by
Izulu, a creature who can change into various animal
shapes to serve its master (p. 86). Native doctors have
various remedies for exorcising evil spirits from individuals (pp. 101 ff.).

1600. Shepperson, George   "Comment on E. M. McClelland's
      1966a   'The Experiment in Communal
                               Living at Aiyetoro.'" Compara-
                               tive Studies in Society and
                               History 9, no. 1: 29-32.

This is a critique of the preceding article in the
same journal written on the Aiyetoro community in
Nigeria, an African independent church movement. The
critique focusses on the lack of discussion about the use
of ecstatic trance, possession by the Holy Spirit, and
glossolalia.

1601. Shepperson, G.   "Ethiopianism and African Na-
      1966b   tionalism (1953)." In Social
                               Change: The Colonial Situation,
                               edited by Immanuel Wallerstein,
                               pp. 478-88. New York: John
                               Wiley & Sons.

Although spirit possession is not explicitly mentioned,
the article deals in depth with the "Zionist" church
movement in Africa.

1602. Shooter, Rev. Joseph   The Kafirs of Natal and the Zulu
      1857   Country. London: E. Stanford.

Chapter 6 includes several accounts of the practices of
"prophets" who claim to be in communication with the
spirits among the Kafirs of South Africa. Also given is
a description of the initial "calling" of an individual
by the spirits.

1603. Short, Robin   African Sunset. London: Johnson
      1973   Publications.

      Although spirit possession is not explicitly labelled,
description is given of men   called Chintemu among the
Ndembu of Zambia who can change themselves into spirits
and, in that form, steal food (p. 175).

1604. Shorter, Aylward   "The Migawo: Peripheral Spirit
      1970   Possession and Christian Pre-
                              judice." Anthropos 65, nos.
                              1-2: 110-26.

      The migawo spirit possession guild among the Kimbu and
southern Nyamwezi (Tanzani) is described in detail. Dissociation is induced by music and drugs. Women in particular seek membership to escape situations of "conflict,
rivalry and frustration." Migawo is not a religious
ritual, but a healing practice.

1605. Shorter, Aylward   "Symbolism, Ritual and History:
      1972   An Examination of the Work of
                              Victor Turner." In The Histori-
                              cal Study of African Religion,
                              edited by T. O. Ranger and I. N.
                              Kimambo, pp. 139-49. (Bib.
                              1442.)

      The Swezi and Migawo spirit possession guilds and
their diffusion are analyzed for the following East African kingdoms: Buha (Ha), Usumbwa (Sumbwa), Usukuma
(Sukuma), Unyamwezi (Nyamwezi), Ukimbu (Kimbu), and Pare
(in Uganda, Rwanda, Burundi, and Tanzania, p. 146).

1606. Shorter, Aylward   African Culture and the Chris-
      1973   tian Church. London:
                              Geoffrey Chapman.

      The uses of spirit possession in both traditional Afri-
can religions and the African Christian Churches are explored on pages 23-24, 134-35, 143-44.

1607. Shorter, Aylward   African Christian Theology--
      1975   Adaptation or Incarnation?
                              London: Geoffrey Chapman.

      Spirit possession is briefly mentioned in the introduc-
tion to this general philosophical work on the interrelationship between Christianity and traditional African
religions (pp. 13, 16).

1608. Shropshire, Rev. Denys "The Initiation of a Doctor of
      1929   the Wa Barwe Tribe." Man, vol.
                              29.

313

Southern Rhodesia. A case of a Wa Barwe (Barwe) man
who fell ill, and was diagnosed as possessed by a shawe
spirit. Curing ceremony described in which the possessed
became initiated into the priestly class (p. 205).

1609. Shropshire, Rev. Denys   "A 'Kupemha' Shawe of the
      1930   Wabarwe Tribe." Man 30, no. 7:
                               125-26.

Report of a Wabarwe (Barwe) (Rhodesia) woman possessed
of a Kupemha Shawe (beggar spirit). The woman's possession was diagnosed by a diviner, and she was initiated
to the doctor status. Shawe dancing described.

1610. Shropshire, Denys W. T. The Church and Primitive
      1938   Peoples. London: Society for
                               Promoting Christian Knowledge.

Spirit possession is discussed both in terms of being
a case of disease and in terms of being a part of religious ecstatic ritual. Ethnic groups mentioned are the
Mashona (Shona) (Rhodesia), Ba-Ila (Ila) (Zambia),
Konde (Ngondi) (Zambia), and Zulu (South Africa) (pp.
120-27, 199-207, 404).

1611. Sibisi, Harriet   "The Place of Spirit Possession
      1975   in Zulu Cosmology." In Religion
                               and Social Change in Southern
                               Africa, edited by M. G. Whisson
                               and M. West, pp. 48-57.
                               (Bib. 1870.)

Spirit possession among the Nguni-speaking Zulus of
South Africa is examined historically with special emphasis on the colonial period.

1612. Sibley, James L., and   Liberia - Old and New. Garden
      D. Westerman   City, N.Y.: Doubleday, Doran &
      1928   Co.

Possession by evil spirits is said to cause illness
among the peoples of Liberia--no specific ethnic group
cited (pp. 208 ff.).

1613. Sibree, J.   Madagascar and Its People.
      1870   London.

During February 1863, the European residents at
Tananarive (Madagascar) heard of new disease called
Imanenjana, dancing mania. People would dance to the
music, and those affected were primarily from the lower
classes. Mostly women aged fourteen to twenty-five com-
plained of pain in different parts of the body, and to
the sound of music would begin to dance. The reporter

314

says these people seemed possessed and their attention
was not on what was going on around them (p. 561).
[Cited by Jeffreys (1953, Bib. 853).]

1614. Sicard, Harald von   "The Origin of Some of the
       1951   Tribes in the Belingwe Re-
                            serve." Nada (Salisbury) 28:
                            5-25.

Spirit possession and mediumship among the Romwe of
Rhodesia are discussed in this article on the origin of
these people (pp. 16 ff.).

1615. Sidhom, Swailem   "The Theological Estimate of
       1969   Man." In Biblical Revelation
                            and African Beliefs, edited by
                            K. A. Dickson and P. Elling-
                            worth, pp. 83-115. (Bib. 450.)

Possession by the Jok spirit among the Dinka in the
Súdan is mentioned on page 102.

1616. Sieber, Roy   "Figure Carvings Used in Healing
       1974   Contexts among the Goemai and
                            Montol of Northern Nigeria."
                            Paper presented at the meeting
                            of the American Anthropological
                            Association, Mexico City, 19-24
                            November.

Carved figures are used among the Goemai and Montol of
northern Nigeria as integral parts of various healing
practices. Included among these are treatments for illness caused by a spirit force, Kwompten, "catching" or
possessing an individual.

1617. Sigerist, Henry   A History of Medicine. Vol. 1.
       1951   London: Oxford University Press.

Chapter 2, part 2, is a general discussion of spirit
possession and its treatment (pp. 193-213).

1618. Silla, Ousmane   "Religion traditionnelle et
       1968a   techniques therapeutiques des
                            Lébou du Sénégal." Bulletin de
                            l'Institut fondamental d'Afrique
                            noire (Dakar) 30(B), no. 4:
                            1566-80.

A detailed description is given of the Lébou (Lebu) (of
Cape Vert, Senegal) beliefs concerning the spirits called
tuur, who govern the destiny of villages, clans, lineages, and the rab ancestral spirits, who control the actions of men and the forces of nature. The possession
ceremonies involved with these spirits are outlined.

1619. Silla, Ousmane   "Structure familiale et menta-
      1968b   lité religieuse des Lebou du
                              Sénégal." Notes africaines de
                              l'Institut français d'Afrique
                              noire (Dakar), no. 119, pp. 79-
                              83. Ill.

   Among the Lébou (Lebu), fertility and an ancestor cult
play a significant role, and all illness and misfortune
come from ritual transgressions against the spirits; thus
the importance of possession cults among these people.

1620. Silla, Ousmane   "Language et techniques théra-
      1969   peutiques des cultes de posses-
                              sion des Lebou du Sénégal."
                              Bulletin de l'Institut fonda-
                              mental d'Afrique noire (Dakar)
                              31(B), no. 1: 215-38.

   The Lébou (Lebu) possession cults in Senegal, tuuru
and ndöp, are described in detail, and transcriptions of
various sacred songs are presented. Comparisons are made
to group therapy.

1621. Silverman, Julian   "A Paradigm for the Study of
      1968   Altered States of Conscious-
                              ness." British Journal of
                              Psychiatry 114, no. 515: 1201-18.

   A theoretical model of altered states of consciousness
is presented that emphasizes differing modes of attention. Includes discussion of trance states.

1622. Simmonds, R. G. S.   "Charewa, Voice of the Rain
      1964   God." Nada (Salisbury) 9, no.
                              1: 60-63.

   Spirit mediumship among the vaBudjga (Budya) peoples in
Rhodesia exists as the means of communication between the
rain god (the spirit of a famous chief) and the living.

1623. Simpson, G. E.   "The Vodun Service in North
      1940   Haiti." American Anthropolo-
                              gist 42, no. 2: 236-54.

   The theology of the Vodun cult comes to life in the
Vodun service. Description of religious service and discussion of regional variations in Haiti. Spirit possession is discussed.

1624. Simpson, G. E.   "The Belief System of Haitian
      1945   Vodun." American Anthropolo-
                              gist 47, no. 1: 35-59.

Some discussion of the historical and political correlates to the start of the Vodun cult in Haiti. Discusses
the religious ritual and the role of spirit possession in
it.

1625. Simpson, G. E.   "Two Vodun Related Ceremonies."
      1948   Journal of American Folklore 61,
                              no. 239: 49-52.

      Description of the Festival of June 24, St. John's
      birthday, celebrated at the house of a famous Hangan
      (vodun) priestess (Haiti). Description of the festival
      with details on spirit possession.

1626. Simpson, G. E.   "Magical Practices in Northern
      1954   Haiti." Journal of American
                              Folklore 67:395-403.

      Voodoo spirits, called Loa, are worshipped in rural
      Haiti. The Loa possess people and use them to communi-
      cate with their worshippers. The first possession of a
      person by a Loa may be violent. The Hougan ("cult
      leader") uses various methods to calm the violence of
      the first possession, including speaking in a special
      language, presumably an African dialect. The Loa is
      then "tamed"; that is, the person is taught to control
      his trances.

1627. Simpson, G. E.   "Jamaican Revivalist Cults."
      1956   Social and Economic Studies 5:
                              353-4.

      Not available for annotation.

1628. Simpson, George Eaton   "The Acculturative Process in
      1960   Jamaican Revivalism." In Men
                              and Cultures, edited by
                              Anthony F. C. Wallace, pp. 332-
                              41. Selected Papers of the
                              Fifth International Congress of
                              Anthropological and Ethnological
                              Sciences (1956). Philadelphia:
                              University of Pennsylvania
                              Press.

      The African influence in the Jamaican revivalist cults
      is seen in their emphasis on the spirit realms and in
      their use of possession trance.

1629. Simpson, George Eaton   "The Ras Tafari Movement in
      1962a   Jamaica in Its Millennial As-
                              pect." In Millennial Dreams in
                              Action, edited by Sylvia L.
                              Thrupp, pp. 160-65. The Hague:
                              Mouton & Co.

317

Briefly mentioned is the relationship between the
Jamaican Ras Tafari movement that has no possession practice and the Afro-Jamaican cults of Pocomania, Revivalist, Revival Zion, Cumina, and Convince, all of which
practice some form of spirit possession. These cults in
general are "outlet[s] for pent-up emotions" (p. 164).

1630. Simpson, George E.   "The Shango Cult in Nigeria and
         1962b   Trinidad." American Anthropolo-
                                  gist 64, no. 6: 1204-19.

The Shango cult exists among the Yoruba of Nigeria and
among lower-class people of African descent in Trinidad,
and comparisons are drawn between the use of temples,
rituals, divination, and social organization in the two
manifestations of the cult. Description of the possession state, with particular emphasis on the erē state,
intermediary between deep trance and complete recovery
(pp. 1209-13).

1631. Simpson, George Eaton   "The Acculturative Process in
         1964   Trinidadian Shango." Anthropo-
                                  logical Quarterly 37, no. 1: 16-
                                  27.

The syncretic Shango cult on Trinidad in the Caribbean
is examined for its African roots in the Yoruba culture,
and for its European, Christian elements. Ritual para-
phernalia and cultic ceremonies, including spirit possession, are described.

1632. Simpson, George E.   "Selected Yoruba Rituals: 1964."
         1965a   Nigerian Journal of Economic and
                                  Social Studies (Ibadan) 7, no.
                                  3: 311-24.

Various annual Yoruba religious ceremonies are described
from field work conducted in 1964 in Nigeria. Spirit possession does not occur in the Orumila or in the Ogun
ceremonies, but is practiced in the Shango, Sonponna,
Osanyin, and Obatala ceremonies.

1633. Simpson, G. E.   "The Shango Cult in Trinidad."
         1965b   African Notes (Ibadan) 3, no.
                                  1: 11-21.

Among Yoruba and others of African descent in Trinidad,
the Shango Cult of Nigeria is widespread. Spirit possession occurs during many of the cult's ceremonies.
The phenomenon of spirit possession in general is discussed.

1634. Simpson, George Eaton   "Baptismal, 'Mourning' and
         1966a   'Building' Ceremonies of the

318

Shouters in Trinidad." Journal
of American Folklore 79, no.
311: 537-50.

Possession by the Holy Spirit and other trance states
are discussed for the Shouters or Spiritual Baptists on
Trinidad in the Caribbean. African religious elements
are traceable.

1635. Simpson, George E.   "The Vodun Cult in Haiti."
      1966b   African Notes (Ibadan) 3, no.
                                    2: 11-21.

Detailed account of the Haitian Vodun cult in which
its African origins, rites and beliefs, history and
social significance are discussed.

1636. Simpson, George Eaton   "The Acculturative Process in
      1970a   Jamaican Revivalism." In
                                    Caribbean Papers, Sondeos,
                                    edited by G. E. Simpson, pp.
                                    3/3-3/12 (Bib. 1637.)

The Afro-American religious cults in Jamaica (Revival
Zion, Pocomania, and Cumina) are discussed. Greatest
emphasis is placed on Cumina, which uses spirit possession.

1637. Simpson, George Eaton,   Caribbean Papers, Sondeos.
      ed.   CIDOC, no. 70. Cuernavaca.
      1970b

      Includes in this bibliography:
               1636   G. E. Simpson (1970a)
               1638   G. E. Simpson and P. B. Hammond
                             (1970c)
               1639   G. E. Simpson (1970d)
               1640   G. E. Simpson (1970e)
               1641   G. E. Simpson (1970f)
               1644   G. E. Simpson (1970i)
               1658   M. G. Smith (1970)

1638. Simpson, George Eaton,   "Discussion" following paper by
      and Peter O. Hammond   M. G. Smith, "The African Heri-
      1970c   tage in the Caribbean." In
                                    Caribbean Papers, Sondeos,
                                    edited by G. E. Simpson, pp.
                                    1/51-1/58 (Bib. 1637.)

In response to comments made by M. G. Smith in the
above-cited article (Bib. 1658) concerning the nature of
spirit possession in the Caribbean, the authors discuss
it with regard to African cultures (pp. 1/53-1/54).

319

1639. Simpson, George Eaton   "Folk Medicine in Trinidad."
      1970d   In Caribbean Papers, Sondeos,
                                   edited by G. E. Simpson, pp.
                                   4/14-4/23. (Bib. 1637.)

      Spirit possession as a cause of illness among the in-
habitants of Trinidad in the Caribbean is discussed
along with the folk remedies that are used to cure such
illnesses.

1640. Simpson, George Eaton   "Haitian Magic." In Caribbean
      1970e   Papers, Sondeos, edited by G. E.
                                   Simpson, pp. 2/53-2/58.
                                   (Bib. 1637.)

      Spirit possession in the vôdoun cult of Haiti is dis-
cussed.

1641. Simpson, George Eaton   "Loup Garou and Loa Tales from
      1970f   Northern Haiti." In Caribbean
                                   Papers, Sondeos, edited by G. E.
                                   Simpson, pp. 2/44-2/52. (Bib.
                                   1637.)

      The Haitian spirit possession cult is discussed in this
compilation of loup garou and loa tales.

1642. Simpson, George E.   "Religious Changes in South-
      1970g   western Nigeria." Anthropolo-
                                   gical Quarterly 43, no. 2: 79-
                                   92.

      Possession by the Atinga spirit in the "reformative"
Atinga cult, which arose in southwestern Nigeria in the
early 1950's, is mentioned on page 84.

1643. Simpson, G. E.   Religious Cults of the Caribbean:
      1970h   Trinidad, Jamaica and Haiti.
                                   Rio Piedras, Puerto Rico:
                                   Institute of Caribbean Studies,
                                   University of Puerto Rico.

      Not available for annotation.

1644. Simpson, George Eaton   "The Shango Cult in Trinidad."
      1970i   In Caribbean Papers, Sondeos,
                                   edited by G. E. Simpson, pp.
                                   4/3-4/13. (Bib. 1637.)

      The African slaves brought to the Caribbean island of
Trinidad were mainly Yoruba. The Shango cult, which
practices spirit possession, is directly related to the
Yoruba religion.

320

1645. Simpson, George Eaton   "Afro-American Religions and
      1972   Religious Behavior." Caribbean
                               Studies 12, no. 2: 5-30.

     A general, yet detailed, survey of Afro-American reli-
gious cults is presented here, along with a discussion
of the different issues concerned with the understanding
of spirit possession. The cults discussed are: Haitian
Vodun, Cuban Santeria, Brazilian Candomble, Trinidadian
Shango, and Jamaican Pocomania, Revival Zionists, Cumina,
and Convince.

1646. Simpson, George Eaton   "The Kele (Chango) Cult in St.
      1973   Lucia." Caribbean Studies 13,
                               no. 3: 110-16.

     The kele ceremony of the Chango (Shango) cult on St.
Lucia in the Caribbean involves spirit possession by the
ancestors. Similarities in beliefs and practices with
other Afro-American cults are traced, including the
Trinidadian Shango and the Grenadan and Carriacauan "Big
Drum Dance."

1647. Singleton, Michael   "Medicine Men and the Medical
      1975   Missionary." Cultures et dé-
                               veloppement (Louvain) 7, no. 1:
                               33-52.

     Spirit possession as a cause of illness is mentioned in
the context of a presentation of native medical practices in Mpanda, a small town in Tanzania (p. 39).

1648. Sion, Etienne   "The Charismatic Nature of the
      1976   Local Church." Afer: African
                               Ecclesiastical Review (Eldoret)
                               18, no. 3:160-65.

     Possession by the Holy Spirit is discussed within the
theological context of the Charismatic movement in Christianity.

1649. Sithole, Ndabaningi   Obed Mutezo: The Mudzimu Chris-
      1970   tian Nationalist. Nairobi:
                               Oxford University Press.

     Throughout this book and in the introduction written by
Terence Ranger, the roles of the midzimu spirits of the
dead and their mediums in the life of Obed Mutezo, a
Rhodesian nationalist, are described. The life of this
man is traced from its ancestral roots to his present
situation in Rhodesia (Zimbabwe).

321

1650. Slaski, J.
1951

Peoples of the Lower Luapula
Valley. Ethnographic Survey of
Africa, edited by Daryll Forde,
East Central Africa, pt. 2.
London: International African
Institute.

The Lamba people of Northern Rhodesia (Zambia) practice three different types of spirit possession: (1) by
woodland spirits who enhance dancing abilities; (2) by
professional hunting spirits; and (3) by Lenje (Lenge)
chiefs who give healing prophetic powers (pp. 63-64).

1651. Smartt, C. G. F.
1958a

"An African Witchhunt." In
Mental Disorders and Mental
Health in Africa South of the
Sahara, pp. 183-90. CCTA/CSA-
WFMH-WHO, Pub. no. 35. Bukavu.

Very descriptive account of the activities of an
African in Tanganyika (Tanzania), skilled in witchcraft,
who hunts out those practicing evil against others. Possession is mentioned briefly.

1652. Smartt, C. G. F.
1958b

"Psychiatry in Tanganyika." In
Mental Disorders and Mental
Health in Africa South of the
Sahara, pp. 59-61. CCTA/CSA-
WFMH-WHO, Pub. no. 35. Bukavu.

The most severe mental illness cases come from the 10
percent of the Tanganyikans (now Tanzanians) who live in
the growing urban centers. The rural 90 percent of the
population who have a socially patterned and regulated
environment live "a happy and carefree existence. In
spite of its disadvantages, I think that the African mind
is protected rather than harmed by his animistic religion" (p. 60).

1653. Smith, Edwin W.
1923

The Religion of the Lower Races
as Illustrated by the African
Bantu. New York: Macmillan Co.

Written by a missionary, this work deals generally with
the Bantu-speaking peoples of Africa. With regard to
their religion, both spirit possession and mediumship are
mentioned on pages 40-43.

1654. Smith, Edwin W., ed.
1950

African Ideas of God: A Symposium. London: Edinburgh House
Press.

Includes in this bibliography:
710   R. Guillebaud (1950)
1683   R. C. Stevenson (1950)

322

1655. Smith, M. F.   Baba of Karo: A Woman of the
      1955   Muslim Hausa. New York:
                       Philosophical Library.

In this autobiographical account of a Muslim Hausa
woman of Nigeria, the bori cult of spirit possession
practiced exclusively by women is described within its
social context (see book's index under "bori" for page
citations).

1656. Smith, M. G.   "The Hausa of Northern
      1965   Nigeria." In Peoples of Africa,
                       edited by James L. Gibbs, Jr.,
                       pp. 121-55. New York: Holt,
                       Rinehart & Winston.

Brief mention is made of the bori spirit possession
cult among the Hausa of northern Nigeria (pp. 151-52).

1657. Smith, M. G.   "A Hausa Kingdom: Maradi under
      1967   Dan Baskore, 1854-1875." In
                       West African Kingdoms in the
                       Nineteenth Century, edited by
                       D. Forde and P. M. Kaberry, pp.
                       93-122. (Bib. 592.)

The "Queen Mother" or Iya was chosen among the senior
royal kinswomen in the Hausa kingdom of Maradi, Niger, to
preside over many ritual ceremonies including those of
the pre-Islamic cult of spirit worship through possession
by the bori spirits (pp. 95, 108).

1658. Smith, M. G.   "The African Heritage in the
      1970   Caribbean." In Caribbean Pa-
                       pers, Sondeos, edited by G. E.
                       Simpson, pp. 1/39-1/51.
                       (Bib. 1637.)

Spirit possession in the Caribbean and African cultural influence are discussed on pages 1/41, 1/45.

1659. Smith, T. Lynn   Brazil: People and Institutions.
      1947   Baton Rouge: Louisiana State
                       University Press.

The Afro-American spirit possession cults in Brazil are
discussed on pages 708-28. Specific mention is made of
the Gêge-Nagô cults.

1660. Smith, T. Lynn   Brazilian Society. Albuquerque:
      1974   University of New Mexico Press.

The spirit possession trances in the syncretic religions of Brazil which are heavily influenced by African
cultures are discussed on pages 133-49.

323

1661. Soga, John Henderson   The Ama-Xosa: Life and Customs.
      n.d. [1931]   Lovedale: Lovedale Press.

Although not so labelled, it appears that the Ama-Xosa
(Xosa) of South Africa have some belief in spirit possession, particularly in the case where evil spirits
enter an individual, causing illness, and must be exorcised (pp. 185 ff.).

1662. Souffrant, Claude   "Religion et développement."   In
      1972   Les Religions africaines comme
                              source de valeurs de civilisa-
                              tion, Colloque de Cotonou
                              (August 1970), pp. 205-11.
                              (Bib. 358.)

The relationship between religion and socioeconomic
development is examined with reference mainly to Haiti.
Spirit possession is mentioned on page 211.

1663. Sousberghe, L. de   "De la signification de quelques
      1960   masques pende. 'Shave' des
                              Shona et 'mbuya' des Pende."
                              Zaïre: Belgian African Review
                              (Bruxelles) 14, nos. 5-6: 505-
                              31.

The connection between the mbuyu masks of the Pende and
the shave spirits of the Shona, both in Rhodesia, is explored here. Spirit mediumship among the Shona is mentioned (pp. 508 ff.).

1664. Southall, Aidan W.   Alur Society: A Study in Pro-
      1954   cesses and Types of Domination.
                              Cambridge: W. Heffer & Sons.

Among the Alur of Uganda and Zaïre, spirit possession
is used in their religious practices and is cited as a
cause of illness (pp. 93, 118, 370, 375).

1665. Southall, Aidan   "Spirit Possession and Medium-
      1969   ship among the Alur."   In
                              Spirit Mediumship and Society in
                              Africa, edited by J. Beattie and
                              J. Middleton, pp. 232-72.
                              (Bib. 150.)

Among the Alur of Uganda, diseases may be caused by
Jok spirits. In such cases, the spirit is exorcised by
inducing it to possess its victim and then entertaining
it with a dance, thus persuading it to leave. Dancers
may themselves become possessed on such occasions. There
are also diviner-mediums who conduct possession séances
as a curative technique.

324

1666. Spencer, Sidney   Mysticism in World Religion.
      1963   Baltimore: Penguin Books.

      Discussion of spirit possession among the Nuer (Sudan)
      is to be found in chapter 1, devoted to a discussion of
      mysticism in primitive religions (pp. 13-16).

1667. Spring, Anita   "Epidemiology of Luvale Spirit
      1974   Possession - Alternatives to
                             Procreation." Paper presented
                             at the American Anthropological
                             Association meeting, Mexico City,
                             November. 26 pp.

      In response to the articles by I. M. Lewis (1966, Bib.
      1036) and P. J. Wilson (1967, Bib. 1895) in Man, the
      author discusses the epidemiology of spirit possession in
      terms of its physiological ramifications for the matri-
      lineal Luvale of Zambia.

1668. Sseguya, L.   "The Concept of Death and Future
      1974   Life among the Ganda." Occa-
                             sional Research Papers in Afri-
                             can Traditional Religion and
                             Philosophy (Makerere University,
                             Kampala), vol. 23, no. 230.

      Among the Ganda (Baganda) of Uganda, spirits are
      thought to communicate with the living through trees,
      the wind, and sick people (p. 18).

1669. Ssekamwa, John C.   "Witchcraft in Buganda Today."
      1967   Transition (Kampala) 6, no.
                             30: 31-9. Ill.

      Current assessment of the range of influence of witch-
      craft practiced by medicine men and women who act as
      spirit mediums in Buganda (Ganda) (Uganda) states that
      there is a practitioner for every three villages, and
      projects that when the elite and non-elite come up against
      problems insoluble by Western medicines and methods,
      they will increasingly turn to the traditional witch-
      craft.

1670. Staewen, C., and   Kulturwandel und Angstentwick-
      F. Schönberg   lung bei den Yoruba Westafrikas.
      1970   München: Weltforum Verlag.

      The level of anxiety among the Yoruba of Nigeria has
      risen in recent years and is due to the contact with
      European culture. In order to make this assessment, the
      traditional Yoruba religion and its use of the Ifa
      Oracle are examined. Spirit possession is not explicitly
      labelled. [Cited in Transcultural Psychiatric Research
      Review (Bruges) 8 (October 1971): 162-64.]

                             325

1671. Stainbrook, Edward   "Some Characteristics of the
      1952   Psychopathology of Schizophrenic
                                  Behavior in Bahian Society."
                                  American Journal of Psychiatry
                                  109:330-35.

      Spirit possession in the Candomblé cult in Bahia,
      Brazil, is analyzed psychologically (p. 334).

1672. Stappers, Leo   "Le Fétiche kasango chez les
      1951a   Bamilembwe." Kongo-Overzee
                                  (Antwerpen) 17, nos. 4-5:373-78.

      Ceremony of installation of the fetish often involves
      possession by the spirit of the fetish among the
      Milembwe (Zaïre).

1673. Stappers, L.   "Le Fétiche mpunga." Zaïre 5,
      1951b   no. 4: 351-69.

      Article includes a description of spirit possession
      among the Ba-Ngombe of Zaïre.

1674. Stappers, Leo   "Note sur le fétiche ntambwe du
      1951c   Kasai." Aequatoria
                                  (Coquilhatville) 14, no. 3: 90-
                                  92.

      Buanga fetish described; ceremonies associated with
      this fetish involve spirit mediumship among the Kasanga
      (Zaïre). [Cited in African Abstracts, vol. 4, no. 366.]

1675. Stayt, H. A.   The Vavenda. London: Oxford
      1931   University Press.

      Stayt reports that possession cults were rare among
      the Venda (South Africa) until about 1914. Discussion of
      possession dances in relation to medicine and magic
      (p. 302).

1676. Stebbing, M.   "'Mamhepo' - Spirit Possession
      1972   among the Shona." Paper pre-
                                 sented at the Conference on the
                                 History of Central African Reli-
                                 gious Systems, Lusaka,
                                 30 August - 8 September.

      Mamhepo spirit possession is a form of witchcraft
      among the Shona of Rhodesia. The "mother," a witch
      (muroyi), sends zvidhoma spirits - souls of dead children -
      to possess and eventually kill the victim by their pre-
      sence. Control over these spirits is passed from mother
      to eldest daughter. Evidence is given that this is a re-
      cent phenomenon (since the 1950's) and is to be distin-
      guished from the traditional possessions by midzimu, an-
      cestral spirits, and mashave, usually foreign spirits.

326

1677. Stefaniszyn, B.   "African Reincarnation Re-exam-
      1954   ined." African Studies
                         (Johannesburg) 13, nos. 3-4:
                         131-46.

   Both communication with and possession by the spirits
are involved in the African notion of reincarnation.

1678. Stefaniszyn, Bronislaw   Social and Ritual Life of the
      1964   Ambo of Northern Rhodesia.
                               London: Oxford University Press.

   Chapter 7, "Religion and Divination," deals with spirit
possession among the Ambo (Northern Rhodesia, now Zambia).
Description of: onset of illness, curing ceremonies involving possession dances, the possessing spirits, influences from neighboring tribes.

1679. Steger, Hanns-Albert   El Trasfondo revolucionario del
      1972   sincretisma criollo: Aspectos
                              sociales de la transformacion
                              clandestina de la religion en
                              Afroamerica colonial y post-
                              colonial. Cuernavaca (Mexico):
                              CIDOC, Sondeos, No. 86.

      Not available for annotation.

1680. Stevens, Phillips   "Orisha-nla Festival." Nigeria
      1966   Magazine (Lagos) 90:184-99.
                              Ill.

   A description of the main beliefs surrounding the Ife
(Nigeria) gods Orisha-nla and his wife Yemoo. At an
annual festival at their main shrine, a priest is possessed by Yemoo's spirit.

1681. Stevens, Phillips, Jr.   "The Danubi Ancestral Shrine."
      1976   African Arts (Los Angeles) 10,
                               no. 1: 30-37.

   The Bachama of eastern Nigeria believe that if one
meets a spirit one risks being possessed by it and wan-
dering around aimlessly until death (p. 31).

1682. Stevenson, R. C.   "The Nyamang of the Nuba Moun-
      1940   tains of Kordofan." Sudan Notes
                             and Records 23:75-98.

   Spirit possession in the Sudan and its relation to initiation to the priesthood (p. 97).

1683. Stevenson, R. C.   "The Doctrine of God in the Nuba
      1950   Mountains." In African Ideas
                                of God, edited by E. W. Smith.
                                (Bib. 1654.)

    Spirit possession among the Koalib of the Nuba Moun-
tains (Sudan) (pp. 210, 217-23).

1684. Stevenson, R. C.   "Some Aspects of the Spread of
      1966   Islam in the Nuba Mountains
                                (Kordofan Province, Republic of
                                the Sudan)." In Islam in
                                Tropical Africa, edited by I. M.
                                Lewis, pp. 208-27. (Bib. 1035.)

    Spirit possession of shamans among the Kadura (Kadero)
and Dilling peoples of the Sudan is mentioned on page
218.

1685. Stewart, John   "Where Goes the Indigenous Black
      1974   Church?" In Is Massa Day Dead?
                                by Orde Coombs, pp. 189-203.
                                Garden City, N.Y.: Anchor
                                Press-Doubleday.

    In discussing the black churches in Trinidad, the
author describes the decline in importance of spirit possession to the Baptists and Shangoists. Author relies on
the views of a pastor who served as one of the informants.

1686. Stokes, Eric, and   The Zambesian Past. Manchester:
      Richard Brown, eds.   Manchester University Press.
      1966

      Includes in this bibliography:
                        6   D. P. Abraham (1966)
                      627   G. K. Garbett (1966)
                     1436   T. Ranger (1966a)
                     1437   T. Ranger (1966b)

1687. Stoll, Otto   Suggestion und Hypnotismus in
      1904   der Völkerpsychologie. 2d ed.
                                Leipzig.

    Account of animal possession: men who from time to
time leave their homes and wander about filled with the
delusion that they are changed into lions (p. 282).

1688. Stonelake, Alfred R.   Congo Past and Present. London:
      1937   World Dominion Press.

    The outbreak of the Lilwa cult among the Congo (Kongo)
of the Belgian Congo (Zaïre) during the first part of
this century is recorded by a missionary. The cult focussed around spirit possession and trance states (p. 15).

328

1689. Strelcyn, S.   "Magie, médecine et possession
      1972   à Gondar." Journal of Religion
                            in Africa (Leiden) 4, no. 3:
                            161-70.

Centered around a critique of Maxime Rodinson's book
Magie, médecine et possession à Gondar (1967, Bib. 1499),
this is a discussion of zar spirit possession in
Ethiopia.

1690. Summers, Montague   The History of Witchcraft and
      1926   Demonology. New York: Alfred
                            A. Knopf.

The Haitian voodoo possession cult is mentioned on
pages 26, 158, and 163 in this general work on witchcraft and demonology.

1691. Sundkler, B. G. M.   Bantu Prophets in South Africa.
      1961a   London: Oxford University Press.

Religion and social background of the Zulus (South
Africa); the rise of the independent church movement;
worship and healing; church and community. Possession
phenomena reported, with particular discussion of
glossolalia (pp. 120, 143, 238-47).

1692. Sundkler, B. G. M.   "The Concept of Christianity in
      1961b   the African Independent
                            Churches." African Studies
                            (Johannesburg) 20, no. 4: 203-
                            13.

The Bantu (South Africa) Zionist practice of
glossolalia is mentioned in this general article on African independent churches (p. 204).

1693. Swabey, M. H.   Government Report Bamenda Divi-
      1928   sion, Cameroons Province, Annual
                            Report.

Discusses the Makka movement in Cameroon, manifested in
frenzied dancing in which both men and women joined.
The dancers would gyrate in a frenzy and would shake as
if in epileptic fit. Anyone who fell down in a trance
was admitted to the society. On recovery, such a person
appeared to be endowed with supernatural powers and went
about the villages denouncing people as witches. People
claimed that they had found a new God. [Cited by
Jeffreys (1953, Bib. 853).]

1694. Swantz, Marja-Liisa   "The Spirit Possession Cults and
      1968   Their Social Setting in a Zaramo
                            Coastal Community." Makerere

329

Institute of Social Research,
Conference Paper no. 477.
Kampala. 15 pp.

A detailed analysis of the spirit possession cults among the Zaramo of Ethiopia is presented. Influenced greatly by Islamic beliefs, these cults focus on exorcising spirits by having them fully possess the individual.

1695. Świderski, Stanislaw   "Le Bwiti, société d'initiation
1965   chez les Apindji, au Gabon."
    Anthropos 60, nos. 1-6: 541-76.

Although spirit possession is not explicitly labelled, the sorcerer among the Apindji (Puni) of Gabon goes into trance during the Bwiti ceremony with the aid of music, and then prophesies.

1696. Swiderski, Stanislaw   "Notes Biographiques sur le
1973   fondateurs et les guides
    spirituels des sectes syncreti-
    ques au Gabon." Anthropologica
    15, no. 1: 38-87.

    Not available for annotation.

1697. Sy, Moussa Oumar   "Considérations sur les
1971   principes constitutifs de la
    personnalité chez les Negro-
    Africains." Bulletin de l'in-
    stitut fondamental d'Afrique
    noire (Dakar), ser. B, 33, no.
    1: 14-62.

In this general article on the African concept of personality, spirit possession is discussed on pages 40 ff.

1698. Sykes, Frank W.   With Plumer in Matabeleland.
1969 (1897)   New York: Negro Universities
    Press.

Written by a Trooper in the late nineteenth century, this account mentions the M'Limo cult among the Matabele (Ndebele) of Rhodesia, but spirit mediumship is not explicitly labelled (pp. 254-62).

1699. Tabler, Edward C.   The Far Interior. Cape Town:
1955   A. A. Balkema.

The Makalanga (Kalanga) hereditary priests and their function as mediums for the Mwari cult in Rhodesia are mentioned briefly on pages 112-13.

1700. Tait, David   "A Sorcery Hunt in Dagomba."
      1963   Africa: Journal of the Interna-
                             tional African Institute
                             (London) 33, no. 2: 136-47.

      Although not specifically labelled as spirit posses-
      sion, "seers" go into a trance state in order to deter-
      mine who among the Dagomba of the Gold Coast (Ghana)
      are sorcerers (pp. 136-37).

1701. Talbot, D. A.   Woman's Mysteries of a Primitive
      1968 (1915)   People. London: Frank Cass &
                             Co.

      Evidence for spirit mediumship among the Ibibio priests
      of Nigeria is given on pages 182-83.

1702. Talbot, P. A.   In the Shadow of the Bush. New
      1912   York: George H. Doran Co.

      Discussion of spirit possession by the spirits of the
      Ju Ju tree (chap. 3, pp. 31, 40). Information for the
      Efik and Ekoi people of Nigeria.

1703. Talbot, P. A.   Tribes of the Niger Delta.
      1967 (1932)   London: Frank Cass & Co.

      Among the Kalabari of Nigeria, sacred snake spirits are
      said to possess their priestesses and manifest them-
      selves in a frenzied dance. Also, the python goddess
      speaks through her priestess-mediums as an oracle (pp.
      38-43).

1704 Tallant, Robert   Voodoo in New Orleans. New
      1946   York: Macmillan Co.

      The voodoo spirit possession cult, which originated in
      Haiti, is described as it appears in New Orleans.

1705. Tanner, R. E. S.   "Hysteria in Sukuma Medical
      1955   Practice." Africa: Journal of
                             the International African In-
                             stitute (London) 25, no. 3:
                             274-79.

      Two practices of magicians among the Sukuma of Tan-
      ganyika (now Tanzania) are described. Magicians, who
      are chosen for their profession because of possession by
      ancestor magicians, enter self-induced trances in order
      to divine the cause of a patient's illness. After a
      period of dissociation (probably feigned, according to
      the author) in which the magician mutters in what is
      claimed to be a spirit language, indicating that the an-
      cestor spirit has entered his body, the magician pro-
      nounces the diagnosis. The magician then returns to nor-

                             331

mal and discusses the diagnosis with the patient. Magicians may also induce trances in patients who are suspected of being possessed by ancestor spirits. After putting the patient in a trance, in which the patient's body is wholly taken over by the spirit, the medium demands of the spirit its name and grievance, so that a cure may be diagnosed.

1706. Tanner, R. E. S.　　　　"The Magician in Northern
　　　　1957　　　　　　　　Sukumaland, Tanganyika." South-
　　　　　　　　　　　　　　western Journal of Anthropology
　　　　　　　　　　　　　　13, no. 4: 334-51.

　　　　The role of the magician in Sukuma (Tanganyika, now Tanzania) society and the nature of his work. A magician obtains power to practice when he is "caught" by his ancestor spirits. Discussion of possession and glossolalia.

1707. Tanner, R. E. S.　　　　"The Theory and Practice of
　　　　1969　　　　　　　　Sukuma Spirit Mediumship." In
　　　　　　　　　　　　　　Spirit Mediumship and Society in
　　　　　　　　　　　　　　Africa, edited by J. Beattie and
　　　　　　　　　　　　　　J. Middleton, pp. 273-89.
　　　　　　　　　　　　　　(Bib. 150.)

　　　　Among the Sukuma of Tanzania, spirit mediums are usually men who have been possessed by an ancestor spirit. They are able to diagnose the problems of others through the spirit's aid. Some, but not all, mediums are members of mediumship cults. Possessed mediums speak a jumble of monosyllables said to be Kinaturu, a foreign language.

1708. Tarantino, A.　　　　　"Notes on the Lango." Uganda
　　　　1949　　　　　　　　Journal (Kampala) 13, no. 2:
　　　　　　　　　　　　　　145-53.

　　　　Describes ceremonies of exorcism in cases of possession among the Lango (Uganda) (p. 151).

1709. Tardits, Claude　　　　"Religion, Epic, History."
　　　　1962　　　　　　　　Diogenes (Montreal), no. 37,
　　　　　　　　　　　　　　pp. 16-27.

　　　　The Dahomean, Yoruban, Fon, and Gun [Nigeria, Dahomey (Benin), Togo] spirit possession religions are discussed in detail.

1710. Tart, Charles T., ed.　　Altered States of Consciousness.
　　　　1969　　　　　　　　Garden City, N.Y.: Doubleday &
　　　　　　　　　　　　　　Co.

　　　　Includes in this bibliography:
　　　　　　　　432　　　A. J. Deikman (1969)
　　　　　　　1070　　　A. Ludwig (1969)

1711. Tasie, G. O. M.   "Priesthood and Social Change in
      1970   the Traditional Religion of the
                              Kalabari People." Journal of
                              Religion in Africa (Leiden) 3,
                              no. 2: 96-105.

Only one of the three forms of priesthood among the
Kalibari people of Nigeria remains strong due to its concern with personal problems in modern living. Qualifica-
tions for the two male and one female priesthoods involving possession by the deity are seriousness of purpose and high standards of moral behavior.

1712. Tasie, G. O. M.   "Africans and the Religious Di-
      1976   mension: An Appraisal."
                              Africana Marburgensia 9, no. 1:
                              34-70.

In this general theoretical article on religion in
Africa, spirit possession is briefly mentioned on page
56.

1713. Tauxier, L.   La Religion bambara. Paris:
      1927   Librairie orientaliste Paul
                              Geuthner.

Spirit possession by the evil suba spirit, which de-
vours the human soul, is one of the explanations of
sorcery among the Bambara of the French Sudan (Mali)
(pp. 57 ff.). Spirit mediumship is used in the Bambara
religious society called the Komo (pp. 275 ff.).

1714. Tauxier, L.   Religion, moeurs, et coutumes
      1932   des Agnis de la Côte d'Ivoire.
                              Paris: Librairie orientaliste
                              Paul Geuthner.

Mediumship and divine possession trance are outlined
for the Agni (Anyi) of the Ivory Coast on pages 76 ff.

1715. Tax, Sol, ed.   Acculturation in the Americas.
      1952   Chicago: University of Chicago
                              Press.

Includes in this bibliography:
                  97   R. Bastide (1952)
                1838   R. A. Waterman (1952)

1716. Taylor, Brian K.   The Western Lacustrine Bantu.
      1962   Ethnographic Survey of Africa,
                              edited by Daryll Forde. London:
                              International African Institute.

In Bunyoro (Nyoro), Uganda, mediums of the spirits of a
dynasty of hero-gods called Bachwezi initiate men and women into a secret spirit possession cult. Mediums of the
spirits often act as diviners (pp. 38-39).

333

1717. Taylor, John V.   The Growth of the Church in
      1958   Buganda. London: SCM Press.

      Chapter 11 deals with aspects of spirit possession
      among the Baganda (Ganda) (Uganda). Three forms of pos-
      session are described, and each is discussed.

1718. Taylor, John V., and   Christians of the Copperbelt.
      Dorothea A. Lehmann   London: SCM Press.
      1961

      The relationships between the traditional beliefs in
      possession by the ngulu spirits among the peoples of
      Northern Rhodesia (Zambia) and the African independent
      church movements are discussed in various places (see
      book's index under "Ngulu (spirits)" for page citations).

1719. Taylor, John V.   The Primal Vision: Christian
      1963   Presence amid African Religion.
                            London: SCM Press.

      Spirit possession and mediumship are mentioned for the
      Buganda (Ganda) of Uganda, and a description of a séance
      with a medium is given (pp. 148-51, 158).

1720. Temples, Placide   Bantu Philosophy. Paris:
      1959   Présence africaine.

      Examines spirit possession and its place in Bantu re-
      ligious ideas (pp. 57, 71, 74, 83).

1721. Ten Raa, Eric   "The Moon as a Symbol of Life
      1969   and Fertility in Sandawe
                            Thought." Africa: Journal of
                            the International African In-
                            stitute (London) 39, no. 1:
                            24-53.

      Although the Sandawe and Rimi of central Tanzania have
      many similar rituals and beliefs, they have very differ-
      ent perceptions of the sun. The Rimi see the sun as
      beneficial, a giver of fertility and exorciser of sor-
      cery. The Sandawe, however, see the sun as ambiguous.
      They attribute fertility to the moon, and they exorcise
      sorcery by means of a spirit, or state of possession,
      which is called Simbó (p. 52).

1722. Terranova, R., and   "Aspects psychopathologiques et
      B. Ratsifandrihamanana psychosociaux de l'épilepsie dans
      1970   un milieu transculturel." Afri-
                            can Journal of Medical Sciences
                            (Oxford) 1, no. 2: 213-19.

      Spirit possession is discussed as being the usual Afri-
      can explanation for epilepsy (p. 215).

                            334

1723. Tewfik, G. I.   "Problems of Mental Illness in
      1958   Uganda." In Mental Disorders
                         and Mental Health in Africa
                         South of the Sahara, pp. 62-68.
                         CCTA/CSA-WFMH-WHO, Pub. no.
                         35. Bukavu.

One of the most frequent mental illnesses in Uganda is
a transient form of psychosis lasting one to two months
which is traditionally ascribed to possession by evil
spirits of the dead, and whose symptoms include a wild,
vacant look, shouting, crying, restlessness, loss of all
fear, delusions and hallucinations, great strength, and
speaking in foreign tongues.

1724. Theuws, P. J. A.   "Le Styx ambigu." Problèmes
      1968   sociaux congolais (Lubumbashi),
                          no. 81, pp. 3-33.

     In a detailed description of Luba (Zaïre) attitudes to-
wards death and the dead, possession is cited as one
means of communication between the living and the dead,
along with the appearance of the spirits in dreams either
in the guise of an animal or in their human form.

1725. Theuws, P. T. J.   "Rites et religion en Afrique."
      1965   Revue du clergé africain
                          (Inkisi) 20, no. 3: 205-37.

     In this general theoretical article, the use of spirit
possession in African religions is dicussed on pages
230 ff.

1726. Theuws, Th.   "Le réel dans la conception
      1961   Luba." Zaïre: Belgian African
                         Review (Bruxelles) 15, no. 1:
                         13-44.

     In this long and very detailed discussion of the world-
view of the Luba (Zaïre), mention is made of a sorcerer's
ability to leave his human form and take possession of an
animal's body temporarily in order to carry out his evil
sorcery (p. 19).

1727. Thiel, Josef Franz La Situation religieuse des
      1972   Mbiem. Ser. 2, vol. 1.
                          Bandumbu: Centre d'études
                          ethnologiques.

     Although spirit possession is not explicitly labelled
for the Mbiem (Mbim) of Zaïre, the calling of a diviner
involves speaking with the spirits of the dead, and once
initiated, the diviner may act as an oracle (pp. 85-86).
Spirit mediumship is mentioned on page 112.

1728. Thion, Serge   Le Pouvoir pâle. Paris:
      1969   Éditions du seuil.

Possession by the Holy Spirit among the members of the
Zionist Church of South Africa is described as a collective trance state (p. 252).

1729. Thomas, Elizabeth   The Harmless People. New York:
      Marshall   Alfred A. Knopf.
      1959

The medicine dance of the Kalihari !Kung Bushmen of
Southwest Africa and Bechuanaland (Botswana) is described
in chapter 8. By means of dancing the Bushmen work themselves into a trance state where either their soul will
leave their body or they will begin to heal while in
trance.

1730 Thomas, H. B., and   Uganda. London: Oxford Univer-
      Robert Scott   sity Press.
      1949

The female priestesses of the Alur in Uganda go into
trance and then are possessed by the supreme deity,
Jok, who makes pronouncements and gives omens through
their lips (pp. 289-90).

1731. Thomas, L. V.   "Sociologie et psychiatrie:
      1965   Problèmes posés par l'Afrique
                           noire." Psychopathologie
                           africaine (Dakar) 1, no. 3:
                           443-85.

A general theoretical presentation is given of the relationship in Africa between sociological and psychiatric aspects of modern society. After a detailed discussion of traditional beliefs and practices, including
those surrounding spirit possession systems (pp. 446
ff.), the conclusion is reached that for psychiatry to
be useful at all, it must take these traditional systems
into consideration when dealing with African patients.

1732. Thomas, L. V.   "La Mort et la sagesse afri-
      1967   caine." Psychopathologie
                           africaine (Dakar) 3, no. 2: 13-
                           80.

African philosophical ideas about death are explored
extensively in this article. The phenomenon among Wolof
and Lébou (Lebu) of Senegal of an ancestor possessing
and in that way being reincarnated in the form of a
small child, termed nit ku bon, is mentioned on page 33.

1733. Thomas, Louis-Vincent,   Les Religions d'Afrique noire.
      and René Luneau   Paris: Fayard.
      1969a

      In this general work on African religions, spirit pos-
      session and exorcism are mentioned in various contexts
      throughout; pages 145-50 specifically deal with the use
      of spirit possession, and examples of texts and invoca-
      tions are given from the Serer (Senegal) Lup spirit pos-
      session rituals.

1734. Thomas, L. V.   "Société africaine et santé
      1969b   mentale." Psychopathologie
                                africaine (Dakar) 5, no. 3:
                                355-94.

      Spirit possession, both as a curative procedure and as
      a cause of illness requiring exorcism, is mentioned in
      this general article on mental health in African socie-
      ties (pp. 359, 364, 376 ff., 390-91).

1735. Thomas, Louis-Vincent,   La Terre africaine et ses reli-
      and René Luneau   gions. Paris: Librairie
      1975   Larousse.

      In this general theoretical work on African religions,
      spirit possession is discussed for various ethnic
      groups, including: Songhay (Songhai) (Niger); Ethiopians
      (Gondar); Yoruba and Fon (Nigeria and Benin); Serer,
      Wolof, and Lebu (Senegal); Haitian voodoo cult; Hausa
      (Nigeria); Mitsogo and Fang (Gabon); Mosi (Mossi) (Upper
      Volta); Dogon (Mali); and Ashanti (Ghana) (pp. 170-81;
      see book's index under "Possession" for further page
      citations).

1736. Thomas, Thomas Morgan   Eleven Years in Central South
      1971   Africa. 2d ed. London: Frank
                                Cass & Co.

      Written by a missionary around 1870, this account
      focusses on the Amandebele (Ndebele) people of South
      Africa. Although spirit possession and mediumship are
      not explicitly labelled, the cave dwelling oracle, the
      Umlimo of these people, is discussed on pages 288 ff.
      The trance state during which the diviner communicates
      with the spirit worlds is described on pages 299-300.

1737. Thompson, A. Y., and   "The Zar in Egypt." The Muslim
      E. Frank   World 3:275-90.
      1903

      Not available for annotation.

337

1738. Thompson, Robert Farris   African Art in Motion. Los
      1974   Angeles: University of Califor-
                                 nia Press. Ill.

    Chapter 3, entitled "Icon and Act," deals with the use
of African art in its traditional settings. Spirit possession and mediumship are discussed, and numerous ethnic
groups are mentioned.

1739. Thurnwald, Richard C.   Black and White in East
      1935   Africa. London: George
                                 Routledge & Sons.

    Spirit possession by Sheytân or evil spirits among the
Tonga (Mozambique). Exorcism rituals described. Possession mostly affects women; however, men can become
possessed by Pepo spirits, a variety of demons (p. 384).

1740. Tiemo, G. O. E.   Egbena-Ijo Customs and Tradi-
      1968   tions. Institute of African
                                 Studies, University of Ibadan,
                                 Occasional Paper no. 17.
                                 Ibadan.

    Spirit possession of priests among the Egbena group of
the Igo (Ijaw) in Nigeria may be accompanied by immer-
sion under water for long periods of time, during which
they commune with the water spirits (p. 15).

1741. Tindall, P. E. N.   A History of Central Africa.
      1968   London: Longmans.

    The religious practices among the Bantu in Central
Africa during the nineteenth century included the office
of spirit medium to the important tribal spirits who
were concerned with the general welfare of the people,
their crops, and the rainfall (pp. 76-79). The role
that these mediums played during the Matabele (Ndebele)
and Mashona (Shona) rebellions in the late nineteenth
century in Southern Rhodesia is outlined on pages 167-
68, 170, 175.

1742. Tinling, David C.   "Voodoo, Root Work, and Medi-
      1967   cine." Psychosomatic Medicine
                                 29, no. 5: 483-90.

    "Root work" is a North American derivative of the
Haitian voodoo cult of African origins. This article
explores the relationships between voodoo and "root
work" beliefs in hexing and modern medicine as manifested in American Blacks.

1743. Toker, Eugene   "Mental Illness in the White
      1966   and Bantu Populations of the
                                    Republic of South Africa."
                                    American Journal of Psychiatry
                                    123, no. 1: 55-65.

The general psychiatric problems in South Africa are
discussed, among which is the phenomenon of epilepsy.
The Bantu-speaking peoples believe that epileptics are
bewitched and possessed, and they may become medicine
men (p. 61).

1744. Tooth, G. C.   Studies in Mental Illness in the
      1950   Gold Coast. London: Her
                                    Majesty's Stationery Office.

The study describes many illnesses whose symptomatology
is very similar to spirit possession among the peoples of
the Gold Coast (Ghana).

1745. Torelli, P. Ubald   "Notes ethnologiques sur les
      1973   Banya-Mwenge du Toro (Uganda)."
                                    Annali Lateranensi (Vatican
                                    City) 37:461-559.

Although spirit possession is not explicitly labelled,
exorcism practiced by a diviner during an epidemic a-
mong the Banya-Mwenge of Uganda is described on pages
555-56.

1746. Torrey, E. Fuller   "The Zar Cult in Ethiopia."
      1967   International Journal of Social
                                    Psychiatry (London) 13, no. 3:
                                    216-23.

The Zar possession cult in Ethiopia is analyzed as
having three distinct varieties: conversion Zar--charac-
terized by a conversion hysteria reaction mainly in
women; seer Zar--emphasizing fortune-telling and practiced usually by a man; and group therapy Zar--a group
of individuals afflicted by Zar spirits, directed in
ritual practices by a male or female leader.

1747. Torrey, E. Fuller   The Mind Game: Witchdoctors and
      1971   Psychiatrists. New York:
                                    Emerson Hall.

This book investigates and compares the witch-doctor,
the psychiatrist, and other types of psychotherapists to
discover their personality types and their methodologies.
The Zar spirit-possessed priest (Ethiopia) and other
traditional healers are mentioned. [Cited in Transcultural Psychiatric Research Review (Bruges) 8 (October
1971): 118-19.]

339

1748. Tracey, Hugh   "What Are Mashawi Spirits?"
      1934   Nada (Salisbury) 12:39-52.

      A psychological analysis of the shawi spirits among the
      Mashona (Shona) of Rhodesia is conducted here·   Spirit
      possession is discussed.

1749. Traoré, Dominique   Comment le noir se soigne-t-il?
      1965   ou médecine et magie africaines.
                              Paris: Présence africaine.

      Writing on traditional African medical practice in
      general, the author describes spirit possession on pages
      556-58.

1750. Tredgold, Sir Robert C. The Rhodesia that Was My Life.
      1968   London: George Allen & Unwin.

      The author, a judge in Rhodesia, discusses a case he
      presided over involving a witch-doctor. Spirits are
      mentioned, and although not explicitly labelled, spirit
      possession is implied (pp. 80-82).

1751. Tremearne, Major   Hausa Superstitions and Customs.
      A. J. N.   London: John Bale, Sons, &
      1913   Danielsson.

      The bori spirit possession cult among the Hausa of
      Nigeria is discussed in detail (pp. 109, 145-52, 530-40).

1752. Tremearne, A. J. N.   The Ban of the Bori. London:
      1914   Heath, Cranton.

      Included in the study is a description of spirit pos-
      session among the Moslem Hausa (Nigeria) in the early
      part of this century.

1753. Trimingham, J. Spencer Islam in the Sudan. London:
      1949   Oxford University Press.

      The role of spirit possession in causing illnesses in
      the Islamic cultures of the Sudan is described on pages
      166-78.

1754. Trimingham, J. Spencer Islam in Ethiopia. London:
      1952   Oxford University Press.

      The zar spirit possession cult in Ethiopia is discussed
      on pages 258 ff.

1755. Trimingham, J. Spencer Islam in West Africa. Oxford:
      1959   Clarendon Press.

      The bori spirit possession cult among the Hausa of
      Nigeria is discussed on pages 44, 59, 61, 94, 109-11.

340

1756. Trincaz, Jacqueline   "Mythes, sens et représentations
      1973   de la maladie chez les Mancagne
                             de Casamance (Sénégal)." Psy-
                             chopathologie africaine (Dakar)
                             9, no. 1: 79-109.

The phenomenon of spirit possession among the Mancagne
(Mankanya) of Senegal is interpreted as being more sociological than psychological in origin: the possessed is
taking on the ills of the society and finds an outlet
for this anxiety through symbolic identification with the
spirits.

1757. Trouillot, Hénock   "Introduction a une historie du
      1970   Vodou." Revue de la société
                             haitienne d'historie et de
                             géographie (Port-au-Prince) 34:
                             33-182.

      Not available for annotation.

1758. Tucker, S.   "The Divining Basket of the
      1940   Ovimbundu." Journal of the
                             Royal Anthropological Institute
                             of Great Britain 70, no. 2: 171-
                             201.

Part of this study deals with the Ovimbundu (Mbundu)
(Angola) diviner and how he receives his calling to the
profession through spirit possession.

1759. Tuden, Arthur   "Leadership and the Decision-
      1966   Making Process." In Political
                             Anthropology, edited by Marc
                             J. Swartz, Victor W. Turner,
                             and Arthur Tuden, pp. 275-83.
                             Chicago: Aldine Publishing Co.

The political role of the territorial spirits and the
mediums they possess among the Ila of northwestern Zambia
are discussed on pages 278-79.

1760. Tuden, Arthur, and   Social Stratification in Africa.
      Leonard Plotnicov,   New York: Free Press.
      eds.
      1970

      Includes in this bibliography:
                  1031   H. S. Lewis (1970)
                  1381   M. L. Perlman (1970)

1761. Tulanalwo, P.   "The Kerewe Beliefs in Super-
      1974   natural Beings." Occasional
                             Papers in African Traditional

Religion and Philosophy
(Makerere University, Kampala),
vol. 22, no. 217.

On the largest island in Lake Victoria live the Kerewe
(Uganda), who believe that one may become possessed by
the muzimu bad spirits and that such possession causes
illness and misfortune for the individual. If the possession is severe, a mufumu specialist is called in to
"calm" the muzimu. The relationship between these beliefs and Christianity is discussed.

1762. Turner, Arthur   "The Effects of Urban Conditions
      1972   on Indigenous Zambian Religious
                              Institutions in Kabwe." Paper
                              presented at the Conference on
                              the History of Central African
                              Religious Studies, Lusaka,
                              30 August - 8 September.

From a three-month (March-May 1972) period of inten-
sive interviews with eighty African residents of Kabwe,
Zambia, on the topic of possession and religious beliefs,
the author comes to the following conclusion: ". . . my
data shows that impersonal anonymous spirits which are
immediately at hand serve as a more readily available explanation for forces which are beyond the control of urban Africans, and that there seems to be a direct correlation between the impersonality of the spirit involved
and the degree to which the urban inhabitant fails to
perceive the source of his problem" (p. 30).

1763. Turner, Harold W.   "Pagan Features in West African
      1965   Independent Churches." Practi-
                              cal Anthropology 12, no. 4: 145-
                              51.

The relationship between pagan and Christian elements
in independent African churches is discussed; among the
pagan practices listed are: divination through revelation, ecstatic worship and spirit possession, purification procedures, etc.

1764. Turner, H. W.   History of an African Indepen-
      1967a   dent Church. 2 vols. Oxford:
                             Clarendon Press.

Spirit possession in the African independent church
movements, and in particular the Church of the Lord
(Aladura) in Nigeria, is mentioned in connection with the
Holy Spirit and is accompanied by trance and glossolalia
(vol. 1: pp. 49, 138 ff.; vol. 2: see book's index
under "Possession" for page citations).

1765. Turner, H. W.   "A Typology for African Reli-
      1967b   gious Movements." _Journal of_
                                   Religion in Africa (Leiden) 1,
                                   no. 1: 1-34.

Various categories of modern African religious movement are discussed in an attempt to distinguish between
the different mixtures of Christian and traditional beliefs and practices found in each. Various uses of
spirit possession are presented.

1766. Turner, Harold W.   "Bibliography of Modern African
      1968/70   Religious Movements--Supple-
                                  ment." _Journal of Religion in_
                                  Africa (Leiden), Supplement I,
                                  1, no. 3: 173-211; Supplement
                                  II, 3, no. 3: 161-208.

These are updated supplements to the original bibliography on modern African religious movements compiled by
Robert Cameron Mitchell and H. W. Turner (Bib. 1218).

1767. Turner, Harold W.   "Pentecostal Movements in
      1972   Nigeria." _Orita_ (Ibadan) 6,
                                  no. 1: 39-47.

The rise and development of the Pentecostal movements
in Nigeria during this century are discussed. All employ
some form of glossolalia, faith healing, spirit possession.

1768. Turner, V. M.   _The Lozi Peoples of North_
      1952   _Western Rhodesia_. Ethnographic
                                 Survey of Africa, edited by
                                 Daryll Forde, vol. 3, no. 3.
                                 London: International African
                                 Institute.

Exorcism rites described; spirit possession and spirit
mediumship discussed for the Lozi of northwestern
Rhodesia (Zambia) (pp. 52-53).

1769. Turner, V. M.   "Lunda Rites and Ceremonies."
      1953   _Occasional Papers of the Rhodes-_
                                Livingstone Museum, no. 10.

Discussion of curative cults among the Lunda (Zambia)
(pp. 53-56).

1770. Turner, Victor W.   _Schism and Continuity in an_
      1957   _African Society_. Manchester:
                                Manchester University Press.

The _Chihamba_ ritual among the Ndembu (Zambia), during
which one who has been "seized" by a spirit and thus made
ill is cured, is described in detail from page 293 on (see

book's index under "Ritual" for further page citations).

1771. Turner, Victor W.   "Lunda Medicine and the Treat-
      1964a   ment of Disease." Occasional
                                 Papers of the Rhodes-Livingstone
                                 Museum, no. 15.

     Spirit possession as cause of disease among the Ndembu
of Zambia is briefly mentioned on page 3.

1772. Turner, V. W.   "An Ndembu Doctor in Practice."
      1964b   In Magic, Faith and Healing,
                                 edited by A. Kiev. (Bib. 902.)

     Study of a Ndembu (Zambia) doctor; divination tech-
niques; therapeutic rites; the Ihamba cult; spirit possession by the spirits of Europeans or of alien tribesmen
(p. 242).

1773. Turner, Victor W.   The Forest of Symbols. Ithaca,
      1967   N.Y.: Cornell University Press.

     Being "seized" by a spirit among the Ndembu of north-
western Zambia can cause illnesses and misfortunes,
leading one to participate in certain "cults of affliction" or to follow a path towards initiation as a
"doctor" or "diviner" (mentioned throughout book, but
especially pages 9, 11-15, 142 ff., 282 ff., 360 ff.).

1774. Turner, Victor W.   The Drums of Affliction.
      1968   Oxford: Clarendon Press.

     Spirit possession may cause illness, but may also lead
one to become a diviner among the Ndembu of Zambia (see
book's index under "Divination," "Rituals of Affliction," "Shades," etc., for page citations).

1775. Turner, Victor W.   The Ritual Process. London:
      1969   Routledge & Kegan Paul.

     Among the Ndembu (Zambia), women may be "caught" by
shades and thus afflicted with illness or misfortune.
The Isoma cult aims at propitiating that shade and exorcising all other evil influences from the individual
(pp. 11 ff.).

1776. Turner, Victor W.   Dramas, Fields, and Metaphors.
      1974   Ithaca, N.Y.: Cornell University
                                 Press.

     Spirit mediumship among the Shona of Rhodesia and its
political importance is discussed on pages 184-85. The
recent introduction of the Tukuku cult among the Ndembu
of Zambia which involves possession by alien spirits is
mentioned on pages 249-50.

344

1777. Turner, Victor W.   Revelation and Divination in
      1975   Ndembu Ritual. Ithaca, N.Y.:
                                Cornell University Press.

      Among the Ndembu of Zambia, spirits may "catch" an in-
      dividual and by doing so send him illness and misfor-
      tune; the "cults of affliction" perfom rituals to exor-
      cise these influences. In divination, the diviner
      "trembles" under the influcnce of the spirits (see
      book's index under "Cult Affliction," "Divination,"
      "Spirit Affliction," etc., for page citations).

1778. Twumasi, P. A.   "Ashanti Traditional Medicine."
      1972   Transition (Accra) 8, no. 41:
                                50-63.

      Medical practitioners among the Ashanti of Ghana and
      the Ivory Coast receive their calling in the form of
      possession by a deity. Training of practitioners and the
      diagnoses and treatments of illnesses are outlined.

1779. Tyler, Rev. Josiah   Forty Years among the Zulus.
      1891   Boston: Congregational Sunday
                                School & Publishing Society.

      Written by a missionary, this work includes an account
      of Zulu "diviners" or "spirit doctors" in South Africa,
      who think that they are in communication with the
      spirits, and thus have extraordinary powers to find out
      the causes of misfortune (pp. 99 ff.).

1780. Tylor, E. B.   Primitive Culture. Vol. 1. New
      1889   York: Henry Holt & Co.

      Spirit possession among the Zulus (South Africa) dis-
      cussed on page 98.

1781. Tylor, E. B.   Anthropology. New York: D.
      1898   Appleton & Co.

      Discussion of demoniacal possession as a disease
      theory; hysteria and epilepsy as they relate to spirit
      possession.

1782. Ustrof, Werner   Afrikanische Initiative: Das
      1975   aktive Leiden des propheten
                                Simon Kimbangu. Bern: Herbert
                                Lang; Frankfurt: Peter Lang.

      Description and analysis of the Simon Kimbangu move-
      ment in the Belgian Congo (Zaïre) is presented in this
      monograph. Mention is made of spirit possession and
      trance behavior on pages 86 ff. in discussing the socio-
      religious tradition of the Bakongo under colonial rule.
      Missionaries as early as 1703 (p. 89) noted folk move-
      ments involving visions and trances.

1783. Vail, H. Leroy   "Religion, Language and the
      1972   Tribal Myth: The Tumbuka and
                          Cewa of Malawi." Paper pre-
                          sented at the Conference on the
                          History of Central African Reli-
                          gious Systems, Lusaka,
                          30 August - 8 September.

No mention is made of possession, but the historical
connection between the Tumbuka- and Cewa-speaking
(Chewa) peoples of Malawi is traced through their similar religious beliefs. Linguistic analyses are given to
support hypothesis that although languages may differ between two peoples, cultural elements do not necessarily
do so also. Hereditary priests of the snake spirit
Chikang'ombe (Tumbuka), intermediary between men and the
high god Chinta (Tumbuka), are described.

1784. Valerio, Cicero   Feneomenos parapsicologicos e
      1962   espiritas. São Paulo: Editora
                           Pirantiniga.

Not available for annotation.

1785. Vambe, Lawrence   An Ill-fated People. London:
      1972   Heinemann.

In this historical analysis of the Shona people in
Zimbabwe (Rhodesia), particularly in relation to the
white government, the role of the spirit medium is discussed in chapters 5 (pp. 57-73), 9 (pp. 113-30), and 13
(pp. 175-94).

1786. Vambe, Lawrence   From Rhodesia to Zimbabwe.
      1976   Pittsburgh: University of Pitts-
                           burgh Press.

In this autobiographical account of a young African of
Shona (Rhodesia) origin, mention is made of a healer who
is possessed by a shave spirit in order to treat illnesses (pp. 18-19), and of the mhondoro or lion mediums
of these people (p. 66).

1787. Van der Kerken, M. G.   "Religion, science et magie au
      1938   pays des Mongo." Bulletin des
                                 séances, Institut royal colonial
                                 belge (Bruxelles) 9, no. 2: 202-
                                 92.

Among the Bakutshu (Kutshu) of Zaïre, the future priests
of the wetshi, the spirits of the air and the sun, become possessed as a sign that they are to be initiated
into the cult (pp. 236-37).

1788. van der Walde, Peter   "Trance States and Ego Psycho-
      H.   logy." In Trance and Possession
      1968   States, edited by R. Prince,
                                   pp. 57-68. (Bib. 1421.)

      Trance states, including possession trance, are exam-
ined in light of the research on hypnosis and the theoretical position of ego psychology.

1789. Van Everbroeck, N.   "Mbombo'ipoku: Le Seigneur à
      1961   l'abîme." Archives d'ethno-
                                   graphie, Musée royal de
                                   l'Afrique centrale (Tervuren),
                                   no. 3.

      The Bolia, Sénegele (Sengele), and Ntómba (Ntomba) of
Zaïre share a common belief in bélimá, spirit beings, of
whom Mbomb'ipoku is considered to be the greatest. Many
other spirit beings occupy the worlds of these peoples,
including those who cause illness by means of possession
and must be exorcised (pp. 51-123).

1790. Van Geluwe, H.   Les Bira et les peuplades limi-
      1957   trophes. Ethnographic Survey of
                                  Africa, edited by Daryll Forde.
                                  London: International African
                                  Institute.

      The Bira of Equatorial Guinea maintain that the spirits
of the dead, after having been near the deities, rede-
scend to earth and possess a member of their clan (p.
149).

1791. Van Noten, Francis   "!King Bosjesmannen in der
      1965   Kalahari." Africa-Tervuren 11,
                                  no. 2: 40-48. Ill.

      The healing trance dances of the !Kung Bushmen
(Bechuanaland, now Botswana) are described, during which
contact is made with the spirits of the dead who send
sickness and death to the living. Those in trance expell
and protect against the evil spirits by applying their
hands upon their companions.

1792. van Pelt, P.   "A Few Cases of 'Spirit Posses-
      1976   sion.'" Tanzania Notes and
                                  Records (Dar es Salaam), nos.
                                  77-78, pp. 45-49.

      Several cases of spirit possession are mentioned here
from Tanzania; sorcery-sent possession illness, spirits
being attracted to a person by their own accord, and mass
possession are all discussed.

1793. Vansina, Jan   Les Tribus Ba-Kuba et les
      1954   peuplades apparentées. London:
                                      International African Institute.

      Among the Ba-Kuba (Kuba) of Zaïre the "magician of
      God" is one who regularly goes into trance, and has
      spirit friends with whom he communicates. He can also
      predict the outcome of the day's hunt (p. 48).

1794. Vansina, J.   "Les Croyances religieuses des
      1958   Kuba." Zaire: Belgian African
                                      Review (Bruxelles) 12, no. 7:
                                      725-58.

      Those individuals among the Kuba of Zaïre who have been
      summoned to serve the ngesh spirits through a dream or
      an illness are termed "shamans" by the author. These
      practitioners can communicate with the spirits in various
      ways, including through spirit possession (pp. 737-42).

1795. Vansina, Jan   Introduction à l'ethnographie du
      1966   Congo. Bruxelles: Editions
                                      universitaires du Congo.

      Spirit possession and mediumship appear among the
      Ngbandi, Mbanja (Mbandja), and Ngbaka (pp. 34-37) and
      among the Lunda, Cokwe (Chokwe), Lwena (Luvale), Ruund,
      and Mbagani (p. 183), all of Zaire.

1796. Vansina, Jan   "Les Mouvements religieux kuba
      1971   (kasai) a l'epoque coloniale."
                                      Études d'histoire africaine
                                      (Kinshasa), no. 2, pp. 155-87.

      The spirit possession trance in the cult surrounding
      the ngesh spirit among the Kuba of Zaïre is described
      on pages 175-76.

1797. Van Wing, J.   "Études Bakongo - II. Religion
      1938   et Magie." Mémories de
                                      l'Institut royal colonial belge
                                      (Bruxelles) 9, no. 1: 1-301.

      The beliefs, symbols, rites and practices of the reli-
      gion of the Bakongo (Kongo) of Zaïre are presented here,
      and spirit possession and exorcism are described on
      pages 23, 26, 198 ff.

1798. Van Wing, J.   "Bakongo Magic." Journal of the
      1941   Royal Anthropological Institute
                                      of Great Britain and Ireland 71,
                                      nos. 1-2: 85-97.

Mention of belief in individuals among the Bakongo
(Kongo) (Zaire) who possess evil power and who can spirit
possess other individuals. Discussion of the role of the
diviner in detecting the source of possession.

1799. Van Wing, J.   "Le Kimbanguisme vu par un
      1958   témoin." Zaire: Belgian African
                              Review (Bruxelles) 12, no. 6:
                              563-618.

The first pages of this extensive article on Simon
Kimbangu and the evolution of the cult that grew up a-
round him in Zaire deal with trance and spirit possession.

1800. van Wyk, J. Alex   "Independent African Churches:
      1964   Sects Spontaneous Development?"
                              Ministry (Morija, Basutoland)
                              4, no. 2: 58-63.

The relationship of the use of spirit possession in the
Zionist churches of Africa to its use in the traditional
African religion is traced on pages 60-61.

1801. Vedder, H.   "The Berg Damara." In The Na-
      1966a   tive Tribes of South West
                              Africa, edited by C. H. L. Hahn,
                              H. Vedder, and L. Fourie, pp.
                              37-78. (Bib. 715.)

Among the Berg Damara of Angola, the witch-doctor
"trembles" when he communicates with the spirits, suggesting a mediumship trance (p. 64).

1802. Vedder, Heinrich   South West Africa in Early Times.
      1966b   Translated and edited by Cyril
                              G. Hall. New York: Barnes &
                              Noble.

In this nineteenth-century account, the beliefs of the
Ovambo tribes of South West Africa are described. These
people believe that illness and death may be caused
through possession of an individual by evil ancestor
spirits, or through contact with one possessed by evil
spirits such as a witch or sorcerer. Treatment by means
of exorcism are described (pp. 75-77).

1803. Verger, Pierre   Dieux d'Afrique. Paris: Paul
      1954a   Harmann éditeur. Ill.

Pictorial illustrations of Voodoo worship and individuals in states of possession, trance, etc. Introduction by Théodore Mono and Roger Bastide. Bibliographical
footnotes. 160 photographs.

1804. Verger, Pierre   "Rôle joué par l'état d'hébétude
      1954b   au cours de l'initiation des
                        novices aux cultes des Orisha et
                        Vodun." Bulletin de l'Institut
                        fondamental d'Afrique noire
                        (Dakar), ser. B, 16, nos. 3-4:
                        322-40.

The initiations in the Yoruba Orisha and Vodun cults
in Nigeria and Dahomey (Benin), which involve spirit possession trance, are described. Various theorists who
have written about possession are then criticized, followed by the author's own analysis.

1805. Verger, Pierre   "Yoruba Influences in Brazil."
      1955   Odu (Ibadan), vol. 3-11.

Describes ceremonies for African (Yoruba) divinities in
Brazil in which spirit possession occurs, and gives some
information on spirit mediumship.

1806. Verger, P.   "Notes sur le culte des Orisha
      1957   et Vodun." Mémoires de
                        l'Institut Français d'Afrique
                        noire (Dakar), no. 51.

Description of spirit possession and various trance
states for Brazil and West Africa (chaps. 2 and 3).

1807. Verger, Pierre   "Trance States in Orisha Wor-
      1963   ship." Odu (Ibadan) 9:13-20.

In Dahomey (Benin) and Nigeria, the Yoruba worship of
Orisha involves spirit possession. The trance state is
not regarded as being abnormal or psychotic, but the
practitioner appears to have a double personality.

1808. Verger, Pierre   "Les Religions traditionnelles
      1965   africaines sont-elles compati-
                        bles avec les formes actuelles
                        de l'existence?" In Les Reli-
                        gions africaines tradition-
                        nelles, Rencontres internation-
                        ales de Bouaké (October 1962),
                        pp. 97-118. (Bib. 1466.)

In this theoretical article, the African-Brazilian cultural and religious interchange is examined, and the
practice of spirit possession is mentioned both in the
article itself and in the discussion following it.

1809. Verger, Pierre   "The Yoruba High God." Odu
      1966   (Ibadan) 2, no. 2: 19-40.

The concept of a high god among the Yoruba of Nigeria is analyzed, employing historical accounts by missionaries and anthropologists. The possession of human beings by the orișa (Orisha), or divine being, is described on pages 37-38.

1810. Verger, Pierre   "Trance and Convention in Nago-
      1969   Yoruba Spirit Mediumship." In
                            Spirit Mediumship and Society in
                            Africa, edited by J. Beattie
                            and J. Middleton, pp. 50-66.
                            (Bib. 150.)

Possession trances occur regularly among the Nago-Yoruba and Fon people of Dahomey (Benin). The mediums of the gods are called iyaworisha or vodunsi--"wife of the orisha" or "wife of the vodun" (the sex of the medium, however, may be male or female). Description of several social rituals involving possessed mediums.

1811. Verger, Pierre   "Raisons de la survie des reli-
      1972   gions africaines au Bresil."
                            In Les Religions africaines
                            comme source de valeurs de civi-
                            lisation. Colloque de Cotonou
                            (August 1970), pp. 172-84.
                            (Bib. 358.)

Spirit possession among the African-influenced religious cults of Brazil is mentioned on page 176.

1812. Vergiat, A. M.   Les Rites secrets des primitifs
      1936   de l'Oubangui. Paris: Payot.

Chapter 10 deals with exorcism practices used when a person is made ill through being possessed by a spirit among the Manja, Banda,Gbaya (Baya), Sango (Sangu), and Nzakara peoples of Zaire and the Central African Empire.

1813. Vesme, Caesar de   Primitive Man. Vol. 1. London:
      1931   Rider & Co.

In chapter 5 the author cites reports of Europeans who have witnessed séances by Africans. Trances and possession do occur among Africans, and that seems to be proof to the author that the African is a spiritualist. Some ethnographic accounts of spirit possession.

1814. Viaene, L.   "La Religion des Bahunde (Kivu)."
      1952   Kongo-Overzee (Antwerpen) 18,
                            no. 5: 388-425.

The Bahunde (Hunde) of Zaïre believe in a supreme being who guides the world through Bazimu spirits. The communication between these spirits and the people goes through diviners who are the spirits' mediums. [Cited in African Abstracts, vol. 5, no. 457.]

1815. Viard, Capitaine René   Les Guérés: Peuple de la forêt.
      1934   Paris: Société d'éditions.

Among the Guéres (Ngere) of the Ivory Coast, the witch-doctor ("féticheur") entrances an assistant medium, who begins to tremble and then is possessed by a spirit. Hypnotism is thought by the author to explain the phenomenon (pp. 58-59).

1816. Vig, Lars   Les Conceptions religieuses des
      1973   anciens Malagaches.
                              by Bruno Hübsch. Tananarive:
                              Imprimerie catholique Tanana-
                              rive.

The relationship between spirit possession and physical illnesses (and the curative rites of exorcism) is mentioned for the peoples of Madagascar on pages 20-24, 52. The author was a missionary at the turn of this century.

1817. Vilakazi, Absolom   Zulu Transformations.
      1962   Pietermaritzburg: University
                              of Natal Press.

Spirit possession by ancestor spirits among the Sibisi of South Africa is mentioned on page 90 in connection with differing clan affiliations of husband and wife resulting in differing ways of worshipping the ancestors.

1818. Villermont, Comtesse   Magie et sorcellerie africaines.
      Simon de   Paris: Omnium littéraire.
      1951

Spirit possession and mediumship are mentioned in this short survey of African beliefs in magic and sorcery (pp. 14 ff.).

1819. Vincent, Jeanne-   "Divination et possession chez
      Françoise   les Mofu, Montagnards du Nord-
      1971   Cameroun." Journal de la
                            . Société des africanistes (Paris)
                              41, no. 1: 71-132.

The complex interrelationship between various divination techniques and spirit possession among the Mofu of north Cameroon is described in detail. Different spirits possess men and women in the process of divining the cause of a problem.

1820. Vincent, Jeanne-   Le Pouvoir et le sacré chez les
      Françoise   Hadjeray du Tchad. Paris:
      1975   Éditions anthropos.

The Hadjeray (Hadjerai) of Chad practice spirit possession as a part of their religion. Main references:
pages 76 ff., 86 ff., 174-80.

1821. Vittoz, Pierre   "Le Mouvement pentecostiste."
      1975   Flambeau (Yaoundé), no. 47,
                                pp. 146-55.

Speaking in tongues and possession by the Holy Spirit
are both discussed in this theoretical article on the
Pentecostal Movement in Africa.

1822. Vivier, L. M.   Glossolalia. Thesis for the
      1960   degree of Doctor of Medicine,
                                University of Witwatersrand.

Very helpful in defining phenomenon of glossolalia.
Psychological testing given to members of the Pentecostal
churches, in South Africa, who have claimed to have
spoken in tongues.

1823. Vivier, L. M.   "The Glossolalic and His Perso-
      1969   nality." In Beitrage zur
                                Ekstase, edited by T. Spoerri
                                [Bibliotheca Psychiatrica et
                                Neurologica 134:153-75]. Basel:
                                S. Karger.

An in-depth psychological examination of a group of
South African Pentecostals who speak in tongues when possessed by the Holy Spirit reveals that they are neither
neurotic nor hypnotically suggestible, nor do they have
a tendency to dissociate.

1824. Vyncke, J.   "L'Assistance psychiatrique au
      1958   Ruanda-Urundi." In Mental Dis-
                                orders and Mental Health in
                                Africa South of the Sahara,
                                pp. 52-55. CCTA/CSA-WFMH-WHO,
                                Pub. no. 35. Bukavu.

Traditionally in Ruanda-Urundi (Rwanda, Burundi), all
mental illnesses were thought to be caused by spirit possession, an external source of disease. At times, initiation into cults such as Imandwa was called for and included the use of a plant of the Datura stamonium family--
the extreme effects of which are considered to be similar
to modern electric shock therapy.

1825. Waddell, H. M.   Twenty-nine Years in the West
      1863   Indies and Central Africa.
                              London: T. Nelson & Sons.

      Discussion of African traditional beliefs and the re-
vival of Myalism and Obeah as preferred forms of worship. In Guinea there were reports of spirit possession
by the devil. Information for Jamaica and Nigeria.
[Cited by Jeffreys (1953, Bib. 853).]

1826. Wagner, Günter   The Bantu of North Kavirondo.
      1949   Vol. 1. London: Oxford Univer-
                              sity Press.

      A cause of mental illness among the Bantu of north
Kavirondo in Kenya is believed to be possession by
spirits (p. 222).

1827. Wagner, Günter   "The Abaluyia of Kavirondo
      1954   (Kenya)." In African Worlds,
                              edited by D. Forde, pp. 27-54.
                              (Bib. 588.)

      Witches are believed to be possessed by evil forces
among the Abaluyia (Abalyhya) of Kavirondo, Kenya (p.
46).

1828. Waldmeier, Theophilus   The Autobiography of Theophilus
      1886   Waldmeier. London.

      Possession cases for Abyssinia (Ethiopia) reported by
Waldmeier of the Bale Missionary Society. In Abyssinia
(Ethiopia), people were often possessed by evil spirits
which were called Boudah. Description of exorcism ceremonies witnessed by the author.

1829. Walker Art Center   Art of the Congo. Minneapolis.
      1967   Walker Art Center. Ill.

      In this discussion of art in Zaïre, mention is made of
spirit worship, and mediumship is implied though not
specifically stated. Ethnic groups mentioned are: Kongo,
Yaka, Pende, Cokwe (Chokwe) and Luba (p. 16).

1830. Walker, Sheila S.   Ceremonial Spirit Possession in
      1972   Africa and Afro-America.
                              Leiden: E. J. Brill.

      The phenomenon of spirit possession as manifested in
African and Afro-American religions is analyzed from the
perspectives of neurophysiology, hypnosis, initiation
and socialization processes, culture, mental illness,
and philosophy.

354

1831. Wallace, A. F. C.   "Cultural Determinants of Re-
      1959   sponses to Hallucinatory Ex-
                            perience." AMA Archives of
                            General Psychiatry 1:58-69.

A discussion of the use of the terms "hallucination"
and "possession" and the terminological problem of the
kind of phenomena that are being denoted by these terms.

1832. Wallace, A. F. C.   Religion: An Anthropological
      1966   View. New York: Random House.

Spirit possession is discussed in general terms and
with specific reference to the Haitian voodoo cult and to
the Zulus of South Africa (see book's index under "Possession" for page citations).

1833. Wallis, Wilson D.   Religion in Primitive Society.
      1939   New York: F. S. Crofts & Co.

Description of the ceremonies and training involved in
consecrating a priest of the Ashanti (of Ghana). Nearly
all Ashanti priests are qualified for the profession by
susceptibility to spirit possession (pp. 71-72). Suto
(South Africa), Ganda (Uganda), and peoples of Northern
Rhodesia (Zambia) have spirit mediums who are visited by
the spirits of dead rulers and medicine men (pp. 82-83).

1834. Ward, Barbara E.   "Some Observations on Religious
      1956   Cults in Ashanti." Africa:
                            Journal of the International
                            African Institute (London) 26,
                            no. 1: 47-61.

Among the Ashanti of the rural Gold Coast (Ghana) the
growth of the Christian Church has been slow. One cause
of this may be the prohibition by the missionary churches
(mostly Presbyterian) against spirit possession and other
practices involving emotional outbursts and active participation by the worshippers.

1835. Warmelo, N. J. van,   Contributions towards Venda His-
      ed.   tory, Religion and Tribal
      1950   Ritual. South Africa Native
                             Affairs Department, Ethnological
                             Publications, vol. 3. Pretoria.

Verbatim translations of the accounts given by Venda
(South Africa) informants concerning their religious life
are presented here. Spirit mediumship is practiced in
order to discover the reason why an ancestor has possessed
and thus made an individual ill (pp. 141-50).

355

1836. Warren, Donald, Jr.   "Spiritism in Brazil." Journal
      1968   of Inter-American Studies 10,
                               no. 3: 393-405.

      Largely focussed on the spiritist cult of Allan Kardec
      in Brazil, mention is made of the Afro-Brazilian cults
      of Candomblé and Umbanda. All of these cults involved
      spirit possession and mediumship.

1837. Wasungu, P.   "Sorcellerie et possession en
      1972   Afrique." Ethno-Psychologie
                                (Le Havre) 27, nos. 2-3: 323-55.

      This general theoretical article discusses the distinc-
      tions drawn between sorcery and witchcraft and presents
      material on spirit possession. Data are taken from
      many groups in Africa.

1838. Waterman, Richard Alan   "African Influence on the Music
      1952   of the Americas." In Accultura-
                                tion in the Americas, edited by
                                S. Tax, pp. 207-18.
                                (Bib. 1715.)

      Although spirit possession is not directly discussed,
      this article deals with the music of the Afro-American
      possession cults including that of the Haitian vodun
      religion.

1839. Wavell, Steward, Audrey   Trances. New York: E. P.
      Butt, and Nina Epton   Dutton & Co.
      1967

      Chapters 6, 17, and 27 record experiences of communi-
      cation with spirits through possession and mediumship in
      North Africa, witnessed by Nina Epton. Included are the
      Gnaoua ethnic group in Morocco and the Sufi brotherhoods
      of Aissaoua and Derquaoua of Morocco.

1840. Weatherby, J. M.   "Inter-tribal Warfare on Mount
      1962   Elgon in the 19th and 20th
                                Centuries." Uganda Journal
                                (Kampala) 26, no. 2: 200-212.

      The main emphasis of this essay is on the Sebei of
      Kenya, although mention is made of many other groups who
      moved into the area around Mount Elgon during the nine-
      teenth and twentieth centuries. The Sebei have a tradi-
      tion of prophets who are possessed and have the gift of
      second sight.

1841. Webster, Hutton   Primitive Secret Societies. 2d
      1908   ed. London: Macmillan & Co.

356

Discussion of initiation to West African spirit cults after individuals become possessed (p. 174).

1842. Webster, J. B.   "Independent Christians in
      1969   Africa." Tarikh (London) 3,
                          no. 1: 56-83.

The various independent Christian church movements over Africa are given detailed historical analyses. The role of such traditional elements as spirit possession in these new churches is mentioned.

1843. Weeks, John H.   Among the Primitive Bakongo.
      1914   London: Seeley, Service & Co.

In order to become a witch-doctor among the Bakongo (Kongo) of Zaïre, one must be possessed by the fetish of the witch-doctor who is one's teacher. The witch-doctor also cures persons who have been possessed and made ill by evil spirits, using a technique that combines a possession trance with exorcism. Finally, witches are considered to be "possessed" by the evil spirits they use to harm others (pp. 215 ff., 223 ff., 226 ff., 280 ff.).

1844. Weinberg, S. Kirson   "Mental Healing and Social Change
      1964   in West Africa." Social Pro-
                              blems 2, no. 3: 257-59.

In this general article, Christian faith healing, Western psychiatric practices, and traditional African methods of treating mental illnesses in Ghana are compared. [Cited in Transcultural Psychiatric Review (Bruges) 4 (October 1967): 155-58.]

1845. Weinberg, S. Kirson   "'Mental Healing' and Social
      1967   Change in West Africa." In
                              The Sociology of Mental Dis-
                              orders, edited by S. Kirson
                              Weinberg, pp. 341-50. Chicago:
                              Aldine Publishing Co.

Traditional West African techniques of healing mental illnesses are discussed and compared with the more recent introduction of Western-trained psychiatrists and Christian faith healers. Spirit possession is presented as a cause of illness whose cure is exorcism.

1846. Weinberg, S. Kirson   Culture and Communication in Dis-
      n.d.   order and Psychotherapy in
                              Ghana, West Africa. Mimeographed.
                              16 pp.

Although not explicitly labelled, spirit possession is implied as being a cause of illness among Africans living in Accra, Ghana, West Africa. The relationship between traditional and Western healing practices, as affected

357

by sociocultural change, is emphasized. [Cited in Trans-cultural Psychiatric Research Review (Bruges) 7 (April 1970): 37-39.]

1847. Weingertner, L.   Umbanda-synkretische kulte in
      1969   Brasilien. Erlander:
                             Evangelical Lutheran Mission.

Not available for annotation.

Weinrich, A. K. H., also publishes under Aquina, Sister
Mary O. P. (Bib. 44-48).

1848. Weinrich, A. K. H.   "Karanga History and the Mwari
      1969-70   Cult." Cultures et developpe-
                             ment (Louvain) 2, no. 2: 389-
                             405.

Spirit mediumship and possession in the Karanga Mwari
cult in Rhodesia are discussed in their relationship to
political institutional changes.

1849a. Weinrich, A. K. H.   Chiefs and Councils in Rhodesia.
       1971   London: Heinemann.

The relationship between the spirit mediums and the
chiefs of the Karanga in Rhodesia is discussed in terms
of their political history (pp. 61, 78, 86-87, 107, 113).

1849b. Weinrich, A. K. H.   The Tonga People on the Southern
       1977   Shore of Lake Kariba. Gwelo,
                             Rhodesia: Mambo Press.

Spirit possession is discussed in chapter 7 which deals
with traditional religion. Possession is particularly
mentioned in connection with rain spirits and Mpande
spirits of the Tonga (Thonga) (Rhodesia).

1850. Welbourn, F. B.   East African Rebels. London:
      1961   SCM Press.

This volume studies in great detail the Buganda (Ganda)
(Uganda) and Kikuyu (Kenya) independent church movements,
both historically and psychologically. Spirit possession,
though not specifically indexed, is mentioned in various
places throughout the text (p. 178; see book's index
under "Religion" for further page citations).

1851. Welbourn, F. B.   "Some Aspects of Keganda Reli-
      1962   gion." Uganda Journal
                             (Kampala) 26, no. 2: 171-82.

Possession by ancestral spirits; mediums who interpret
the wishes of the spirits form a cult among the Keganda
(Ganda) (Uganda).

1852. Welbourn, F. B.   "The Importance of Ghosts." In
      1963   African Independent Church Move-
                               ments, edited by V. E. W. Hay-
                               wood, pp. 15-26. World Council
                               of Churches Research Pamphlet
                               no. 11. London: Edinburgh
                               House Press.

      Spirit possession is briefly mentioned in this general
article on the importance of ghosts and ancestor spirits
in African religions (p. 16).

1853. Welbourn, F. B.   East African Christian. London:
      1965   Oxford University Press.

      In this historical work on Christianity in East Africa,
mention is made of the Jaluo (Luo) and Buganda (Ganda)
traditional beliefs in spirit possession (pp. 34-35).

1854. Welbourn, F. B., and   A Place to Feel at Home. London:
      B. A. Ogot   Oxford University Press.
      1966

      Spirit possession by the Holy Spirit is mentioned in
various contexts in this study of two African independent
churches of Kenya: the Church of Christ in Africa and
the African Israel Church Nineveh (see book's index under
"Spirit Possession" for page citations).

1855. Welbourn, F. B.   "Spirit Initiation in Ankole and
      1969   a Christian Spirit Movement in
                               Western Kenya." In Spirit Me-
                               diumship and Society in Africa,
                               edited by J. Beattie and J.
                               Middleton, pp. 290-306.
                               (Bib. 150.)

      Among the Ankole (Nkole) (Kenya) there is a mediumship
cult for spirits called Cwezi. Membership in the cult
follows an initiation ceremony. Possession is feigned
in this initiation, but diviners may become actually possessed in private sessions. Among the Luo of western
Kenya a group of members of the Anglican church broke
away and formed their own churches which included spirit
possession in the services.

1856. Welch, James W.   "The Isoko Tribe." Africa:
      1934   Journal of the International
                               African Institute (London) 7, no.
                               2: 160-73.

      Among the Isoko, who inhabit the northwest corner of
the Niger delta (Nigeria), the most important religious
figure is the obueva (obu meaning doctor, and eva

359

meaning charm). Among several means of selection for
this office is possession by a spirit during a frenzy
brought on by dancing; an obueva, however, has to serve
an apprenticeship of not less than a year. The obueva is
consulted in cases of doubt or calamity (p. 165).

1857. Welch, Sidney R.   Portuguese Rule and Spanish
      1950   Crown in South Africa 1581-1640.
                            Cape Town: Juta & Co.

In a calendrical ritual among the Kafir of South Africa,
the chief would go into a trance, utter glossolalia,
"the dialects of many tribes," and, possessed by a spirit,
would prophesy (p. 155). The witch-doctors among the
Kafir, in order to detect thieves, would become seemingly
"crazy" and then, inspired by the spirits, would utter
the name of the thief (p. 171).

1858. Werbner, Richard P.   "Atonement Ritual and Guardian
      1964   Spirit Possession among
                             Kalanga." Africa: Journal of
                             the International African In-
                             stitute (London) 34, no. 3:
                             206-23.

Among the Kalanga of Southern Rhodesia (now Rhodesia)
hereditary guardian spirits known as Mazenge (sing.
zenge) often possess women. Description of the ceremonies
to cure victims. Discussion of the role of women in
Kalanga society and why they would be liable to spirit
possession.

1859. Werbner, Richard P.,   Regional Cults. (A. S. A.
      ed.   Monograph 16.) New York:
      1977   Academic Press.

This volume of collected essays was not available in
its entirety for annotation. In the editor's introduction, the stated area of concentration is south-central
Africa, specifically the regional cults of the peoples of
Zambia and Zimbabwe, which employ both spirit possession
and mediumship. The following scholars have contributed
articles dealing with spirit possession: Elizabeth Colson (Bib. 368b); J. M. Schoffeleers; G. Kingseley
Garbett; and Richard Werbner.

1860. Werner, A.   The Natives of British Central
      1906   Africa. London: Archibald Con-
                             stable & Co.

Spirit possession and mediumship among the Yao of
Rhodesia are mentioned throughout chapters 3 and 4.
Specific description is given of the Mbona spirit medium
on pages 60-61.

1861. Werner, Alice   Myths and Legends of the Bantu.
      1933   London: George G. Harrap & Co.

      A description of spirit possession and trance states
      among the Lamba (Zambia) (chap. 16).

1862. Werner, Douglas   "Some Developments in Bemba Re-
      1971   ligious History." Journal of
                             Religion in Africa (Leiden) 4,
                             no. 1: 1-24.

      The introduction of spirit possession and spirit me-
      diumship among the Bemba of northeastern Zambia and the
      development of these religious practices is analyzed
      historically within the broader context of Bemba reli-
      gion (pp. 6-7, 18-23).

1863. Westcott, Joan, and   "The Symbolism and Ritual Con-
      Peter Morton-Williams text of the Yoruba Laba Shango."
      1962   Journal of the Royal Anthropolo-
                             gical Institute of Great Britain
                             and Ireland 92, pt. 1: 23-37.

      Spirit possession in the Yoruba religion (Nigeria) is
      mentioned throughout this article.

1864a. West, Martin   "People of the Spirit: The
       1974   Charismatic Movement among Afri-
                             can Independent Churches."
                             Journal of Theology for Southern
                             Africa (Cape Town) no. 7, pp.
                             23-29.

      Glossolalia, spirit possession, and mediumship are dis-
      cussed in the context of the Zionist African independent
      churches. Comparison is made with the use of spirit pos-
      session in traditional African religions and the depriva-
      tion theory proposed by I. M. Lewis (Bib. 1036-38).

1864b. West, Martin   "African Churches in Soweto,
       1975a   Johannesburg." In Urban Man in
                             Southern Africa, edited by Clive
                             Kileff and Wade Pendleton.
                             Gwelo, Rhodesia: Mambo Press.

      Author discusses a number of characteristics of spirit
      churches, one of which is spirit possession (South
      Africa) (p. 25).

1864c. West, Martin   Bishops and Prophets in a Black
       1975b   City: African Independent
                             Churches in Soweto, Johannesburg.
                             Cape Town: David Philip.

The author discusses spirit possession (on pages 18, 29, 35, 36, 40, 45, 60, 93, 123, 176-77, 183, 188) in the context of the independent churches having an all-African membership and leadership (South Africa).

1865. Westermann, Diedrich   "The Value of the African's
        1926   Past." International Review of
                              Missions 15, no. 59: 418-37.

Spirit possession in African religion is discussed briefly in this general theoretical article written by a missionary (p. 425).

1866. Westermarck, Edward   The Belief in Spirits in Morocco.
        1920   Åbo: Finnish Literary Society.

The jnûn spirits are believed by Moroccans to be able to assume any shape including the human form. They can cause illnesses and madness by possessing an individual, but can also be the messengers of the saints. Very detailed data are given.

1867. Westgarth, J. N.   Qua Ibo. (Belfast) (November).
        1927

Description of a spirit movement in Nigeria in 1927. The movement was called "the shakers," not to be confused with the English movement in the time of Charles I. [Cited in Jeffreys (1953, Bib. 853).]

1868. Westgarth, J.   The Holy Spirit and the Primi-
        1946   tive Mind. London: Victory
                              Press.

Not available for annotation.

1869. Whisson, Michael G.   "Some Aspects of Functional Dis-
        1964   orders among the Kenya Luo."
                              In Magic, Faith and Healing,
                              edited by A. Kiev, pp. 283-304.
                              (Bib. 902.)

Clear discussion of spirit possession as one kind of disease causing mental disorder among the Luo of Kenya (pp. 283-304).

1870. Whisson, Michael G.,   Religion and Social Change in
   and Martin West, eds.   Southern Africa. Cape Town:
        1975   David Philip.

Includes in this bibliography:
           1259   C. Murray (1975)
           1611   H. Sibisi (1975)

1871. White, A.   "Threatening Voices: Auditory
      1968/69   Hallucinations of Psychiatric
                           Outpatients at the Mulayo Mental
                           Health Center." Sociology
                           Papers, University of East Afri-
                           ca Social Sciences Council Con-
                           ference, pp. 513-24. Kampala:
                           Makerere Institute of Social
                           Research.

      A Western psychiatric analysis is made of auditory
hallucinations among the outpatients of the Mulago Mental Health Center (Uganda). These patients, mainly
diagnosed as schizophrenics or depressives, feel that
they are communicating with the spirit realms.

1872. White, C. M. N.   "Witchcraft, Divination and Magic
      1948   among the Balovale Tribes."
                           Africa: Journal of the Interna-
                           tional African Institute
                           (London) 18, no. 2: 81-104.

      On the basis of nine years of fieldwork among the Balo-
vale tribes--Lunda, Lwena (Luvale), Luchazi, and Chokwe--
of northwest Northern Rhodesia (Zambia), the author presents a general outline of witchcraft and divination
practices along with a linguistic analysis of relevant
native terms. Possession and exorcism are mentioned in
the context of the relationship between witches (male or
female) and their familiars.

1873. White, C. M. N.   "Stratification and Modern
      1949   Changes in an Ancestral Cult."
                           Africa, vol. 19.

      Discussion of the Mahamba ancestral spirits associated
with the Balovale (Luvale) tribes of Northern Rhodesia
(Zambia). Some discussion of possession and exorcism
dances.

1874. White, C. M. N.   "Elements in Luvale Beliefs and
      1961   Rituals." Rhodes-Livingstone
                           Papers (Manchester), no. 32.

      Spirit possession among the Luvale of Northern
Rhodesia (Zambia) is a form of punishment sent by the ancestors and can be the cause of illness. The Mahamba
cults are organized to deal with such problems (pp. 47
ff.).

1875. White, J. D.   "History and Customs of the
      1971   Urungwe District." Nada
                           (Salisbury) 10, no. 3: 33-72.

363

A detailed history is given of the various migrations
and events occurring in the Urungwe District of Rhodesia.
Spirit mediumship is mentioned as a practice of the Va-
Sori (Sori) peoples (p. 47).

1876. Whiteley, Wilfred   Bemba and Related Peoples of
      1950   Northern Rhodesia. Ethnographic
                              Survey of Africa, edited by
                              Daryll Forde. London: Interna-
                              tional African Institute.

      Description of forms of spirit possession; the nature
of the possessing spirits and ritual cures among the
Bemba of Northern Rhodesia (Zambia).

1877. Willems, Emilio   "Religious Mass Movements and
      1966   Social Change in Brazil." In
                              New Perspectives of Brazil,
                              edited by Eric N. Baklonoff,
                              pp. 205-32. Nashville: Vander-
                              bilt University Press.

      Discussed is the role of spirit possession and medium-
ship in the African-influenced Brazilian cults of
Umbanda, Macumba, Candomblé, and Xango (Shango).

1878. Willis, C. A.   "The Cult of Deng." Sudan Notes
      1928   and Records 11:195-208.

      Discusses the prophets of the Nuer (Sudan). These
prophets appear to be epileptics or reproduce the appearance of epileptic fits; they are supposed to be possessed by the spirit of Deng.

1879. Willis, Roy G.   "Changes in Mystical Concepts
      1968   and Practices among the Fipa."
                              Ethnology 7, no. 2: 139-57.

      The change in types of spirits and their influence
upon the living from pre- to post-colonial times is outlined for the Bantu-speaking Fipa of southwest Tanzania.
Attention is paid to those spirits for whom individuals
act as mediums for divinatory purposes, and those which
cause illness by means of possession.

1880. Willis, R. G.   "Instant Millennium: The Socio-
      1970a   logy of African Witch-cleansing
                              Cults." In Witchcraft Confes-
                              sions and Accusations, edited
                              by M. Douglas, pp. 129-39.
                              (Bib. 476.)

      Briefly mentioned is the spirit-possessed ngunza
prophet among the Kongo (Zaire).

1881. Willis, R. G.   "Kaswa: Oral Tradition of a
      1970b   Fipa Prophet." Africa: Journal
                             of the International African
                             Institute (London) 40, no. 3:
                             248-56.

An historical analysis of the oral traditions centering
on Kaswa, the famous nineteenth-century Fipa prophet of
southwest Tanzania, who prophesied the destruction of the
old social order and "its replacement by the values and
technology of a capitalist society" (p. 284). The
various spirit mediumship cults thriving at the same time
are briefly outlined.

1882. Willis, Roy   Man and Beast. New York: Basic
      1974   Books.

Communication with and possession by the spirits are
discussed for the Nuer and Dinka of the Sudan, the Lele
of Zaïre, and the Fipa of Tanzania (see book's index
under "Spirits" for page citations).

1883. Willoughby, W. C.   Race Problems in the New Africa.
      1923   Oxford: Clarendon Press.

Trance, spirit possession, and mediumship among the
Bantu-speaking peoples of Africa are mentioned on pages
70-72.

1884. Willoughby, W. C.   The Soul of the Bantu. New
      1928   York: Doubleday, Doran & Co.

Discussion of spirit possession appears in chapter 2.
Describes several prophet movements such as the Kimbangu
movement of Zaire.

1885. Willoughby, W. C.   Nature-Worship and Taboo.
      1932   Hartford, Conn.: Hartford
                             Seminary Press.

Discusses Zulu (South Africa) belief in spirit possession by a ghost of a murdered man (pp. 19, 29,. 34-45,
109-11, 175).

1886. Wilmeth, Marilyn Walton, "Theatrical Elements in Voodoo:
      and J. Richard   The Case for Diffusion."
      Wilmeth   Journal for the Scientific
      1977   Study of Religion 16, no. 1:
                              27-37.

The growth and development of the Afro-Haitian Voodoo
religion are traced. Mention is made of spirit possession.

365

1887. Wilmot, A.   The History of South Africa.
      1901   London: Kegan Paul, Trench,
                          Trübner & Co.

In 1857, a certain witch-doctor of the Kafir peoples
of South Africa received a message from the spirits that
all the cattle his people owned should be killed in order
that their wealth be increased. This message was received through a girl acting as a spirit medium (pp. 21-
22).

1888. Wilson, Bryan   Religious Sects. London:
      1970   Weidenfeld & Nicolson.

Spirit possession and mediumship are mentioned in the
Nigeria independent movement of Aladura (pp. 176-77) and
in the Brazilian Candombé cult (p. 221).

1889. Wilson, Bryan   Magic and the Millennium. St.
      1975   Albans: Paladin.

In this detailed theoretical account of religious
movements, spirit possession in Africa and the Caribbean
is discussed for the following groups: Zionist sects
(Zulu tradition), South Africa (p. 58); Pocomania,
Jamaica (p. 59); Fang, Gabon (pp. 80-81); the Twelve
Society (Luvale influence), Barotseland (Zambia) (pp.
92-93); Brazilian possession cults (pp. 108-14, 124);
Mumbo movement, Luo and Kisii (Gusii) western Kenya (p.
262); and general information on Africa (pp. 107, 160).
Spirit mediumship is presented for Brazilian cults (pp.
113, 117-18); Ndebele and Shona, Mashonaland (p. 214);
and general information for Africa (p. 94).

1890. Wilson, George   The History of the Universities'
      Herbert   Mission to Central Africa.
      1936   Letchworth, Hertfordshire:
                          Garden City Press.

Possession by evil spirits is mentioned as occurring on
Pemba Island off the coast of Zanzibar (p. 139).

1891. Wilson, Godfrey   "An African Morality." In
      1960   Cultures and Societies of
                          Africa, edited by S. and P.
                          Ottenberg, pp. 345-64.
                          (Bib. 1335.)

Brief mention is made of a form of divination among the
Nyakyusa of Tanzania which involves a "speaking cala-
bash," interpreted by the author as being a form of ventriloquism (p. 349).

366

1892. Wilson, Monica   Communal Rituals of the
      1959   Nyakyusa. London: Oxford Uni-
                               versity Press.

   Among the Nyakyusa of Tanganyika (Tanzania) the future
of society is often predicted by special dreamers, called
Abakunguluka. There are also others, called abakom'
amalago, who prophesy while in a trance or while having
fits; these people are mostly women. Speaking of a woman
prophesying in this manner, men say, "The shade has
entered her" or "Kyala catched hold of her that she may
speak of the matter" (pp. 71-72).

1893. Wilson, Monica Hunter   Reaction to Conquest. London:
      1961   Oxford University Press.

   Although spirit possession is not explicitly labelled,
the ancestors send illness to those they wish to become
diviners among the Pondo of South Africa. Initiation involves a trance state (chap. 7).

1894. Wilson, Monica   Religion and the Transformation
      1971   of Society. Cambridge: Cam-
                               bridge University Press.

   Spirit mediumship and possession are discussed in
chapter 2. Mention is made of the following central and
southern African peoples: Nguni, Nyakyusa, and Ndembu.

1895. Wilson, Peter J.   "Status Ambiguity and Spirit Pos-
      1967   session." Man (London), n.s. 2,
                               no. 3: 366-78.

   Theoretical discussion of spirit possession employing
data from several African groups and focussing on the relationship between possession and status ambiguity.
Discussion is given of I. M. Lewis's hypothesis (Man
1966, Bib. 1036) concerning the linkage between possession
and inequalities between the sexes. [Lewis's response to
Wilson's article, and Wilson's reply to it, are given in
Man (1967) 2, no. 4: 626-29.]

1896. Wilson-Haffenden,   The Red Men of Nigeria. London:
      Captain J. R.   Seeley, Service & Co.
      1930

   Possession by evil spirits among the Kwotto (Panda) of
Nigeria is the explanation given of wer-animals, men who
are able to transform themselves into animals in order to
attack other humans (pp. 158 ff.).

1897. Winter, Edward H.   Bwamba. Cambridge: W. Heffer
      1956   & Sons.

Description of the Amba (Uganda) beliefs concerning
spirit possession, occurring mainly in women, as a sign
for formal indoctrination by "putting the god on her
head" (pp. 111 ff.).

1898. Winter, Edward H.   Beyond the Mountains of the
      1959   Moon. London: Routledge & Kegan
                             Paul.

The Amba of Uganda feel that spirits "catch" women when
they are away from home collecting firewood or water, and
must then fully possess the women if illness, death, or
other misfortunes are to be avoided (pp. 22 ff.).

1899. Wintrob, R., and   "Magic and Witchcraft in
      E. D. Wittkower   Liberia; Their Psychiatric Im-
      1966a   plications." Paper presented at
                             the Association for the Advance-
                             ment of Psychotherapy meeting,
                             Atlantic City, 8 May. Mimeo-
                             graphed. 14 pp.

Following a presentation of the various beliefs in
witchcraft and magic found in Liberia, several hypotheses
are formulated to explain their prevalence. [Cited in
Transcultural Psychiatric Research Review and Newsletter
(Bruges) 3 (October 1966): 149-52.]

1900. Wintrob, R. M.   "Psychosis in Association with
      1966b   Possession by Genii in Liberia."
                             Psychopathologie africaine
                             (Dakar) 2, no. 2: 249-58.

Spirit possession among the Mandingo (Malinke) peoples
of Liberia is of two types: possession by "Mammy
Water," a spirit with the form of a beautiful white woman
who is thought to bring fame and wealth; and possession
by genii, malevolent spirits who cause illness and misfortune. Two case studies are presented, along with
Western psychiatric diagnoses.

1901. Wintrob, Ronald M.   "Sexual Guilt and Culturally
      1968a   Sanctioned Delusions in Liberia,
                             West Africa." American Journal
                             of Psychiatry 125, no. 1: 127-
                             33.

Two cases from Liberia are presented: one of a Bissa
woman and one of a Kpelle girl. Both individuals believed that they had been possessed by genii. Clinical
diagnoses are given.

1902. Wintrob, R., and   "Witchcraft in Liberia and Its
      E. D. Wittkower   Psychiatric Implications." In
      1968b   An Evaluation of the Results of
                               the Psychotherapies, edited by
                               Stanley Lesse, pp. 305-17.
                               Springfield, Ill.: Charles C
                               Thomas, Publishers.

Spirit possession and witchcraft in Liberia are approached from a psychiatric viewpoint, and traditional
African beliefs and practices are analyzed.

1903. Wipper, Audrey   "The Cult of Mumbo." East Afri-
      1966   can Institute of Social Research
                               Conference Papers, no. 374, pp.
                               1-34.

The Mumbo cult of South Nyanza (Kenya) is examined in
detail. Drawing adherents from mainly the Luo and
Kisii (Gusii), the practices include spirit possession
and glossolalia (pp. 2, 14-15, 22).

1904. Wipper, Audrey   "The Gusii Rebels." In Protest
      1970   and Power in Black Africa,
                               edited by A. A. Mazuri, pp. 377-
                               426. (Bib. 1520.)

The Mumbo cult, in which followers are possessed by the
Mumbo snake spirit, is discussed as an anticolonial protest movement among the Gusii of Kenya.

1905. Wise, R.   "Marriage Guidance by Exorcism."
      1962   Tanganyika Notes and Records
                               58/59:40-42.

A local witch diviner in Tanzania, after inducing a
cataleptic state in himself, casts out devils, especially
matrimonial troubles. When the crowd is gripped by mass
hysteria, he casts out the devil by tapping the women on
the shoulder. Thus the couple is reconciled. [Cited in
African Abstracts, vol. 14, no. 580.]

1906. Wishlade, R. L.   Sectarianism in Southern Nyasa-
      1965   land. London: Oxford University
                               Press.

Possession by the Holy Spirit in the Kimbangu movement
of southern Nyasaland (Malawi) is mentioned on page 138.

1907. Wittkower, E. D.   "Spirit Possession in Haitian
      1964   Vodun Ceremonies." Acta Psycho-
                               therapeutica et Psychosomatica
                               (Basel) 12, no. 1: 72-80.

A Vodun ceremony in Haiti is presented, and subsequent
analysis of spirit possession compares it to hypnosis,
epilepsy, and hysteria, but suggests that none of these
descriptions is entirely accurate.

1908. Wittkower, E. D., and   "Transcultural Psychiatry."
      H. Rin   Archives of General Psychiatry
      1965   13, no. 5: 387-94.

This is a general article outlining the approaches and
difficulties of practicing psychiatry transculturally.
Various mental illnesses are discussed, including
Haitian voodoo spirit possession under the heading of
"Atypical Psychoses" (pp. 392-93).

1909. Wittkower, E. D.   "Transcultural Psychiatry." In
      1968   Modern Perspectives in World
                              Psychiatry, edited by John G.
                              Howells, pp. 617-712. New
                              York: Brunner/Mazel.

Haitian voodoo spirit possession is discussed briefly
in this general article on transcultural psychiatry (pp.
705-6).

1910. Wittkower, E. D.   "Trance and Possession States."
      1970   International Journal of Social
                              Psychiatry (London) 16, no. 2:
                              153-60.

After presenting brief descriptions of the possession
states observed in Haiti--the Voodoo cult, in Monrovia,
Liberia--the Prophet Healers, and in Brazil--the Candomblé
cult, the author proceeds to outline the essential features of the trance and possession states in comparison
with psychotic, neurotic, and hypnotic states.

1911. Wolfe, Alvin W.   In the Ngombe Tradition: Con-
      1961   tinuity and Change in the Congo.
                              Evanston, Ill.: Northwestern
                              University Press.

Among the Ngombe of Zaïre, strange spirits are thought
to enter one's body and cause illness, and specialists
are able to exorcise them. However, the healer who himself has had the "disease of spirits," who has been
cured, and who enters into a possession trance so as to
cure others is a relatively new phenomenon (pp. 79-80).

1912. Wood, A. V.   The Bantu Reaction to Christia-
      n.d. [1962]   nity. Prism Pamphlet no. 3.
                              London: Insight Publication.

In this short tract, the relationship between the traditional Bantu (South Africa) beliefs concerning religious

370

matters and Christianity is examined. Zionism is spoken of as being "a battery which is steadily charged with the suppressed energies of the Bantu" (p. 14), and speaking in tongues (possession by the Holy Spirit) is discussed on pages 11 ff.

1913. Wooding, Charles J.   "The Winti-Cult in the Para-
      1972   District." Caribbean Studies
                               12, no. 1: 51-78.

The in-depth analysis of the Winti-Cult in Surinam is presented. Based on African traditional ideas, the cult mainly concentrates on healing, and spirit possession is the major element in the ceremonies. Psychological analysis is given.

1914. Woollacott, R. C.   "Pasipamire--Spirit Medium of
      1975   Chaminuka, the 'Wizard' of
                              Chitungwiza." Nada (Salisbury)
                              11, no. 2: 154-67.

The extraordinary powers and the life history of the Chaminuka spirit medium, Pasipamire, of the Shona in Rhodesia, who lived during the second half of the nineteenth century, are examined here utilizing mainly oral sources.

1915. Wright, Marcia   "Nyakyusa Cults and Politics in
      1972   the Later Nineteenth Century."
                              In The Historical Study of Afri-
                              can Religion, edited by T. O.
                              Ranger and I. N. Kimambo, pp.
                              153-71. (Bib. 1442.)

Spirit mediumship in the Kyala cult among the Nyakyusa of Tanzania is analyzed historically (pp. 159 ff.).

1916. Wyllie, R. W.   "Introspective Witchcraft among
      1973   the Effutu of Southern Ghana."
                              Man (London), n.s. 8, no. 1:
                              74-79.

Spirit mediumship and possession along with exorcism rituals are discussed with regard to "introspective" or confession-oriented witchcraft among the Effutu of southern Ghana.

1917. Wyllie, R. W.   "Pastors and Prophets in
      1974   Winneba, Ghana: Their Social
                              Background and Career Develop-
                              ment." Africa: Journal of the
                              International African Institute
                              (London) 44, no. 2: 186-93.

371

The origination, composition, and social characteristics of the various churches in Winnebu, Ghana, are analyzed. Messages sent by the Holy Ghost in dreaming or waking experiences are cited as frequent reasons for initiating healing activities and, at times, for the founding of a new sect.

1918. Wyllie, R. W.   "Some Contradictions in Missio-
      1976   nizing." Africa: Journal of the
                      International African Institute
                      (London) 46, no. 2: 196-204.

Spirit healing and speaking in tongues are briefly mentioned as occurring in the African independent churches (p. 200).

1919. Wymeersch, P.   "Les 'Apostolos': Notes sur un
      1973   mouvement syncrétique de la
                      région de Lubumbashi (Rep. du
                      Zaïre)." Africa-Tervuren
                      (Tervuren) 19, no. 1: 6-15. Ill.

Possession by the Holy Spirit and glossolalia are described for the Apostolos of Zaïre, a syncretic African independent church movement in the Lubumbashi region (pp. 11 ff.).

1920. Yap, P. M.   "The Possession Syndrome: A
      1960   Comparison of Hong Kong and
                      French Findings." Journal of
                      Mental Science [British Journal
                      of Psychiatry] (London) 106, no.
                      442 (n.s. no. 406): 114-37.

Although African and Afro-American possession cults are only mentioned briefly in the first paragraph of this article, a general review of the literature on spirit possession is presented and analyzed.

1921. Young, Allan   "Magic as a 'Quasi-Profession':
      1975a   The Organization of Magic and
                      Magical Healing Among Amhara."
                      Ethnology 14, no. 3: 245-66.

The author describes the role of the debtera, a magician-healer who is an ecclesiastic of the Ethiopian Orthodox Church. The article concerns the Amhara area around the old imperial capital of Gondar, in Begemder province north of Lake Tana in Ethiopia. A detailed description is offered of spirit possession, often associated with Zar cults, and the role of the magician-healer in dealing with the spirits.

1922. Young, Allan
      1975b

"Why Amḥara get Kureynya: Sick-
ness and Possession in an
Ethiopian Zar Cult." American
Ethnologist 2:567-87.

Not available for annotation.

1923. Zahan, Dominique
      1970

Religion, spiritualité et pensée
africaines. Paris: Payot.

Chapter 6 deals with the "Messagers de l'inconnu" who
include diviners and spirit mediums. Ethnic groups mentioned in this general theoretical work are the Lulua,
Bassonge (Songe), and Baluba (Luba) (Zaïre).

1924. Zaretsky, Irving, and
      Mark P. Leone, eds.
      1974

Religious Movements in Contemporary America. Princeton, N.J.:
Princeton University Press.

      Includes in this bibliography:
            247   E. Bourguignon (1974a)
            657b   L. G. Gerlach (1974)
            682   F. D. Goodman (1974b)
            1116b   M. Marks (1974)

1925. Zempleni, A., and
      J. Rabain
      1965

"L'Enfant nit ku bon: Un Tableau
psychopathologique traditionel
chez les Wolof et Lébou du
Sénégal." Psychopathologie
africaine (Dakar) 1, no. 3: 329-
441.

Given here is a detailed presentation of a case of a
peculiar type of spirit possession found among the Wolof
and Lébou (Lebu) of Senegal: a child is thought of as
being possessed by, or as being a reincarnation of, an
ancestor spirit. The differences and similarities between this type of possession and the more usual transi-
tory ones are given on pages 331-80.

1926. Zempleni, A.
      1966

"La Dimension therapeutique du
culte des rab, ndöp, tuuru et
samp, rites de possession chez
les Lébou et les Wolof."
Psychopathologie Africaine
(Dakar) 2, no. 3: 295-439. Ill.

The therapeutic aspects of the ndöp ritual among the
Lébou (Lebu) and Wolof of Senegal are discussed. The possession phenomenon is followed from the initial symptoms,
to the ritual activities, to, finally, the full possession by the rab, ancestral spirits. Also included are
brief descriptions of two variants of the ritual, the
tuuru and the samp.

1927. Zempleni, A.   "Sur l'alliance entre la personne
      1967   et le rab dans le n'dop."
                            Psychopathologie africaine
                            (Dakar) 3, no. 3: 441-450.

Explored here is the relationship between two intercon-
nected rituals among the Wolof of Senegal. These are the
cheit ceremonies, performed when a bride sets up her own
household, and the n'dop rituals, where a practitioner becomes possessed by the rab, ancestor spirits.

1928. Zempleni, A.   "La Thérapie traditionelle des
      1969   troubles mentaux chez les Wolof
                            et les Lébou (Sénégal)." Social
                            Science and Medicine 3:191-205.

Given here are the basic principles behind the traditional beliefs and curing practices of the Wolof and
Lébou (Lebu) in Senegal. A major cause of illness is
possession by various types of spirits, including the rab
and tuur ancestral spirits, and the jinne and seytanne
of Islamic origin. [Cited in Transcultural Psychiatric
Research Review (Bruges) 7 (April 1970): 29-32.]

1929. Zempleni, Andras   "Pouvoir dans la cure et pouvoir
      1973   social." Pouvoirs, Nouvelle
                            Revue de Psychanalyse 8:141-78.
                            Ill.

The women's healing cults among the Moundang (Mundang)
of the Chad Republic, which employ spirit possession, are
discussed here. Emphasis is placed on their healing
rituals in order to show that a sociological analysis
such as that conducted by I. M. Lewis (Bib. 1038) is not
a sufficient explanation. [Cited in Transcultural
Psychiatric Research Review (Montreal) 12 (April 1975):
63-67.]

1930. Zempleni, Andras   "From Symptom to Sacrifice: The
      1977   Story of Khady Fall." Trans-
                            lated by Karen Merveille. In
                            Case Studies in Spirit Posses-
                            sion, edited by V. Crapanzano
                            and V. Garrison, pp. 87-139.
                            (Bib. 391.)

An in-depth case study of Khady Fall, a possessed
priestess of the Wolof people in Senegal, is given here.
Both her own history and the cult of the rab in which she
participates are described.

1931. Zempleni, A.   L'Interprétation et la thérapie
      n.d.   traditionnelle du désordre men-
                            tal chez les Wolof et les Lébou,
                            Sénégal. 2 vols. Paris:
                            Université de Paris.

A very detailed presentation, both theoretical and descriptive, is given of the traditional interpretations and therapies of mental disorders among the Wolof and Lébou (Lebu) of Senegal. Spirit possession is an often-cited cause of mental illness. [Cited in Transcultural Psychiatric Research Review (Bruges) 6 (April 1969): 69-74.]

1932. Zenkovsky, S.   "Zar and Tambura as Practiced by
       1950   the Women of Omdurman." Sudan
                             Notes and Records 31, no. 1: 65-
                             81.

Several cases are reported of spirit possession by Zar spirits in the Sudan. Also, cases are reported of possession by devils; however, the latter do not respond to the curing ceremony of the Zar cult.

1933. Zuesse, Evan M.   "Divination and Deity in African
       1975   Religions." History of Reli-
                             gions vol. 15, no. 2.

Not available for annotation.

1934. Zuure, Père Bernard   Croyances et pratiques reli-
       n.d.   gieuses des Barundi.

Cited by Rosemary Guillebaud (Bib. 710) in connection with the practices of the Ryangombe cult, which practices spirit possession in Barundi (Rundi) (Burundi).

1935. Zvobgo, Chengetai   "Shona and Ndebele Response to
       J. M.   Christianity in Southern
       1976   Rhodesia, 1897-1914." Journal
                             of Religion in Africa (Leiden)
                             8, no. 1: 40-51.

The strong resistance to the Christian missionaries among the Shona and Ndebele of Southern Rhodesia is analyzed for the period from 1897 to 1914. Mention is made of the political role of the traditional spirit mediums.

PORTUGUESE CITATIONS FROM BRAZIL

1936. Ab 'D'Ruanda   Banhos, defumações e amacís na
       1954a   Umbanda. Rio de Janeiro:
                             Editôra Espiritualista Ltda.

1937. Ab 'D'Ruanda   Lex Umbanda catecismo. Rio de
       1954b   Janeiro: Grafica Editôra Aurora,
                             Ltda.

1938. Alva, Antonio de   Como desmanchar trabalhos de
       1967a   Quimbanda. 2 vols. Rio de
                             Janeiro: Editôra Eco.

375

1939. Alva, Antonio de
      1967b

O livro dos exus; kimbas e eguns.
Rio de Janeiro: Editôra Eco.

1940. Alva, Antônio de
      1971

Ogum o Orixá guerreiro. Rio de
Janeiro: Editôra Espiritualista,
Ltda.

1941. [Anonymous]
      1965

Banhos de descarga e amacís
defumações e oferendãs. Rio de
Janeiró: Editôra Eco.

1942. [Anonymous]
      1973

2000 pontos ricados e cantados
na Umbanda e Candomblé. Rio de
Janeiro: Editôra Eco.

1943. [Anonymous]
      n.d.

Cantigas de boiadeiro. Rio de
Janeiro: Edições Crença.

1944. [Anonymous]
      n.d.

Cantigas de caboclos. Rio de
Janeiro: Edições Crença.

1945. [Anonymous]
      n.d.

Cantigas de exu. Rio de
Janeiro: Edições Crença.

1946. [Anonymous]
      n.d.

Cantigas de orixás. Rio de
Janeiro: Edições Crença.

1947. [Anonymous]
      n.d.

Cantigas de prêtos velhos. Rio
de Janeiro: Edições Crença.

1948. Bandeira, Cavalcanti
      1970

O que é a Umbanda. Rio de
Janeiro: Editôra Eco.

1949. Barcelos, Mãrio
      1968

Aruanda. Rio de Janeiro:
Editôra Eco.

1950. Barcelos, Mãrio
      1970

O livro do exército branco de
oxalá. Rio de Janeiro: Editôra
Eco.

1951. Barreto, Ary
      1974

Os deuses umbandistas. São
Paulo: Editôra Lance, Ltda.

1952. Bettiol, Leopoldo
      1963

Do batuque e das origens da
Umbanda. Rio de Janeiro:
Gráfica Editôra Aurora, Ltda.

1953. Bittencourt, Jose Maria
      1970

No reino dos exus. Rio de
Janeiro: Editôra Eco.

1954. Braga, Lourenço
      1961

Umbanda, magia branca et
Quimbanda, magia negro. Rio de
Janeiro: Edicões Spiker.

1955. Camargo, Candido Procopio Ferreira de 1961 — Kardecismo e Umbanda. São Paulo: Livraria Pioneira Editôra.

1956. Conguê, Babaô n.d. — Pontos de Candomblé. Rio de Janeiro: Editôra Eco.

1957. Costa, Fernando 1974 — A prática do Candomblé no Brasil. Rio de Janeiro: Editôra Renes.

1958. Dias Sobrinho, J. 1972 — Forças ocultas, luz e caridade. Rio de Janeiro: Editôra Espiritualista, Ltda.

1959. Efigênio, Jamil 1973 — Sob a luz da Umbanda. Rio de Janeiro: Editôra Espiritualista, Ltda.

1960. Farelli, Maria Helena 1972 — As 7 fôrças da Umbanda. Rio de Janeiro: Editôra Eco.

1961. Farelli, Maria Helena 1974 — As 7 giras de exu. Rio de Janeiro: Editôra Eco.

1962. Felix, Candido Emanuel 1965 — A cartilha da Umbanda. Rio de Janeiro: Editôra Eco.

1963. Felix, Candido Emanuel n.d. — O manuel de rezas e mandingas. Rio de Janeiro: Editôra Eco.

1964. Fontenelle, Aluizio 1963. — A Umbanda através dos séculos. Rio de Janeiro: Gráfica Editôra Aurora, Ltda.

1965. Fontenelle, Aloysio 1964 — Umbanda, 320 pontos cantados. Rio de Janeiro: Editôra Livro S. A.

1966. Franco, Florisbela M. Sousa 1964 — Umbanda. Rio de Janeiro: Editôra Espiritualista, Ltda.

1967. Freitas, Byron Tôrres de, and Tancredo da Silva Pinto 1963 — Guia e ritual para organização de terreiros de Umbanda. Rio de Janeiro: Editôra Eco.

1968. Freitas, Byron Tôrres de, and Vladimir Cardoso de Freitas 1965 — Na gira de Umbanda. Rio de Janeiro: Editôra Eco.

377

1969. Freitas, Byron Tôrres   Na gira de Umbanda e das almas.
       de, and Vladimir   Rio de Janeiro: Editôra Eco.
       Cardoso de Freitas
       1969

1970. Freitas, Byron Tôrres   Doctrine e ritual de Umbanda.
       de, and Tancredo da   Rio de Janeiro: Editôra
       Silva Pinto   Espiritualista, Ltda.
       1970

1971. Freitas, Byron Tôrres   Os orixás e a lei de Umbanda.
       de, and Vladimir   Rio de Janeiro: Editôra Eco.
       Cardoso de Freitas
       n.d.

1972. Freitas, João de   Xangô Djacutá. Rio de Janeiro:
       1968   Editôra Eco.

1973. Freitas, João de   Exu na Umbanda. Rio de Janeiro:
       1971   Editôra Espiritualista, Ltda.

1974. Freitas, João de   Curimbas da Umbanda. Rio de
       1974   Janeiro: Editôra Baptista de
                                 Souza.

1975. Freitas, João de   Camba de Umbanda. Rio de
       n.d.   Janeiro: Gráfica Editôra Aurora,
                                 Ltda.

1976. Freitas, João de   Ogum Megê. Rio de Janeiro:
       n.d.   Editôra Eco.

1977. Lapassade, Georges,   O segredo da Macumba. Rio de
       and Marco Aurélio   Janeiro: Editôra Paz e Terra
       Luz   S. A.
       1972

1978. Louza, Francisco   Os Orixás governam o seu
       1973   destino. Rio de Janeiro:
                                 Editôra Espiritualista, Ltda.

1979. Maciel, Silvio   Umbanda mista. Rio de Janeiro.
       Pereira
       1951

1980. Magno, Oliveira   Antigas orações da Umbanda. Rio
       n.d.   de Janeiro: Editôra Espiritua-
                                 lista, Ltda.

1981. Mello, Hamilton   Iaô. Rio de Janeiro: Editôra
       Vallente de, and   Espiritualista, Ltda.
       Tancredo da Silva
       Pinto
       1975

1982. Miranda, Roberto dos   Candomblé, Umbanda e suas
       Santos   obrigações. Rio de Janeiro:
       n.d.   Editôra Espiritualista, Ltda.

1983. Molina, N. A.   Feitiços de prêto velho. Rio de
       1972a   Janeiro: Editôra Espiritualista,
                                  Ltda.

1984. Molina, N. A.   Saravá a linha das almas. Rio
       1972b   de Janeiro: Editôra Espiritua-
                                  lista, Ltda.

1985. Molina, N. A.   Saravá Exu. Rio de Janeiro:
       1972c   Editôra Espiritualista, Ltda.

1986. Molina, N. A.   Saravá Ibejada. Rio de Janeiro:
       1972d   Editôra Espiritualista, Ltda.

1987. Molina, N. A.   Saravá o povo d'água. Rio de
       1972e   Janeiro: Editôra Espiritua-
                                  lista, Ltda.

1988. Molina, N. A.   Saravá o rei das 7
       1972f   encruzilhadas. Rio de Janeiro:
                                  Editôra Espiritualista, Ltda.

1989. Molina, N. A.   Saravá Ogun. Rio de Janeiro:
       1972g   Editôra Espiritualista, Ltda.

1990. Molina, N. A.   Saravá Oxoce. Rio de Janeiro:
       1972h   Editôra Espiritualista, Ltda.

1991. Molina, N. A.   Saravá seu tranca ruas. Rio de
       1972i   Janeiro: Editôra Espiritua-
                                  lista, Ltda.

1992. Molina, N. A.   Saravá Xangô. Rio de Janeiro:
       1972j   Editôra Espiritualista, Ltda.

1993. Molina, N. A.   Saravá Maria Padilha. Rio de
       1973a   Janeiro: Editôra Espiritua-
                                  lista, Ltda.

1994. Molina, N. A.   Saravá Obaluaiê. Rio de
       1973b   Janeiro: Editôra Espiritua-
                                  lista, Ltda.

1995. Molina, N. A.   Saravá Pomba Gira. Rio de
       1973c   Janeiro: Editôra Espiritua-
                                  lista, Ltda.

1996. Molina, N. A.   Como cortar o olho grande. Rio
       1974a   de Janeiro: Editôra Espiritua-
                                  lista, Ltda.

1997. Molina, N. A.   Manual de oferendas e despachos
      1974b   na Umbanda e na Quimbanda. Rio
                             de Janeiro: Editôra Espiritua-
                             lista, Ltda.

1998. Molina, N. A.   Manual do Babalaô e Yalorixá.
      1974c   Rio de Janeiro: Editôra Espiri-
                             tualista, Ltda.

1999. Molina, N. A.   Pontos cantados e riscados de
      1974d   exus. Rio de Janeiro: Editôra
                             Espiritualista, Ltda.

2000. Molina, N. A.   Pontos cantados e riscados
      1974e   oxôssi. Rio de Janeiro: Editôra
                             Espiritualista, Ltda.

2001. Molina, N. A.   Pontos cantados e riscados de
      1974f   pretos velhos. Rio de Janeiro:
                             Editôra Espiritualista, Ltda.

2002. Molina, N. A.   Saravá seu caveira. Rio de
      1974g   Janeiro: Editôra Espiritualista,
                             Ltda.

2003. Molina, N. A.   Saravá seu marabô. Rio de
      1974h   Janeiro: Editôra Espiritualista,
                             Ltda.

2004. Molina, N. A.   Saravá seu tiriri. Rio de
      1974i   Janeiro: Editôra Espiritualista,
                             Ltda.

2005. Molina, N. A.   Como frazer e desmanchar
      n.d.   trabalhos de Quimbanda. Rio de
                             Janeiro: Editôra Espiritualista,
                             Ltda.

2006. Molina, N. A.   Saravá Iemanjá. Rio de Janeiro:
      n.d.   Editôra Espiritualista, Ltda.

2007. Molina, N. A.   Saravá Oxum. Rio de Janeiro:
      n.d.   Editôra Espiritualista, Ltda.

2008. Nunes Filho, Átila   Umbanda religião-desafio. Rio
      1970   de Janeiro: Editôra Espiritua-
                             lista, Ltda.

2009. Oliveiro, Jorge de   Magias da Umbanda. Rio de
      1970a   Janeiro: Editôra Eco.

2010. Oliveiro, Jorge de   O evangelho na Umbanda. Rio de
      1970b   Janeiro: Editôra Eco.

2011. Oliveiro, Jorge de   Umbanda transcendental. Rio de
      1971   Janeiro: O Cruzeiro S. A.

2012. Oliveiro, Jorge de   Ritual prático do Candomblé e
      1973   seus mistérios. Rio de Janeiro:
                              Editôra Espiritualista, Ltda.

2013. Pessoa, Laudemir   Ritual de terreiro umbandista.
      n.d.   Rio de Janeiro: Editôra Eco.

2014. Pinto, Altair   Dicionário da Umbanda. Rio de
      1971   Janeiro: Editôra Eco.

2015. Pinto, Tancredo da   Cabala umbandista. Rio de
      Silva   Janeiro: Editôra Espiritualista,
      1971a   Ltda.

2016. Pinto, Tancredo da   Minas sob a luz da Umbanda.
      Silva, and Antônio   Belo Horizonte: Editôra G.
      Pereira Camêlo   Holman, Ltda.
      1971b

2017. Pinto, Tancredo da   O eró (segrêdo) da Umbanda. Rio
      Silva   de Janeiro: Editôra Eco.
      n.d.

2018. Ribeiro, René   Cultos afrobrasileiros do Recife.
      1952   Recife: Gráfica Editôra do
                              Recife S/A.

2019. Rosa, Celso   Babalaôs e Ialorixás. Rio de
      1967a   Janeiro: Editôra Espiritualista,
                              Ltda.

2020. Rosa, Celso   Umbanda de caboclos. Rio de
      1967b   Janeiro: Editôra Eco.

2021. Scliar, Marcos   Umbanda magia branca. Rio de
      1971   Janeiro: Editôra Eco.

2022. Seljan, Zora, A. O.   Imanjá e suas lendas. Rio de
      1967   Janeiro: Gráfica Record Editôra.

2023. Seljan, Zora, A. O.   Iemanjá Mãe dos orixás. São
      1973   Paulo: Editôra Afro-Brasileira.

2024. Silva, W. W. da   Doutrina secreta da Umbanda. Rio
      Matta e   de Janeiro: Livraria Freitas
      1967   Bastos S.A.

2025. Silva, W. W. da   Macumbas e Candomblés na Umbanda.
      Matta e   Rio de Janeiro: Livraria Freitas
      1970   Bastos S.A.

2026. Silva, W. W. da
Matta e
1974

Umbanda de todo nós. Rio de
Janeiro: Livraria Freitas
Bastos S.A.

2027. Silva, W. W. da
Matta e
n.d.

Mistérios e práctica da lei de
Umbanda. Rio de Janeiro:
Livraria Freitas Bastos S.A.

2028. Souza, José Ribeiro de
1963

Dicionário africano de Umbanda.
Rio de Janeiro: Gráfica Editôra
Aurora, Ltda.

2029. Souza, José Ribeiro de
1969a

O ritual africano e seus
misterios. Rio de Janeiro:
Editôra Espiritualista, Ltda.

2030. Souza, José Ribeiro de
1969b

Omulu o Senhor do Cemitério.
Rio de Janeiro: Editôra Espiritualista, Ltda.

2031. Souza, José Ribeiro de
1969c

Pontos cantados nos Candomblés.
Rio de Janeiro: Editôra
Espiritualista, Ltda.

2032. Souza, José Ribeiro de
1970a

Oxalá O Médium Supremo. Rio de
Janeiro: Editôra Espiritualista,
Ltda.

2033. Souza, José Ribeiro de
1970b

Pomba-Gira mirongueira. Rio de
Janeiro: Editôra Espiritualista,
Ltda.

2034. Souza, José Ribeiro de
1972

Dicionário africano de Umbanda.
Rio de Janeiro: Editôra Espiritualista, Ltda.

2035. Souza, José Ribeiro de
1973

Culto malê. Rio de Janeiro:
Editôra Espiritualista, Ltda.

2036. Souza, José Ribeiro de
1974a

Catimbo de Zé Pilintra. Rio de
Janeiro: Editôra Espiritualista,
Ltda.

2037. Souza, José Ribeiro de,
and Celso Rosa
1974b

Trancas ruas das almas. Rio de
Janeiro: Editôra Eco.

2038. Souza, José Ribeiro de
n.d.

As festas dos eguns. Rio de
Janeiro: Editôra Eco.

2039. Souza, José Ribeiro de
n.d.

Ceremônias da Umbanda e do
Candomblé. Rio de Janeiro:
Editôra Eco.

2040. Sparta, Francisco
1970

A dança dos orixás. São Paulo:
Editôra Herder.

2041. Teixeira, Antônio Alves
1965

Umbanda dos pretos velhos. Rio
de Janeiro: Editôra Eco.

2042. Teixeira, Antônio Alves
1966

Pomba Gira. Rio de Janeiro:
Editôra Eco.

2043. Teixeira, Antônio Alves
1969a

Umbanda e suas engiras. Rio de
Janeiro: Editôra Espiritualista,
Ltda.

2044. Teixeira, Antônio Alves
1969b

Despachos e oferendas na
Umbanda. Rio de Janeiro:
Editôra Eco.

2045. Teixeira, Antônio Alves
1972

Omulu-o médico das pobres. Rio
de Janeiro: Editôra Eco.

2046. Teixeira, Antônio Alves
1973

Impressionantes casos de magia
negra. Rio de Janeiro:
Editôra Eco.

2047. Teixeira, Antônio Alves
1974

Exu-o gênio do bem e do mal.
Rio de Janeiro: Editôra Espiritualista, Ltda.

2048. Teixeira, Antônio Alves
n.d.

Oxossi (São Sebastião). Rio de
Janeiro: Editôra Eco.

2049. Teixeira, Antônio Alves
n.d.

Umbandismo. Rio de Janeiro:
Gráfica Editôra Aurora, Ltda.

2050. Varella, João
Sebastião das Chagas
1970

Orixás e obrigaçoes. Niterói:
Gráfica Vasconcellos Ltda.

2051. Varella, João
Sebastião das Chagas
1973

Ervas sagradas na Umbanda. Rio
de Janeiro: Editôra Espiritualista, Ltda.

2052. Zespo, Emanuel
1953

O que é a Umbanda? Rio de
Janeiro: Biblioteca Espiritualista Brasileira.

2053. Zespo, Emanuel
1971

777 pontos cantados e riscados
da Umbanda. Rio de Janeiro:
Editôra Espiritualista, Ltda.

2054. Zespo, Emanuel
n.d.

Pontos cantados e riscados da
Umbanda. Rio de Janeiro:
Editôra Espiritualista, Ltda.

INDICES

The indices which follow are the editors' efforts to organize this bibliography and to provide the reader with major classifications of the citations. These indices, as with the bibliography as a whole, are aimed at giving the reader only an entrée into the field. The sources sited, as well as their annotations in this bibliography, may include additional information not indexed here. Therefore, the reader is well advised to leaf through the bibliography as a whole for any topic not indexed. For example, since in virtually every citation women figure prominently, the role of women in spirit possession and spirit mediumship is so pervasive as to render an index of it redundant of the bibliography as a whole. The decision to index the specific topics below is based on the editors' assessment of professional interest in these topics, and on a significant number of relevant entries.

In order to deal with the problematic issue of spellings of foreign words, names of ethnic groups, and cult names, we have followed the orthography as it appeared in the original text. Cross-checking these original spellings with Murdock, George Peter, Africa: Its Peoples and Their Cultural History (New York: McGraw-Hill Book Co., 1959 edition), alternative spellings, wherever relevant, have been included.

Each index is comprehensive of all the citations in the bibliography relevant to the topic of the index, as outlined in the explanatory paragraph preceding it.

INDEX 1

Africa: Ethnic Groups.
(Including Political or Geographic Location.)

Listed alphabetically are African ethnic groups, with alternative names and spellings, their subunits, and political or geographic location. Ethnic Groups followed by an asterisk(*) were mentioned in the original texts but were not found in any of the standard secondary sources we used for cross-checking orthography and location of groups. Prefixes to African ethnic groups such as "Ba-," "Ma-," "Wa-," etc., have been dropped and the group appears under the first letter of the stem, i.e., "Shona" not "Mashona." The alternative spellings are listed under the main name.

Ethnic group	Alternative names and spellings	Subunits of ethnic group	Political or geographic location	Citations
Abalyhya	Abaluyia		Kenya	1827
Acholi			Uganda	195, 196, 199, 208, 662, 1309, 1447
Adangme			Benin, Ghana, Togo	570
Adhola			Uganda	1337
Akan			Ghana, Ivory Coast, Togo	54, 249, 267, 268, 449, 512, 917, 1108, 1114, 1193, 1194, 1195, 1291, 1326, 1355, 1492, 1527, 1559
Alur	Lur		Uganda, Zaire	527, 1165, 1664, 1665, 1730
Amba			Uganda	698, 1897, 1898
Ambian- iandro			Madagascar	412
Ambo			Zaire, Zambia	1678
Ambo	Ovambo		Angola, South West Africa	528, 531b, 716, 1802
Amhara			Ethiopia	1921, 1922
Anuak	Annuak		Sudan	540
Antaimoro	Antemoro		Madagascar	446
Antaisaka	Antesaka		Madagascar	446
Anyi	Agni		Ivory Coast	29, 1714
Ashanti			Ghana, Ivory Coast	16, 249, 295, 315, 424, 426, 566, 567, 568, 570, 595, 598, 698, 822, 1079, 1105, 1291, 1427, 1428, 1453, 1735, 1778, 1833, 1834
Awori			Nigeria	1065
Azande	Zande		Central Africa, Central African Empire, Sudan, Zaire	416, 474, 537, 542, 544, 949, 1107, 1108, 1356, 1388, 1406

Ethnic group	Alternative names and spellings	Subunits of ethnic group	Political or geographic location	Citations
Bachama			Nigeria	819, 1159, 1681
Bambara			Mali	350, 353, 452,
			Senegal	708, 1227, 1713
Bamileke	Bameleke, Meleke		Cameroon	501, 1054
Banda			Zaire	1812
Bandibu			Zaire	1385
Bangwa			Cameroon	252
Banya-Mwenge			Uganda	1745
Banyang			Nigeria, West Africa	1531, 1532
Baoule	Baoulé		Ivory Coast	533, 947
Bara			Madagascar	554, 555
Bari			Sudan	1267
Barwe	Wabarwe		Rhodesia	1608, 1609
Bashi			Burundi, Rwanda, Zaire	348, 1247, 1249, 1250, 1251
Bata			Nigeria	919, 1159
Baya	Gbaya		Central African Empire	1812
Bayel			Sudan	1262
Bemba			Zambia	263, 419, 786, 913, 1302, 1484, 1495, 1862, 1876
Berg Damara			Angola	1801
Bete	Bété		Ivory Coast	661, 1363, 1364
Beti			Cameroon, Equatorial Guinea	23
Betsileo	Batsileo		Madagascar	412, 492
Bhaca			South Africa	725, 727, 728
Bira			Cameroon, Equatorial Guinea	1790
Bissi			Liberia	1901
Bolia			Zaire	1789
Boma			Zaire	1587
Bondei			Tanzania	405
Bubi			Equatorial Guinea	434, 435

Ethnic group	Alternative names and spellings	Subunits of ethnic group	Political or geographic location	Citations
Budya	Babudja Budjga VaBudjga Wabudya		Rhodesia	36, 1234, 1257, 1622
Bulu	Boulou		Cameroon, Equatorial Guinea	23
Bushmen	San		Botswana, South Africa, South West Africa, Southern Africa	190, 200, 463, 709
		Gcwi		312
		Kung		698, 995, 1127, 1128, 1729, 1791
		Zhû/-twâsi		190, 884, 885
Chaga	Chagga		Tanzania	1299
Chewa	Cewa Cêwa Chêwa		Central Africa, Malawi, Mozambique, Rhodesia, Zambia	474, 960, 961, 962, 1048, 1050, 1141, 1396, 1434, 1572, 1573, 1783
Chiga	Bakiga Kiga		Uganda, Zaire	172b, 259, 494, 698, 1245, 1439, 1485
Chikwaka			Zambia	650
Chokwe	Cokwe Tchokwe Tehokwe		Angola, Zaire, Zambia	123, 124, 526, 753, 1795, 1829, 1872
Chonyi			Kenya	867
Chopi			Mozambique	1396
Dagomba			Ghana	1700
Danda	Wadondo		Rhodesia	1175
Darasa			Ethiopia	1156
Datwenawa			Niger	1018
Dida			Ivory Coast	796, 999
Digo			East Africa, Kenya	657b, 673
Dikidiki			Burundi, Rwanda, Zaire	979
Dilling			Sudan	1684
Dinka			Sudan	705, 1046, 1109, 1156, 1584, 1585, 1615, 1882

Ethnic group	Alternative names and Spellings	Subunits of ethnic group	Political or geographic location	Citations
		Padang Dinka		157, 207
Diola	Dyola		Senegal	350, 353, 708, 895, 1228
Dogon			Mali, Upper Volta	451, 1010, 1351, 1735
Dolbo-hanta	Dulba-hente		Somalia	1033
Duala			Cameroon	289
Dushane	imiDushane		South Africa	726
Dye	Dyé		Togo	615
Edo	Benin		Nigeria	966
Effutu			Ghana	1916
Efik			Nigeria	1702
Ekoi			Nigeria	1702
Enga	Baenga Baenya		Congo, Zaire	56
Ewe			Benin, Ghana, Togo, West Africa	425, 513, 584, 1355
Fang	Pahouin		Cameroon, Equatorial Guinea, Gabon	23, 71, 558, 981, 1735, 1889
Fanti	Fante		Ghana	261, 337
Fipa	Wafipa		Tanzania, Uganda	1299, 1380, 1494, 1879, 1881, 1882
Fő			Benin	1556
Fon	Dahomey Dan-homê Lake Dahomey		Benin, Nigeria, Senegal, Togo, West Africa	14, 20, 86, 100, 233, 255, 327, 403, 511, 676, 721, 760, 761, 765, 779, 1174, 1176, 1187, 1351, 1357, 1557, 1709, 1735, 1810
Fulani	Peul		Senegal	350, 353, 455, 708
Ga	Gã		Ghana	564, 567, 569, 570, 578, 733, 822, 908, 909, 910, 911, 912, 914, 935, 1291, 1356, 1357

Ethnic group	Alternative names and spellings	Subunits of ethnic group	Political or geographic location	Citations
Galla	Gaila		Ethiopia	33
		Macha Galla		925
		Shoa Galla		1031
Ganda	Baganda Buganda Keganda Kiganda		East Africa, Tanzania, Uganda	258, 373, 553, 577, 609, 698, 875, 897, 913, 917, 1063, 1072, 1074, 1106, 1150, 1156, 1246, 1297, 1310, 1311, 1328, 1358, 1381, 1457, 1501, 1504, 1509, 1510, 1589, 1668, 1669, 1717, 1833, 1850, 1851, 1853
Garwe	Vagarwe		Rhodesia	1384
Gbande			Liberia, Sierra Leone	440
Gbundi	Gbunde		Liberia, Sierra Leone	1053
Gcaleke			Rhodesia	1084
Ge	Mina		Benin, Togo	1374, 1556
Gidole			Ethiopia	331
Giryama	Giriama		Kenya	1293, 1346
Gisu	Bagesu Bagishu Gishu		Uganda	876, 948, 1504, 1508
Godye	Godię Godie		Ivory Coast	661, 927
Goemai			Nigeria	1616
Gogo			Tanzania	1311, 1490
Guha	Bagua Bagwe		Tanzania	632
Gun			Benin, Nigeria, Togo	1709
Gurage			Ethiopia	1022, 1038, 1594, 1595, 1596
Guro	Gouro		Ivory Coast	437, 1280

Ethnic group	Alternative names and spellings	Subunits of ethnic group	Political or geographic location	Citations
Gusii	Kisii		Kenya, Uganda	1298, 1889, 1903, 1904
Gwambe			South Africa	622
Ha			Tanzania	379, 1299, 1567, 1605
Hadjerai	Haderay		Chad	621, 1820
Hangaza			Tanzania	1299
Hausa			Benin, Niger, Nigeria	2, 179, 180, 249, 271, 345, 520, 929, 972, 1034, 1055, 1163, 1213, 1225, 1266, 1283, 1284, 1315, 1354, 1538, 1539, 1540, 1655, 1656, 1657, 1735, 1751, 1752, 1755
		Goberawa	Niger	1018
		Maguzawa	Nigeria	686, 700
Haya	Bahaya Baziba Kiziba Ziba		Tanzania, Uganda	172b, 1077, 1236, 1295, 1299
Hehe			Tanzania	274, 498, 698, 1463
Hera			Rhodesia	600
Herero			Angola	500
Heviosso*			Benin, Nigeria	685
Hima	Bahima		Uganda	1502
Hlengwe			Rhodesia	819
Hunde	Bahunde		Zaire	1814
Hungana			Burundi, Rwanda, Zaire	979
Hutu	Hum		Burundi, Rwanda, Zaire	777, 979
Ibibio			Nigeria	855, 1701
		Anang Ibibio		1179, 1180, 1181
Ibo			Nigeria	415, 503, 839, 854, 861
Idoma			Nigeria	49
Ife			Nigeria	1680

390

Ethnic group	Alternative names and spellings	Subunits of ethnic group	Political or geo- graphic location	Citations
Igala			Nigeria	221
Igbira			Nigeria	280
Igbo			Nigeria	844, 1290
		Aro		842
Ijaw	Ijo			
	Ịjọ		Nigeria	19
		Egbena		
		Ịjọ		1740
Ila	Baila		Zambia	793, 1610,
	Ba-Ila			1759
Isala	Sisala		Ghana	1168
Isoko			Nigeria	251, 1856
Iwa			Zambia	1519
Jita			Tanzania	1299
Jonam			Uganda	1535
Jukun			Nigeria, Sudan	1160
Kabre	Kabrè		Togo	615
Kadero	Kadaru		Sudan	1684
Kaffa			Sudan	797
Kaguru			Tanzania	158, 160
Kalabari			Nigeria	39, 809, 810, 811, 812, 813, 815, 816, 817, 1109, 1703, 1711
Kalanga	Amakalanga Makalaka Makalanga		Rhodesia, South Africa	154, 290, 344, 600, 718, 801, 1314, 1446, 1699, 1858
Kamba	Akamba		Kenya	498, 788, 789, 1038, 1047, 1198, 1201, 1277, 1311
Kamberi			Nigeria	1539
Kanda	Okanda		Zaire	202
Kanuri			Nigeria	49
Karanga	Karonga Vakaranga		Mozambique, Rhodesia, Zambia	5, 35, 36, 45, 46, 47, 332, 600, 649, 657a, 819, 1049, 1261, 1433, 1451, 1848, 1849
Kasanga			Zaire	1674
Kerebe			Tanzania	743, 1299
Kerewe			Tanzania, Uganda	1761
Keyu	Elgeyo		Kenya	1145

Ethnic group	Alternative names and spellings	Subunits of ethnic group	Political or geographic location	Citations
Khoi-khoi	Hottentot		South Africa	744
Kikuyu	Akikuyu Gikuyu		Kenya, Tanzania	698, 744, 789, 891, 892, 1156, 1260, 1311, 1539, 1850
Kimbu			Tanzania	7, 1604, 1605
Kingwe*	Bakingwe		Uganda	66
Kirdi			Nigeria	966
Kissi			Guinea, Ivory Coast, Liberia, Senegal	795, 1362
Koalib			Sudan	1683
Kololo	Makololo		Rhodesia, Zambia	1564
Kongo	Bakongo Bokongo Congo		Angola, Congo, Zaire	70, 71, 75, 127, 283, 284, 370, 489, 527, 782, 783, 850, 951, 1092, 1093, 1094a, 1094b, 1248, 1251, 1446, 1461, 1549, 1688, 1797, 1798, 1839, 1880
Konkomba			Togo	615
Konnawa			Niger	271
Kono			Guinea	794
Konongo			Tanzania	7
Konso			Ethiopia	331, 719
Korekore	Makore- kore		Rhodesia	228, 229, 230, 311, 600, 620, 627, 628, 629, 641, 657a
Kota	Bakota		Gabon, Rhodesia, Zambia	1383, 1564
Kotoko			Chad	992
Kpelle			Liberia	1329, 1901
Kran	Krã		Liberia	738
Krobo			Benin, Ghana, Togo	824
Kuba			Zaire	783, 786, 1793, 1794, 1796

Ethnic group	Alternative names and spellings	Subunits of ethnic group	Political or geographic location	Citations
Kukuya			Congo	215
Kulu	Kulũ		Nigeria	1162
Kuluwe	Wakuluwe		Malawi	1166
Kumam			Uganda	534, 1535
Kumu			Zaire	188
Kutshu	Bakutshu N'Kutshu		Zaire	257, 1787
Kwangwa	Makwangwa		Zambia	937
Labadi			Ghana	1425
Lala	Balala		Zaire	952
Lamba			Togo	457, 615
Lamba			Zambia	526, 753, 913, 1650, 1861
Lambo*	Balambo		Zaire	878
Lango			Kenya, Uganda	33, 195, 751, 1156, 1447, 1708
Lebu	Lebou Lebou		Gambia, Senegal	67, 68, 350, 353, 354, 355, 356, 455, 624, 691, 708, 896, 1196, 1228, 1289, 1331, 1577, 1618, 1619, 1620, 1732, 1735, 1925, 1926, 1928, 1931
Lele	Bashilele		Central Africa, Zaire	472, 473, 474, 477, 964, 1109, 1882
Lenge	Lenje		Zambia	1038, 1650
Lobi			Ghana	448
Lokele			Zaire	991
Loko	Lokko		Sierra Leone	1086
Londo	Balonda Londe		Angola	1564
Lovedu			South Africa	783, 932, 933
Lozi	Barotse Malozi		Zambia	665, 666, 937, 1255, 1472, 1768
Luapula			Zambia	399
Luba	Baluba Louba		South Africa, Zaire	216, 219, 294, 526, 527, 753, 783, 786, 966, 1327, 1725, 1726, 1829, 1923

Ethnic group	Alternative names and spellings	Subunits of ethnic group	Political or geographic location	Citations
Lubale	Malubale		Angola, Zambia	937
Luchazi			Zaire, Zambia	1872
Lugbara			Congo, Zaire, Zambia	916, 1038, 1107, 1156, 1197, 1199, 1200, 1202, 1203, 1204, 1206, 1207
Luguru	Uluguru		Tanzania	1565
Lulua	Bena Lulua		Zaire	527, 1085, 1923
Lumbu	Bilumbu		Zaire	527
Lunda			Zaire, Zambia	786, 1087, 1167, 1769, 1795, 1872
Lungu	Beni-Marungu		Zaire	881
Luo	Jaluo		East Africa, Kenya, Tanzania, Uganda	198, 1038, 1296, 1299, 1382, 1447, 1853, 1855, 1869, 1889, 1903
Lusa	Balusa		Zaire	1251
Luvale	Balovale Lwena		Central Africa, Malawi, Zaire, Zambia	474, 1667, 1795, 1872, 1873, 1874, 1889
Makua			Tanzania	1299
Malinke	Mandingo Mandingue		Liberia, Senegal	350, 1900
Mambo			Rhodesia	36
Manganja	Mang'anja		Malawi, Mozambique	1435, 1569, 1571, 1574
Manianga			Zaire	1385
Manja			Zaire	1812
Mankanya	Mancagne		Senegal	1756
Mano			Liberia, Sierra Leone	1053
Manyika			Rhodesia	657a
Maravi	Amaravi Maraves		Malawi	609, 1450
Marina			Madagascar	1142
Masa	Massa		Cameroon	1015
Masai			Kenya, Tanzania	804, 1293, 1311

394

Ethnic group	Alternative names and spellings	Subunits of ethnic group	Political or geographic location	Citations
Masasi			Tanzania	1444
Mawri*			Niger	1389
Mbagani			Zaire	1795
Mbaka	M'baka		Central African Empire	459
Mbala	Bambala		Zaire, Zambia	527, 793
Mbandja	Mbanja		Zaire	292, 1795
Mbedzi			Rhodesia	600
Mbim*	Mbîm Mbiem		Zaire	1586, 1587, 1727
Mbire			Rhodesia	600
Mbowe	Mambowe		Zambia	937
Mbukushu	Hambukushu		Zambia	971
Mbula			Nigeria	919
Mbundu	Ovimbundu		Angola	722, 746, 1088, 1758
Mende			Liberia, Sierra Leone	698, 742, 1052, 1053, 1086
Meru			Kenya	1156
Milembwe	Bamilembwe		Zaire	1672
Mitsogo	Mitsogho		Gabon	671, 672, 1735
Moba			Togo	615
Mofu			Cameroon	1819
Mongo			Congo, Zaire	56, 1251, 1533
Montol			Nigeria	1616
Mora			Cameroon	966
Moru			Sudan	126, 1156
Mossi	Mosi		Upper Volta	436, 1034, 1735
Mum	Bamum		Cameroon	1156
Mundang	Moundang		Chad	1929
Murle			Sudan	1030
Nago			Benin, Nigeria	20, 1693
Nandi			Kenya	805
Ndau	vaNdau		Central Africa, Mozambique, Rhodesia, South Africa	204, 206, 494, 495, 783, 872, 873, 1378, 1396, 1467
Ndebele	Amandebele Matabele		Rhodesia	36, 40, 154, 187, 203, 288, 395, 409, 429, 800, 823, 826, 880, 941, 1156, 1279, 1287, 1436, 1530, 1736,1889,1935

Ethnic group	Alternative names and spellings	Subunits of ethnic group	Political or geographic location	Citations
Ndembu			Angola, Central Africa, Rhodesia, Southern Africa	474, 1107, 1406, 1446, 1603, 1771, 1772, 1773, 1774, 1775, 1776, 1777, 1894
Ndogo			Sudan	1548
Ngbaka			Zaire	292, 1593, 1795
Ngbandi			Zaire	292, 1795
Ngere	Guere		Ivory Coast	225, 661, 1815
Ngizim			Nigeria	1161
Ngombe	Bangombe		Zaire	292, 1673,1911
Ngondi	Konde		Malawi, Zambia	1096, 1610
Ngoni	Ngona		Central Africa, Malawi, Rhodesia, South Africa, Southern Africa, Zambia	22, 495, 515, 557, 600, 1454, 1462
Ngoro			Cameroon	26
Ngungela			Angola	124
Nguni			South Africa, Southern Africa	711, 730, 731, 732, 1894
Nkole	Ankole Banyankole		Kenya, Uganda	74, 917, 1503, 1507, 1856
Nkouna*			Angola	433
Nkoya			Zambia	193
Nsenga	Senga		Central Africa, Zambia	605, 1253
Ntinde	amaNtinde		South Africa	726
Ntomba	Ntómbá		Zaire	1789
Nuba	Nouba		Egypt, Sudan	124, 749, 783, 888, 889, 1038, 1294, 1537
Nuer			Sudan	207, 298, 375, 439, 536, 538, 541, 543, 698, 821, 1029, 1109, 1585,1666, 1878, 1882

Ethnic group	Alternative names and spellings	Subunits of ethnic group	Political or geographic location	Citations
Nupe			Nigeria	589
Nyakyusa	Nyakusa		Tanzania, Southern Africa	372, 1000, 1093, **1299**, 1892, 1894, 1915
Nyambo			Tanzania	1299
Nyamwezi			Tanzania	7, 380, 1299, 1604, 1605
Nyaneka	Nhyneka-Humba Nyaneka-Humbe		Angola	433, 526, 528, 531a, 573
Nyanja			Tanzania	1299
Nyiha			Tanzania	265
Nyima	Nyamang Nyimang		Sudan	698, 934
Nyombgwe	WaNayombgwe WaNyombgwe		Rhodesia	750
Nyoro	Banyoro Bunyoro		Uganda	72, 73, 74, 130, 131, 132, 133, 134, 135, 136, 137, 138, 139, 140, 141, 142, 143, 144, 145, 146, 147, 148, 151, 152, 153, 487, 517, 689, 698, 1038, 1108, 1113, 1272, 1273, 1381, 1503, 1505, 1506, 1716
Nzakara			Central African Empire, Congo	978, 1468, 1469, 1470, 1812
Nzima	Nzema N'zima		Ghana, Ivory Coast	428, 706, 707
Omiéné			Gabon	748
Padhola			Uganda	1304, 1597
Panda	Kwotto		Nigeria	1896
Pare			Kenya, Tanzania	1299, 1311, 1605
Pedi			Rhodesia, South Africa, Southern Africa	600, 731, 1266, 1580

Ethnic group	Alternative names and spellings	Subunits of ethnic group	Political or geographic location	Citations
Pemba			Kenya, Tanzania	695, 1891
Pende	Bapende		Rhodesia, Zaire	527, 1663, 1829
Pogoro	Pagoro Wapogoro		Tanzania, Uganda	1, 857, 1076, 1104
Pondo	Mpondo		South Africa, Southern Africa	731, 828, 1038, 1893
Puni	Apindji		Gabon	1695
Qhayi	imiQhayi		South Africa	726
Reshe	Gungawa		Nigeria	1540
Rimi			Tanzania	1721
Rolong	Barolong		Botswana, South Africa	326
Romwe			Rhodesia	1614
Ronga	Baronga		South Africa	869, 870
Rovouma			Angola	124
Rozwi	Rozvi Warozwi		Rhodesia	600, 823, 1451
		Sangaan		823
Ruanda	Banyaruanda Banyarwanda Nyarwanda Rwanda		Malawi, Rwanda, Tanzania, Zaire	181, 781, 784, 874, 958, 1109, 1115, 1247, 1250, 1251, 1299, 1369, 1370, 1371
Rundi	Barundi Burundi		Burundi	611, 1109, 1247, 1250, 1934
Runga			Tanzania	1299
Ruri			Tanzania	1299
Ruund			Zaire	1795
Sabei	Mbai Sebei		Uganda	599
Sakalava	Sakalave		Madagascar	631, 1336, 1534
Sakata	Basakata		Congo, Zaire	300, 347, 527, 1587
Sala	Basala		Zambia	793
Sandawe			Tanzania	1721
Sangu	Sango		Zaire	1812
Sara			Chad, Uganda	551, 1513
Sebei			Kenya, Uganda	498, 1840
Segeju			Tanzania	696, 697
Sena			Malawi, Mozambique	1569

Ethnic group	Alternative names and spellings	Subunits of ethnic group	Political or geographic location	Citations
Sengele	Séngele		Zaire	1789
Serer	Sérer		Gambia,	167, 168, 350
	Sérèr		Senegal	353, 455, 624,
	Sereer			691, 692, 693,
	Sérère			694, 708, 896,
				1228, 1289,
				1331, 1733,
				1735
Shilluk			Egypt,	298, 539, 820,
			Sudan	1045
Shioko	Batshioko		Zaire	216
Shona	Mashona		Central	6, 40, 48, 124,
			Africa,	129, 174, 175,
			Rhodesia	176, 187, 210,
				211, 286, 287,
				288, 291, 394,
				395, 396, 407,
				409, 410, 411,
				526, 580, 600,
				625, 626, 634,
				635, 636, 637,
				638, 639, 640,
				642, 643, 644,
				645, 646, 647,
				648, 651, 652,
				653, 655, 656,
				753, 802, 823,
				827, 880, 941,
				975, 976, 1102,
				1103, 1138,
				1144, 1147,
				1178, 1243,
				1256, 1279,
				1404, 1436,
				1437, 1438,
				1439, 1441,
				1445, 1446,
				1448, 1451,
				1460, 1610,
				1663, 1676,
				1748, 1776,
				1785, 1786,
				1889, 1914,
				1935
		Enhla		941
		Lozwi		941
		Zanzi		941
Sibisi			South Africa	1817
Sidamo			Ethiopia	266, 724, 1056

Ethnic group	Alternative names and spellings	Subunits of ethnic group	Political or geographic location	Citations
Soga	Basoga		Uganda	551, 552, 1503
Somali			Ethiopia, Somali	1036, 1037
Songe	Bassonge		Zaire	1923
Songhai	Songay Songhay Sonrai		Benin, Mali, Niger, Sudan	2, 34, 226, 490, 720, 781, 1034, 1521, 1522, 1524, 1525, 1526, 1735
Sori	Vasori		Rhodesia	1875
Sotho	Basotho Basuto Suto		Botswana, South Africa, Southern Africa	52, 53, 326, 343, 491, 506, 731, 931, 985, 1259, 1580, 1598, 1833
Subi	Shubi		Tanzania	1299
Suk	Pokot		Kenya	498
Suku	Basuka		Zaire	1586
Sukuma	Sakuma		Tanzania	7, 378, 380, 783, 1212, 1299, 1605, 1705, 1706, 1707
Sukwa	Basukwa		Malawi	958
Sumbwa	Sumba		Tanzania, Uganda	7, 74, 379, 1299, 1605
Swahili			Tanzania	124, 314, 526
Swazi			Swaziland	81, 159, 161, 596, 913, 938, 939, 940, 944, 1580
Tallensi			Ghana	598, 698
Tande	Vatande		Rhodesia	1148
Tawara	Tavara Watawara		Rhodesia	36, 120, 229, 232, 600
Teita	Taita		Kenya	739, 1038
Teke			Zaire	1587
		Teke Tsaayi		488
Tembu			South Africa	977
Temne			Sierra Leone	423, 461, 462, 1100
Teso			East Africa, Kenya, Uganda	984
Tetela	Batetela		Zaire	527

Ethnic group	Alternative names and spellings	Subunits of ethnic group	Political or geographic location	Citations
Thonga	Bathonga Batonga Tonga		Central Africa, Mozambique, Rhodesia, South Africa, Southern Africa, Zambia	367, 744, 781, 783, 852, 871, 1038, 1083, 1244, 1396, 1739, 1849b
		Gwembe Tonga		365, 368a, 368b
		Inhambane Thonga		1467
		Plateau Tonga		360, 361, 363, 364, 366, 368b, 474
		Shangana Tonga		306, 791, 932, 1580
		Valley Tonga		1036
Tiriki			Kenya	1547
Togbo			Central African Empire	978
Toro	Batooro Batoro Tooro		Uganda	877
Torwa			Rhodesia	600
Tsonga			Mozambique, South Africa	731, 859, 860
Tswa	Batswa		Mozambique	1378, 1396
Tswana	Bechuana Twana		Botswana, Rhodesia, South Africa, Southern Africa	275, 463, 600, 744, 1156, 1365, 1580
Tuareg			Mali, Niger	605,1282,1496
Tuburi	Toupouri Tupuri		Cameroon, Nigeria	1015
Tukulor	Toucouleur Tukulër		Senegal	350, 353, 455, 708, 1289
Tumbuka			Central Africa, Malawi	1783
Turkana			Kenya	698, 1156
Tutsi	Batutsi Watutsi		Rwanda, Zaire	777, 1575

401

Ethnic group	Alternative names and spellings	Subunits of ethnic group	Political or geographic location	Citations
Twa	Batwa		Rwanda, Zambia	777, 793
Urhobo			Nigeria	251
Venda	Bavenda		Rhodesia, South Africa	201, 344, 510, 600, 731, 1038, 1446,1675,1835
Vezi			Madagascar	521
Vezo			Madagascar	1211
Vili	Loango		Congo, Zaire	715
Wasu			East Africa	414
Wembe			Zambia	687
Wolof			Gambia, Senegal	86, 350, 353, 355, 356, 455, 460, 624, 708, 896, 1196, 1330, 1331, 1332, 1576, 1577, 1732, 1735, 1925, 1926, 1927, 1928, 1930, 1931
Xosa	amaXosa Xhosa		South Africa, Southern Africa	584, 731, 851, 1153, 1222, 1368, 1580,1661
		Qaba		270
Xwala			Benin	1556
Yaka	Maiaca		Angola, Zaire	1208, 1586, 1829
Yako	Yakö		Nigeria	591, 1109
Yanzi	Bayansi Yansi		Zaire	441, 527, 1586, 1587
		Bakeni		1587
		Nsala-Mbanda		1587
Yao			Central Africa, Malawi, Mozambique, Rhodesia, Tanzania	474, 1860
Yauri			Nigeria	740
Yombe			Zambia	213
Yoruba			Benin, Nigeria, Togo, West Africa	11, 12, 51, 87, 93, 100, 119, 122, 162, 163, 164, 165, 416, 513, 514, 522

Ethnic group	Alternative names and spellings	Subunits of ethnic group	Political or geographic location	Citations
				523, 546, 547, 548, 550, 781, 783, 808, 833, 834, 913, 917, 968, 982, 1004, 1005, 1055, 1066, 1080, 1097, 1099, 1163, 1187, 1192, 1228, 1239, 1240, 1241, 1242, 1300, 1348, 1350, 1352, 1355, 1375, 1376, 1400, 1413, 1414, 1415, 1416, 1419, 1420, 1422, 1555, 1556, 1631, 1632, 1670, 1709, 1735, 1804, 1807, 1809, 1810, 1863
Zaramo			Ethiopia, Tanzania	837, 1694
Zavala			Mozambique	1464
Zerma			Benin, Niger	2, 490, 720, 1173, 1390, 1391
Zezuru			Rhodesia	600, 620, 657a
Zigua	Wazigua		Tanzania	125
Zinza			Tanzania, Uganda	1299
Zulu			South Africa, Southern Africa	80, 170, 172b, 282, 305, 306, 560, 563, 664, 667, 668, 669, 698, 731, 856, 869, 870, 926, 930, 996, 997, 1038, 1060, 1069, 1281b, 1294, 1318, 1427, 1580, 1610, 1611, 1691, 1779, 1780, 1832, 1885

Africa: Miscellaneous Groups.

Included in this index are groups mentioned in the
original texts, which are: 1) religious brotherhoods,
e.g., Ḥamadsha; 2) religious groups, e.g., Hindu; 3)
generic names for large linguistic groups, e.g., Bantu;
and 4) generic names for populations, e.g., Berber.

Group	Alternative name or subunit	Political or geographic location	Citations
Aisaoua		Algeria, Morocco, Tunisia	483, 688, 1839
Arab	Shaiquiya	North Africa, Sudan	849, 1221
Bantu		Cameroon, Congo, Gabon, Kenya, Nigeria, Rhodesia, South Africa, Zaire	217, 306, 496, 502, 574, 731, 791, 1019, 1061, 1117, 1146, 1224, 1367, 1386, 1471, 1528, 1599, 1692, 1741, 1743, 1826, 1912
Berber		North Africa	13, 1028
Derquaoua		Morocco	1839
Falascha		Ethiopia	13
Gnaoua		Morocco	1839
Ḥamadsha		Morocco	249, 388, 389, 393
Hindu		Malawi, Rhodesia, South Africa, Uganda, Zambia	471, 942, 943, 1164
Kaffir	Kafir	South Africa	281, 799, 856, 1024, 1098, 1602, 1857, 1887
Nomads		Niger	2
Oman		Egypt	330

Africa: Ethnic Groups in Political Units.

Listed alphabetically are the political units and
the ethnic groups found within them.   Each country is
designated by its standard name as of 1977, except for
Rhodesia-Zimbabwe and South West Africa-Namibia which
are listed under Rhodesia and South West Africa respec-
tively.

The citations which in some cases follow the name
of the country include:

1) Sources that do not mention a specific ethnic
group but do refer to the population of the
country as a whole.

2) Sources that describe populations in very general terms, such as the "Bantu."

3) Sources that discuss colonial and post-colonial
religious movements and independent African
churches which may draw their adherents from a
variety of ethnic groups within a political
unit. These sources are also listed in Index
14.

The scholar should note that some ethnic groups appear in countries other than those in which they are
traditionally located. This is due to a variety of
reasons, among which are: changing political boundaries
in contemporary Africa, and rural-urban and international
migration patterns. The standard reference for the traditional location of ethnic groups in Africa is Murdock,
George Peter, Africa: Its Peoples and Their Cultural
History (New York: McGraw-Hill Book Co., 1959 edition).

POLITICAL UNIT/Ethnic Group   Citation

ABYSSINIA   (under Ethiopia)
ALGERIA,   Democratic and Popular
             Republic of   34, 483, 1424
ANGOLA,   People's Republic of   468, 530, 747, 973,
                                    1473, 1483, 1549
             Ambo (Ovambo)   528, 531b, 716
             Berg Damara   1801
             Chokwe (Cokwe,
                     Tehokwe)   123, 124, 526, 753
             Herero   500
             Kongo (Bakongo)   1248, 1251, 1549
             Londa (Balonda)   1564
             Mbundu (Ovimbundu)   722, 746, 1088, 1758
             Ngungela   124
             Nkouna   433
             Nyaneka-Humbe   433, 526, 528, 531a,
                                    753
             Rovouma   124
             Yaka (Maiaca)   1208
BAROTSELAND (under Zambia, Republic of)
BECHUANALAND (under Botswana, Republic of)
BENIN,   People's Republic of   425, 741, 1067, 1351,
             (formerly Dahomey)   1555, 1591
             Ewe   425, 584
             Fõ   1556

405

POLITICAL UNIT/Ethnic Group	Citation
Fon (Dahomey, Dan- homê, Lake Dahomey)	14, 20, 100, 233, 255, 327, 403, 448, 511, 676, 721, 760, 761, 765, 779, 1174, 1176, 1351, 1357, 1557, 1709, 1735, 1810
Ge (Gɛ)	1556
Gun	1709
Hausa	1055
Heviosso	685
Nago	20, 1693
Songhai (Sonrai)	226
Xwla	1556
Yoruba	100, 122, 514, 550, 917, 1055, 1228, 1240, 1555, 1556, 1709, 1735, 1804, 1807, 1810
Zerma	1173
BOTSWANA, Republic of (formerly Bechuanaland)	1365
Bushmen (Gcwi, Kung, San, Zhû/twâsi)	190, 200, 312, 463, 710, 884, 885, 995, 1729, 1791
Tswana (Bechuana, Twana)	463, 1156, 1365
BURUNDI, Republic of (formerly Urundi)	216, 710
Dikidiki	979
Hungana	979
Hutu (Hum)	979
Rundi (Barundi)	611, 1109, 1247, 1252, 1934
CAMEROON, United Republic of	778, 1019, 1110, 1693
Bamileke (Bameleke, Meleke)	501, 1054
Bangwa	252
Beti	23
Bulu (Boulou)	23
Duala	289
Fang	23
Masa (Massa)	1015
Mofu	1819
Moru	966
Ngoro	26
Tuburi (Toupouri)	1015
CENTRAL AFRICAN EMPIRE (formerly Central African Republi‹	
Baya (Gbaya)	1812
Mbaka (M'baka)	459
Nzakara	978, 1468, 1469, 1470, 1812
Togbo	978
CENTRAL AFRICAN REPUBLIC (under Central African Empire)	
CHAD, Republic of	1110

POLITICAL UNIT/Ethnic Group   Citation

        Hadjerai   621, 1820
        Kotoko   992
        Mundang (Moundang)   1929
        Sara   1513
CONGO, The Belgian (under Zaire, Republic of)
CONGO, People's Republic of the   70, 576, 658, 715,
        (formerly French Equatorial 1019, 1516, 1579
        Africa)
        Bashi   1250
        Enga (Baenga)   56
        Kukuya   215
        Mongo   56
        Nzakara   1469, 1812
        Sakata (Basakata)   300
DAHOMEY, Republic of (under Benin,
        People's Republic of)
DJIBOUTI (formerly French Territory
        of the Afars and Issas)   980
EGYPT, Arab Republic of   3, 4, 285, 330, 549,
                                     957, 1067, 1278, 1307,
                                     1308, 1497, 1498,1558,
                                     1582, 1737
        Nuba   888
        Shilluk   298
EQUATORIAL GUINEA (formerly
        Spanish Guinea)   674
        Beti   23
        Bubi   434, 435
        Bulu (Boulou)   23
        Fang   23
ETHIOPIA (formerly Abyssinia)   4, 13, 249, 307, 329,
                                     330, 493, 595, 614,
                                     659, 703, 713, 717,
                                     806, 1006, 1007, 1008,
                                     1009, 1012, 1013, 1021,
                                     1023, 1055, 1124, 1182,
                                     1237, 1238, 1347, 1499,
                                     1515, 1552, 1558, 1689,
                                     1735, 1746, 1747, 1754,
                                     1828
        Amhara   1051, 1921, 1922
        Darasa   1156
        Galla (Gaila, Shoa
                Galla)   33, 925, 1031
        Gidole   331
        Gurage   1022, 1038, 1594,
                                     1595, 1596
        Konso   331, 719
        Sidamo   266, 724, 1056
        Somali   1036
        Zaramo   1684
FRENCH EQUATORIAL AFRICA (under Congo, People's
        Republic of the)

                            407

POLITICAL UNIT/Ethnic Group	Citation

FRENCH SUDAN (under Mali, Republic of)
FRENCH TERRITORY OF THE AFARS AND
  ISSAS (under Djibouti)

GABON Republic	562, 674, 1019, 1452, 1696
Fang (Pahouin)	71, 558, 981, 1735, 1889
Kota (Bakota)	1383
Mitsogo	671, 672, 1735
Omiéné	748
Puni (Apindji)	1695
GAMBIA, The	
Serer	624
Wolof	624
GHANA, Republic of (formerly Gold Coast)	63, 64, 156, 249, 260, 261, 268, 424, 425, 565, 570, 571, 593, 594, 613, 923, 965, 1034, 1292, 1324, 1325, 1411, 1493, 1546, 1744, 1846, 1917
Adangme	570
Akan	54, 249, 267, 268, 449, 512, 917, 1108, 1114, 1193, 1194, 1195, 1291, 1326, 1355, 1492
Ashanti	16, 249, 295, 315, 424, 426, 566, 567, 568, 570, 595, 598, 698, 761, 822, 1079, 1105, 1291, 1427, 1428, 1453, 1735, 1778, 1833, 1834
Baoule (Baoulé)	947
Dagomba	1700
Effutu	1916
Ewe	425, 1355
Fanti	261, 337
Ga (Gã)	564, 567, 569, 570, 578, 733, 822, 908, 909, 910, 911, 912, 914, 935, 1114, 1291, 1356, 1357
Isala (Sisala)	1168
Krobo	824
Labadi	1425
Lobi	448
Nzima (Nzema)	428, 706, 707
Tallensi	598, 698
GOLD COAST, (under Ghana, Republic of)	
GUINEA, Republic of	832, 1027
Kissi	795, 1362
Kono	794

POLITICAL UNIT/Ethnic Group	Citation
IVORY COAST, Republic of the	27, 60, 445, 532, 661, 894, 1001, 1364, 1395, 1527
Akan	917, 1527, 1559
Anyi (Agni)	28, 1714
Ashanti	1428, 1778
Baoule (Baoulé)	533
Bete (Bété)	661, 1363, 1364
Dida	796, 999
Godye (Godie, Godié)	661, 927
Guro (Gouro)	437, 1280
Ngere (Guéré)	225, 661, 1815
KENYA, Republic of	918, 1260, 1303, 1382, 1456, 1552, 1826, 1850, 1854, 1855, 1889, 1903
Abalyhya (Abaluyia)	1827
Chonyi	867
Digo	673
Giryama (Giriama)	1293, 1346
Gusii (Kisii)	1889, 1903, 1904
Haya (Kiziba)	1077
Kamba (Akamba)	498, 786, 789, 1038, 1047, 1198, 1201, 1277
Keyu (Elgeyo)	1145
Kikuyu (Akikuyu, Gikuyu)	698, 744, 789, 891, 892, 1156, 1260, 1529, 1850
Lango	1447
Lenge (Lenje)	1038
Luo	192, 1038, 1296, 1382, 1447, 1855, 1869, 1889, 1903
Masai	804, 1293
Meru	1156
Nandi	805
Nkole (Ankole)	1855
Pare	1605
Sebei	1840
Suk (Pokot)	498
Teita (Taita)	739, 1038
Tiriki	1547
Turkana	698, 1156
LIBERIA, Republic of	603, 736, 737, 1612, 1899, 1902, 1910
Bissi	1901
Gbande	440
Gbundi (Gbunde)	1053
Kpelle	1329, 1901
Kran (Krã)	738
Malinke (Mandingo)	1901
Mano	1053
Mende	1053
MADAGASCAR, Democratic Republic of	43, 96, 346, 427, 447, 734, 1101, 1223, 1430, 1613, 1816

POLITICAL UNIT/Ethnic Group　　　Citation

Ambianiandro	412
Antaimoro (Antemoro)	446
Antaisaka (Antesaka)	446
Bara	554, 555
Betsileo (Batsileo)	412, 492
Marina	1142
Sakalava (Sakalave)	631, 1336, 1534
Vezi	521
Vezo	1211
MALAWI, Republic of (formerly	471, 606, 863, 1570,
Nyasaland)	1906
Chewa (Cewa, Cêwa,	960, 961, 962, 1048,
Chêwa)	1050, 1141, 1434,
	1572, 1573, 1783
Guha (Bagwe)	632
Haya (Bahaya)	1236
Karanga (Karonga)	1049
Kuluwe (Wakuluwe)	1166
Manganja (Mang'anja)	1435, 1569, 1571, 1574
Maravi (Amaravi)	609, 1450
Ngondi (Konde)	1096
Ngoni	1454, 1462
Ruanda (Rwanda)	781
Sena	1569
Sukwa (Basukwa)	958
Tumbuka	1783
MALI, Republic of (formerly	
French Sudan)	702
Bambara	452, 1227, 1713
Dogon	451, 1010, 1735
Songhai	34
Tuareg	1282, 1496
MOROCCO, Kingdom of the West	3, 95, 223, 249, 335,
	388, 389, 390, 393,
	483, 702, 907, 1149,
	1424, 1839
MOZAMBIQUE, People's Republic of	868, 1378
Chewa (Cewa)	961, 1396
Chopi	1396
Karanga	1433
Manganja (Mang'anja)	1571, 1574
Ndau (VaNdau)	872, 1378, 1396, 1467
Thonga (Bathonga,	
Tonga)	1038, 1396, 1739
Tswa (Batswa)	1378, 1396
Zavala	1464
NAMIBIA (under South West Africa-	
Namibia)	
NIGER, Republic of the	2, 177, 1044
Datwenawa	1018
Hausa (Goberawa)	2, 271, 1018, 1225,
	1657

POLITICAL UNIT/Ethnic Group	Citation
Konnawa	271
Mawri	1389
Songhai (Songay, Songhay)	2, 34, 490, 720, 781, 1034, 1521, 1522, 1524, 1525, 1526, 1735
Zerma	2, 490, 720, 1390, 1391
NIGERIA, Federal Republic of	10, 37, 55, 76, 106, 251, 279, 397, 404, 518, 524, 525, 545, 557, 704, 723, 745, 818, 836, 838, 839, 840, 841, 848, 889, 890, 953, 954, 972, 1005, 1016, 1064, 1067, 1139, 1163, 1179, 1180, 1181, 1219, 1220, 1313, 1348, 1373, 1375, 1376, 1377, 1412, 1600, 1642, 1764, 1767, 1825, 1888
Awori	1065
Bachama	919, 1159, 1681
Bata	919, 1159
Efik	1702
Ekoi	1702
Fon (Dahomey)	100, 1709, 1735
Goemai	1616
Gun	1709
Hausa (Maguzawa)	179, 180, 249, 345, 520, 686, 700, 929, 972, 1034, 1163, 1213, 1266, 1283, 1284, 1315, 1354, 1538, 1539, 1540, 1655, 1656, 1735, 1751, 1752, 1755
Ibibio (Anang Ibibio)	855, 1179, 1180, 1181, 1701
Ibo	415, 503, 839, 854, 861, 1290
Idoma	49
Ife	92, 1680
Igala	221
Igbira	280
Igbo	842, 844
Ijaw (Ịjọ, Egbena Ịjọ)	19, 1740
Isoko	251, 1856
Jukun	1160
Kalabari	39, 809, 810, 811, 812, 813, 815, 816, 817, 1109, 1703, 1711
Kamberi	1539

411

POLITICAL UNIT/Ethnic Group   Citation

                    Kanuri   49
                    Kirdi   966
                    Kulu (Kulū)   1162
                    Mbula   919
                    Montol   1616
                    Ngizim   1161
                    Nupe   589
                    Panda (Kwotto) 1896
                    Reshe (Gungawa) 1540
                    Urhobo   251
                    Yako (Yakö)   591, 1109
                    Yauri   740
                    Yoruba   11, 12, 51, 87, 93,
                                    100, 119, 122, 162,
                                    163, 164, 165, 416,
                                    485, 514, 522, 523,
                                    546, 547, 548, 781,
                                    783, 808, 833, 834,
                                    913, 917, 968, 982,
                                    1004, 1005, 1066,
                                    1080, 1097, 1099, 1163,
                                    1187, 1192, 1239, 1240,
                                    1241, 1242, 1300, 1348,
                                    1350, 1352, 1355, 1357,
                                    1375, 1376, 1400, 1413,
                                    1414, 1415, 1416, 1419,
                                    1420, 1422, 1630, 1632,
                                    1670, 1709, 1735, 1804,
                                    1807, 1809, 1863
NORTHERN RHODESIA (under Zambia,
        Republic of)
NYASALAND (under Malawi, Republic of)
RHODESIA-ZIMBABWE (formerly   44, 45, 47, 201, 328,
        Southern Rhodesia)   382, 394, 396, 408,
                                     409, 410, 411, 421,
                                     471, 583, 655, 759,
                                     807, 863, 882, 1146,
                                     1257, 1386, 1545,
                                     1649, 1750, 1859
        Barwe (Wabarwe)   1608, 1609
        Budya (Babudja, Budjga,36, 1234, 1257, 1622
          Vabudjga, Wabudya)
        Chewa (Cêwa)   1141
        Chikwaka   650
        Danda (Wadondo)   1175
        Garwe (Vagarwe)   1384
        Gcaleka   1084
        Hera   600
        Hlengwe   819
        Kalanga (Amakalanga,   154, 290, 344, 600,
          Makalaka, Makalanga)   718, 801, 1314, 1446,
                                     1699, 1858

                    412

POLITICAL UNIT/Ethnic Group	Citation
Karanga (Vakaranga)	5, 35, 36, 45, 46, 47, 332, 600, 649, 657a, 819, 1261, 1451, 1848, 1849
Kololo (Makololo)	1564
Korekore (Makorekore)	228, 229, 230, 311, 600, 620, 627, 628, 629, 641, 657a
Kota (Bakota)	1564
Mambo	36
Manyika	657a
Mbedzi	600
Mbire	600
Ndau (VaNdau)	204, 494, 1467
Ndebele (AmaNdebele, Matabele)	36, 40, 154, 187, 203, 288, 395, 409, 429, 800, 823, 826, 880, 941, 1156, 1279, 1287, 1436, 1530, 1698, 1736, 1741, 1889, 1935
Ngoni (Ngona)	600
Nyombgwe (Wanyomgbwe)	750
Pedi	600
Pende	1663
Romwe	1614
Rozi (Warozwi)	600, 823, 1451
Shona (Mashona)	6, 40, 48, 124, 129, 174, 175, 176, 187, 210, 211, 228, 286, 287, 288, 291, 394, 395, 396, 407, 409, 410, 411, 526, 580, 600, 625, 626, 634, 635, 636, 637, 638, 639, 640, 642, 643, 644, 645, 646, 647, 648, 651, 652, 653, 655, 656, 753, 802, 823, 827, 880, 941, 975, 976, 1102, 1103, 1138, 1144, 1146, 1178, 1243, 1256, 1279, 1404, 1436, 1437, 1438, 1439, 1441, 1446, 1451, 1460, 1610, 1663, 1676, 1741, 1748, 1776, 1785, 1786, 1889, 1914, 1935
Sori (VaSori)	1875
Tande (Vatande)	1148
Tawara (Tavara, Watawara)	36, 120, 229, 232, 600

413

POLITICAL UNIT/Ethnic Group	Citation
Thonga (Gwembe Tonga, Inhambane Tonga, Shangaan Tonga)	365, 368, 823, 852, 1467, 1849b
Torwa	600
Tswana	600
Venda	344, 600
Wembe	687
Yao	1860
Zezuru	600, 620, 657a
RUANDA (under Rwanda, Republic of)	
RWANDA, Republic of (formerly Ruanda)	216, 325, 710, 1026, 1387, 1485, 1824
Bashi	1247, 1249
Dikidiki	979
Hungana	979
Hutu (Hum)	777, 979
Ruanda (Banyarunda, Banyarwanda, Nya-runda, Nyarwanda, Rwanda)	181, 777, 784, 874, 958, 1109, 1115, 1247, 1249, 1250, 1251, 1369, 1370, 1371, 1387
Tutsi	777
Twa	777
SENEGAL, Republic of	57, 349, 352, 453, 508, 1085, 1140, 1407, 1566
Bambara	350, 353, 708
Diola (Dyola)	350, 353, 708, 895, 1228
Fon (Dahomey)	86
Fulani (Peul)	350, 353, 455, 708
Lebu (Lebou, Lébou)	67, 68, 350, 353, 354, 355, 356, 455, 624, 691, 708, 896, 1196, 1228, 1289, 1331, 1577, 1618, 1619, 1620, 1732, 1735, 1925, 1926, 1928, 1931
Mankanya (Mancagne)	1756
Malinke (Mandingue)	350
Serer (Sérer, Sérèr, Sereer, Sérère)	167, 168, 350, 353, 455, 624, 690, 691, 692, 693, 694, 708, 896, 1228, 1289, 1331, 1733, 1735
Tukulor (Toucouleur, Tukulër)	350, 353, 455, 708, 1289
Wolof	86, 350, 353, 355, 356, 455, 460, 624, 708, 896, 1196, 1330, 1331, 1332, 1576, 1577, 1732, 1735, 1925, 1926, 1927, 1928, 1930, 1931

POLITICAL UNIT/Ethnic Group	Citation
SIERRA LEONE, Republic of	25, 76
Gbundi (Gbunde)	1053
Loko (Lokko)	1086
Mano	1053
Mende	698, 742, 1052, 1053, 1086, 1561
Temne	423, 461, 462, 1100
SOMALIA, Democratic Republic of	329, 330, 1514
Dolbohanta	1033
Somali	1036, 1037
SOUTH AFRICA, Republic of	173, 214, 222, 278, 281, 327, 339, 482, 484, 502, 560, 562, 563, 574, 630, 754, 791, 799, 856, 887, 942, 943, 964, 986, 1019, 1045, 1058, 1061, 1098, 1132, 1154, 1164, 1305, 1318, 1322, 1471, 1512, 1536, 1542, 1578, 1599, 1602, 1691, 1692, 1728, 1743, 1822, 1823, 1857, 1887, 1912
Bhaca	725, 727, 728
Dushane (imiDushane)	726
Gwambe	620
Kalanga (Makalanga)	801
Khoi-khoi (Hottentot)	744
Lovedu	783, 932, 933
Luba	783
Ndau (VaNdau)	206, 494, 783, 872, 873
Ndebele (Amandebele)	1736
Ngoni	515
Nguni	711, 732
Ntinde (AmaNtinde)	726
Pedi	1226, 1580
Pondo	828, 1038, 1893
Qaba	270
Qhayi (imiQhayi)	726
Rolong (Barolong)	326
Ronga (Baronga)	869, 870
Sibisi	1817
Sotho (Basotho, Basuto, Southern Sotho, Suto)	52, 53, 326, 343, 491, 506, 931, 985, 1259, 1580, 1833
Tembu	977
Thonga (Bathonga, Shangana Tonga, Tonga)	744, 781, 783, 791, 871, 932, 1580
Tsonga	859, 860
Tswana (Bechuana)	274, 744, 1580
Venda (Bavenda)	201, 510, 1038, 1446, 1675, 1835

POLITICAL UNIT/Ethnic Group   Citation

     Xosa (AmaXosa, Xhosa)   270, 504, 851, 1153,
                              1222, 1368, 1580, 1661
     Zulu (Amazulu)   80, 170, 172b, 282,
                              305, 307, 482, 560,
                              563, 664, 667, 668,
                              669, 698, 856, 869,
                              870, 926, 930, 996,
                              997, 1038, 1060, 1069,
                              1281b, 1294, 1318,
                              1427, 1580, 1610, 1611,
                              1691, 1779, 1780, 1832,
                              1885, 1889
SOUTHERN RHODESIA (under Rhodesia-
          Zimbabwe)
SOUTH WEST AFRICA-NAMIBIA
     Ambo (Ovambo)   1802
     Bushmen (Kung)   698, 1127, 1128, 1729
SPANISH GUINEA (under Equatorial Guinea)
SUDAN, Democratic Republic of   4, 61, 62, 79, 516,
                              1014, 1221, 1263,
                              1264, 1265, 1558,
                              1682, 1753, 1932
     Anuak (Annuak)   540
     Azande (Zande)   416, 537, 542, 544,
                              1107, 1108, 1356,
                              1388, 1406
     Bari   1247
     Bayel   1262
     Dilling   1684
     Dinka (Padang Dinka)   157, 207, 705, 1046,
                              1109, 1156, 1537,
                              1584, 1585, 1615, 1882
     Kadero (Kadaru)   1684
     Kaffa   797
     Koalib   1683
     Moru   126, 1156
     Murle   1030
     Ndogo   1548
     Nuba (Nouba)   124, 749, 783, 889,
                              1038, 1294, 1537
     Nuer   207, 298, 375, 439,
                              536, 538, 541, 543,
                              698, 821, 1029, 1109,
                              1585, 1666, 1878, 1882
     Nyima (Nyimang)   698, 934
     Shilluk   298, 539, 820, 1045
     Songhai   34
SWAZILAND, Kingdom of
     Swazi   81, 159, 161, 596,
                              913, 938, 939, 940,
                              944, 1580
TANGANYIKA (under Tanzania, United Republic of)

                         416

POLITICAL UNIT/Ethnic Group	Citation
TANZANIA, United Republic of	712, 994, 1382, 1440,
(formerly Tanganyika,	1547, 1647, 1651,
including Zanzibar)	1652, 1792, 1905
[ZANZIBAR]	843, 1905
Bondei	405
Chaga (Chagga)	1299
Fipa (Wafipa)	1299, 1494, 1879,
	1881, 1882
Ganda (Baganda)	1311
Gogo	1311, 1490
Ha	379, 1299, 1567, 1605
Hangaza	1299
Haya	172b, 1299
Hehe	274, 498, 698, 1463
Jita	1299
Kaguru	158, 160
Kamba (Akamba)	1311
Kerebe	743
Kerewe	1299
Kikuyu (Gikuyu)	1311
Kimbu	7, 1604, 1605
Konongo	7
Luguru (Uluguru)	1565
Luo	1299, 1382
Makua	1299
Masai	1311
Masasi	1444
Nyakyusa	372, 1000, 1093, 1221,
	1891, 1892, 1915
Nyambo	1299
Nyamwezi	7, 380, 1299, 1604,1605
Nyanja	1299
Nyiha	265
Pare	1299, 1311, 1605
Pemba	695, 1890
Pogoro (Pagoro, Wapo-	
goro)	1, 857, 1076
Rimi	1721
Ruanda (Nyaruanda)	1299
Runga	1299
Ruri	1299
Sandawe	1721
Segeju	696, 697
Subi (Shubi)	1299
Sukuma (Sakuma)	7, 378, 380, 783,
	1212, 1299, 1605, 1705,
	1706, 1707
Sumbwa (Sumba)	7, 379, 1299, 1605
Swahili	124, 314, 526
Tiriki	1547
Zaramo	837
Zigua	125
Zinza	1299

417

POLITICAL UNIT/Ethnic Group	Citation
TOGO, Republic of	425, 996
Akan	917
Dye (Dyé)	617
Edo (Benin)	966
Ewe	425
Fon	1357, 1709
Ge (Mina)	1374
Gun	1709
Kabre (Kabrè)	615
Konkomba	615
Lamba	615
Moba	615
Yoruba	122, 1555, 1709
TUNISIA, The Republic of	483, 688, 921, 1424
UGANDA, The Second Republic of	78, 181, 400, 662, 883, 915, 1073, 1075, 1235, 1310, 1485, 1491, 1723, 1850, 1871
Acholi	195, 196, 199, 208, 662, 1309, 1447
Adhola	1337
Alur (Lur)	1165, 1664, 1665, 1730
Amba	698, 1897, 1898
Banya-Mwenge	1745
Chiga (Kiga)	172b, 259, 494, 698, 1245, 1485
Fipa	1380
Ganda (Baganda, Buganda)	258, 373, 553, 577, 609, 698, 875, 897, 913, 917, 1063, 1072, 1074, 1106, 1150, 1156, 1246, 1297, 1328, 1358, 1381, 1457, 1501, 1504, 1509, 1510, 1589, 1668, 1669, 1717, 1719, 1833, 1850, 1851
Gisu (Bagesu, Bagishu, Gishu)	875, 948, 1503, 1508
Gusii	1298
Haya (Baziba, Ziba)	1295
Hima (Bahima)	1502
Jonam	1535
Kerewe	1761
Kingwe (Bakingwe)	66
Kumam	534, 1535
Lango	33, 195, 751, 1156, 1447, 1708
Lugbara	916, 1038, 1107, 1197, 1199, 1200, 1202, 1203, 1204, 1206, 1207
Luo	1427
Nkole (Ankole, Banyankole, Nyankole)	74, 917, 1503, 1507

418

POLITICAL UNIT/Ethnic Group   Citation

        Nyoro (Banyoro,   72, 73, 74, 130, 131,
               Bunyoro)   132, 133, 134, 135,
                                    136, 137, 138, 139,
                                    140, 141, 142, 143,
                                    144, 145, 146, 147,
                                    148, 151, 152, 153,
                                    195, 487, 516, 689,
                                    698, 1038, 1108, 1113,
                                    1272, 1273, 1381,
                                    1503, 1505, 1716
        Padhola   1304, 1597
        Pogoro (Pagoro,
               Wapogoro)   1104
        Sara   599
        Sabei (Mbai)   599
        Sebei   498
        Soga (Basoga)   551, 552, 1503
        Sumbwa   74, 1605
        Toro, Batooro, Tooro)   877
UPPER VOLTA, Republic of   456, 879, 894
        Dogon   451, 1351
        Mossi (Mosi)   436, 1034, 1735
URUNDI (under Burundi, Republic of)
ZAIRE, Republic of (formerly The   21, 32, 42, 75, 123,
        Belgian Congo)   127, 171, 189, 220,
                                    227, 370, 377, 519,
                                    539, 600, 601, 602,
                                    850, 862, 863, 864,
                                    865, 866, 906, 974,
                                    1017, 1020, 1091,
                                    1094b, 1135, 1137,
                                    1394, 1782, 1799,
                                    1884, 1919
        Alur (Lur)   527
        Azande   949, 1406
        Banda   1812
        Bandibu   1385
        Bashi   348, 1250, 1251
        Bira   1790
        Bolia   1789
        Boma   1586, 1587
        Chiga (Kiga)   1439
        Chokwe (Cokwe)   1795, 1829
        Dikidiki   979
        Hunde (Bahunde)   1814
        Hungana   979
        Hutu (Hum)   979
        Kanda (Okanda)   202
        Kasanga   1674
        Kongo (Bakongo)   70, 71, 75, 127, 283,
                                    284, 370, 489, 527,
                                    782, 783, 850, 951,
                                    1092, 1093, 1094a,

                        419

POLITICAL UNIT/Ethnic Group	Citation
	1094b, 1446, 1461, 1688, 1782, 1797, 1798, 1829, 1843, 1880
Kuba	786, 1793, 1794, 1796
Kutshu (Bakutshu, N'Kutshu)	257, 1787
Lala (Balala)	952
Lambo (Balambo)	878
Lele (Bashilele)	472, 473, 477, 964, 1109, 1882
Lokele	991
Luba (Baluba)	216, 219, 294, 526, 527, 753, 786, 966, 967, 1327, 1725, 1726, 1829, 1923
Lugbara	1038, 1156
Lulua (Bena Lulua)	527, 967, 1085, 1923
Lumba (Bilumba)	527
Lunda	786, 1795
Lunga (Beni-Marungu)	881, 1251
Lusa (Balusa)	1251
Luvale (Lwena)	1795
Manianga	1385
Manja	1812
Mbagani	1795
Mbala (Bambala)	527
Mbandja	292
Mbîm (Mbiem, Mbîm)	1586, 1587, 1727
Milembwe	1672
Mongo	1251, 1533
Ngbaka	292, 1593, 1795
Ngbandi	292, 1795
Ngombe	292, 1673, 1911
Ntomba	1789
Pende (Bapende)	527, 1829
Ruanda (Banyaruanda, Nyarwanda)	1251
Ruund	1795
Sakata (Basakata)	347, 527, 1587
Sangu	1812
Sengele	1789
Shioko (Batshioko)	216
Songe (Bassonge)	1923
Suku	1586
Teke (Teke Tsaayi)	488, 1587
Tetela (Batetela)	527
Tutsi	1576
Yaka	1586, 1829
Yanzi (Bayansi, Keni, Nsala-Mbanda)	441, 527, 1586, 1587

POLITICAL UNIT/Ethnic Group   Citation

ZAMBIA, Republic of (formerly   9, 194, 262, 471, 863,
     Northern Rhodesia; in-   967, 998, 1255, 1386,
     cluding Barotseland)   1483, 1517, 1519, 1718,
                                 1762, 1859, 1883, 1889
     Ambo   1678
     Bemba   263, 419, 786, 913,
                                   1302, 1484, 1495,
                                   1862, 1876
     Chewa   961
     Chokwe (Cokwe)   1872
     Diola   895
     Ila (Ba-Ila, Baila)   793, 1610, 1759
     Iwa   1519
     Karanga (Vakaranga)   1433
     Kwangwa   937
     Lamba   457, 526, 753, 913,
                                   1650, 1861
     Lenge   1650
     Lozi (Barotse, Malozi) 665, 666, 937, 1255,
                                   1472, 1768
     Luapula   399
     Lubale   937
     Luchazi   1872
     Lunda   1087, 1167, 1769, 1872
     Luvale (Balovale,   1667, 1872, 1873,
         Lwena)   1874, 1889
     Mbala (Bambala)   793
     Mbowe   937
     Mbukushu (Hambukushu)   971
     Ndembu   1107, 1406, 1446, 1603,
                                   1770, 1771, 1772, 1773,
                                   1774, 1775, 1776, 1777
     Ngondi (Konde)   1610
     Ngoni   22
     Nkoya   193
     Nsenga   1253
     Sala (Basala)   793
     Thonga (Batonga,   360, 361, 363, 366,
         Plateau Tonga,   367, 368a, 368b, 1036,
         Valley Tonga)   1083, 1244
     Twa (Batwa)   793
     Yombe   213
ZANZIBAR (under Tanzania, United Republic of)
ZIMBABWE (under Rhodesia-Zimbabwe)

INDEX 4

Africa: Ethnic Groups in Major Regions.
(No specific political unit mentioned.)

     The African continent has been roughly divided into
five regions: Central, East, North, Southern, and West

("Southern" is used to distinguish the region from the
country of South Africa). The citations in this index
refer to works whose authors describe the location of
ethnic groups regionally rather than within political
units. Index 3 places these ethnic groups, but not the
citations listed below, within specific political units.

422

INDEX 5

Africa: General Sources.
(No specific political unit or ethnic group mentioned.)

All references in this index discuss spirit possession or spirit mediumship in general terms for the
African, or the African continent.   Much of this literature is of a general descriptive or philosophic nature.

8, 15, 28, 38, 50, 104, 105, 112, 117, 149, 155, 166,
172a, 172b, 185, 186, 191, 205, 212, 218, 231, 238, 247,
293, 299, 322, 323, 339, 340, 351, 357, 376, 404, 406,
417, 418, 444, 454, 467, 505, 508, 509, 582, 585, 607,
608, 617, 618, 633, 654, 663, 698, 699, 735, 779, 798,
825, 835, 845, 846, 847, 858, 905, 954, 969, 970, 974,
983, 1003, 1039, 1071, 1078, 1081, 1082, 1089, 1095,
1111, 1112, 1143, 1155, 1157, 1158, 1210, 1258, 1270,
1274, 1276, 1281a, 1288, 1301, 1306, 1312, 1322, 1348,
1351, 1353, 1366, 1423, 1429, 1443, 1458, 1465, 1518,
1523, 1554, 1560, 1562, 1568, 1588, 1601, 1606, 1607,
1653, 1677, 1697, 1712, 1720, 1722, 1723, 1731, 1732,
1733, 1734, 1735, 1738, 1747, 1749, 1813, 1818, 1830,
1837, 1844, 1845, 1852, 1883, 1889, 1895, 1900, 1933

INDEX 6

Afro-America: Regions, Political Units, Religious
Movements and Ethnic Groups.

The scholar will notice that ethnic groups are not
frequently mentioned for Afro-America, because many of
the religious movements are in urban centers and have di-
versified ethnic memberships.

REGION/ POLITICAL UNIT	Religious movement	Ethnic group	Citation
BAHAMAS			398
CARIBBEAN			85, 657b, 956, 1258, 1286, 1638, 1658
CUBA			89, 91, 303, 1129, 1333
	Abakuá		486, 1090
	Babalu		420
	Bembe		485
	Chango		1286
	Lucumi		302

423

REGION/ POLITICAL UNIT	Religious movement	Ethnic group	Citation
ST. VINCENT			677
	Shakers		241, 755, 756, 757, 1041
TRINIDAD			758, 769, 773, 1639
	Shango		1215, 1401, 1630, 1631, 1633, 1644, 1645, 1685
	Shouters		1401, 1634
		Congo (Kongo)	324
		Dahomey (Fon)	324
		Ibo	324
		Mandingo (Malinke)	324
		Yoruba	94, 504, 1214, 1630, 1633, 1644
CENTRAL AMERICA			1403
YUCATÁN (MEXICO)			677, 678, 679, 680, 681, 682, 684, 1041, 1541
SOUTH AMERICA			85, 1404
BRAZIL			308, 499, 829, 924
	Afro-Brazilian Cults-General		30, 91, 97, 98, 101, 104, 108, 116, 579, 766, 767, 768, 773, 775, 956, 1286, 1393, 1399, 1426, 1431, 1476, 1478, 1479, 1480, 1481, 1500, 1659, 1660, 1784, 1806, 1808, 1811, 1889, 2018
		Bantu	106, 318, 529
	Batuque		987, 988, 990
	Caboclo		319, 612, 955
	Candomblé		99, 100, 102, 106, 107, 111, 115, 118, 301, 317, 318, 319, 320, 321, 339, 381, 485, 493, 612, 772, 774, 808, 955, 988, 1068, 1187, 1334, 1393, 1475, 1482, 1592, 1645, 1671, 1836, 1877, 1910, 1942, 1956, 1957, 1977, 1982, 2012, 2025, 2031, 2036, 2037, 2039
		Fon	100, 106
	Gêge-Nagô Cults		1659
	Kardecism (Espiritismo)		30, 310, 1836, 1955, 1958

INDEX 7

Afro-America: General Sources.
(No specific political unit or ethnic group mentioned.)

All references in this index discuss spirit possession or spirit mediumship in general terms for Afro-
America. Much of this literature is of a general descriptive or philosophic nature.

Citations: 85, 106, 110, 115, 117, 183, 238, 247, 341, 384, 675, 763, 770, 776, 779, 956, 969, 1286, 1645, 1679, 1830, 1920.

INDEX 8

World Areas outside Africa and Afro-America.

Included here are peripheral citations to Europe, the Middle East, the Far East, the Arabian Peninsula, and North America, which contain information of comparative value for African research.

WORLD AREA/Religious Movement	Citations
ARABIAN PENINSULA	293
Zar	1558
EUROPE	316, 952, 1126, 1396, 1511
MIDDLE EAST	
Hebrew	566, 568
NORTH AMERICA	
Pentecostal	85, 657b, 677, 1486, 1541
Voodoo	31, 1379, 1704, 1742
FAR EAST	
China	1105
Malaysia	265
Singapore	1105

INDEX 9

Theoretical Sources on Spirit Possession and Spirit Mediumship.

All general source material dealing with the theoretical analysis of spirit possession and spirit mediumship are included.

Citations: 24, 58, 113, 121, 142, 192, 194, 224, 235, 236, 239, 240, 242, 243, 244, 246, 247, 248, 250, 269, 293, 304, 340, 392, 508, 573, 595, 604, 770, 771, 780, 790, 814, 903, 925, 936, 993, 1002, 1043, 1062a, 1123, 1188, 1209, 1216, 1271, 1301, 1323, 1343, 1395, 1477, 1480, 1617, 1648, 1687, 1781, 1803, 1908, 1909, 1920

Music.

These references deal with the role of music in spirit possession and spirit mediumship experiences in Africa and Afro-America.

Citations: 17, 19, 41, 216, 371, 384, 403, 422, 665, 744, 768, 831, 832, 846, 859, 915, 950, 968, 979, 1116b, 1176, 1177, 1271, 1342, 1528, 1588, 1597, 1838

Religious Movements.
Including Independent Christian Churches and other colonial and post-colonial syncretic movements.

This index gives a complete list of the citations of all religious movements in Africa or Afro-America that practice spirit possession, spirit mediumship, or glossolalia.

Citations: 10, 21, 32, 37, 41, 42, 44, 45, 47, 55, 60, 63, 64, 69, 70, 75, 76, 77, 78, 82, 127, 128, 155, 173, 178, 184, 186, 213, 214, 249, 251, 256, 260, 261, 276, 277, 278, 279, 327, 328, 370, 387, 394, 396, 408, 409, 410, 411, 413, 424, 425, 430, 445, 448, 468, 478, 484, 518, 524, 525, 530, 533, 546, 556, 557, 559, 560, 561, 563, 570, 595, 603, 655, 661, 662, 701, 704, 745, 754, 782, 803, 818, 836, 838, 839, 840, 841, 848, 850, 862, 863, 864, 865, 866, 886, 915, 918, 945, 964, 965, 967, 986, 997, 1005, 1017, 1020, 1058, 1095, 1130, 1131, 1132, 1133, 1134, 1135, 1136, 1137, 1138, 1139, 1143, 1179, 1180, 1181, 1219, 1220, 1255, 1257, 1260, 1268, 1305, 1313, 1316, 1317, 1318, 1319, 1320, 1321, 1322, 1348, 1351, 1359, 1364, 1365, 1367, 1375, 1376, 1377, 1382, 1394, 1395, 1440, 1456, 1518, 1519, 1527, 1542, 1546, 1547, 1555, 1562, 1578, 1579, 1600, 1601, 1606, 1607, 1642, 1648, 1691, 1692, 1718, 1728, 1763, 1764, 1765, 1766, 1767, 1800, 1821, 1822, 1823, 1842, 1844, 1846, 1850, 1854, 1855, 1864b, 1864c, 1866, 1884, 1888, 1889, 1903, 1906, 1910, 1912, 1917, 1918, 1919

MAJOR REGION/POLITICAL UNIT	Citation
ETHIOPIA	4, 13, 249, 329, 330, 493, 595, 703, 713, 980, 1006, 1007, 1008, 1009, 1012, 1013, 1021, 1023, 1033, 1034, 1051, 1055, 1124, 1182, 1237, 1238, 1372, 1498, 1499, 1515, 1552, 1558, 1689, 1746, 1747, 1754, 1921, 1922
SOMALIA	329, 330, 1032, 1033
SUDAN	4, 61, 62, 79, 516, 889, 1221, 1558, 1932

INDEX 18

Zionism.

This African independent church movement, mainly located in Southern Africa, is cited separately owing to its widespread influence.

Citations: 44, 69, 173, 184, 408, 413, 448, 560, 563, 754, 886, 997, 1130, 1132, 1133, 1305, 1359, 1367, 1440, 1578, 1601, 1691, 1728, 1800, 1889, 1912

LISTS OF JOURNALS, NEWSLETTERS, PERIODICALS SURVEYED.

The journals, newsletters and periodicals cited below were surveyed in the following manner. List 1 contains publications investigated from their initial publication date up through December 1977. Over the years,
they have been outlets for material on spirit possession
and spirit mediumship. List 2 includes publications
which were surveyed only when we had references from
other sources to articles which they contained. Upon
surveying the publications in List 3, no relevant topical
materials on spirit possession and spirit mediumship
were uncovered. We investigated these publications in
hopes of finding material on spirit possession and spirit
mediumship which may previously have escaped scholarly
notice. These publications, however, did not yield relevant information. They are cited herein so that the
scholar may avoid an unproductive search.

List 1: <u>Journals, Newsletters and Periodicals -
Thoroughly Investigated and Relevant</u>

Abstracts in Anthropology
Acta Psychotherapeutica et Psychosomatica (Basel)
    [becomes in 1965 Psychotherapy and Psychosomatics]
Acta Psychiatrica Scandinavica (Copenhagen)
Afer: African Ecclesiastical Review (Eldoret)
Africa: Journal of the International African Institute
    (London)
Africa (Madrid)
Africa: Rivista trimestrale di studi e documentazione
    dell'istituto italo-africano (Rome)
Africa Quarterly (New Delhi)
African Research Bulletin (Exeter)
Africa-Tervuren (Tervuren)
African Abstracts (London)
African Affairs: Journal of the Royal African Society
    (London)
African Arts (Los Angeles)
African Diary (New Delhi)
African Historian (Ibadan)
African Historical Studies (Boston)
African Journal of Medical Science (Oxford)
African Notes (Ibadan)
African Social Research (Lusaka)
    [formerly Rhodes-Livingstone Journal]
African Studies (Johannesburg)
African Studies Association (Boston)
Africana Bulletin (Warsaw)
Africana Marburgensia (Marburg)
Afrique contemporaire (Paris)
Afrique documents (Dakar)

Afrique et l'Asie (Paris)
American Anthropologist
American Anthropological Association Memoirs
American Journal of Psychiatry
American Journal of Psychotherapy
American Sociological Review
Annales du Musée royal du Congo belge (Tervuren)
Annales médico-psychologiques (Paris)
Annali Lateranensi (Vatican City)
Anthropological Quarterly
Anthropos
Archives d'ethnographie, musée royal de l'Afrique
    centrale (Tervuren)
Archives de sociologie des religions (Paris)
Archives of General Psychiatry
Azania (Nairobi)

Bantu Studies
Belgian Congo Today (Brussels)
Boston University Papers on Africa
Botswana Notes and Records (Gaborone)
British Medical Journal
Bulletin de l'Institut fondamental d'Afrique noire
    (Dakar)
Bulletin des séances, Institut royal colonial belge
Bulletin of the School of Oriental and African Studies

Cahiers d'études africaines (Paris)
Cahiers d'outre-mer (Bordeaux)
Cahiers du C.E.D.A.F. [Centre d'etude et de documenta-
    tion africaine] (Bruxelles)
Cahiers de l'homme (Paris)
Cahiers des religions africaines (Kinshasa)
Cahiers economiques et sociaux (Leopoldville)
Canadian Journal of African Studies
Caribbean Quarterly
Caribbean Studies
Centre d'analyse et de recherche documentaires pour
    l'Afrique noir (Paris)
Civilisations (Bruxelles)
Comparative Studies in Society and History
Comptes rendus de l'Academie des sciences coloniales
    d'outre-mer (Paris)
Confinia Psychiatrica (Basel)
Congo: Revue generale de la colonie belge (Bruxelles)
Congres international des africanistes (Dakar)
Cultures en Zaïre et en Afrique (Kinshasa)
Cultures et developpement (Louvain)
Current Anthropology (Chicago)

Dina na Mila (Kampala)
Diogenes
Dissertation Abstracts International

East African Institute of Social Research Conference
    Papers
East African Studies (Nairobi)
Éthiopiques (Dakar)
Ethnology
Études congolaises, Institut national d'études
    politiques (Bruxelles)
Études d'histoire africaine (Kinshasa)
Etudes dahoméennes (Porto Novo)
Études nigériennes (Paris)

Flambeau (Yaoundé)
Folklore (London)
Fort Hare Papers (South Africa)

Genève-Afrique
Ghana Bulletin of Theology
Gold Coast Review

Harvard African Studies
Hespéris-Tamuda (Rabat)
Hibbert Journal
Historical Association of Tanzania Papers (Nairobi)
History of Religions (Chicago)
History Papers, University of East Africa

Ibadan (Ibadan)
Institute for the Study of Man in Africa Publications
    (Johannesburg)
International African Institute Monographs (London)
International African Seminar (Dar es Salaam)
International Archives of Ethnography
International Journal of African Historical Studies
    (Boston)
International Review of Missions

Journal de la Société des africanistes (Paris)
Journal for the Scientific Study of Religion
Journal of African History
Journal of African Studies
Journal of Asian and African Studies (Leiden)
Journal of Ethiopian Studies (Addis Ababa)
Journal of Religion in Africa (Leiden)
Journal of Social Science (Blantyre)
Journal of the Royal Anthropological Institute of
    Great Britain and Ireland (London)
Journal of Theology for Southern Africa (Braamfontein,
    Transvaal)

Kale (Dar es Salaam)
Kano Studies (Nigeria)
Kenya Historical Review (Nairobi)

Lagos Notes and Records
Liberian Studies Journal (Greencastle, Ind.)

Makerere Historical Journal (Kampala)
Man (London)
Mawazo (Kampala)
Mbioni (Dar es Salaam)
Mémoires de l'Académie royale des sciences coloniales
    d'outre-mer (Bruxelles)
Ministry (Morija)
Mission Field
Monde non-chrétien (Paris)
Musées de Genève

Nada: The Rhodesian Ministry of Internal Affairs Annual
    (Salisbury)
Nigeria Magazine (Lagos)
Nigerian Journal of Economics and Social Studies
Notes africaines: Bulletin d'information et de
    correspondence de l'Institut francais d'Afrique noire
    (Dakar)
Nyasaland Journal (Blantyre)
    [becomes in 1965 Society of Malaŵi Journal]

Occasional Research Papers in African Traditional Reli-
    gion and Philosophy (Kampala)
Odu (Ibadan)
Organization of African Unity: Scientific, Technical
    and Research Commission (London)
Orita (Ibadan)

Pount (Djibouti)
Practical Anthropology
Presence africaine (Paris)
Problèmes sociaux congolais (Bruxelles/Lubumbashi)
Problèmes sociaux zaïrois (Lubumbashi)
Proceedings of the Royal Society of Medicine (London)
Psychiatrica Clinica (Basel)
Psychopathologie africaine (Dakar)
Publications of the Institute for the Study of Man in
    Africa (Johannesburg)

Recherches africaines (Conakry)
Religious Studies Papers (Kampala)
Research Review (Legon)
Revue congolaise (Bruxelles)
Revue du clerge africain (Inkisi)
Rhodes-Livingstone Institute Communications, Journal,
    Papers (Lusaka)
Rhodesiana History (Salisbury)
Rhodesiana (Salisbury)

Sierre Leone Bulletin of Religion (Freetown)
Sociology Papers (Kampala)
South African Journal of Science
South African Medical Journal
Southern Rhodesian Native Affairs Department Annual
    (Salisbury)

435

Southwestern Journal of Anthropology
Sudan Notes and Records (Khartoum)

Tanganyika Notes and Records (Dar es Salaam)
  [becomes Tanzania Notes and Records]
Tarikh (London)
Thought and Practice (Nairobi)
Transafrican Journal of History (Nairobi)
Transcultural Psychiatric Research Review (Bruges/
  Montreal)
Transition (Kampala)
Travaux et mémoires de l'Institut d'ethnologie (Paris)

Uganda Journal (Kampala)

West African Religion (Nsukka)
West African Review

Zaïre: Belgian African Review (Bruxelles)
Zaïre-Afrique: Économie, culture, vie sociale (Kinshasa)

List 2: Journals, Newsletters, Periodicals - Investi-
         gated for Cited Articles.

Abhandlungen und Berichte des Staatlichen Museums für
  Völkerkunde (Dresden)
Acta Neuropsquiatrica Argentina
Acta Tropica (Basel)
Aequatoria
Aethiopica (New York)
African Music
African Review
African World (London)
Afrique chrétienne; le monde religieuse
AMA Archives of General Psychiatry
American Ethnologist
American Imago (Boston)
American Sociological Review
Americas
Anais do 31 Congresso Internacional de Americanistas
  (São Paulo)
Annales de l'universite de Madagascar
Anthropologica
Archivio per l'Antropologia e la Etnologia (Firenze)
Baessler Archiv (Berlin)
Band (Leopoldville)
Belgique d'outre-mer (Bruxelles)
Bibliotheque universelle (Switzerland)
Boletim da Sociedade de estudos da colonia de
  Moçambique (Lourenço Marques)
British Journal of Delinquency
Bulletin de juridictions indigènes et du droit coutumier
  congolais (Elizabethville)

436

Bulletin de l'Académie malagasche (Tananarive)
Bulletin de la Société des recherches congolaises
    (Brazzaville)
Bulletin de C.E.P.S.I.
Bulletin militaire
Bulletin of the History of Medicine (Baltimore)
Bulletin of the International Committee on Urgent Anthro-
    pological and Ethnological Research
Bulletin of the University College of Addis Ababa Ethno-
    logical Society

Cahiers congolais de la recherche et du développement
Cahiers internationaux de sociologie (Paris)
Caribbean Review (San Juan)
Central African Journal of Medicine (Salisbury)
Chine, Madagascar (Lille)
Communications from the School of African Studies (Cape
    Town)
Comptes rendus sommaires des séances de l'Institut
    français d'anthropologie (Paris)
Congo-Afrique: Économie, culture, vie sociale (Kinshasa)
Congo Mission News (Leopoldville)
Critique (Paris)

Dance Perspectives
Diogene

Eastern Anthropologist
Éducation africaine (Dakar)
Electroencephalography and Clinical Neurophysiology
L'Encephale (Paris)
Ethno-Psychologie (Le Havre)
Ethnos (Stockholm)
Ethos
Évolution psychiatrique

Field Museum of Natural History, Anthropological Series
Folia Orientalia (Cracow)

Ghana Bulletin of Religion
Grands lacs

L'Homme
Human Biology
Human Organization

International Journal of Clinical and Experimental
    Hypnosis
International Journal of Psychiatry (New York)
International Journal of Social Psychiatry (London)

Jamaican Journal
Journal de la Société des américanistes de Paris
Journal of Abnormal and Social Psychology

Journal of American Folklore
Journal of East Africa and Uganda Natural History Society
Journal of Health and Human Behavior
Journal of Inter-American Studies
Journal of Mental Science
Journal of Negro History
Journal of Transpersonal Psychology
Journal of the African Society (London)
Journal of the Historical Society of Nigeria (Ibadan)
Journal of the Society for Psychical Research

Kongo-Oberzee (Antwerpen)

Language and Speech

Mélanges Louis Massignon (Damas)
Memorias do Instituto de investigação cientifica de
  Moçambique
Mémoires de l'Institut fondamental d'Afrique noire
  (Dakar) (formerly Institut français d'Afrique noir)
Mémoires de l'Institut royal colonial belge
Memoires du Centre des hautes etudes d'administration
  musulmane
Mémoires O.R.S.T.O.M. [Office de la recherche scientifique
  et technique outre-mer] (Paris)
Memoirs of the American Anthropological Association
Mensario administrativo (Luanda)
Minotaure (Paris)
Mission: Cattoliche (Milano)
Moçambique - documentário trimestral (Lourenço Marques)
Musical Quarterly
Muslim World

Nigerial Field
Nigrizia (Verona)

Occasional Papers of the Rhodes-Livingstone Museum
  (Livingstone)
Octogenarian Dicata (Mexico City)
Optima (Johannesburg)

Paideuma (Frankfurt)
Papers of the Michigan Academy of Science, Arts and
  Letters
Portugal em Africa
Primitive Man
Proceedings of the Society for Psychic Research (London)
Psyché (Paris)
Psychedelic Review
Psychiatry
Psychoanalytical Review
Psychologia Africana (Johannesburg)
Psychosomatic Medicine
Publications de la Faculté des lettres et sciences
  humaines de Paris, Série "Recherches"

Race
Reviews in Anthropology
Revista brasileira de psiquiatria
Revue de la Societe haitienne d'histoire et de geographie
Revue de psychologie des peuples (La Havre)

Social and Economic Studies
Social Compass
South Africa: Native Affairs, Ethnological Publications
South African Journal of Science (Johannesburg)
Southern Folklore Quarterly
Studia Ethnographica Upsaliensia (Uppsala)
Studies in African History (The Hague)
Sudan Society (Khartoum)

Theoria (Pietermaritzburg)
Tomorrow
Transactions of the New York Academy of Sciences
Transcultural Research in Mental Health Problems
Travel (New York)

Ultramar (Lisbon)

Voix du Congolais

Wiener völkerkundliche Mitteilungen
World Health Organization Papers

Zambesi Mission Records
Zambezia (Salisbury)
Zeitschrift fur Ethnologie

List 3: Journals, Newsletters, Periodicals - Investi-
         gated but Not Relevant.

Abbia revue culturelle camerounaise (Yaoundé)
Abstracta Islamica
Acta Africana (Genève)
    [becomes Geneve-Afrique]
Acta Neurologica et Psychiatrica Belgica
Africa (New York)
    [becomes Africa Confidential]
Africa and the World (London)
Africa Confidential (London)
Africa Contemporary Record (London)
Africa Currents (London)
Africa Digest (London)
Africa Institute Bulletin and Communications (Pretoria)
Africa 1966 (Tunis)
Africa Report (Washington, D.C.)
Africa South (London)
Africa South of the Sahara (London)

Africa Today (New York)
African Affairs (London/Carbondale)
African and Black American Studies (Littleton, Colo.)
African Association, Proceedings (London)
African Classical Association Proceedings (Salisbury)
African Forum (New York)
African Journal of Education Research (Ibadan)
African Language Review (London)
African Recorder (New Delhi)
African Religious Research (Los Angeles)
African Research Monographs (Paris)
African Research Studies (Boston)
African Review (Accra)
African Review (Dar es Salaam)
African Scholar
African Studies Bulletin
African Studies Association of the United Kingdom
  (Birmingham)
African Studies Association of the West Indies
  (Kingston)
African Studies Review (East Lansing, Mich.)
African Transcripts (Philadelphia)
African Urban Notes (East Lansing, Mich.)
African Women (London)
African World Annual (London)
African World (New York)
Africana Newsletter (Stanford)
Afrika-Bücher (Pretoria)
Afrika Rundschau (Hamburg)
Afrika Spectrum (Hamburg)
Afrikanische Gesellschaft in Deutschland
Afrique littéraire et artistique (Paris)
Afrique medicale (Dakar)
Afro-Asia
American Academy of Political and Social Science
American Museum of Natural History, Anthropology Papers
American Universities Field Staff Reports
Anales de antropología
Annales africaines (Paris)
Annales de l'universite d'Abidjan (Ivory Coast)
Année africaine (Paris)
Année politique africaine (Dakar)
Annuaire de l'Afrique du nord (Paris)
Anthropological Journal of Canada
Anthropologie (Oosterhout)
Anthropology Tomorrow
Archives of Neurology and Psychiatry (Chicago)
Archivos de Instituto de estudios africanos (Madrid)
Asia and Africa Review
Atlanta University Center for African and African-Ameri-
  can Studies

Bergbauliche Ressourcen im südlichen Afrika (Hamburg)
Bibliotheca Africana
Black Orpheus
Black Review

Blackfriars (Oxford)
Bulletin de correspondance africaine (Algiers)
Bulletin de l'Association française pour les recherches
    et études camerounaise (Bordeaux)
Bulletin de Madagascar
Bulletin of African Studies in Canada
Bulletin of the Society for African Church History
    (Nsukka)

Cahiers de Tunisie
Cahiers nord-africains (Paris)
Cahiers O.R.S.T.O.M. [Office de la recherche scientifique
    et technique outre-mer]
Canadian Review of Sociology and Anthropology
Central Africa
Central African Examiner (Salisbury)
Central African Historical Association (Salisbury)
Central African Research (London)
Centre de recherche et d'information sociopolitiques
    (Bruxelles)
Christian Century
Chronologie politique africaine (Paris)
Collection d'études politiques (Léopoldville)
Comité d'études historiques et scientifiques de
    l'Afrique occidentale française (Paris)
Conch (Austin)
Coryndon Memorial Museum Papers (Nairobi)
Courrier africain (Bruxelles)
Cuadernos africanos y orientales (Madrid)
Cuadernos de estudios africanos (Madrid)

Drum

East Africa and Rhodesia (London)
East African Institute of Social Research (Kampala)
East African Journal (Nairobi)
East African Publishing House Historical Studies (Nairobi)
East African Academy (London)
East African Universities Social Science Council (Nairobi)
Encyclopédie coloniale et maritime mensuelle (Paris)
Epilepsia Amsterdam
Estudios ultramarinos (Lisbon)
Ethiopia Observer
Études (Paris)
Europe-France outre-mer (Paris)

Foyer chrétien (Abidjan)
France outre-mer (Paris)

Ghana Journal of Sociology (Legon)
Ghana Notes and Queries (Kumasi)
Ghana Today (Accra)
Ghanaian
Guinea Española (Santa Isabel)

Historical Pamphlets on Africa

Ikenga (Ibadan)
Insight and Opinion (Ghana)
Institut d'études centrafricaines (Brazzaville)
International Congress of Group Psychotherapy (Milan)
International Congress of Psychiatry (Zurich)
Issue - African Studies Association (Waltham, Mass.)

Jahrbuch: Asien, Afrika, Lateinamerika (Berlin)
Jeune Afrique (Paris)
Journal de psychologie normale et pathologique (Paris)
Journal for Social Research (Pretoria)
Journal of African and Asian Studies (New Delhi)
Journal of African Languages
Journal of Ethiopian Studies
Journal of General Psychology
Journal of Nervous Mental Disease
Journal of the Royal Army Medical Corps
Journal of Tropical Medical Hygiene
Journal of West African Languages (London)

Lesotho (Morija)
Lesotho Quarterly (Morija)

Nairobi Historical Studies (Nairobi)
Nations nouvelles (Yaoundé)
Neues Afrika (München)
New African (London)
New Nation (Pretoria)
New Orient (Prague)
News Check (Johannesburg)
Nigerian Opinion (Ibadan)
Nkanga (Kampala)
Nordiska Afrikainstitutet Research Report (Uppsala)
Notes et documents voltaïques (Ouagadougou, Upper Volta)

Objective: Justice (New York)

Pamphlets on Africa South of the Sahara
Pan-African Journal
Papers in International Studies, Africa Series (Ohio)
Phylon
Policy Abstracts Newsletter (Kampala)
Proceedings of the Royal Society of Medicine
Provisional Council for the Social Sciences in East
   Africa
Psychanalyse
Psychiatry
Psychoanalytic Review
Psychoanalytic Studies Society

Race Relations News (Johannesburg)
Reality (Pietermaritzburg)

442

Recherches et études camerounaises (Yaoundé)
Recherches voltaïques (Paris)
Remarques africaines (Bruxelles)
Report from South Africa (London)
Reporter (Nairobi)
Revue africaine (Alger)
Revue congolaise d'administration (Kinshasa)
Revue des deux mondes (Paris)
Revue tunisienne de sciences sociales (Tunis)
Rhodesia and Eastern Africa (London)
Rhodesian Commentary (Salisbury)

Sechaba (South Africa)
South Africa-Bantu Affairs Commission Report (Pretoria)
South Africa International (Johannesburg)
South Africa Today (Johannesburg)
South African Digest (Pretoria)
South African Institute of Race Relations (Johannesburg)
South West Africa Annual (Windhoek)
Southern Africa (New York)
Survey of Race Relations in South Africa (Johannesburg)
Syracuse University, Program of East African Studies,
    Papers

Terre malgache (Tany)
Transactions of the Historical Society of Ghana (Legon)

United States Department of State, African Series
Utafiti (Dar es Salaam)

West Africa (London)
West Africa Annual (Lagos)
West African Journal (Exeter)
West African Language Monograph Series (London)

Zambia Papers (Manchester)

443